Alfredian Prologues and Epilogues

Alfredian
Prologues and Epilogues

edited by
SUSAN IRVINE

OXFORD
UNIVERSITY PRESS

Great Clarendon Street, Oxford, OX2 6DP,
United Kingdom

Oxford University Press is a department of the University of Oxford.
It furthers the University's objective of excellence in research, scholarship,
and education by publishing worldwide. Oxford is a registered trade mark of
Oxford University Press in the UK and in certain other countries

Editorial matter © Susan Irvine 2023

The moral rights of the author have been asserted

All rights reserved. No part of this publication may be reproduced, stored in
a retrieval system, or transmitted, in any form or by any means, without the
prior permission in writing of Oxford University Press, or as expressly permitted
by law, by licence or under terms agreed with the appropriate reprographics
rights organization. Enquiries concerning reproduction outside the scope of the
above should be sent to the Rights Department, Oxford University Press, at the
address above

You must not circulate this work in any other form
and you must impose this same condition on any acquirer

Published in the United States of America by Oxford University Press
198 Madison Avenue, New York, NY 10016, United States of America

British Library Cataloguing in Publication Data

Data available

Library of Congress Control Number: 2023940369

ISBN 978–0–19–969210–1

Printed and bound in the UK by
Clays Ltd, Elcograf S.p.A.

Links to third party websites are provided by Oxford in good faith and
for information only. Oxford disclaims any responsibility for the materials
contained in any third party website referenced in this work.

Acknowledgements

'Consider the beginnings and ends of things, the greatest and the smallest, how they all conspire to baffle thee' (Laurence Sterne, Sermon 44: The Ways of Providence Justified to Man). Sterne's words, albeit not penned with Old English prologues and epilogues in mind, nevertheless carry a certain resonance for anyone working on these texts. In attempting to counter my frequent bafflement, and to make the Alfredian prologues and epilogues more accessible to students and scholars, I have benefitted from the generous help of many people and institutions. Their contributions have been invaluable in the preparation of this book.

I owe a particular debt of gratitude to those scholars who commented on early versions of parts of the book, answered queries, or provided materials, including Anya Adair, Helen Appleton, Michael Bintley, Nicole Discenza, Tony Edwards, Dora Faraci, Richard Gameson, Malcolm Godden, Mark Griffith, Rohini Jayatilaka, Stefan Jurasinski, Francis Leneghan, Leslie Lockett, Richard North, Winfried Rudolf, Paul Szarmach (†), Paolo Vaciago, and Greg Waite. Three others, Amy Faulkner, Richard Marsden, and Christine Rauer, read and commented on the entire manuscript, and I am extremely grateful to them for taking this on and for the improvements they made. Any errors that remain are entirely my own.

Many other scholars and students have helped through comments and questions in seminars and lectures I have given on versions of work preparatory to the book. I would like to thank the audiences at Cambridge, Cluj, Harvard, Göttingen, King's College London, Leiden, Leipzig, Oxford, Rome, UCL, and Valladolid for their insights.

I have consulted many medieval manuscripts in the course of preparing this book and would like to thank the staff of the British Library, the Bodleian Library, Cambridge University Library, Trinity College Library, Cambridge, the Parker Library, and Rochester Cathedral Library, who have been uniformly supportive. I am also grateful to my own institution, UCL, for funding a symposium on the topic of Medieval Prologues and Epilogues, to the Lichtenberg-Kolleg, University of Göttingen, Germany, for appointing me to a Senior Research Fellowship in 2017 to work on this book project, to the Universita' Degli Studi Roma Tre in Rome for offering me a Visiting Professorship in 2019, and to the Alexander von Humboldt Foundation for its support through an Anneliese Maier Research Award. I would also like to thank the editorial and production team at Oxford University Press, and particularly Eleanor Collins, who has been unwaveringly patient and encouraging throughout the preparation of this book.

I am immensely grateful to my husband John for his constant support, and to my family generally for offering both encouragement and diversion along the way. This book is dedicated to my grandson Solly, whose arrival as the project draws to its close brings a welcome new prologue.

Contents

Abbreviations	xi
General Introduction	1
The Influence of Earlier Traditions	3
Alfred's Reign and the Vernacular Translation Programme	8
The Place of the Prologues and Epilogues in the Authorship Debate	12
Overview of the Corpus of Alfredian Prologues and Epilogues	14
Language	17
Early Medieval Reception History	20
Editorial Procedure and Conventions	23
The Old English *Dialogues*	25
Prose and Verse Prefaces; Gregorian Preface; Incipits and Explicits	25
Introduction	27
The Work and its Contexts	27
Manuscripts and Previous Editions	29
The Prose Preface to the *Dialogues*	31
The Verse Preface to the *Dialogues*	33
The Gregorian Preface to the *Dialogues*	33
The Incipits and Explicits of the *Dialogues*	34
Note on the Texts	35
Texts and Translations	36
The Prose Preface to the *Dialogues*	36
The Verse Preface to the *Dialogues*	38
The Gregorian Preface to the *Dialogues*	40
Summary of Book I of the *Dialogues*	46
Book I Explicit	48
Book II Incipit	48
Summary of Book II of the *Dialogues*	48
Book II Explicit	50
Book III Incipit	50
Summary of Book III of the *Dialogues*	50
Book III Explicit	52

viii Contents

Book IV Incipit	52
Summary of Book IV of the *Dialogues*	52

The Old English *Pastoral Care* — 55
Prose and Verse Prefaces; Gregorian Preface and Epilogue; Verse Epilogue — 55

Introduction	57
The Work and its Contexts	57
Manuscripts and Previous Editions	58
The Prose Preface to the *Pastoral Care*	61
The Verse Preface to the *Pastoral Care*	64
The Gregorian Preface to the *Pastoral Care*	66
The Gregorian Epilogue to the *Pastoral Care*	67
The Verse Epilogue to the *Pastoral Care*	67
Note on the Texts	69
Texts and Translations	70
The Prose Preface to the *Pastoral Care*	70
The Verse Preface to the *Pastoral Care*	76
The Gregorian Preface to the *Pastoral Care*	78
Summary of the *Pastoral Care*	80
The Gregorian Epilogue to the *Pastoral Care*	82
The Verse Epilogue to the *Pastoral Care*	84

The Old English *Boethius* (Prose and Prosimetrical Versions) — 87
Prose and Verse Prefaces; Prose and Verse *Vitae*; Epilogue — 87

Introduction	89
The Work and its Contexts	89
Manuscripts and Previous Editions	92
The Prose Preface to the *Boethius*	93
The Verse Preface to the *Boethius*	95
The Prose and Verse *Vitae*	97
The Epilogue to the *Boethius*	99
Note on the Texts	100
Texts and Translations	102
The Prose Preface to the *Boethius*	102
The Verse Preface to the *Boethius*	104
The Prose *Vita* of the *Boethius*	106
The Verse *Vita* of the *Boethius*	108

Summary of the *Boethius*	114
The Epilogue to the *Boethius*	116

The Old English *Soliloquies* — 119
Preface; Incipits and Explicits — 119
Introduction — 121
- The Work and its Contexts — 121
- Manuscripts and Previous Editions — 123
- The Preface to the *Soliloquies* — 124
- The Incipits and Explicits of the *Soliloquies* — 128

Note on the Texts — 129
Texts and Translations — 130
- The Preface to the *Soliloquies* — 130
- Summary of Book I of the *Soliloquies* — 132
- Book I Explicit — 134
- Book II Incipit — 134
- Summary of Book II of the *Soliloquies* — 134
- Book II Explicit — 136
- Book III Incipit — 136
- Summary of Book III of the *Soliloquies* — 136
- Book III Explicit — 138

The *Laws* of Alfred — 141
Preface — 141
Introduction — 143
- The Work and its Contexts — 144
- Manuscripts and Previous Editions — 145
- The Preface to the *Laws* of Alfred — 146

Note on the Text — 150
Text and Translation — 152
- The Preface to the *Laws* of Alfred — 152
- Summary of the *Laws* of Alfred — 164

The Old English *Bede* — 165
Preface and Epilogue — 165
Introduction — 167
- The Work and its Contexts — 167
- Manuscripts and Previous Editions — 168

The Preface to the *Bede*	170
The Epilogue to the *Bede*	174
Note on the Texts	175
Texts and Translations	176
The Preface to the *Bede*	176
Summary of the *Bede*	180
The Epilogue to the *Bede*	182

Textual Notes   **185**

The *Dialogues*	185
The *Pastoral Care*	188
The *Boethius*	190
The *Soliloquies*	192
The *Laws* of Alfred	193
The *Bede*	195

Commentary   **197**

The *Dialogues*	197
The *Pastoral Care*	201
The *Boethius*	205
The *Soliloquies*	208
The *Laws* of Alfred	211
The *Bede*	216

Glossary and List of Proper Names	221
Bibliography	281

Abbreviations

BT, BTS	Bosworth, Joseph, and T. Northcote Toller, *An Anglo-Saxon Dictionary* (Oxford: Clarendon Press, 1898); T. Northcote Toller, *Supplement* (Oxford: Clarendon Press, 1972), with *Revised and Enlarged Addenda* by A. Campbell (Oxford: Clarendon Press, 1972).
DOE	*Dictionary of Old English: A to I online*. Edited by Angus Cameron, Ashley Crandell Amos, Antonette diPaolo Healey, et al. (Toronto: Dictionary of Old English Project, 2018).
Fontes Anglo-Saxonici	*Fontes Anglo-Saxonici: A Register of Written Sources Used by Anglo-Saxon Authors*, https://www.st-andrews.ac.uk/~cr30/Mercian/Fontes.
Parker on the Web	*Parker Library on the Web: Manuscripts in the Parker Library at Corpus Christi College, Cambridge*, https://parker.stanford.edu/parker/.

General Introduction

Prologues (or prefaces) and epilogues have featured in English literary culture from its very beginnings.[1] A tradition of framing works written in English with these introductory and concluding pieces was established in the ninth century and continued to develop through the early medieval period and beyond.[2] Amongst the surviving examples in Old English are the mid-ninth-century Codex Aureus Inscription,[3] the prologues and epilogues written to accompany the works associated with the reign of Alfred the Great (871–99), two prefatory poems known as *Aldhelm* (composed in English, Latin, and Greek) and *Thureth*, probably from the tenth and eleventh centuries respectively,[4] and the prose prefaces to sets of homilies, saints' lives, and other writings by the prolific late tenth- and early eleventh-century writer Ælfric.[5] The focus of this book is on the prologues, epilogues, and other frame texts linked to works associated with Alfred's reign, which are edited here as a group for the first time.[6] Highly varied, enigmatic, and not always reliable in the claims they make, these

---

[1] The terms prologue and preface are used interchangeably here; see *Oxford English Dictionary*, entry for 'prologue'; Frantzen (2003), p. 124. I have adhered to modern convention in using preface rather than prologue for the titles of Old English texts belonging to this genre.

[2] The development of the genre of the prologue in the medieval period, early and late, has been addressed in a number of studies: see, for example, Stephens (1960); Minnis (1988); J. Wilcox (1994); Evans (1999); Frantzen (2003); Galloway (2005); Thijs (2007b); Godden (2009a) and (2013); S. Irvine (2015a) and (2017); Copeland (2016); and Dearnley (2016).

[3] The Codex Aureus Inscription is on fo. 11r of Stockholm, National Library of Sweden, MS A. 135; the text is edited by Sweet and Whitelock (1967), p. 175.

[4] *Aldhelm* is attached to a copy of Aldhelm's work *De uirginitate* (*On Virginity*). *Thureth* is a poem of intercession for someone named Thureth preceding the canons of the Council of Enham in London, British Library, Cotton MS Claudius A. iii. The two poems are edited by Jones (2012), pp. 126–9.

[5] For an edition of Ælfric's prefaces, see J. Wilcox (1994).

[6] The Old English works whose frame texts are edited here are referred to by the titles (Old English) *Dialogues*, *Pastoral Care*, *Boethius*, *Soliloquies*, *Laws*, and *Bede* respectively. Where the main Latin sources of these works are referred to, the Latin titles are used (*Dialogi*, *Cura pastoralis*, *De consolatione Philosophiae*, *Soliloquia*, and *Historia ecclesiastica*).

pieces offer intriguing glimpses not only into the authorship and circumstances of composition, translation, or transmission of the works written in or around Alfred's reign but also more generally into the relationship between writer and reader in Anglo-Saxon England.

This edition aims to showcase for a broad audience the extraordinary range of framing material found in the manuscripts containing the works associated with Alfred's reign, and to offer the opportunity to explore links between the different kinds of material. Amongst the frame texts are some which belong to the category of 'translators' prologues': these are written (or purportedly written) by the translator of the main work, and designed to be circulated with that work from the outset. Other frame texts were written later, perhaps by a scribe or reader of the work, and added in the course of transmission over the two centuries or so following Alfred's reign. In cases where only late copies of works survive, it is not always easy to distinguish between original framing material and later additions or interpolations. A third type of framing material derives from the Latin sources themselves, which contain their own prologues and epilogues, rendered into Old English as part of the translation of the main work.[7] These vernacular versions of Latin frame texts not only serve as important models for the translators' own compositions, but also sometimes participate in a layered framing structure in which the translated pieces intersect provocatively with those that were composed independently.

Like prologues and epilogues throughout the medieval period (and beyond), the Alfredian frame texts have an inherently paradoxical status. Ostensibly standing apart from the main work, they are nevertheless integral to it, justifying its existence and shaping its reception.[8] In organizing the prologues and epilogues in terms of their relationship to the work they frame, this book aims to acknowledge how closely they are associated with that main work. In presenting them as a set of texts detached from their

---

[7] Where a prologue or epilogue translated from a Latin original is cited here, the Latin author is acknowledged in the title (for example, the Gregorian Preface to the *Dialogues*) to distinguish that frame text from the independent prologues and epilogues, except in the case of the frame texts to the *Bede* where there is no risk of confusion.

[8] On the role of 'paratext' more generally, see Genette (1997). Genette's focus, however, is the printed book, and anything for which the author or author's associate is not responsible is considered irrelevant; see also S. Irvine (2015a), pp. 169–70.

main works, however, it also aims to suggest that the meanings and functions of these pieces are in some respects dependent upon their generic relationship to each other and the models they drew on. Stamping their own mark on well-established genres, the Alfredian frame texts as a group provide uniquely striking witnesses to literary self-representation, textual authority, and audience reception in early medieval England.

The Influence of Earlier Traditions

The taste for prologues and epilogues as accompaniments to vernacular works clearly responded to a rich classical and continental tradition of furnishing works with frame texts. The desire to confer on works in English the literary authority enjoyed by Latin classical and early medieval works circulating both on the Continent and in their own country led authors and scribes to emulate their predecessors' compositional techniques. In providing prologues and epilogues for their works, the Old English authors mainly take their cue both from the Latin works on which their own writings are based and from other Latin works and collections of works that featured such framing texts. They may also have been influenced, as we shall see, by the use of frame texts in translations of the Bible into Germanic languages written on the Continent in the ninth century.

Although it is clear that the authors of the vernacular prologues and epilogues to Alfredian works had access to a range of classical, patristic, and continental precedents, the exact models they drew on cannot always be identified. The evidence tells us which kinds of sources they knew or used but the actual works often remain obscure. For their knowledge of classical rhetoric, these authors seem not to have had available to them works by authors such as Cicero, Quintilian, and Horace, which offered theoretical approaches to the composition of the prologue and (less commonly) the epilogue.[9] Their familiarity with the forms and conventions of these genres probably derived mainly therefore from the rich array of examples available

---

[9] On the knowledge of classical rhetorical works in early medieval England, see Stanton (2002), pp. 73–8. On the rhetorical background to medieval translation more generally, see Copeland (1991).

to them in the works of the Christian Latin tradition.[10] As well as knowing the original frame texts of the works translated around the end of the ninth century—including Gregory's *Dialogi* and *Cura pastoralis*, and Bede's *Historia ecclesiastica*—they might have known the prologues to various saints' lives available in England,[11] and the prologues and epilogues accompanying other works by authors such as Aldhelm, Abbot of Malmesbury at the end of the seventh century, and Alcuin of York (b. 724), whose writing career was mainly spent at the court of Charlemagne. With Alcuin and other later Carolingian writers such as Walahfrid Strabo (*c.*805–49), Hrabanus Maurus (780–856), and Smaragdus (*c.*770–*c.*840), a practice of combining prologues in both prose and verse seems to have developed.[12] Combinations of epilogues in prose and verse also occurred: in Alcuin's treatise on the nature of the soul (*De ratione animae*), the main work is followed by two poems, a prose piece, a litany, and a short final address in verse.[13] Although there is no manuscript evidence to prove that any of these Carolingian precedents were available in England in Alfred's reign, the idea that they might have been known, or at least known of, in Alfredian literary circles would fit well with the lively intellectual exchange that evidently existed between Carolingian Europe and late ninth-century England.

For their use of the vernacular in their frame texts, the Old English authors may have been influenced by the biblical translations into Old Saxon and Old High German that were being produced on the Continent in the ninth century.[14] Amongst these translations is an Old High German poetic version of the Gospels known as the *Evangelienbuch*, composed by the monk Otfrid of Weissenburg sometime between 863 and 871.[15] The *Evangelienbuch* is amply supplied with framing material: it contains four prologues (including the first chapter of the work proper, in which Otfrid justifies his decision to write in German), and an epilogue. Three of the four prologues are written in Old High German verse; the other, a Latin prose

---

[10] On the conventions of the Latin prefatory tradition, see Janson (1964).
[11] Frantzen (2003), p. 126.   [12] Godden (2011), pp. 443–4.
[13] Curry (1966), pp. 65–72.   [14] Godden (2011), pp. 455–8.
[15] See Bostock (1976), pp. 190–212; Haug (1997), pp. 29–41.

letter to Liutbert, Archbishop of Mainz, succeeds the first verse prologue. The epilogue is written in Old High German verse. As with the Latin Carolingian works, no evidence exists that the *Evangelienbuch*, or other works in Old High German or Old Saxon, were known in England in the late ninth century, but the presence of scholars from the Continent at Alfred's court (such as Grimbald of St Bertin) certainly makes it feasible.[16]

In producing their own frame texts, the Old English authors imitate and adapt the conventions of structure, form, and rhetoric established by their predecessors. The framing structures of some Alfredian works show the influence of Carolingian writers (such as Alcuin) in their combination of prose and verse texts. The *Pastoral Care*, for example, is supplied with two prefaces—prose and verse respectively—independent of its source (Gregory's *Cura pastoralis*), as well as a translation (in prose) of Gregory's own Latin preface. It also has two epilogues: the prose translation of Gregory's own epilogue followed by an independent verse epilogue. The prosimetrical *Boethius* opens with both a prose preface and a verse preface, leading into a biographical-historical introduction in verse that is also added independently in the Old English version.

In their forms, too, the Alfredian prologues and epilogues rely on earlier precedents. Written in the form of a letter, the Prose Preface to the *Pastoral Care* can be situated within the classical tradition of the epistolary preface, defined by Tore Janson as an introduction 'with the formal characteristics of a letter, namely a salutatory phrase at the beginning and/or the word *uale* or corresponding at the end'.[17] The form of the epistolary preface is also used in the Old English Gregorian Preface to the *Pastoral Care* and the Preface to the *Bede*, which address 'you, dearest brother' (Bishop John of Ravenna) and King Ceolwulf respectively.

The Alfredian provision of epilogues in the form of petitions or prayers is similarly based on long-established convention. Like the Latin original from which it is translated, the Gregorian Epilogue to the *Pastoral Care* is in the form of a petition to John of Ravenna. The Verse Epilogue to the *Pastoral Care* serves as a petition to readers to imbibe the wisdom taught by

---

[16] See the Prose Preface to the *Pastoral Care*, line 63 and Commentary.
[17] See Janson (1964), p. 106 n. 2.

Gregory. The *Bede* closes with two prose petitions (based on the Latin source), to God and the readers of the work respectively, and a supplementary verse petition, probably written by a scribe, occurs in one eleventh-century copy of the work. The only surviving copy of the all-prose version of the *Boethius* (made in about 1100) ends with a metrical prayer, probably composed and added in the eleventh century.

A range of topoi, or rhetorical motifs, commonly used in the Latin tradition are also exploited in the Alfredian frame texts. The modesty formula (where the author's unworthiness is asserted) underlies the depiction of Wulfsige as a 'poor servant' of God in the Verse Preface to the *Dialogues*, and the king's acknowledgement of his helpers in the Prose Preface to the *Pastoral Care*. The commission motif (the claim to be writing for someone in particular) occurs in the Verse Preface to the *Dialogues*, and also in an inverted form in the Prose Preface to the *Dialogues* in which King Alfred claims to have asked others to translate the work for him. Several prefaces allude to translation technique in terms of a 'word-for-word, sense-for-sense' formula, reflecting a distinction articulated by Cicero and Jerome amongst others.[18] This topos is used in the Gregorian Preface to the *Dialogues* (in this case following the work's Latin source), and in the prose prefaces to the *Pastoral Care* and the *Boethius*.

Peculiar to the prefaces written in verse is the use of the motif of book as speaker. The topos can again be traced to the Latin tradition, though it occurs only rarely. Alcuin's verse preface to his late eighth-century work *De dialectica* (*On Dialectics*) provides one precedent for its use by a Carolingian writer that may conceivably have been known in England by the end of the ninth century.[19] Amongst the Alfredian prefaces the book speaks out in the first person in the verse prefaces to both the *Dialogues* and the *Pastoral Care*, and possibly also in the Verse Preface to the *Boethius*.[20] The appeal of

---

[18] See, for example, Copeland (1991), pp. 42–55; Stanton (2002), pp. 75–7 and 82–3. For an overview of the evidence of knowledge in Anglo-Saxon England of Jerome's Letter 57 to Pammachius, in which Jerome uses these terms, see Gittos (2014), p. 244 n. 46.

[19] See Godden (2011), pp. 462–4.

[20] On this topos in the verse prefaces, see, for example, Earl (1994). On 'voice' in written texts more generally, see Schaefer (1992).

this device to the writers of vernacular prefatory poems (evinced later too in *Aldhelm* and *Thureth*) can perhaps be linked to familiarity with the use of a first-person voice for inanimate objects in other Old English poems, such as the Exeter Book riddles—in one riddle the speaking object is a book[21]—and *The Dream of the Rood* where the cross speaks out.[22] The first-person voice of the book is also a feature of some vernacular scribal colophons, the brief notes left by scribes at the beginning or end of manuscripts. One eleventh-century scribe, for example, helpfully jotted the note 'Wulfwi me wrat' (Wulfwi wrote me) in London, British Library, Cotton MS Otho C. i.[23] We might also compare the material objects from the early medieval period whose inscriptions give them a voice: the Alfred Jewel, for example, housed in the Ashmolean Museum, Oxford, is inscribed with the message 'Ælfred mec heht gewyrcan' (Alfred ordered me to be made).[24]

In relying so firmly on an extensive body of conventions derived from the Latin tradition, the Alfredian prologues and epilogues strive to invest the English works they frame with the authority and prestige of the Latin originals. In adhering, to a lesser or greater extent, to a set of well-established conventions, the frame texts clearly prioritize the rhetorical over the documentary. This affects how we read them. However reliable these texts may seem, the statements they make cannot necessarily be taken at face value. Claims of personal authorship by a king, and the idea that vernacular translation was done for the unlearned, are rhetorical tropes inherited from the Latin tradition. The prefaces that make such claims are, as Malcolm Godden has shown, 'literary creations in this period, with a long history of using their own conventions and tropes and not always a close regard for fact'.[25] We cannot assume that the frame texts accurately record who the works

---

[21] Krapp and Dobbie (1936), pp. 193–4 (Riddle 26).
[22] On speaking objects in Old English literature, see Paz (2017). On parallels between the Alfredian verse prefaces and riddles, see Earl (1994); O'Brien O'Keeffe (2005); and Orton (2005).
[23] See Gameson (2002), p. 45.
[24] On the Alfred Jewel and other material objects associated with Alfred's reign, see, for example, Hinton (2008). On the possible link between the Alfred Jewel and the *æstel* (or book-pointer) mentioned in the Prose Preface to the *Pastoral Care*, see the Commentary on that text, line 60.
[25] Godden (2009a), p. 94. See also Godden (2013); Gittos (2014).

were written by, who their intended audiences were, or what circumstances prompted their composition. The interpretation of these frame texts may have very little to do with historical truth, whatever they seem to suggest to the contrary.[26]

Alfred's Reign and the Vernacular Translation Programme

The works framed by the prologues and epilogues edited in this volume were composed in or around the reign of the king now known as Alfred the Great. Alfred, son of King Æthelwulf and his first wife Osburh, succeeded his brother Æthelred as king of the West Saxons in AD 871. Much of the first part of Alfred's reign was dominated by attempts to fight off the Vikings whose raids on Wessex (and other Anglo-Saxon kingdoms) presented a constant threat.[27] Attempts to negotiate peace with the raiders finally paid off in 878, when terms favourable to Alfred and Wessex were agreed with the Danes. The period of relative calm that followed allowed the king to put in place strategies to reform and strengthen the kingdom of Wessex. Although the development of military strategies must have been the most urgent priority, cultural reform was clearly also high on his agenda.

The widespread and repeated Viking depredations inevitably took their toll on the culture of Latin learning in Anglo-Saxon England. The middle decades of the ninth century apparently saw a severe slump in literary activity, with only three surviving manuscripts datable to that period.[28] Though older manuscripts continued to be available, book production itself seems largely to have gone into abeyance, and illiteracy affected even the scribes responsible for copying charters.[29] Only the kingdom of Mercia, it seems, successfully sustained Latin learning through the ninth century.[30] Given Mercia's closeness, both political and geographical, to Wessex in this

---

[26] See further the section on 'The Place of the Prologues and Epilogues in the Authorship Debate' below.

[27] Asser's biography and the *Anglo-Saxon Chronicle* are important sources of information for Alfred's reign. For a fuller account of the historic context, accompanied by a translation of Asser's biography, see Keynes and Lapidge (1983). See also Keynes (2015).

[28] Lapidge (1996), p. 416. See also Gneuss (1986).   [29] Lapidge (2006), p. 45.

[30] See, for example, Brown and Farr (2001).

period,[31] it is unsurprising, perhaps, that it was to Mercia that Alfred turned, probably in the early 880s, to find scholars who would help him improve learning in his kingdom (namely Plegmund, Wærferth, Athelstan, and Werwulf). Other scholars were brought in from Wales (Asser, his biographer) and the Continent (Grimbald, and John 'the old Saxon').

The Prose Preface to the *Pastoral Care* presents the king's response to the decline in learning that he saw around him. It sets out a scheme to establish a translation programme by which 'certain books most necessary for all people to know' were to be made available in English. The question of exactly which books were in the writer's mind here remains a matter of conjecture,[32] but the success of the programme as a means of promoting learning can reasonably be inferred from the survival of a range of vernacular works composed in or around Alfred's reign.[33] The majority of these are translations into English of Latin works. The *Dialogues* (translating Gregory the Great's *Dialogi*) is thought to have been written at Alfred's request, before the education programme itself was implemented, by the Mercian bishop Wærferth (on the evidence of Asser's biography of Alfred).[34] The *Pastoral Care*, *Boethius*, *Soliloquies*, and *Prose Psalms* (translating respectively Gregory's *Cura pastoralis*, Boethius' *De consolatione Philosophiae*, Augustine's *Soliloquia*, and the first fifty psalms of the Psalter) have traditionally been attributed to the authorship of Alfred himself, though the extent of Alfred's contribution has been much disputed in recent years.[35] More loosely linked to the Alfredian programme are two other translations: the *Bede* (translating Bede's *Historia ecclesiastica*), apparently Mercian in origin,[36] and the *Orosius* (translating Orosius' *Historiarum adversum paganos Libri VII*).[37] Other works in English, which may be new

---

[31] See Keynes (1998).

[32] Most scholars link the phrase 'certain books' to the *Pastoral Care* and other contemporary translations. Anlezark (2017) has recently argued that it refers to the books of the Bible.

[33] See Jayatilaka (2012) for a list of 'the collective body of writings associated with the ninth-century court of Alfred' (p. 670).

[34] Stevenson (1959), ch. 77.

[35] See especially Godden (2007) and the response in Bately (2009). For further discussion of the authorship issue, see the section below on 'The Place of the Prologues and Epilogues in the Authorship Debate'.

[36] See, for example, Rowley (2011), p. 2; see further the chapter on the *Bede* below.

[37] For the *Orosius*, see Godden (2016).

compositions or compilations rather than translations, have also been linked with varying degrees of certainty to the Alfredian programme: they include the *Laws* of Alfred, the Parker version of the *Anglo-Saxon Chronicle*, a collection of medical texts known as Bald's *Leechbook*, the *Old English Martyrology*, and the *Dialogues of Solomon and Saturn*.[38]

Scholars engaged with the translation project had good reason to emphasize the king's enthusiasm for the production of works in English. Latin had long been the established language of literary authority in England. From the end of the sixth century onwards, following the arrival of Augustine and his fellow missionaries in Kent, who brought with them all the trappings of a Latin literary culture, it was Latin that had served as the primary language of learning. The respect for Latin and everything it represented was deeply instilled. With Latin carrying such cultural prestige, the proposal that English should be used as a language of learning, even just as a stepping-stone to further education, required powerful backing to be implemented successfully. The king's support of and participation in the translation programme helped to lend to the vernacular texts a measure of the authority hitherto enjoyed mainly by Latin.

Historical precedent served as justification for proposing a vernacular translation programme. The Prose Preface to the *Pastoral Care* presents the policy of translation as fitting into a long history of such activity across a range of languages: from Hebrew to Greek, from Greek to Latin, and from Latin to other vernaculars. Recent precedents might have included the works translated into the vernacular in Carolingian Europe. The emperor Charlemagne apparently commissioned a series of Old High German model translations of works such as Matthew's Gospel and Isidore of Seville's *De fide catholica*,[39] and Otfrid of Weissenburg, as we saw earlier, firmly advocated writing in his native tongue of German in the prefatory material of his *Evangelienbuch*.[40]

---

[38] For the Parker version of the *Chronicle*, see Bately (1986); for Bald's *Leechbook*, see Wright (1955); for the *Old English Martyrology*, see Rauer (2013); for the *Dialogues of Solomon and Saturn*, see Anlezark (2009).

[39] Haug (1997), pp. 28–9; Godden (2011), pp. 455–6.   [40] See above pp. 4–5.

In advocating the use of the vernacular, the Alfredian programme may also have been influenced by models of vernacular literary production available in England itself. Translation of Latin works into English was already under way as early as the first part of the eighth century at the monastery of Jarrow, to judge by a contemporary report that Bede was working on a translation of the Gospel of St John at the time of his death.[41] Bede's story of the cowherd Cædmon, who is miraculously granted the ability to render the scriptures into English verse,[42] hints at an early interest in vernacular translation. A number of Old English poems, including *Genesis A* and *B*, *Exodus*, and *Daniel*, offer verse paraphrases of biblical material. In Mercia, where the transmission of learning had continued through the ninth century, there seems to have been a tradition of producing prose works in Old English before Alfred's programme, one with which the *Bede* and the *Dialogues* can perhaps be associated.[43] A pre-existing tradition of this kind is likely to have paved the way for the acceptance of a more formal translation programme.

For the vernacular authors, the act of translation built on a process of learning and interpreting the text, as articulated in the Prose Preface to the *Pastoral Care*: 'Siððan ic hie ða geliornod hæfde, swæ swæ ic hie forstod, ond swæ ic hie andgitfullicost areccean meahte, ic hie on Englisc awende' (When I had learned it as I understood it and as I could most intelligibly interpret it, I translated it into English).[44] Not surprisingly, the works produced by this process translate their sources more literally in some places than in others. Each of the vernacular authors shows a willingness to move between what Robert Stanton refers to as 'the two poles of literality and looseness' that underpin translation theory.[45] Nevertheless there is considerable variety amongst the translations in their closeness overall to their main sources. The two works that can be linked to the Mercian tradition, the *Dialogues* and the *Bede*, show a tendency to be more literal and Latinate in

---

[41] See 'Cuthbert's Letter on the Death of Bede', in Colgrave and Mynors (1969), pp. 582–3; cf. Stanton (2002), pp. 56–7.
[42] Colgrave and Mynors (1969), Book IV, ch. 24.
[43] Brown and Farr (2001); Fulk (2012); Waite (2014); Rowley (2015); Rauer (2021).
[44] The Prose Preface to the *Pastoral Care*, lines 64–5.   [45] Stanton (2002), p. 82.

their approach. The earliest of the works that can be identified with the translation programme itself, the *Pastoral Care*, also remains close to its source. Later works, the *Boethius* and *Soliloquies*, show a more interpretive and independent approach. Christine Thijs has rightly argued that it cannot be assumed that faithful translations would have been considered inferior in this period;[46] the inclusion of more 'original' material might not in itself have been perceived as a sign of intellectual advancement. The apparent shift in the works towards greater independence may nevertheless point to an increasing confidence in the use of the vernacular as a means of disseminating learning.

The audiences envisaged for the vernacular works presumably ranged quite widely, given the differences amongst the works in scope and ambition. The frame texts offer few clear pointers to help identify these intended audiences. In some cases their evidence is apparently inconsistent and even contradictory. The Prose Preface to the *Dialogues*, for example, suggests that the work was translated for one person's private reading, while the Verse Preface to the *Dialogues* indicates that the work had been put into wider circulation.[47] The two scenarios are not of course mutually exclusive. The Prose Preface to the *Pastoral Care* seems to envisage the work being made available via learned bishops to a broad spectrum of society, while the Verse Preface to the same work implies that it is the bishops' own lack of Latin that has prompted the need for the translation.[48] Such differences of emphasis underline the need for caution in accepting at face value any evidence for intended audiences that the prologues and epilogues might seem to provide.

The Place of the Prologues and Epilogues in the Authorship Debate

An association between King Alfred and the production of writings in the vernacular was established from an early date. Alfred's name seems to have become synonymous with the tradition of the eloquent ruler, one

---

[46] Thijs (2007a).   [47] See further Johnson (2006).
[48] See further Godden (2009a).

of the defining features of Carolingian court culture which he and his circle were keen to emulate.[49] A number of the frame texts make claims for Alfred's role in the composition of particular works, and their existence has traditionally been used as evidence of the king's authorship of the *Pastoral Care*, *Boethius*, and *Soliloquies*, and at least part of the *Laws*. The *Pastoral Care* has a prose preface, in which the first-person voice of Alfred lays claim to the composition of the main work, and a verse preface which (in the voice of the book) attributes the translation to Alfred. The *Boethius* has a prose preface that identifies Alfred as the translator of both the prose and prosimetrical versions, and a verse preface that celebrates his poetic skill. The *Soliloquies* has a preface that describes in the first person a process of compilation and construction (alluding to literary production); the unnamed speaker is commonly assumed to be Alfred, whose name is mentioned in an explicit at the end of the third book. The *Laws* contains a preface in which the first-person voice of Alfred claims to have selected these laws himself.

The unreliability of such claims can be exemplified by the Prose Preface to the *Dialogues* which, though it purports to be composed by the king, is generally agreed on stylistic grounds not to be by him. While it may have suited those responsible for promoting and circulating works in English at the end of the ninth and beginning of the tenth centuries to present the king as their author, the historical reality was perhaps rather different. External evidence offers further reasons for exercising caution in assuming that Alfred took an authorial role. We might note, for example, that literary activity on the Continent includes a number of precedents for ghost-writing in the name of a ruler.[50] Moreover, Asser's biography of Alfred, which ends in AD 893, suggests that the king did not learn Latin until his late 30s,[51] and makes no mention of a programme of translation. Although Asser's evidence leaves open the possibility that Alfred translated a series of works between 893 and his death in 899, it also raises questions as to whether the king, as a relatively later learner of Latin and a bearer of many other

---

[49] See Stanton (2002), pp. 91–100. [50] See Godden (2007).
[51] Stevenson (1959), ch. 87.

responsibilities, could realistically have composed in those six years the substantial corpus of works attributed to him. It is worth noting too that other early medieval authors who refer to Alfred's authorial activity—Ælfric, Æthelweard, and William of Malmesbury, for example—attribute works to the king which he could not have written, such as the *Bede*, and therefore cannot be treated as trustworthy.

The case for Alfred's authorial role has been kept alive mainly by the evidence for shared authorship amongst two or more of the works. Most scholars would agree that the *Boethius* and the *Soliloquies* are likely to have been the work of the same author, on the grounds of their linguistic and stylistic similarities and their overlapping interests.[52] For some scholars, linguistic and stylistic evidence suggests further that the author of these two works was the same person who translated the *Pastoral Care* and the *Psalms*. The position of those who take the latter view is summed up by Janet Bately:

> [B]ehind the translations, or rather renderings of the *Pastoral Care*, *Consolation*, *Soliloquies*, and *Psalms* there was one mind at work (though probably never entirely on its own), and given the existence of a first-person prefatory letter by the king himself, claiming authorship of *Pastoral Care*, I continue to maintain that it is reasonable to conclude that that mind was King Alfred's.[53]

Bately's comment serves as a salutary reminder of just how central the frame texts are to the authorship debate. Their evidence, though, remains controversial. This edition, while acknowledging the significance of the royal imprimatur in any reading of the framing material, does not assume that any of these pieces (or the works which they furnish) was composed by Alfred himself, or that any two or more of them were the work of the same author.

Overview of the Corpus of Alfredian Prologues and Epilogues

The Alfredian prologues, epilogues, and other frame texts all have in common their occurrence in copies of works associated with the court of

---

[52] Godden and Irvine (2009), I.135–6.
[53] Bately (2009), p. 209. See also Pratt (2007); Bately (2015). For an 'Annotated Bibliography on the Authorship Issue', see Discenza and Szarmach (2015), pp. 397–415.

King Alfred. Both the frame texts translated from the original Latin works and the framing material independent of the main Latin sources are an integral part of the framing structure. The corpus of works associated with Alfred's court includes those traditionally attributed to the king as author—the *Pastoral Care*, *Boethius*, *Soliloquies*, and (at least in part) the *Laws*—and also those that have been linked to the literary production of his reign but not attributed to him personally, namely the *Dialogues* and the *Bede*.

The relationship between the Alfredian frame texts and the main works they accompany is sometimes complex and uncertain. In some cases the frame texts were composed around the same time as the main work and circulated with it from an early date: the prefaces and epilogue to the *Pastoral Care*, and the prefatory *Vitae* (or Lives) to the *Boethius*, belong to this category, and probably too the prefaces to the *Soliloquies* and *Laws*. In other cases, the frame texts were composed at a later date for a particular manuscript copy, as exemplified by the Verse Preface to the *Dialogues* and the verse part of the Epilogue to the *Bede*. Such frame texts may provide important evidence for the history and transmission of the work. It is not, though, always easy to determine whether or not a work's frame texts are contemporary with its composition. The status of the Prose Preface to the *Boethius*, for example, remains a subject for debate:[54] was it perhaps written later than the main work but designed to look as though it were contemporary, or might it represent a later adaptation of an original preface?

Some of the frame texts included here mark off sections of works rather than a whole work. They serve as extended incipits and explicits of individual books within a work. Like the prologues and epilogues to whole works, these internal frame texts are of interest in terms of the presentation of the text, since they give access to an author's or scribe's conception of the work in relation to the contemporary audience. Frame texts of this kind occur in the *Dialogues* and the *Soliloquies*.

While every effort has been made in this edition to do justice to the wide range of material that might constitute a 'prologue' or 'epilogue' in a medieval text, the imposition of some boundaries has been necessary. The edition does not include pieces which might be interpreted in a general sense as

---

[54] See further the chapter on the *Boethius* below.

'prefatory' within a particular manuscript context (when, for instance, their interests can be seen to coincide with the subsequent 'main work'), but which either have an uncertain relationship with that main work or exist independently elsewhere. This is the case with the various kinds of prefatory material that accompany the *Anglo-Saxon Chronicle*, a work associated with Alfred's reign and possibly commissioned by him. One version of the *Anglo-Saxon Chronicle*, known as the C Text, is preceded in its manuscript by two poems, the *Menologium* and *Maxims II* (a metrical calendar and list-like poem of gnomic wisdom respectively), which have been interpreted as 'preliminary matter' to the *Chronicle* itself.[55] Notwithstanding their intriguing correspondences, there is no explicit or clear relationship between these poems and the *Chronicle*. The so-called 'Genealogical Preface' of the Parker manuscript (or the A Text) of the *Anglo-Saxon Chronicle* consists of a genealogical and regnal list.[56] Although its function was presumably to shape the way in which the *Chronicle* was read and interpreted,[57] it is one of a number of such genealogical tables circulating in a variety of contexts, and probably existed independently before the *Chronicle* itself was compiled.[58] The D, E, and F Texts of the *Anglo-Saxon Chronicle* have a different 'preface' which also exists elsewhere in a separate context:[59] it consists entirely of a brief vernacular summary of Book I, chapter 1, of Bede's *Historia ecclesiastica*.

The rendering of the first fifty psalms, known as the *Prose Psalms* and traditionally attributed to Alfred, has no prologue (though the possibility that it had one which has been lost in transmission cannot be ruled out).[60] Each of the vernacular prose psalms is preceded by a short argument or introduction explaining how it should be interpreted (from literal-historical

---

[55] Dobbie (1942), p. lx. The manuscript is London, British Library, Cotton MS Tiberius B. i (also known as the C Text of the *Anglo-Saxon Chronicle*). It is edited by O'Brien O'Keeffe (2001).

[56] The Parker Chronicle is in Cambridge, Corpus Christi College MS 173 (also known as the A Text). It is edited by Bately (1986).

[57] See, for example, S. Irvine (2015b), p. 353.

[58] S. Irvine (2015b), pp. 353–4.

[59] D Text: London, British Library, Cotton MS Tiberius B. iv; E Text (the Peterborough Chronicle): Oxford, Bodleian Library, MS Laud Misc. 636; F Text: London, British Library, Cotton MS Domitian A. viii. For editions, see (for D) Cubbin (1996); (for E) S. Irvine (2004); and (for F) Baker (2000).

[60] For editions of the *Prose Psalms*, see O'Neill (2001) and (2016).

and allegorical perspectives). These introductions, though of considerable interest in relation to the vernacular renderings of the psalms, are distinct from the prologue tradition and have meaning only as an explanation of the psalm they introduce. They are also therefore not included in this edition.

Language

Surviving Old English texts are traditionally attributed to four major dialects: Kentish (in the south-east), West Saxon (in the south-west), Mercian (in the midland territories of Mercia), and Northumbrian (in the north). This undoubtedly presents a simplified picture of how linguistic differences interacted with geographical and political boundaries in early medieval England. It nevertheless remains a useful framework in assessing the linguistic evidence that may contribute to establishing when and where an Old English work was composed. The language of the frame texts, insofar as it is possible to establish their linguistic character from relatively small amounts of evidence, predominantly exhibits features characteristic of the late West Saxon dialect. This is because the manuscripts in which they occur mainly date from the tenth and eleventh centuries when late West Saxon was widely adopted as the literary standard.

The mainly late West Saxon (lWS) features of the majority of the surviving copies, however, belie the earlier and more dialectally varied origins of many of the frame texts. In the case of the *Pastoral Care*, linguistic evidence for this can be gleaned from an early copy (890 × 896) of the main work and its contemporary frame texts, preserved in Oxford, Bodleian Library, MS Hatton 20 (on which the texts edited here are based).[61] The manuscript shows many spellings characteristic of the early West Saxon dialect, including the common use of *io* for lWS *eo* (e.g. *gehioldon, giorne*),[62] and the use of *ie* for lWS *y* (e.g. *hieder, ieldran*). Some non-West Saxon orthographical features also occur, such as *a* for WS *ea* before *l* and a following consonant (e.g. *onstal*); *e* for WS *ie/i/y* as a product of *i*-mutation of *ea* (e.g. *lefdon*);

---

[61] For a detailed account of the language of the *Pastoral Care* manuscripts, see Schreiber (2003), pp. 83–182.

[62] The Hatton 20 examples are from the Prose Preface to the *Pastoral Care*.

back mutated *i* for WS *i* (e.g. *siodo, ongiotan*). These non-West Saxon spellings can probably be attributed to Mercian influence, as Carolin Schreiber suggests, especially given the geographical proximity and political ties between the West Saxon and Mercian kingdoms towards the end of ninth century.[63]

In the case of works where no contemporary or near-contemporary copies survive, the late West Saxon dialect of the scribes makes the linguistic origins of the frame texts more difficult to assess. While it is generally agreed that the *Dialogues* and *Bede* were originally translated in the Mercian dialect, their frame texts are more diverse linguistically. The language of the Prose Preface to the *Dialogues* suggests that this piece, though written in Alfred's voice, was composed by the translator of the main work (probably Wærferth).[64] The Verse Preface evidently had a later origin since it was composed to accompany a copy of the *Dialogues* commissioned in the late ninth century by Wulfsige, Bishop of Sherborne. In keeping with this, it retains linguistic features reflecting composition in the early West Saxon dialect (e.g. *geliefeð, biesene, hiora, resðe,* and *selesða*).[65] The framing texts of the *Bede* have a similarly complex relationship to the main work. Linguistic differences between the Preface to the *Bede* and the main text suggest, as Greg Waite has argued, that the preface-writer was not the translator of the main work. The Preface to the *Bede* was perhaps composed sometime later, by someone familiar with Anglian usage but working in West Saxon circles.[66] The Epilogue to the *Bede* has separate origins for its prose and verse parts. The prose sections are, as Waite notes, 'consistent in style and lexis with the work of the *OE Bede* translator, not with that of the Preface translator'.[67] They were presumably produced at the same time and by the same author as the main work. The language of the poem added at the end of the copy in Cambridge, Corpus Christi College MS 41 gives little indication of dialect or date, but is at least compatible with this being an eleventh-century composition by a West Saxon scribe.

---

[63] Schreiber (2003), p. 109.

[64] Godden (1997). See also Bately (2003), pp. 113–17, who argues that it may have been composed by a colleague of Wærferth's or someone in Alfred's entourage.

[65] Sisam (1953c), p. 225.   [66] Waite (2015).   [67] Waite (2015), p. 56.

General Introduction 19

The *Boethius*, *Soliloquies*, and *Laws* survive only in copies of the mid-tenth century or later, but linguistic evidence suggests that they are probably West Saxon in origin. The prose version of the *Boethius* (in Oxford, Bodleian Library, MS Bodley 180, from around 1100), containing the Prose Preface and Prose *Vita*, mainly shows features of the late West Saxon dialect, along with some non-West Saxon and transitional features.[68] Though the curiously retrospective viewpoint (*on his dagum*, 'in his days') presented in the Prose Preface suggests that at least some of it may have been a later addition to the main body of the work, the linguistic evidence does not support or refute this.[69] The prayer written at the end of the work, perhaps in the hand of the main scribe, is probably an eleventh-century composition.[70] It contains a few lexical usages that stand out from basic Old English (e.g. *galnysse*, *gehyrsumnesse*, *toforan*, and *gewissigan*), all of them typical of late West Saxon.[71] The prosimetrical version of the *Boethius* (a mid-tenth-century copy in London, British Library, Cotton MS Otho A. vi), containing the Prose Preface, Verse Preface, and Verse *Vita* of the prosimetrical *Boethius*, mainly shows features of the early and late West Saxon dialects, along with some Kentish and possibly Mercian features.[72] The sole surviving witness to the *Soliloquies*, whose preface was probably composed contemporaneously with the rest of the work, is a copy made in the first half of the twelfth century: its language is essentially late West Saxon, combined with features characteristic of the South Eastern dialect of Early Middle English.[73] Examples of those features in this preface include *æce* (for *ece*, 'eternal'), *meihte* (for *meahte*, verb 'might'), *while* (for *hwile*, 'while'), and *weig* (for *wæg*, 'way'). The language of the Preface to the *Laws* of Alfred, edited here from the mid-tenth-century copy in Cambridge, Corpus Christi College MS 173, fits with composition and transmission within West Saxon circles.

---

[68] Godden and Irvine (2009), I.170–83.
[69] Bately (2003), p. 114, suggests that the word *earfoþrime* reflects an 'Alfredian mannerism' and that overall the preface's 'Alfredian credentials are linguistically impeccable'.
[70] Bredehoft (2009), pp. 175–9.   [71] Bately (2003), pp. 118–19.
[72] Godden and Irvine (2009), I.152–70.
[73] See Carnicelli (1969), pp. 3–24; Stanley (1970), pp. 111–12; and Lockett (2022), pp. 311–12.

Early Medieval Reception History

A number of the Alfredian frame texts clearly attracted the attention of contemporary and later readers and writers. This is evident both from annotations in copies of the texts and from their influence on later compositions. The prefatory material in particular made its mark on early medieval literary culture.

Evidence of the interest of later readers in the framing material of the *Pastoral Care* is well exemplified by the copy in the oldest surviving manuscript, Oxford, Bodleian Library, Hatton 20, produced for Bishop Wærferth of Worcester. The Preface to the *Pastoral Care* in this copy was annotated in the early eleventh century by Archbishop Wulfstan himself, probably as a way of clarifying the meaning of the text.[74] Further annotations were added in the first half of the thirteenth century by the scribe known as the Worcester Tremulous Hand.[75] This copy was annotated in the early modern period too, most extensively in the late sixteenth century by John Joscelyn, secretary to Archbishop Parker, who also collated its text with copies in other manuscripts.[76] Early readers of MS Hatton 20 showed an interest as well in framing material other than the Prose Preface to the *Pastoral Care*. There is also evidence of early readerly engagement with its copy of the Verse Epilogue to the *Pastoral Care* on folio 9v. The last six lines of the poem, probably inspired by the Gospel of John 4:7–26 (the story of the meeting between a Samaritan woman and Christ), prompted one tenth-century reader of this copy to write out John 4:13–14 (in Latin) further down on the same page. A closing colophon on the page, 'Koenwald monachus. Ælfric clericus hoc conposuit' (The monk Koenwald. The cleric Ælfric composed this) may link the entry to Cenwald, Bishop of Worcester from 928/929 to 957/958.[77]

Reception of the Prose Preface to the *Pastoral Care* is also witnessed through its influence on the work of some later vernacular writers. Æthelwold may have drawn on it in composing his prologue (known as

---

[74] See Dance (2004), pp. 37–43; see also Ker (1956), pp. 24–5; Graham (2004), p. 46.

[75] See Graham (2004), pp. 46–8; Franzen (1991), pp. 59–60. As both Graham and Franzen note, the copy of the Prose Preface in Cambridge, Corpus Christi College MS 12, is also glossed by the Tremulous Hand.

[76] See Graham (2004), pp. 48–9.   [77] See Schreiber (2003), p. 54; Whobrey (1991), p. 184.

'King Edgar's Establishment of the Monasteries') to a version of the Old English translation of the Rule of St Benedict, composed in about 870.[78] At the end of the tenth century, the monk and prolific vernacular writer Ælfric also apparently drew on it in producing the preface to his *Grammar*.[79] William of Malmesbury, writing in Latin in the first half of the twelfth century, views this preface as so pivotal for literary development in England that he includes a summary of it in his *Gesta regum Anglorum* (The Deeds of the English Kings), as well as supplying a list of what he believed to be King Alfred's translations.[80]

We can catch glimpses of the reception of other Alfredian prefaces. The Prose Preface to the *Dialogues* was clearly being read in the late tenth or early eleventh century when it was rewritten, along with the rest of the work, by a reviser (as witnessed by the copy in Oxford, Bodleian Library, MS Hatton 76). Interest in the Verse Preface to the *Dialogues* around the middle of the eleventh century is witnessed by a scribal annotation in the only surviving copy (in London, British Library, MS Cotton Otho C. I, vol. 2), which changes the name *Wulfsige* to *Wulfstan*, perhaps referring to Bishop Wulfstan II who may have commissioned the manuscript either as a resource for preaching or for private reading.[81] Around a century and a half later, another reader of the Verse Preface to the *Dialogues* can be identified, this time the Worcester Tremulous Hand who left his mark in glosses here and elsewhere throughout the work.[82]

The relatively few examples of the trope of the book as speaker that have survived may suggest that the Alfredian examples (the Verse Preface to the *Pastoral Care*, the *Dialogues*, and perhaps the *Boethius*) acted as a model for two later non-Alfredian prefatory poems *Aldhelm* and *Thureth*. In *Aldhelm*, Aldhelm's dual role as *byscop* (bishop) and *æpele sceop* (glorious poet) is perhaps influenced by the depiction of Alfred as both *cyning* (king) and *leoðwyrhta* (poet) in the Verse Preface to the *Boethius*.[83] Both poems also reflect on the

---

[78] See Pratt (2012), pp. 167–8.   [79] See Godden (1978) and (2009b), pp. 142–3.
[80] See Mynors, Thomson, and Winterbottom (1998–9), ii.123 (I.192–4).
[81] Johnson (2006), pp. 187–9.   [82] Franzen (1991), p. 64.
[83] *Aldhelm*, lines 3 and 5, in Jones (2012), p. 126; the Verse Preface to the *Boethius*, lines 2 and 3, edited below.

particular difficulties which their 'author' might have in conveying their material.

The introductory *vitae* of the *Boethius* may partly inform Æthelweard's comment, in his tenth-century Latin *Chronicon*, on the reception of the *Boethius*:

> Nam ex Latino rhetorico fasmate in propriam uerterat linguam uolumina, numero ignoto, ita uarie, ita praeopime, ut non tantum expertioribus sed et audientibus liber Boetii lachrymosus quodammodo suscitaretur motus.[84]
>
> For from the ornate Latin tongue he [Alfred] turned unknown numbers of books into his own language with such variety and richness, that not only for scholars, but for any who might hear it read, the tearful passion of the book of Boethius would be in a measure brought to life.

Since the beginning of the work, including the *vita*, focuses on Boethius' sorrow, but this sorrow becomes rapidly less important as the dialogue continues, we might reasonably ask, with Malcolm Godden, whether Æthelweard 'had done more than glance at the beginning'.[85] In any case, the *vita*, along with various passages of lament in the main work, may have informed Æthelweard's perspective here.

Evidence for the reception of the Preface to the *Laws* of Alfred is similarly uncertain. Some parallels in structure and narrative devices between this preface and Æthelwold's 'King Edgar's Establishment of the Monasteries' may suggest that Æthelwold used it as a model (perhaps in conjunction with the Prose Preface to the *Pastoral Care*).[86] The Preface to the *Laws* also shows a number of correspondences with Ælfric's mid-Lent homily (from his second series of *Catholic Homilies*) and the Old English *Heptateuch*.[87] It is tempting to speculate, with Jurasinski and Oliver, that such correspondences point to reception of the Preface to the *Laws* as a scriptural translation as well as a legal text. Ultimately, though, the evidence may point as much to shared access to a common interpretive tradition as to direct consultation of the Alfredian frame text.

---

[84] Æthelweard, *Chronicon*, IV.2, in Campbell (1962), p. 51.

[85] Godden (2008), p. 191 n. 2. See also Szarmach (2012), pp. 221–2. Weaver (2016), p. 235, links Æthelweard's response to the 'hagiographical framework' of the *Boethius* as a whole.

[86] See S. Irvine (2017), p. 16.

[87] For an overview, see Jurasinski and Oliver (2021), pp. 152–6.

Editorial Procedure and Conventions

The texts are organized according to the main work with which they are associated. The ordering of the main works conforms to a chronological sequence that is plausible rather than definitive. For each main work there is a separate introduction, discussing the work and its contexts, the manuscripts and previous editions, and each of the various frame texts in turn. The frame texts themselves follow this introduction. They are ordered according to the layout of the main work, and interposed with summaries of the main work (or part of that work) at the appropriate points in order to establish context. Where a main work has two alternative prologues occurring in separate manuscripts or versions, they are printed one after the other.

The texts are based on fresh examination of the manuscripts in which they survive (unless otherwise stated). In each case the text follows closely the chosen base manuscript, except that word-division, punctuation, capitalization, paragraphing, and metrical lineation (for the verse) are editorial. Abbreviations have been silently expanded in the texts and Textual Notes: for MS 7, I have used *and* or *ond* depending on the linguistic context. Accents have not been reproduced since they often seem to be used arbitrarily in the manuscripts. Folio references to the manuscript on which the text is based are provided.

The facing-page translations are my own, based in some cases on translations I have published elsewhere.

The Textual Notes, located in a separate section after the texts, record significant textual variants and emendations to the base text. Significant features in the layout of the base text are also recorded. The lemma (or portion of the text to which the variant or emendation applies), where supplied, is followed by a square bracket]; a numeral in parentheses after the lemma indicates which usage in the relevant line is being referred to. Every word except the lemmata and variant readings is italicized. An interlinear or marginal insertion is indicated by \ /. Missing or illegible letter(s) are indicated by [ ].

A separate section of Commentary follows the Textual Notes. A complete Glossary to the texts is provided after the Commentary.

The Old English *Dialogues*

Prose and Verse Prefaces
Gregorian Preface
Incipits and Explicits

INTRODUCTION

The *Dialogues* is furnished with a range of framing material. It includes two prefaces independent of the source, one in prose and one in verse. The Prose Preface appears in two copies of the work, one of which is a heavily revised version of the other; the Verse Preface appears only in a separate copy. The Prose Preface is the earlier of the two, purportedly written by King Alfred (but probably in fact by the translator of the main work). The Verse Preface was apparently composed for a copy made after the work was in wider circulation.

The Prose Preface and Verse Preface are supplementary to the Old English work's Gregorian Preface, a translation of Gregory's own prologue to the *Dialogi*, in which Gregory explains the circumstances that prompted the Latin work's composition. In one copy of the *Dialogues*, the phrase *explicit prefatio* (the preface ends [here]) occurs after the Gregorian Preface. Wærferth's translation of Gregory's prologue can therefore be seen to serve as part of a broader framing structure in which an original preface is itself framed by prefatory material independent of the source.[1]

In addition to its prefaces, the work is provided with short frame texts at the beginnings and endings of each of its four books (except for the end of the last book). These extended incipits and explicits, also independent of the main source, were probably part of the Old English work from an early stage. The incipits focus on Gregory's eloquence, the explicits on the dialogue form of the work.

The Work and its Contexts

Gregory the Great's *Dialogi*, which the Old English work translates, comprises a collection of stories about virtuous people and the miracles they were able to perform. It was written around AD 593 and became immensely popular

---

[1] Compare a similar layering of frame texts in the *Pastoral Care*.

in the early medieval period. Divided into four books, its overarching structure is a dialogue between Gregory and his deacon Peter, within which the individual stories act as examples of virtuous living. Evidence from surviving manuscripts and book lists suggests that the work was a staple of the Anglo-Saxon library,[2] its popularity no doubt fostered by the combined narrative and didactic appeal of the stories as well as by the authority of Gregory's name.[3] Within its Alfredian context, there was also perhaps a parallel to be drawn between contemporary England under constant attack from the Vikings and the sixth-century Italy of Gregory's day beset by Lombard invasions.[4]

The evidence of the king's biographer Asser would suggest that the *Dialogues* was the earliest of the Alfredian translations.[5] Since Asser makes no mention of the wider translation programme, it seems likely that the translation was made before the programme properly took shape. The most likely date of composition is between 885 and the end of 887 (when, according to Asser, Alfred began to translate Latin himself).[6] Asser tells us that Wærferth, Bishop of Worcester from around 872 to 915, translated the work at Alfred's command.[7] The use of vocabulary and spellings characteristic of the Mercian dialect is attributable to Wærferth's links to Mercia. The Prose Preface to the *Dialogues* implies that the production of the translation was envisaged as a communal venture by Alfred's 'loyal friends'. This may show modesty on the part of Wærferth (who probably composed this preface as well as the main work).[8] Alternatively it may reflect a model of translation which entails discussion with a team of scholars. If so, we might compare the Prose Preface to the *Pastoral Care* where tribute is paid to Plegmund, Asser, Grimbald, and John, from whom Alfred 'learned' the book.

Wærferth's translation of the *Dialogi* keeps close to its Latin source in both content and style.[9] By using Latinate sentence constructions, combined with alliteration and other word play that exploits the potential of the vernacular idiom, Wærferth apparently attempted to recreate the eloquence for which Gregory was so renowned. Critical opinion is divided on the degree of his success in this regard. His contemporary Asser praised

---

[2] Lapidge (2006), p. 127. [3] See further Dekker (2001).
[4] See, for example, Keynes and Lapidge (1983), p. 293; Dekker (2001), pp. 49–50.
[5] Stevenson (1959), ch. 77. [6] Godden (2013), p. 94.
[7] Stevenson (1959), ch. 77. [8] Godden (1997), p. 37.
[9] See Bately (1988), pp. 120–3.

him for writing *elucabratim et elegantissime* (painstakingly and very elegantly).[10] Modern scholars have been less ready to appreciate Wærferth's largely literal—and not entirely reliable—rendering of Gregory's writing,[11] while acknowledging that faithfulness to the Latin source may have been a sign of respect to the authority of the original author.[12]

The motivation behind the production of the Old English work cannot be easily determined. The Prose Preface states that the work was produced for King Alfred's personal use. The Verse Preface, however, implies that the work has been circulated more widely, with further copies in preparation. It is possible that both prefaces reflect the reality of the time they were written, if the potential benefits of circulating works in English was only a later inspiration. Alternatively, as Malcolm Godden has suggested, the story of Alfred commissioning the *Dialogues* for his personal use may always have been 'a fiction, a way of both lending his authority to the text and justifying the use of the vernacular'.[13] If so, the work was perhaps directed in the first instance towards bishops (such as the one mentioned in the Verse Preface), whose brief was to produce more copies. The recipients of these copies conceivably included lay nobles and secular clergy; eleventh-century manuscript evidence suggests that it was by then at least a useful resource for preaching.[14]

Manuscripts and Previous Editions

The prefatory material, and the incipits and explicits, are witnessed in three manuscript copies of the *Dialogues*:

C Cambridge, Corpus Christi College MS 322 (s. xi^2).[15]
H Oxford, Bodleian Library, MS Hatton 76 (s. xi^1).[16]
O London, British Library, Cotton MS Otho C. i, vol. 2 (s. xi^{in} for Books I and II and s. xi^{med} for Books III and IV).[17]

---

[10] Stevenson (1959), ch. 77.
[11] See Godden (1997), pp. 44–7; for other examples, see Johnson (2007); Johnson (2015), pp. 378–9.
[12] Thijs (2007a).   [13] Godden (2009a), p. 100.
[14] See Dekker (2001); Johnson (2006).
[15] Ker (1957), no. 60; Gneuss and Lapidge (2014), no. 92.
[16] Ker (1957), no. 328A; Gneuss and Lapidge (2014), no. 632.
[17] Ker (1957), no. 182; Gneuss and Lapidge (2014), no. 359.

A fourth witness to the *Dialogues*, Canterbury, Cathedral Library, MS Add. 25 (s. x^ex), known as A, does not contain relevant material; it consists only of two adjacent bifolia containing portions of Book IV of the *Dialogues*.[18]

C contains the only surviving copy of Wærferth's Prose Preface to the *Dialogues* in its original form. O contains the only surviving copy of the Verse Preface to the *Dialogues*. H, which consists of fragments from Books I and II of an extensively revised version of the Old English original, based on a copy related to the one in C, has the Prose Preface.[19]

Both O and C contain copies of the incipits of Books II, III, and IV and the explicits of Books I, II, and III. H's fragments include a revised version of the incipit of Book II. The incipit of Book I appears in O but not in C or H. The passage is likely to have been part of the original work, given how closely it corresponds to the other incipits,[20] and subsequently lost in C's transmission history.[21] In its manuscript context in O, this incipit begins on a new line with a large decorated initial, and runs into the Gregorian Preface with no visual break, creating a sense of continuity between the two. The incipit of Book I is therefore edited here as the opening section of the Gregorian Preface to the *Dialogues*.

The copyist of O views the Gregorian Preface (including the incipit of Book I) as part of the main work rather than prefatory: after a line-break between the end of the Verse Preface and the beginning of the Gregorian Preface, the text runs on without a break to the end of Book I. In C, however, there is no break after the Prose Preface, which runs straight on into the Gregorian Preface, with a section break coming only after the Gregorian Preface. Similarly in H (the revised version of C), the section break comes at the end of the Gregorian Preface (fo. 3r), where the

---

[18] See Ker (1957), no. 96; Gneuss and Lapidge (2014), no. 207; Yerkes (1977).

[19] H's versions of the Prose Preface and of the Book II incipit are not printed in this edition. H's text is printed in a parallel column to C's text in the standard edition of the work by Hecht (1900).

[20] Godden (1997), p. 43 n. 27, responding here to the view expressed by Yerkes (1986), p. 341, that the passage represents linguistically the later Verse Preface in O rather than the rest of the text and is therefore not original.

[21] Conceivably the loss happened either at the point in C's transmission when the Prose Preface was added, or as a result of confusion arising from the repetition of *æresða* in the incipit of Book I and the subsequent *ærestan*.

copyist writes *explicit prefatio* (the preface ends [here]). Unlike O, then, C and H present the Prose Preface and Gregorian Preface as together serving a prefatory function, separate from the main body of Gregory's work.

The Gregorian Preface, the incipits of Books II, III, and IV, and the explicits occur in O and C. Hans Hecht, in what remains the standard edition of the *Dialogues*, bases his text on C rather than O (with H also printed where available in a parallel column),[22] but it is the copy in O that is in fact closer to Wærferth's original.[23] O is therefore used as the base text in this edition, drawing on readings in C where O's text is missing or illegible.

The *Dialogues*, including the Prose Preface and Verse Preface, the Gregorian Preface, and the incipits and explicits, was edited in full by Hecht in 1900. The Verse Preface was edited within the Anglo-Saxon Poetic Records series by Elliott Van Kirk Dobbie in 1942,[24] on its own by David Yerkes in 1980,[25] and in the Dumbarton Oaks Medieval Library series, as one of a number of Alfredian verse prefaces, by Susan Irvine and Malcolm Godden in 2012.[26]

The Prose Preface to the *Dialogues*

Although the Prose Preface to the *Dialogues* uses Alfred's first-person voice, its language and style (particularly the heavy use of word pairs such as 'ongyten and gehyred', and 'godcundan and gastlican') suggest that it, like the main work, was written by Wærferth.[27] It was probably written at the same time as or soon after the translation itself. The reason for the omission of the Prose Preface from O (where the Verse Preface to the *Dialogues* occurs instead) is unclear. The manuscript may have derived from a copy of

---

[22] Hecht (1900).   [23] See Harting (1937). See also Godden (2013), p. 96.
[24] Dobbie (1942), pp. 112–13.   [25] Yerkes (1980).
[26] Irvine and Godden (2012), pp. 404–7.
[27] Other instances in the Prose Preface are 'geleoðigen and gebigen', 'sohte and wilnade', 'þeawum and wundrum', and 'mynegunge and lufe'. On Wærferth's authorship, see Godden (1997), pp. 36–8; and Godden (2009a), p. 96 n. 10. Bately (2003), pp. 116–17, argues that the author may have been one of Wærferth's clergy rather than Wærferth himself.

the work circulated before the Prose Preface was added. Other possible explanations are that the Prose Preface was lost in transmission (either before the Verse Preface was supplied or afterwards), or that the Prose Preface, in implying that Alfred needed a translation for his personal reading, came to be viewed as misleading and was therefore replaced.[28]

The Prose Preface to the *Dialogues* depends heavily upon Gregory's own prologue. Its conceit—the difficulty of reconciling worldly commitments and spiritual contemplation—is drawn from Gregory's description of his own struggles. In attaching a preface which so closely reflects the state of mind expressed by Gregory, Wærferth not only anticipates the translation of Gregory's own preface that will follow, but also presents Alfred as a kind of contemporary equivalent to Gregory the Great.[29] Alfred's and Gregory's parallel one another, investing Alfred with the religious and literary authority that Gregory represents. The effect is enhanced by the repetition of motifs across the two prefaces: Alfred is presented as bemoaning his worldly distractions as king in the same way that Gregory does as pope. Both the Prose Preface to the *Dialogues* and Gregory's own prologue end by turning their attention to book production, creating an implicit parallel between Gregory's and Alfred's literary activities.

The Prose Preface to the *Dialogues* consists of just two sentences, which parallel each other stylistically in their heavy use of subordinate clauses and word pairs. Both sentences culminate in a contrast of the earthly and the divine, and in particular the benefits of engaging with the latter. The preface makes much of Alfred's individual voice: it begins with the word *ic* (I) and first-person singular pronouns also feature prominently in its second half. The first-person plural forms (*us*, *we*, and *ure*) elsewhere in the preface are not the plural of majesty, which was used only from the twelfth century onwards.[30] Rather Alfred is being linked to other leaders, secular and religious, who strive to reconcile their earthly and spiritual responsibilities (including Gregory himself).

---

[28] Godden (2013), p. 95.
[29] Compare the Verse Preface to the *Pastoral Care*, in which Alfred is presented as continuing Gregory's work.
[30] See Mitchell (1987), I.107 (§252).

The Verse Preface to the *Dialogues*

In line 12, one Bishop Wulfsige is named as the person who commissioned the copy of the book for which the Verse Preface to the *Dialogues* was written.[31] Wulfsige was Bishop of Sherborne around the last two decades of the ninth century. Although it is possible that the poem is the work of Wulfsige himself, it makes no claim to his authorship and may have been commissioned rather than composed by him. Its date of composition presumably falls within the period of Wulfsige's episcopacy. A number of lexical parallels with Old English poems including *Andreas* have been identified.[32]

The poem consists of two parts, the first (up to line 15) explaining the function of the book and how it came to be made and the second (line 16 to the end) entreating that those who read the book say prayers for both Wulfsige and his lord King Alfred. It can also be read as tripartite, with each section focusing on a different facet of the book's interaction with others: the individual reader (lines 1–11), the bishop who commissioned the copy (lines 12–22), and King Alfred who gave the exemplar for the copy (lines 23–7).

The preface is written in the voice of the book, a trope occurring in other prefatory verse from the Alfredian period onwards (such as the Verse Preface to the *Pastoral Care* and the poems *Aldhelm* and *Thureth*).[33] The idea of books as sources of wisdom is prominent in the poem, reflected in the image of the book as both physical treasure and spiritual model.[34] The poem also emphasizes the role of the devout as models of spiritual goodness, suggesting that whoever composed it did so with the main work in mind.

The Gregorian Preface to the *Dialogues*

The Gregorian Preface to the *Dialogues* was translated by Wærferth as part of the broader *Dialogues* translation project. It keeps close to Gregory's original Latin prologue, except in its addition of a short opening section (the incipit of Book I and a statement on the content and purpose of the

---

[31] As a result of scribal alteration the manuscript now reads 'Wulfstan'; the case for 'Wulfsige' as the original reading was made by Sisam (1953b), p. 202. See further the Verse Preface to the *Dialogues*, Commentary, line 12.

[32] Bredehoft (2009), pp. 99–101.   [33] See the General Introduction, pp. 6–7.

[34] See further the Verse Preface to the *Dialogues*, Commentary, line 23.

work). The effect of this independent opening is to establish a clear distinction between Wærferth's contemporary voice and Gregory's voice from the past. Reminders of this distinction emerge through the other incipits and explicits that demarcate the individual books.

Structurally the Gregorian Preface resembles the Latin original in taking the form of a dialogue between Pope Gregory and his deacon Peter. The independent opening sentences guide a contemporary audience in how to approach the text, both by supplying information about the work's content and purpose, and by establishing the distinction between Gregory's world and the reader's own. Stylistically, too, the Gregorian Preface reflects its source, abounding in Latinate constructions and sentence structures.[35] Though the ideas expressed in the preface are Gregory's, many of them would have spoken to English audiences in the late ninth century and beyond: conflict between secular and religious responsibilities, the relationship between mind and body, friendship, learning by example, and literary authority.

The Incipits and Explicits of the *Dialogues*

The incipits and explicits that mark the beginnings and endings of the individual books of the *Dialogues* are independent of the Gregorian source. Manuscript and stylistic evidence suggests that they were all part of Wærferth's original. The incipit of Book I occurs only in O (not in C or H), but its imagery is close to that in the incipits of Books II, III, and IV. All four incipits share with the rest of the work stylistic features such as word pairs (often alliterative), including 'gyldenmuða Gregorius' (golden-mouthed Gregory), 'þyrsteð ond lysteþ' (are thirsty and in longing), 'drincan ond gecnawan' (drink and understand), 'geglenged ond getrymed' (adorned and strengthened), 'wera wundrum' (miracles of men), 'gefrætewudu ond awriten' (adorned and written down), and 'wislicum wordum' (with wise words).[36]

The incipits and explicits have no known sources. Janet Bately suggests that the incipits were perhaps 'based on headings in the lost Latin

---

[35] Bately (1988), pp. 120–1.
[36] These examples occur in the incipits of Books II and IV and the explicits of Books II and III of the *Dialogues*.

exemplar'.[37] The metaphor of water running from a spring or well, shared by all the incipits, has traditional associations with the wisdom that leads to eternal life, which can be traced back to St John's Gospel.[38] It also occurs in the Verse Epilogue to the *Pastoral Care*, where its context is similarly the dissemination of God's wisdom.

The attribution of the epithet 'golden-mouthed' to Gregory in the incipits of Books II and III may derive from the Whitby *Life of Gregory the Great*,[39] although, as Patrick Sims-Williams points out, the Whitby *Life* was apparently never widely available, and a more likely explanation is that the anonymous author of the *Life* and Wærferth were both drawing on a now lost (probably Irish) common source.[40] The image of a golden mouth and golden lips used in these two incipits highlights the idea of Gregory's gift for eloquence. Wærferth includes the Greek and Latin terms for 'golden mouth'—*Chrysosthomas* and *Os Aureum* respectively—as part of his effort to invest the text with the authority of early Christian tradition. The image links speech and ornament in a way that seems apt for a work that represents a stylistically enhanced dialogue. The idea of ornament also informs the explicits of Books II and III where the terms *geglenged* (adorned) and *gefrætewudu* (adorned) are linked to the act of speaking.[41]

Note on the Texts

The text of the Prose Preface to the *Dialogues* is based on Cambridge, Corpus Christi College MS 322 [C] (s. xi²), fo. 1r. The text also occurs in an extensively revised version (not printed here) in Oxford, Bodleian Library, MS Hatton 76 (s. xi¹). The text of the Verse Preface to the *Dialogues* is based on London, British Library, Cotton MS Otho C. i, vol. 2 [O] (s. xi^in), fo. 1r. The texts of the Gregorian Preface, and of the incipits and explicits, are based on O (to which folio numbers refer), with text supplied from C where O is defective.

---

[37] Bately (2002), p. 156.   [38] Dekker (2001), pp. 38–9.
[39] Colgrave (1968), pp. 117–19.   [40] Sims-Williams (1990), pp. 187–8.
[41] For further discussion of this image, see S. Irvine (forthcoming).

TEXTS AND TRANSLATIONS

The Prose Preface to the *Dialogues*

Ic Ælfred, geofendum Criste mid cynehades mærnysse geweorðod, habbe gearolice ongyten and þurh haligra boca gesægene oft gehyred, þætte us, þam þe God swa micle heanesse worldgeþingða forgifen hafað, is seo mæste ðearf, þæt we hwilon ure mod betwix þas eorþlican ymbhigdo geleoðigen and gebigen to ðam godcundan and þam gastlican rihte. And forþan ic sohte 5
and wilnade to minum getreowum freondum, þæt hi me of Godes bocum be haligra manna þeawum and wundrum awriten þas æfterfylgendan lare, þæt ic þurh þa mynegunge and lufe gescyrped on minum mode betwih þas eorðlican gedrefednesse hwilum gehicge þa heofonlican.

The Prose Preface to the *Dialogues*

I, Alfred, honoured with the glory of kingship by the grace of Christ, have clearly perceived and frequently heard from statements in holy books that for us, to whom God has granted such high distinction in worldly office, there is a very great need to calm our minds occasionally in the course of these earthly anxieties and turn them to divine and spiritual law. And therefore I sought and asked my true friends to write down for me from God's books the teachings that follow concerning the practices and miracles of holy men, so that, strengthened in my mind through those exhortations and love, I may occasionally reflect on heavenly things amongst these earthly tribulations.

The Verse Preface to the *Dialogues*

Se ðe me rædan ðencð   tyneð mid rihtum geðance.
He in me findan mæg,   gif hine feola lysteð
gastlices lifes   godre biesene,
þæt he ful eaþe mæg   upp gestigan
to ðam heofonlican hame   þar byð a hyht ond wyn,   5
blis on burgum,   þam þe bearn Godes
sielfes hiora eagum   geseon motan.
Þæt mæg se mon begytan,   se þe his modgeðanc
æltowe byþ   ond þonne þurh his ingehygd
to þissa haligra   helpe geliefeð   10
ond hiora bisene fulgað,   swa þeos boc sagað.
Me awritan het   Wulfsige bisceop,
þeow ond þearfa   þæs þe alne þrym aof
ond eac walden is   wihta gehwelcre,
an ece God   eallra gesceafta.   15
Bideþ þe se bisceop   se þe ðas boc begeat,
þe þu on þinum handum nu   hafast ond sceawast,
þæt þu him to þeossum halgum   helpe bidde,
þe heora gemynd heron   gemearcude siendon,
ond þæt him God ællmihtig   20
forgyue þa gyltas   þe he geo worhte
ond eac resðe mid him   se ðe ah ealles rices geweald,
ond eac swa his beahgifan,   þe him ðas bysene forgeaf,
þæt is se selesða   sinces brytta,
Ælfryd mid Englum,   ealra cyninga   25
þara þe he sið oððe ær fore   secgan hyrde,
oððe he iorðcyninga ær   ænigne gefrugne.

The Verse Preface to the *Dialogues*

He who intends to read me will close me with proper understanding.
If he wishes for many good examples
of the spiritual life, he can find them in me,
so that he can very easily ascend
5 to the heavenly home where there is always hope, joy,
and bliss in those dwellings for those who are allowed
to see the Son of God himself with their own eyes.
That can be obtained by any person whose mind
is sound and then through his understanding
10 trusts in the help of these saints
and carries out their example, as this book says.
Bishop Wulfsige commanded me to be written,
the poor servant of him who exalted all glory
and is also the ruler of every creature,
15 one eternal God of all creation.
The bishop who procured this book, which you
now have in your hand and gaze at, requests
that you should pray to these holy men whose
memories are inscribed in it to help him,
20 and ask almighty God
to forgive the sins which he has committed
and also to grant him rest with him who has power over every kingdom,
and also [to grant rest] to his ring-giver who gave him the book's exemplar,
that is Alfred of the English, the best
25 treasure-giver of all the kings
that he has ever heard spoken of,
or of earthly kings that he has previously found out about.

The Gregorian Preface to the *Dialogues*

Her ongynneð se æresða stream þære clænan ond hlutran burnan þurh þone halegan breosð ures fæder ond larheowes þæs apostolican papan sanctus Gregorius up aspringan and forþ yrnan to lare ond to bisene eallum þam þe lysteð feran on liues weg.

Forþon nu æt ærestan we magon gehyran hu se eadega ond se | apostolica wer sanctus Gregorius spræc to hys deacone, þam wæs nama Petrus, be haligra manna þeawum ond life to lare ond to bysene eallum þam þe Godes willan wyrceað ond lufiað. Ond forþon se eadiga sanctus Gregorius ærest wæs sprecende be him sylfum þisum wordum ond þus cwæð:

Sume dæge hit gelamp þæt ic wæs swiðe geswenced mid þam geruxlum ond uneðnessum sumra woruldlicra ymbhogena, for þam underfenge þises biscoplican folgoðes. In þam worldscirum we beoð ful oft genyded þæt we doð þæt þe us genoh gewis ys þæt wæ ne don sceolon. Þa me gelyste ðære diglan stowe þe ic ær on wæs on mynstre. Seo is þære gnornunge freond, forðon mon symble mæg hys sares ond hys unrihtes mæst geþencean gyf he byð ana in digolnesse. Ðær me ætywde openlice hyt sylf eal swa hwæt swa me mislicode be minre agenre wisan, ond þær comon sweotollice beforan þa eagan minre heortan eall þa gedonan unriht, þe gewunedon þæt hig me sar ond sorge ongebrohton.

Witodlice ic sæt þa ðær swyðe geswenced ond longe swigende. Ða com me to min sunu Petrus ond min se leofosta deacon, se wæs gebunden and getogen to me hiwcuðlice mid freondlicre lufan from þære frymðe hys geogoðhades, ond he wæs symble min gefæra to smeaunge þæs halgan wordes ond ðære godcundan lare. Ond he ða lociende on me geseah þæt ic wæs geswenced mid hefige sare minre heortan, ond þa cwæð þus to me: 'Ac la, gelomp þe aht niwes? Forhwon hafast ðu maran gnornunge þonne hyt ær gewuna wæs?'

Ða cwæð ic hym to: 'Eala Petrus, seo gnornung þe ic dreoge daga gehwylce, symble heo ys me eald for gewunan, ond symble heo is me niwe for eacan. Min þæt ungeselige mod is swiðe gecnyssed ond gedrefed for þære wunde his bysgunge, ond gemyneð hwylc hyt ær wæs in mynstre: hu hyt on bæc læt ond forhogode eal ðas | gewitendlican þing, ond hu swiðe hyt oferhlifade eall þas worldþing þe we nu on drohtniað, ond þæt hit ne gewunode noht elles þencean buton þa heofonlican. Ond þær eac hit oferstah,

The Gregorian Preface to the *Dialogues*

Here the first stream of the pure and clear spring begins to gush up and flow through the holy breast of our father and teacher the apostolic pope St Gregory, as a lesson and example to all those who wish to travel on the way of life.

5 Therefore now to begin with we can hear how the blessed and apostolic pope St Gregory spoke to his deacon, whose name was Peter, about the teachings, customs and life of holy people as a lesson and example for all those who do and love God's will. And therefore the blessed St Gregory first spoke these words about himself, saying:

10 It happened one day that I was very worn down by the hubbub and stresses of various worldly responsibilities, on account of undertaking this episcopal position. In worldly affairs we're very often obliged to do things which we know we ought not to do. Then I had a hankering for the secluded place which I had been in previously in the monastery. That (place) is friend
15 to grief because someone can always think most deeply about his sorrow and wrongful behaviour if he is alone in a place apart. There everything I disliked about my own role revealed itself openly, and there came clearly before the eyes of my heart whatever wrongs I had committed that regularly inflicted pain and sorrow on me.

20 Indeed I then sat there very troubled and in silence for a long time. Then my son and dearest deacon Peter, who had been linked and drawn to me intimately with friendly affection from the beginning of his youth, came to me, and he was constantly my companion in the study of holy scripture and divine teaching. And looking at me he saw that I was weighed down by heavy
25 sorrow in my heart, and then said to me as follows: 'So has anything new happened to you? Why are you grieving more than you have in the past?'

Then I said to him: 'Oh Peter, the grief that I suffer every day always remains old for me through my being used to it, and always new because it keeps increasing. My unhappy mind is very battered and troubled because
30 of the wound of its [worldly] activity, and recalls what it had before in the monastery: how it left behind and despised all these transitory things, and how much it rose above all these worldly things that we now engage in, and how it used to think about nothing else except heavenly things. And there

þeah ðe hit behæfd wære in lichomon, þa locu sylf ðæs lichomon mid sceawunge þæs heofenlican lifes. Ond eac þone deað, þe þinceð fulneah eallum mannum wite, þone hit lufade þær gelice swylce lifes ingong ond his gewinnes mede ond edlean.

Ond nu for ðam bysegum þisse bisceoplican scire hyt þrowað þa embehogan worldlicra manna, ond æfter swa fægerre onsyne hys ræste þe hit on wæs, hit is nu afyled mid ði duste eorðlicra dæda. Ond nu, þonne hit tostregdeð ond todæleð hit sylf embe oþera manna wisan for nedþearfe monigra monna, witodlice þonne hit wyle ymbe his agne þencean, buton tweon hit gehwyrfeð þy medmare to his sylfes ðearfe. Genoh georne ic gehicge hwæt ic dreoge, ond hwæt ic anforlet. Ond symble þonne ic geþence þæt ic ær forleas þa diglan stowe, me ðinceð þis þi hefigre þæt ic nu ræfnige.

Geseoh nu, Petrus, þæt me is gelicost þam þe on lefan scype byð, þe byð geswenced mid ðam yþum micles sæs: swa ic eom onstyred mid þam gedrefednessum þisse worldle, ond ic eom gecnysed mid þam stormum þære strongan hreohnesse in þam scype mines modes. Ond þonne ic gemune mines þæs æran lifes þe ic on mynstre ær on wunode, ðonne asworette ic ond ageomorige gelice þam þe on lefan scipe neah londe gelæteð, ond hit þonne se ðoden ond se storm on sæ adrifeð swa feor swa hit æt nehstan nænig lond geseon ne mæg. Ond eac me þinceð þæt nu gyt micle hefigre sy þæt, þonne ic beo slegen ond gedrefed mid ðam unmætum yþum þisra woruldþinga, þæt ic þonne uneaðe mæg a geþencean ond geseon þa hyðe þe ic forlet þa ic of mynstre gewat. Forþon swylce byð þæs monnes modgeþancas, þæt þonne he ærest þæt god forleoseð þæt he ær hæfde, he swa þeah æt fruman gemyneð þæt he hit forleas, ond þonne þæt mod | feor gewiteð ymb oðru þing, æc swylce hit forgiteð his agenes gode hit ær forleas, oððæt þonne æt nehstan hit gewurðeð þæt se monn no ne gemyneð þæs ðe he ær hæfde. Forþon ic spræc ær beforan swa þæt, þonne we liðað feor, æt nehstan we no geseoð þa stilnesse þære hyðe þe we ær from læton.

Ond eac me byð ful oft to gemynde becumen ond geþeoded to eacan mines sares sumera monna lif, þa þe forleton mid ealle mode þas andweardan world. Đonne ic sceawige þara heanesse ond rihtwisnesse, ic geðence hu swiðe ic sylf licge in þisum nyðerlican þingum. Monige þara gelicedon heora scyppende in digolran life þonne ic on eom. Hi ne ealdedon næfre fram hira modes niwnesse ðurh eorðlice dæde, ond ælmihtig God nolde hig abysgian mid þam gewinnum þises middangeardes.

too, though it was confined in the body, it rose above the body's enclosure through contemplation of the heavenly life. And also it loved death, which seems to nearly everyone a torment, as being equivalent to the beginning of a life and a payment and reward for its struggle.

And now because of the affairs of this episcopal office it suffers the troubles of those in secular life, and after enjoying so pleasant a quality of repose, has now been polluted by the dust of earthly deeds. And now, when it disperses and divides itself concerning other people's behaviour because of what many people need, certainly when it wishes to think about its own need, it will doubtless turn the more briefly to that need of its own. I am thinking very intently about what I suffer and what I have lost. And whenever I think that I have lost the secluded place, then what I am now suffering seems to me heavier.

Observe now, Peter, that I am most like someone who is on a frail ship that is buffeted by the waves of a high sea: so I am now afflicted by the troubles of this world, and I am buffeted by the storms of the great turbulence in the ship of my mind. And when I remember that earlier life of mine which I spent previously in a monastery, then I sigh and groan like someone who shapes his course near to land in a frail ship, and then the violent wind and storm drive it so far out to sea that in the end it cannot see any land. And also it seems to me that it may be still more intolerable since, when I am beaten and assailed by the huge waves of these worldly affairs, then only with difficulty can I ever think about and look on the harbour that I abandoned when I departed from the monastery. And likewise are a person's thoughts: when he first loses something good that he previously had, he still remembers at the outset that he has lost it, and then the mind departs far away to deal with other things but also it forgets the good thing of its own which it lost, until then in the end it turns out that the person has no memory of what he had before. For that reason I said thus before, that when we sail far away, we don't in the end see the peace of the harbour which we previously departed from.

And the life of certain people, who with all their heart abandoned this present world, has very often come into my mind and exacerbated my sorrow. When I contemplate those ones' height of perfection and righteousness, I think how much I myself wallow in these lowly things. Many of them pleased their creator in a more secluded life than I live. They never decayed from the newness of their minds through earthly deeds, and almighty God did not wish to bother them with this world's struggles.

Ac nu þa ðe ic embe sprece, ic gecyðe bet, me ðinceð, gif ic gesceade mid 70
mearcunge þara monna naman, þa þe her bæftan gesægd wæron þurh
ascunge ond ondsware.'
    Petrus cwæð to him: 'Ne oncnew ic noht swiðe hwæðer in Longbeardum
æfre ascinon ænigra monna lif mid mægnum ond wundrum. Nat ic hwæðer
eallunga si inæled ond ontihted of ðæra bysene ond wiðmetenesse. Ne 75
tweoge ic noht þæt gode weras wæron on þisum lande; þonne wene ic,
hwæðere, þætte wundru ond mægenu oððe nænige þinga from him
gewordene wæron, oððe hig oð þis forswigode wæron, þæt we nyton hwæðer
hig gewordene wæron oþþe næron.'
    Gregorius him ondswarode: 'Eala Petrus, gif ic þe ana asecge be fulmede- 80
mum ond gecorenum werum þe ic sylf, an yfelic monn, ongeat æt þam |
godum ond þam geleaffullum weron þe hit me cyðdon, eac þa ðe ic þurh me
sylfne oncneow ond geleornade, ic wene þæt þes dæg blinneð ær ðon me þæt
spell ateorige.'
    Petrus him to cwæð: 'Ic wolde la þæt þu me acsiendum sægdest hwæt- 85
hwega be ðam godum werum, ond þæt þe ne þuhte to hefig, þæt þu ongunne
hwæthwega gebrecan in þone wisdom þære recenesse, forðam ne cymeð
noht ungelic trymnes upp ac swiðe geþwærlicu of ðære gemynde godra
mægna. Witodlice in þære gerecenesse we magon ongytan hwylc þæt gode
mægen byð to findenne ond to gehabbanne, ond we magon oncnawan, in 90
þære sægene þara wundra, hu þæt mægen, funden ond gehæfd, bið gemær-
sod. Ful monige menn wæron þa ma inælað ond getihtað al þa bysene godra
wera þonne þa lare to ðære lufan þæs heofenlican eðles. Ond swa gewurðeþ
ful oft þæt þam mode þæs geheredan becymeð twyfeald fultum in þam byse-
num ura fædera: forþon hit bið onbærned of wiðmetenesse godra foregan- 95
gendra to þære lufan þæs toweardan lifes, ond þeah hit wene þæt hit sylf
hwæthwega sig, symble hit byð geeaðmodad þæs þi swyðor ðonne hit
ongyteð ænige beteran wisan be oþrum monnum.'
    Gregorius him ondswarode: 'Þa wisan þæ ic me geacsode æt gesægene
arwurðra wera, untweogendlice ic þe þa secge mid bysene þære halgan 100
aldorlicnesse. We witon þæt us eallum cuð is þæt Marcus ond Lucas writon
þæt godspel nalæs no þi þe hig hit gesawon ac hig hit geleornedon, swa hi
hit gehyrdon of Petres muðe ond of Paules þæra apostola. Swa eac ic wille
animan ond ateon fram þam | þe þas boc rædað þone intingan ælcere

70   But from now on I will relate better the matters of which I'm speaking, I think, if by marking out the names of those men (Gregory and Peter) I distinguish the things that were said through question and answer hereafter.'

Peter said to him: 'I did not know at all whether the lives of any people amongst the Lombards were ever illustrious through virtuous deeds and
75   miracles. I do not know whether I should be inflamed and inspired in every respect by their example and comparison. I do not doubt that there were good men in this country; but I think that no miracles, virtuous deeds, or any things were performed by them, or else they were passed over in silence up till now so that we don't know whether they were performed or not.'

80   Gregory answered him: 'Oh Peter, if I alone tell you about the fully perfect and distinguished men that I myself, a wretched man, learned about from the good and faithful men who made it known to me, and also those whom I knew and learnt about by myself, I think this day will come to an end before my tale will run out.'

85   Peter said to him: 'I would like you to tell me, in response to my questioning, something about those good men and, if you didn't think it too burdensome, to interrupt briefly the wisdom of scriptural exposition, because a not dissimilar but very fitting lesson arises from the memory of fine virtues. Indeed in scriptural exposition we can learn how a fine virtue is to be found
90   and held on to. And we can learn in the account of miracles how virtue, found and held on to, is transmitted. There are very many people who are more inflamed and persuaded to love for the heavenly home by all the examples of good men than by teachings. And thus it happens very often that the mind of the listener receives a double benefit from the examples of
95   our fathers: for it is kindled by comparison with good predecessors to love for the life to come, and though it may think that it is itself something, it is always humbled so much the more when it learns better from comparison with other people.'

Gregory answered him: 'The ways [of behaving] which I learned from
100   the sayings of honourable men, I tell you unhesitatingly with the example of the sacred authority. We know—it is familiar to us all—that Mark and Luke wrote the gospel not from what they saw but from what they learned, as they heard it from the mouths of the apostles Peter and Paul. So I also wish to take and remove from those who read this book the cause of every doubt

tweounge æt ælcum þæra spella þe ic write; ond ic þæt gecyðe æt hwilcum 105
ordfruman ic geacsode þa ðe ic secge. Ic wille þu Petrus þæt þu þæt wite þæt
ic nime in sumum þæt andgyt an, in sumum ða word mid ði andgyte.
Forðam gif ic be eallum þam hadum synderlice þa word animan wolde,
þonne wæron hi forðbroht ceorlisce þeawe, ond hi no seo hand ond þæt
gewrit þæs writendan swa gecoplice onfenge. Ic leornode ond gefrægn æt 110
gesægene swiðe arwurðra witena þæt ðæt ic nu secge.'

Summary of Book I of the *Dialogues*

In Book I, following on from the Preface, Gregory recounts stories about virtuous people in Italy whose holiness has given them extraordinary powers. Some holy individuals are shown to bring the dead back to life, while less extreme examples of miraculous healing include a story in which sight is given to a blind man. Many miraculous stories are told about the self-denying abbot Equitius, including his exorcism of a nun who forgets to bless a lettuce before eating it. A story of a monastic gardener who apprehends a thief by commanding a snake to guard the vegetables is one of a number of stories about miraculous power over animals: elsewhere we hear how Bishop Boniface frees his garden of caterpillars and persuades a fox to stop stealing his mother's hens, and Fortunatus calms a maddened horse. Other stories involve miraculous yield from meagre supplies of oil and grapes, the replenishment of depleted stores, and miraculous predictions.

105 from each of the stories I write, and I will make known every source from which I learned what I say. I wish you to know, Peter, that in some cases I take the sense alone and in some the words as well as the sense. For if I were to take everybody's words individually then they would be produced in an unrefined manner, and the writer's hand and writing would not receive
110 them so suitably. I learned and found out what I am about to say from the account of those who are very honourable and wise.'

Book I Explicit

Nu is geendad sio forme boc hiora tuegra gespreces Gregorius þæs papan ond Petres his diacones, ond her beneoþan onginneð seo æftere boc eac hiora gespræces be monigfealdum wundrum þæs eadigan weres ond þæs æfæstan abbodes sancte Benedictes.

Book II Incipit

Her yrnet upp se æftra stream ðære godcundan spræce, se cymet of ðære burnan ðæs gastlican æspringes ond þam halgan gaste forgifendum gæð þurh þa ofergyldan weleras þæs eadegan ond þæs apostolican weres sancte Gregories, se mid Grecum Crysosthomas is haten, to þon þæt þurh ða toflownesse þæs ilcan streames se onliht ond geþæned þa þoncas geleaffulra breosta. Þisum wordum se ilca gyldenmuða Gregorius wæs sprecende ond þus cwæð.

Summary of Book II of the *Dialogues*

Book II, which follows on from this incipit, is devoted to the life of St Benedict, telling of his flight to the wilderness as a young man, his establishment of twelve monasteries, the advice and rebukes he gives to monks and devout laymen, and the array of miracles that are performed through his prayers. These miracles include the bringing of provisions (e.g. a well is discovered, the flour is provided during one famine and oil during another, and money is supplied to someone heavily in debt), acts of healing and saving lives (e.g. the monk Maurus runs on water to rescue a boy, a monk crushed under a wall is healed, and a farmer's son is brought back to life), and visions and predictions (e.g. Benedict predicts the fall of his monastery to barbarians, sees his sister Scholastica's soul going to heaven in the form of a dove, and foretells the day of his death).

Book I Explicit

Now the first book of the conversation between those two, Pope Gregory and his deacon Peter, is ended, and here below begins the second book too of their conversation about the many wonders of the blessed man and pious abbot St Benedict.

Book II Incipit

Here flows the second stream of that divine discourse which comes from the spring of the spiritual fountain, and, granted by the Holy Ghost, passes through the gilded lips of the blessed and apostolic man St Gregory, who is called *Chrysostom* by the Greeks, so that through the flowing of that same
5 stream the thoughts of faithful breasts may be illuminated and served. With these words that same golden-mouthed Gregory was speaking, saying thus.

Book II Explicit

Ond æfter þisse ongynneð seo þridde, sio is eac mid haligra wera wundrum geglenged ond getrymed mid heora twegea gespræce.

Book III Incipit

Her onginneð se ðridda flod of ðam neorxnawonglican welan, se þurh þone gyldenan muþ forð aarn ðæs haligan papan ond bisceopes sancte Gregorius, þone Romane for þæra fægran worda gyfe Os Aureum nemniað. On þam flode he wæs sprecende be haligra monna wundrum ond þeawum, swa he ær dyde on ðam ærran bocum, ond ðus wæs cweþende.   5

Summary of Book III of the *Dialogues*

In Book III, which follows on from this incipit, Gregory first recounts stories of virtuous people from the Italian past, including Paulinus, Bishop of Nola, who frees his fellow citizens from captivity by the barbarians; Bishop John and Pope Agapitus, who perform acts of healing, and Bishop Datius, who frees a house of an evil spirit. Gregory then returns to the subject of more recent miraculous events. Some of the stories describe miraculous acts of healing, while others detail how the prayers of the devout can affect the physical world: for example, the course of a river is diverted to prevent floods. In other stories the devout are awarded special powers of insight or visions: the blind Sabinus recognizes that an enemy is serving him poisoned wine; the hermit Menas refuses the gift of a wrong-doer anonymously put before him; Bishop Redemptus is warned of imminent earthly destruction in a vision by St Juticus, after which Italy experiences many adversities.

Book II Explicit

And after this begins the third [book], which is also adorned with the holy miracles of men and strengthened by the speech of the two of them.

Book III Incipit

Here begins the third current from the spring of Paradise, which flowed through the golden mouth of the holy pope and bishop St Gregory, whom Romans call *Golden Mouth* because of his gift of fair words. In that current he was speaking about the miracles and practices of holy men, as he did
5 before in the preceding books, and was saying thus.

Book III Explicit

Her endað seo þridde boc þæs apostolican weres sancte Gregories gespreces ond Petres his diacones, ond heræfter onginneþ seo feorðe boc gefrætewudu ond awriten mid wislicum wordum ond on gesprecum þara ylcena witena.

Book IV Incipit

Her aspringeð seo feorðe yþ þare hluttran burnan of þam muðe þæs æþelan lareowes, of þare þam ðe þyrsteð ond lysteþ magon drincan ond gecnawan, þæt ðæs mannes sawul ne farað no þy gemete þe oðera nytena æfter þam gedale þæs lichaman. Be ðon þæs ærgenemda lareow sanctus Gregorius on þisse æfterfyligendan bec þissum wordum bið reccende ond ðus sprecende. 5

Summary of Book IV of the *Dialogues*

Book IV focuses on miracles that point to the continued life of the human soul after death. Some stories tell of the deaths and visions of devout people, including miracles and the fulfilment of deathbed predictions. Stories of people who die but come back to life are recounted, including one Stephen who dies properly three years later and is envisioned crossing a bridge where good and evil spirits tussle over his body (in line with the conflicting tendencies of his life). In other stories the wicked have visions of their future punishments such as dragons devouring them. Some stories describe God strengthening timid souls with revelations to prevent them feeling fear at the time of their deaths. The need to distinguish dreams and illusions is also exemplified. Other stories demonstrate the practices that will and will not benefit the soul after death: while offering Masses can benefit the soul, burial in church is not necessarily a help.

Book III Explicit

Here ends the third book of the conversation between the apostolic man St Gregory and his deacon Peter, and hereafter begins the fourth book, adorned and written down with wise words and in the speeches of those same wise men.

Book IV Incipit

Here the fourth wave of the clear spring gushes up from the mouth of the noble teacher, from which those who are thirsty and in longing can drink and understand that a man's soul does not journey in the same way as other animals after its separation from the body. This aforementioned teacher
5 St Gregory explains and tells about this matter in the following book in these words.

The Old English *Pastoral Care*

Prose and Verse Prefaces
Gregorian Preface and Epilogue
Verse Epilogue

INTRODUCTION

The *Pastoral Care* is furnished with three frame texts independent of its Latin source: two prefaces, one in prose and one in verse, and a verse epilogue. It also retains the original work's own preface and epilogue by Gregory, translated into Old English. With a total of five prefaces and epilogues, the *Pastoral Care* is more amply provided with frame texts than any of the other Alfredian works.

The pieces independent of the source serve as an outer frame enclosing both the main work and the inner Gregorian frame. They show a particular interest in textual production and reception. The Prose Preface to the *Pastoral Care* outlines the motivations which prompted the production of the translation, focusing on Alfred's zest to revive learning in late ninth-century England after its shameful neglect in recent times, and situating the work within the much wider educational programme that Alfred plans to implement. The Verse Preface to the *Pastoral Care* praises Gregory for writing the book, and Augustine for bringing it to England, before reporting Alfred's own role in translating and disseminating the work. The Verse Epilogue to the *Pastoral Care* sets up an elaborate metaphor for the dissemination of knowledge through books and in particular through this book by Gregory.

The Work and its Contexts

The *Pastoral Care* is a close translation of the Latin *Cura pastoralis* (also known as the *Regula pastoralis*) which was composed by Gregory the Great in around AD 590.[1] The *Cura pastoralis* was dedicated to John, Bishop of Ravenna (579–95), who is addressed by Gregory in his prologue and epilogue to the work. Primarily aimed at bishops, the work offers a manual on the responsibilities of the clergy. It is divided into four parts, covering in turn the importance of the bishop's office and of preparing properly for it,

---

[1] On the relationship between the Latin original and its translation, see the recent discussion by Schreiber (2015), pp. 178–90, and references therein.

the kind of lifestyle that is suitable for bishops, best practice for preaching, and finally an exhortation to humility.[2]

Following its completion, the work quickly became popular reading material for bishops across Europe. The Verse Preface to the *Pastoral Care* implies that the Latin original came to England with the mission led by Augustine (later Archbishop of Canterbury) from Rome in AD 597.[3] Certainly it seems to have been known in England by the early eighth century when it was used as a source by the anonymous author of the Whitby *Life of Gregory the Great*.[4] The copy from which the vernacular translation was made might of course have reached Alfred's court independently via Carolingian Francia, perhaps brought over by one of Alfred's advisors such as Grimbald of St Bertin. The work is likely to have been considered a cornerstone of ecclesiastical reform amongst the Anglo-Saxons, since it was apparently the first work translated under the aegis of the Alfredian translation programme.

Manuscripts and Previous Editions

The *Pastoral Care* survives fully or partially in six early manuscripts, ranging in date from the late ninth century to the late eleventh century. They are as follows (ordered according to the approximate manuscript dates):[5]

Tib+K   London, British Library, Cotton MS Tiberius B. xi (890 × 896). This copy was almost entirely destroyed in the Cotton fire of 1731 and a later fire at the British Museum in 1864, but a seventeenth-century transcript by Franciscus Junius up to part-way through chapter 49 is available in Oxford, Bodleian Library, MS Junius 53 [J], which also includes variants from Cotton Otho B. ii and Oxford, Bodleian Library, MS Hatton 20. The Kassel leaf, Kassel, Gesamthochschulbibliothek 4° MS theol. 131 [K], belongs with Cotton Tiberius B. xi.[6]

---

[2] For a more detailed account of the contents of the work, see Schreiber (2003), pp. 2–4.

[3] See the Verse Preface to the *Pastoral Care*, line 1. See further Schreiber (2003), pp. 35–7.

[4] See Colgrave (1968), pp. 164–5 (notes on chapters 30–1 of the Whitby *Life*), and Love (1997).

[5] The sigla here correspond to those used by Schreiber (2003). For a full account of the manuscripts see Schreiber (2003), pp. 51–64. Variants are not normally supplied in my edition from the transcript in J of Tib+K or from J's collations of O.

[6] Ker (1957), no. 195; Gneuss and Lapidge (2014), no. 375.

H	Oxford, Bodleian Library, MS Hatton 20 (890 × 896).[7]
O	London, British Library, Cotton MS Otho B. ii and Otho B. x, ff. 61, 63, 64 (s. x² or x/xi). This manuscript suffered severely in the Cotton fire. Scattered variant readings from it are inserted by Junius in J's margins.[8]
C	Cambridge, Corpus Christi College MS 12 (s. x²).[9]
T	Cambridge, Trinity College MS R. 5. 22 (717), fos. 72–158 (s. x/xi).[10]
U	Cambridge, University Library MS Ii. 2. 4 (s. xi³/⁴).[11]

The earliest manuscripts, H and Tib+K, were copied, probably at Alfred's court, sometime between 890 and 896. The contemporary prose and verse prefaces and epilogue clearly circulated with the work from the outset. Only one manuscript (T), from the end of the tenth or beginning of the eleventh century, does not contain the Prose Preface to the *Pastoral Care*, almost certainly to be explained by loss in transmission. The complete text of the Verse Preface to the *Pastoral Care* survives in four manuscripts (H, C, T, and U).[12] Variant readings supplied in Junius' transcript show that this preface was also included in Tib+K and O. The Verse Epilogue to the *Pastoral Care* survives in just two of the six manuscripts (H and C), but since one of these is a very early copy there is no reason to doubt this epilogue's place in the work as originally disseminated.

Although they circulated with the main work from the outset, the prefaces that are independent of the source were apparently added after the copying of the main work was complete. In the earliest surviving manuscript copies of the *Pastoral Care* (Tib+K and H), the prefaces were written on separate leaves, and in some cases by different scribes, from the main work.[13] In Tib+K the prose and verse prefaces were apparently written in two hands, both different from that of the text of the translation, from which Kenneth Sisam concludes that they were 'pretty certainly on added

---

[7] Ker (1957), no. 324; Gneuss and Lapidge (2014), no. 626.
[8] Ker (1957), no. 175; Gneuss and Lapidge (2014), no. 353.
[9] Ker (1957), no. 30; Gneuss and Lapidge (2014), no. 37.
[10] Ker (1957), no. 87; Gneuss and Lapidge (2014), no. 180.
[11] Ker (1957), no. 19; Gneuss and Lapidge (2014), no. 14.
[12] O'Brien O'Keeffe (1990), pp. 88–95, offers a detailed analysis of the Verse Preface in relation to its manuscript contexts.
[13] See Sisam (1953a), pp. 140–7.

leaves'.[14] In H the prefaces are written in two hands on a separate bifolium added to the manuscript. The Prose Preface in H is written in a hand identical to that of the main scribe of Tib+K; the Verse Preface is written in the same hand as that of the main scribe for the text of the translation, but was possibly written later.[15] This manuscript evidence suggests that the prefaces were attached after the main work had already been copied and gathered into quires. The later addition of the prefaces does not mean that they were not originally conceived as part of the work; it is possible, as Sisam suggests, that it was just more pragmatic to complete them simultaneously with the copying of the main work.[16] In the case of the Verse Epilogue, the manuscript evidence gives no reason for thinking that it was conceived separately from the main work. In its earliest surviving copy (in H), the copying of the piece begins immediately below the main text (with a one-line gap in between), and is carried out by the same two scribes who copied the main text.[17] It seems reasonable to conclude overall that the frame texts are as likely to have been part of the original conception of the work as a later inspiration.

The two late ninth-century manuscripts of the *Pastoral Care* (Tib+K and H) act as significant witnesses to the implementation of the policy to disseminate the translations outlined in the Prose Preface. Records suggest that Tib+K had a blank space at the beginning of its copy of this preface where the name and title of the addressee would normally be included. It also apparently contained a note beside the preface's opening, which suggests that this particular manuscript served as a top copy:

† Plegmunde arcebiscepe is agifen his boc and Swiðulfe biscepe and Wærferðe biscepe.[18]

Archbishop Plegmund has been given his book and Bishop Swithulf and Bishop Wærferth.

H is the copy that was sent to Bishop Wærferth of Worcester. Not only is the preface in that copy addressed to Wærferth by name but also the

---

[14] Sisam (1953a), p. 143.   [15] Ker (1956), p. 22.   [16] Sisam (1953a), p. 143.

[17] The main scribe copies to the bottom of the recto, and the second scribe, who has copied other short sections of text earlier in the manuscript, completes the copying of the Epilogue on the verso. See Ker (1956), pp. 20–1.

[18] The note is recorded in Junius' transcript, fo. xviii. See also Ker (1956), p. 12. It is this note that allows Tib+K and H to be dated so precisely to 890 × 896, since Plegmund became archbishop in 890 and Swithulf, Bishop of Rochester, died in 893 × 896; see Schreiber (2003), p. 52.

destination is specified at the top of the first page: '† ÐEOS BOC SCEAL TO WIOGORA CEASTRE' (this book is to go to Worcester). The fact that the manuscript arrived safely is attested by some annotations made by later Worcester hands.

All the evidence points towards the formulation of a clear plan for sending out copies of the work from a central scriptorium to the various bishops in the English dioceses, and also the implementation of at least part of that plan. The Verse Preface to the *Pastoral Care* suggests that, in addition to the central scriptorium, a number of scriptoria across the kingdom were enlisted to produce copies (lines 12–15).

The standard edition of the *Pastoral Care* (based on two copies, H and J) is Henry Sweet's nineteenth-century edition.[19] N. R. Ker produced a facsimile edition of H (along with two fragments), and Ingvar Carlson edited an early manuscript (O) not edited by Sweet.[20] Parts of the work, including the prologues and epilogues, have also been more recently edited by Carolin Schreiber (with the text based on C).[21] An edition and translation of the whole work by R. D. Fulk (with the text based on Sweet's edition) was published recently in the Dumbarton Oaks Medieval Library series.[22] The Prose Preface to the *Pastoral Care* has been edited separately in a range of Old English readers and guides. The Verse Preface and Epilogue were edited by Elliott Van Kirk Dobbie in the Anglo-Saxon Poetic Records series, by Fred C. Robinson and Eric Stanley in a facsimile edition, and by Irvine and Godden in the Dumbarton Oaks Medieval Library series.[23]

The Prose Preface to the *Pastoral Care*

According to the manuscript evidence, as we have seen, the Prose Preface to the *Pastoral Care* was written between 890 and 896, and was certainly completed before the various copies of the work were sent out to their destinations. The Prose Preface is in Alfred's name and voice. It identifies the king not only as the writer of this preface but also as the inspiration behind the translation programme and the translator of the *Pastoral Care*

---

[19] Sweet (1871). [20] Ker (1956); Carlson (1975–8). [21] Schreiber (2003).
[22] Fulk (2021).
[23] Dobbie (1942), pp. 110–12; Robinson and Stanley (1991); Irvine and Godden (2012), pp. 408–13.

as a whole. Even with a preface written in Alfred's voice, during Alfred's reign and probably at Alfred's court, however, we cannot assume that Alfred was in fact the author.[24] The historical accuracy of the Prose Preface has also been much debated. Scholars have disagreed over whether England's decline in learning at this time was as extensive as described in the Prose Preface.[25] Moreover the Prose Preface's apparent implication that the translation of the *Pastoral Care* was aimed at both secular and ecclesiastical readers has been challenged by other evidence that bishops may in fact have been the primary intended audience.[26]

Various sources and analogues have been proposed for the Prose Preface to the *Pastoral Care*. Bernard Huppé, building on Francis P. Magoun Jr's identification of this preface's epistolary form, showed that its structure (on which see further below) was based on the standard form of the papal epistle.[27] Parallels have also been identified between this preface and various prologues to scriptural material. The idea of translating sometimes word for word and sometimes sense for sense, for example, recalls Jerome's preface to the Vulgate (though the idea was well established as a conventional trope by the end of the ninth century).[28] The Prose Preface has been been compared in more general terms to the Latin prologue to the book of Sirach (or Ecclesiasticus).[29] Parallels have been drawn too with a Latin prose prologue to Paul the Deacon's collection of homilies, written in the voice of the Carolingian emperor Charlemagne but probably composed for him by Alcuin.[30] Such a document would have appealed as a model to a king keen to style himself as an eloquent ruler in the style of Charlemagne,[31] renowned for spearheading a literary renaissance in his kingdom.

---

[24] On the unreliability of prefaces in this period, see the General Introduction, pp. 7–8 and 13–14. Where the name Alfred is used below, it should be taken to refer to the voice of the author as presented in this preface.

[25] Morrish (1986) contends that the Prose Preface presents an exaggerated picture; Gneuss (1986) and Lapidge (1996) argue for its credibility. For the historical context, see 'Alfred's Reign and the Vernacular Translation Programme' in the General Introduction.

[26] See Godden (2011), pp. 459–61, and (2013), pp. 148–9.

[27] Magoun (1948) and (1949); Huppé (1978).

[28] See the General Introduction above at p. 6 and n. 18.

[29] Discenza (1998).   [30] See Godden (2011), pp. 448–61.

[31] Stanton (2002), p. 7.

The Prose Preface to the *Pastoral Care* may also have been influenced by the opening of Gregory's own preface, echoing as it does the latter's epistolary style and its idea of authorial recollection as a basis for the work. The possibility that the influence may have been from the Old English version (the Gregorian Preface) rather than the Latin original is suggested by a verbal echo: the word pair 'luflice ond freondlice' in the Prose Preface (line 1) is reminiscent of the terms of affection used in the Gregorian Preface ('leofusta' and 'suiðe freondlice ond suiðe fremsumlice', line 1).

In its structure the Prose Preface to the *Pastoral Care* resembles the early papal epistle, which conventionally divides into five parts. The Preface begins with a Salutation (line 2), followed by the Proem (lines 3–25), then the Narration (lines 26–56), fourthly the Disposition (lines 57–67), and finally the Conclusion (line 67 to the end). As Huppé notes, however, this preface, though employing the principles of Latin rhetoric, does so 'in a thoroughly English manner'.[32] In particular it makes imaginative use of alliterative word pairs, such as 'mid wige ge mid wisdome' (with war and wisdom, line 9), and 'ge ðone welan ge ðone wisdom' (both the wealth and the wisdom, line 34). The provocative association between *wela* and *wisdom* is echoed in a non-alliterating word pair too: 'maðma ond boca' (treasures and books, line 28). The use of word pairs links the Preface stylistically both to Old English poetry and to prose associated with the Mercian literary tradition, including the *Dialogues* and the *Bede*.

The Prose Preface to the *Pastoral Care* uses a range of different voices to convey its message in a lively and dramatic way. It begins in the third person, with a formal greeting by King Alfred to the book's recipient, but moves quickly into the first person, as befits the personal and reflective tone of the reminiscences that follow. Later, the Prose Preface dramatizes the voice of a previous generation of clerics, imagining them speaking out regretfully at the loss of the wisdom and wealth held by their ancestors: 'Swelce hie cwæden…' (As if they had said…, line 31). Further on still, the Prose Preface sets up a dialogue between Alfred and himself: 'Ac ic ða sona eft me selfum andwyrde ond cwæð…' (But then I immediately answered myself and said…, line 39). At other times the first-person voice is a plural one, the

[32] Huppé (1978), p. 131.

form *we* representing not just the king but also his bishops and even the English community more generally.

The Prose Preface sets up an implicit link between Alfred and Gregory the Great. Perhaps prompted by Gregory, who makes clear at the beginning of his own prologue that he is drawing on his own experience in the past,[33] the Prose Preface makes much of the links between past and present. The educational programme that Alfred proposes is presented as emerging from his recollections of the past (the word *gemunde* 'remembered' is used five times in the preface). The close relationship between learning and teaching is also prominent in the perspectives of both the Prose Preface and Gregory's own prologue.

The idea of kingship informs the Prose Preface throughout. By means of his translation programme Alfred aims to recreate in his kingdom the ideal kingship of the past (described in the first paragraph of the preface). In line with the Carolingian ideal of the eloquent ruler, he sets himself up as a figure of both political and literary authority. This authority is crucial in persuading the Prose Preface's ecclesiastical recipients to endorse a programme of producing and disseminating works in the vernacular at a time when the literary status of English had yet to be established. Through the vernacular translation programme, this preface suggests, Christian learning in England can be revived, and the success and prestige of Alfred's kingdom enhanced.

The Verse Preface to the *Pastoral Care*

The Verse Preface makes no claim itself to be composed by Alfred, although, like the Prose Preface, it attributes the composition of the main work to the king. Its date of composition probably falls within the same period as the *Pastoral Care* itself (that is, between 890 and 896) since it is included in both of the earliest surviving copies, Tib+K and H.

The Verse Preface is written in the voice of the book. In drawing on the trope of book as speaker, it can be compared to the Verse Preface to the *Dialogues* and perhaps also to the Verse Preface to the *Boethius*.[34] The first-person voice in the Verse Preface to the *Pastoral Care* does not speak for a specific manuscript copy, however, as it does in the Verse Preface to the

---

[33] Judic et al. (1992), I.124; cf. the Gregorian Preface (see below), lines 3–4.
[34] On the trope of the book as speaker, see the General Introduction, pp. 6–7.

Dialogues, nor for a particular version either in Latin or Old English, but rather for what Peter Orton calls 'Gregory's book in an essential irreducible form'.[35] Thus it can speak simultaneously as the 'ærendgewrit' (written message) that was brought originally from Rome by Augustine, as the Old English version sent out by Alfred to his scribes for copying, and as any one of the copies that was produced then or later in transmission.

Precedents for a verse preface in the Latin tradition occur in writings of Alcuin.[36] The closest identified to date is Alcuin's short verse preface to his *De dialectica*, a six-line poem which is similarly in the voice of the book and addressed to the reader. The two poems also share imagery and an emphasis on the authority of past writings.

Although the Verse Preface to the *Pastoral Care* is rather uneven stylistically (with the second part much plainer than the first), and metrically irregular in some places, Henry Sweet's term 'curious doggerel' for the poem seems unfairly harsh.[37] The first part of the poem (lines 1–10) makes full use of traditional poetic formulas and diction.[38] The poet imaginatively combines religious and heroic language to alert an audience to the interweaving of secular and spiritual values. Gregory's wisdom, for example, is described in terms of treasure and wealth (his hoard of clever thoughts and his wealth of mind), and his intellectual achievements are described in terms of military success (he is the Lord's champion who wins people for his Lord).

In its intertwining of secular and spiritual perspectives, the poem echoes the preceding Prose Preface. In both prefaces, the pairing of wisdom and wealth serves to connect these intertwining sets of values. Similarly the relationship between the past and the present is emphasized in both prefaces. The account of the text's transmission in the Verse Preface implies that Gregory's wisdom and spiritual authority have been passed down through Augustine to Alfred himself.[39] As in the Prose Preface, the authority of the past is embodied by Alfred whose status as author and king invests him with both literary and political power, transferred implicitly to the vernacular translations themselves.

---

[35] Orton (2005), p. 204.   [36] Godden (2011), pp. 462–4.   [37] Sweet (1871), p. 473.
[38] See O'Brien O'Keeffe (1995), pp. 96–107, and Bredehoft (2009), pp. 99–100, on formulaic overlaps between this poem and other Old English poetry.
[39] Discenza (2001).

Some similarities in structure and content between the Verse Preface to the *Pastoral Care* and the Verse Preface to the *Boethius* may suggest that the author of the latter was familiar with the former. Both refer in their openings to the work they contain ('þis ærendgewrit' and 'ealdspell' respectively), ascribing its composition to a particular writer or writers. Both assert the beneficial effects of the work on its audience, alluding to deficiencies that need addressing (lack of knowledge of Latin and arrogance respectively). The voice of the book is heard at the end of the Verse Preface to the *Pastoral Care*; it is less clear whether the first-person pronoun 'I' at the end of the Verse Preface to the *Boethius* represents the book, but this is perhaps the most convincing of the various possibilities that have been proposed.[40]

The Gregorian Preface to the *Pastoral Care*

The source here is Gregory's own Latin prologue to the *Cura pastoralis*, and the translation was done at the same time as the main work was translated. In the manuscripts of the *Pastoral Care*, the Gregorian Preface is separated from the independent prose and verse prefaces by a list of chapter titles. The chapter titles were probably not drawn up by the main translator but clearly circulated from an early stage with the work.[41] Junius records (on p. 12 of his transcript) that O had the heading 'Prologum' for the Gregorian Preface. Curiously the Gregorian Preface omits the opening dedication found in the Latin original: 'Reverentissimo et Sanctissimi Fratri Ioanni Coepiscopo, Gregorius' (Gregory to his most reverend and most holy brother, John, fellow bishop).[42] This has the effect of obscuring Gregory's authorial role, with readers expected perhaps to have gleaned this information from the Verse Preface. The addressee John is eventually named at the end of the work (in the Gregorian Epilogue).

The Gregorian Preface outlines for readers the four-part structure of the main work, and emphasizes how wary an inexperienced person has to be about taking on the office of teaching. In focusing on the art of teaching and the risks of taking it on without proper preparation, it anticipates the body of the work itself. The style of this preface, with its heavy reliance on subordinate clauses, reflects the syntactic complexity of the Latin. The author's willingness to expand on the Latin is seen in the independent use

[40] See pp. 95–6 below.   [41] Bately (2002), p. 162.   [42] Judic et al. (1992), I.124.

of word pairs such as 'suiðe freondlice ond suiðe fremsumlice' (in a very friendly and kindly way), 'unwærlice ond unryhtlice' (rashly and unjustly), and 'adrifene ond getælde' (driven away and rebuked), which render Latin 'benigna', 'incaute', and 'repellantur' respectively.[43]

The Gregorian Epilogue to the *Pastoral Care*

The source here is Gregory's own epilogue, apparently translated into Old English in the first half of the 890s along with the main body of the *Pastoral Care*. The Gregorian Epilogue, like its source, is brief and highly personal in tone. It divides into two parts, the first a reminder of what the book was about, the second an entreaty to John to intercede for the writer by means of his prayers. The piece presents a dichotomy between Gregory's ability to write eloquently about the ideal teacher and his struggle to correct his own sinfulness. Stylistically it rearranges, adapts, and expands its source material: it prefers the more literal description of the author as a writer to the metaphor of a painter; it develops the metaphor of being tossed around by the waves of sin by introducing the ship-of-the-mind motif; and it adds word pairs such as 'hu fægerne ond hu wlitigne' (how fair and beautiful) for Latin 'pulchrum'.[44]

The Verse Epilogue to the *Pastoral Care*

Like the prose and verse prefaces, the Verse Epilogue to the *Pastoral Care* is included in the earliest surviving manuscripts of the *Pastoral Care* and was probably composed at around the same time as the translation itself. Whether or not this epilogue was composed by the author of the main text is more uncertain. It seems likely that the poet was at least familiar with the main text. The metaphor of a body of water which flows out in channels may derive from the main text: the poet's use of the phrase 'unnyt ut ne tofloweð' (does not flow away useless, line 15), for example, seems to recall the phrase 'lytel unnyttes utfleowe' (little of what is useless may flow away) in chapter 38 of the *Pastoral Care*.[45] Such parallels, however, may be the result of the poet's close knowledge of the translation, or perhaps of versification

---

[43] Judic et al. (1992), I.124, 126.   [44] Judic et al. (1992), II.540–1.
[45] Sweet (1871), p. 279 at line 16, where the phrase represents an independent addition by the translator to the Gregorian source. On this and other examples, see Isaacs (1965); Whobrey (1991), pp. 179–80.

by the poet of material provided by the prose translator, either orally or in written prose, rather than of shared authorship.

Biblical sources also inform this epilogue. The first eight lines offer a close paraphrase of John 7:38–9 as a means of setting up the metaphor of everliving waters springing from the Holy Spirit and flowing from those who believe.[46] For this material, the poet may have recalled the use of the image of flowing waters in earlier depictions of Gregory's eloquence, including the incipits of the individual books of the *Dialogues*. The last six lines of the epilogue, in which the poet bids the reader to fill his vessel with water from the Lord's well, are probably prompted by John 4:7–26 (the story of the Samaritan woman at Jacob's well).[47]

The Verse Epilogue to the *Pastoral Care* builds up a sustained metaphor of spiritual wisdom as a body of water, which the saints and the elect have drawn from and channelled to others through books. The theme of the water of wisdom is developed imaginatively through the poem. Harnessing the vitality of water as a physical commodity, the poet calls attention to the broader spiritual sense of water's 'life-giving quality'.[48] In combining an abstract concept (*wisdom*) with physical imagery (here *wæter* and *wæterscipe*), this epilogue can be compared to the prose and verse prefaces at the beginning of the *Pastoral Care* where ideas of wisdom and wealth are deftly intertwined. In its use of a metaphor so rooted in a practical knowledge of water and watercourses, this epilogue may also be compared to other Alfredian frame texts using practical metaphors to represent the acquisition of learning, such as hunting (in the Prose Preface to the *Pastoral Care*) and the gathering of wood to build a house (in the Preface to the *Soliloquies*). These metaphors serve to give contemporary relevance to the works.

Structurally the Verse Epilogue to the *Pastoral Care* can be divided into three parts. Lines 1–8 explain the image of the body of water in scriptural terms. Lines 9–21 describe various ways that people respond to the wisdom acquired through books. Readers may choose to nurture this wisdom within their own minds, or to circulate it, in which case there is a danger of doing so piecemeal and indiscriminately. Lines 22–30 encourage readers to

---

[46] See Cross (1969); Whobrey (1991), pp. 176–8.   [47] See Whobrey (1991), p. 184.
[48] Magennis (1999), p. 137. On the metaphor of water in the poem, see also Anlezark (2021).

continue their pursuit of wisdom through careful and repeated consultation of Gregory's book.

In projecting the idea of the book as a means of disseminating wisdom in a directed way, the Verse Epilogue employs the traditional Old English poetic motif of mind-as-container. The mind is depicted as a vessel which may retain the water of spiritual wisdom for its own contemplative use, or distribute it to others. This vessel of the mind is to be kept free of leaks so that when it is refilled the water is not then wasted.[49]

The Verse Epilogue makes use of a first-person voice ('us', line 1). The speaker is neither the king nor the book (as in the prefaces to the same work) but one of the 'dwellers on earth' for whom the book is intended. Although the first-person pronoun is not used again after the first line, the conceit of a speaker and listener is maintained through a direct address to the audience at line 22: 'Ac hladað iow nu drincan' (But draw yourselves water now to drink).

Note on the Texts

The text of the Prose Preface is based on Oxford, Bodleian Library, MS Hatton 20 [H] (s. ix²), fos. 1r–2v, with collation of substantial variants in Cambridge, Corpus Christi College MS 12 [C], Oxford, Bodleian Library, MS Junius 53 [J], and Cambridge, University Library MS Ii. 2. 4 [U]. The text of the Verse Preface is based on H, fo. 2v, with collation of substantial variants in C, J, Cambridge, Trinity College MS R. 5. 22 [T], and U. The text of the Gregorian Preface is based on H, fos. 6r–v, with collation of substantial variants in C, J, T, and U. The text of the Gregorian Epilogue is based on H, fo. 98r, with collation of substantial variants in C, T, and U. The text of the Verse Epilogue is based on H, fos. 98r–98v, with collation of substantial variants in C. Later annotations in the manuscripts are not recorded unless they reflect emendations corresponding to other manuscripts which improve the sense. Clear scribal errors in manuscripts other than the base manuscript are not normally recorded unless they are of particular interest. For a full record of variants and annotations, see Schreiber (2003).

---

[49] Mize (2008), pp. 47–53.

TEXTS AND TRANSLATIONS

✠ The Prose Preface to the *Pastoral Care*

ÐEOS BOC SCEAL TO WIOGORA CEASTRE.

Ælfred kyning hateð gretan Wærferð biscep his wordum luflice ond freondlice; ond ðe cyðan hate ðæt me com swiðe oft on gemynd, hwelce wiotan iu wæron giond Angelcynn, ægðer ge godcundra hada ge woruldcundra; ond hu gesæliglica tida ða wæron giond Angelcynn; ond hu ða kyningas ðe ðone onwald hæfdon ðæs folces Gode ond his ærendwrecum hiersumedon; ond hu hie ægðer ge hiora sibbe ge hiora siodo ge hiora onweald innanbordes gehioldon, ond eac ut hiora eðel rymdon; ond hu him ða speow ægðer ge mid wige ge mid wisdome; ond eac ða godcundan hadas hu giorne hie wæron ægðer ge ymb lare ge ymb liornunga ge ymb ealle ða ðiowotdomas ðe hie Gode don scoldon; ond hu man utanbordes wisdom ond lare hieder on lond sohte, ond hu we hie nu sceoldon ute begietan gif we hie habban sceoldon. Swæ clæne hio wæs oðfeallenu on Angelcynne ðæt swiðe feawa wæron behionan Humbre ðe hiora ðeninga cuðen understondan on Englisc, oððe furðum an ærendgewrit of Lædene on Englisc areccean; ond ic wene ðætte noht monige begiondan Humbre næren. Swæ feawa hiora wæron ðæt ic furðum anne anlepne ne mæg geðencean be suðan Temese ða ða ic to rice feng. Gode ælmihtegum sie ðonc ðætte we nu ænigne onstal habbað lareowa.

Ond forðon ic ðe bebiode ðæt ðu do swæ ic geliefe ðæt ðu wille, ðæt ðu ðe ðissa woruldðinga to ðæm geæmetige swæ ðu oftost mæge, ðæt ðu ðone wisdom ðe ðe God sealde ðær ðær ðu hiene befæstan mæge, | befæste. Geðenc hwelc witu us ða becomon for ðisse worulde, ða ða we hit nohwæðer ne selfe ne lufodon ne eac oðrum monnum ne lefdon: ðone naman ænne we lufodon ðætte we Cristne wæren, ond swiðe feawe ða ðeawas.

Ða ic ða ðis eall gemunde, ða gemunde ic eac hu ic geseah, ær ðæm ðe hit eall forhergod wære ond forbærned, hu ða ciricean giond eall Angelcynn stodon maðma ond boca gefylda, ond eac micel mengeo Godes ðiowa ond ða swiðe lytle fiorme ðara boca wiston, forðæm ðe hie hiora nanwuht ongiotan ne meahton forðæm ðe hie næron on hiora agen geðiode awritene.

The Prose Preface to the *Pastoral Care*

THIS BOOK IS TO GO TO WORCESTER.

King Alfred commands Bishop Wærferth to be greeted with love and affection; and I would have you know that it has very often come to my mind what wise men there used to be throughout England, both in ecclesiastical and secular orders; and how happy times were then throughout England; and how the kings who held sway over the people obeyed God and his messengers; and how they maintained their peace, morality, and authority within their borders and also extended their territory outside; and how they succeeded in both war and wisdom; and also how eager the ecclesiastical orders were in teaching and learning, and in all the services which they had a duty to perform for God; and how wisdom and teaching were sought in this country from abroad, and how we now had to obtain that teaching abroad if we were to have it. So entirely had teaching declined in England that there were very few on this side of the Humber who could make sense in English of their religious services or even translate a letter from Latin into English; and I think there were not many beyond the Humber either. There were so few of them that I cannot think of a single one south of the Thames when I succeeded to the kingdom. Thanks be to almighty God that we now have any supply of teachers at all.

And therefore I bid you to do as I believe you would want to do: to free yourself as often as you can from these worldly commitments so that you may apply the wisdom that God gave you wherever you can do so. Think what worldly punishments came upon us when we neither loved learning ourselves nor bequeathed it to others: we loved only the name of being Christian and very few loved the Christian practices.

When I remembered all this, then I also remembered seeing, before everything was plundered and burned, how the churches throughout England were full of treasures and books, and also there was a great multitude of God's servants who derived very little benefit from those books because they could understand nothing of them since they were not written in their

Swelce hie cwæden: 'Ure ieldran, ða ðe ðas stowa ær hioldon, hie lufodon wisdom ond ðurh ðone hie begeaton welan ond us læfdon. Her mon mæg giet gesion hiora swæð, ac we him ne cunnon æfterspyrigean.' Ond forðæm we habbað nu ægðer forlæten ge ðone welan ge ðone wisdom, forðæm ðe we noldon to ðæm spore mid ure mode onlutan. 35

Ða ic ða ðis eall gemunde, ða wundrade ic swiðe swiðe ðara godena wiotona ðe giu wæron giond Angelcynn, ond ða bec ealla be fullan geliornod hæfdon, ðæt hie hiora ða nænne dæl noldon on hiora agen geðiode wendan. Ac ic ða sona eft me selfum andwyrde ond cwæð: 'Hie ne wendon ðætte æfre menn sceolden swæ reccelease weorðan ond sio lar swæ oðfeallan; for 40 ðære wilnunga hie hit forleton, ond woldon ðæt her ðy mara wisdom on londe wære ðy we ma geðeoda cuðon.'

Ða gemunde ic hu sio æ wæs ærest on Ebriscgeðiode funden, ond eft, ða
2r hie Creacas geliornodon, ða wendon hie hie | on hiora agen geðiode ealle, ond eac ealle oðre bec. Ond eft Lædenware swæ same, siððan hie hie gelior- 45 nodon, hie hie wendon ealla ðurh wise wealhstodas on hiora agen geðiode. Ond eac ealla oðra Cristna ðioda sumne dæl hiora on hiora agen geðiode wendon. Forðy me ðyncð betre, gif iow swæ ðyncð, ðæt we eac suma bec, ða ðe niedbeðearfosta sien eallum monnum to wiotonne, ðæt we ða on ðæt geðiode wenden ðe we ealle gecnawan mægen, ond gedon swæ we swiðe eaðe 50 magon mid Godes fultume, gif we ða stilnesse habbað, ðætte eall sio gioguð ðe nu is on Angelcynne friora monna, ðara ðe ða speda hæbben ðæt hie ðæm befeolan mægen, sien to liornunga oðfæste, ða hwile ðe hie to nanre oðerre note ne mægen, oð ðone first ðe hie wel cunnen Englisc gewrit arædan. Lære mon siððan furður on Lædengeðiode ða ðe mon furðor læran wille ond to 55 hieran hade don wille.

Ða ic ða gemunde hu sio lar Lædengeðiodes ær ðissum afeallen wæs giond Angelcynn, ond ðeah monige cuðon Englisc gewrit arædan, ða ongan ic ongemang oðrum mislicum ond manigfealdum bisgum ðisses kynerices ða boc wendan on Englisc ðe is genemned on Læden *Pastoralis*, ond on Englisc 60 'Hierdeboc', hwilum word be worde, hwilum andgit of andgiete, swæ swæ ic hie geliornode æt Plegmunde minum ærcebiscepe ond æt Assere minum
2v biscepe ond æt Grimbolde minum | mæsseprioste ond æt Iohanne minum mæssepreoste. Siððan ic hie ða geliornod hæfde, swæ swæ ic hie forstod, ond swæ ic hie andgitfullicost areccean meahte, ic hie on Englisc awende. Ond to 65

own language. It is as if they had said: 'Our ancestors, who formerly occupied these places, loved wisdom, through which they obtained wealth and left it to us. Here their track can still be seen but we don't know how to follow it.' We have therefore lost both the wealth and the wisdom because we were not willing to stoop to the trail with our minds.

When I remembered all this, then I wondered very greatly that the good and wise men, who once lived throughout England and had thoroughly learned all the books, were not willing to translate any part of them into their own language. But I answered myself straightaway, saying: 'They did not expect that people would ever become so careless and teaching would so decline: they refrained from doing it deliberately, wishing that the more languages we knew, the greater wisdom there would be in this country.'

Then I remembered how the Law was first found in the Hebrew language, and then, when the Greeks learned it, they translated it all into their own language, and also all other books. And so too the Romans translated them all through wise translators into their own language after they had learned them. And also all other Christian peoples translated some part of them into their own language. Therefore it seems better to me, if it seems so to you, that we also translate certain books which are most necessary for everyone to know into the language that we can all understand, and bring to pass, as we very easily can with God's help if we have peace, that all the free-born young people in England who have the means to be able to apply themselves to it may be set to learning, as long as they cannot undertake any other employment, until the time that they know how to read writing in English well. Let the Latin language afterwards be taught as well to those whom one wishes to teach further and bring to a higher office.

When I remembered how the teaching of Latin had fallen off throughout England before this and yet many knew how to read writing in English, then I began amongst the other many and various affairs of this kingdom to translate into English the book which is called *Pastoralis* in Latin, and in English 'Shepherd-book', sometimes word for word, sometimes sense for sense, just as I learned it from my archbishop Plegmund, my bishop Asser, my mass priest Grimbald, and my mass priest John. When I had learned it as I understood it and as I could most intelligibly interpret it, I translated it into English. And I wish to send one to each bishopric in my kingdom,

ælcum biscepstole on minum rice wille ane onsendan, ond on ælcre bið an
æstel, se bið on fiftegum mancessa. Ond ic bebiode on Godes naman ðæt
nan mon ðone æstel from ðære bec ne do, ne ða boc from ðæm mynstre:
uncuð hu longe ðær swæ gelærede biscepas sien, swæ swæ nu, Gode ðonc,
welhwær siendon. Forðy ic wolde ðætte hie ealneg æt ðære stowe wæren, 70
buton se biscep hie mid him habban wille oððe hio hwær to læne sie, oððe
hwa oðre bi write.

and in each there will be a pointer worth fifty mancuses. And I command in God's name that no one take the pointer from the book, nor the book from the church, it being unknown how long there will be such learned bishops as now, thanks to God, are nearly everywhere. Therefore I would like these things always to be in that location unless the bishop wishes to have them with him or it [the book] is somewhere on loan or someone is making a copy of it.

The Verse Preface to the *Pastoral Care*

Þis ærendgewrit   Agustinus
ofer sealtne sæ   suðan brohte
iegbuendum,   swa hit ær fore
adihtode   Dryhtnes cempa,
Rome papa.   Ryhtspell monig   5
Gregorius   gleawmod gindwod
ðurh sefan snyttro,   searoðonca hord.
Forðæm he monncynnes   mæst gestriende
rodra wearde,   Romwara betest,
monna modwelegost,   mærðum gefrægost.   10
Sioððan min on Englisc   Ælfred kyning
awende worda gehwelc,   ond me his writerum
sende suð ond norð,   heht him swelcra ma
brengan bi ðære bisene,   ðæt he his biscepum
sendan meahte,   forðæm hi his sume ðorfton,   15
ða ðe Lædenspræce   læste cuðon.

The Verse Preface to the *Pastoral Care*

Augustine brought this message
from the south over the salt sea
to the island-dwellers, just as the Lord's
champion, the pope in Rome, had composed
it beforehand. The wise Gregory
knew many true doctrines thoroughly
through his mind's intelligence, his hoard of clever thoughts.
Therefore, best of Romans, most wealthy in mind
amongst men, most renowned for his glorious deeds, he won
the greatest number of mankind for the guardian of heaven.
Afterwards King Alfred translated every word
of me into English and sent me south and north
to his scribes, and ordered them to produce more such
copies according to the exemplar, so that he could send them
to his bishops, because some of them
who least knew Latin had need of it.

The Gregorian Preface to the *Pastoral Care*

Þu leofusta broður, suiðe freondlice ond suiðe fremsumlice ðu me tældesð, ond mid eaðmode ingeðonce ðu me ciddesð, forðon ic min mað, ond wolde fleon ða byrðenne ðære hirdelecan giemenne. Ðara byrðenna hefignesse, eall ðæt ic his geman, ic awrite on ðisse andweardan bec, ðy læs hi hwæm leohte ðyncen to underfonne; ond ic eac lære ðæt hira nan ðara ne wilnie 5 ðe hine unwærlice bega; ond se ðe hi unwærlice ond unryhtlice gewilnige, ondræde he ðæt he hi æfre underfenge.

Nu ic wilnige ðætte ðeos spræc stigge on ðæt ingeðonc ðæs leorneres, suæ suæ on sume hlædre, stæpmælum near ond near, oððæt hio fæstlice gestonde on ðæm solore ðæs modes ðe hi leornige; ond forðy ic hi todæle on feower; 10 an is ðara dæla hu he on ðone folgoð becume; oðer hu he ðæron libbe; ðridda is hu he ðæron lære; feorðe is hu he his agene unðeawas ongietan wille ond hira geðæf bion, ðy læs he for ðy underfenge his eaðmodnesse forlæte, oððe eft his lif sie ungelic his ðenunga, oððe he to ðriste ond to stið sie for ðy underfenge his lareowdomes. Ac gemetgige hit se ege his agenra 15 unðeawa, ond befæste he mid his lifes bisenum ða lare ðæm ðe his wordum ne geliefen. Ond ðonne he god weorc wyrce, gemyne he ðæs yfeles ðe he worhte, ðette sio unrotnes, ðe he for ðæm yflan weorcum hæbbe, gemetgige ðone gefean ðe he for ðæm godan weorcum hæfde, ðy læs he beforan ðæs dieglan deman eagum sie ahafen on his mode ond on ofermettum aðunden, 20 ond ðonne ðurh ðæt selflice his godan weorc forleose.

Ac monige sindon me suiðe onlice on ungelærednesse: ðeah ðe hi næfre leorningcnihtas næren, wilniað ðeah lareowas to beonne, ond ðyncet him suiðe leoht sio byrðen ðæs lareowdomes, forðon ðe hi ne cunnon ðæt mægen his micelnesse. From ðære dura selfre ðisse bec, ðæt is from onginne ðisse 25 spræce, sint adrifene ond getælde ða unwaran, ðe him agniat ðone cræft ðæs lareowdomes ðe hi na ne geleornodon.

The Gregorian Preface to the *Pastoral Care*

Most beloved brother, you rebuked me in a very friendly and kindly way, and chided me with humble intention because I hid myself and wanted to escape the burdens of pastoral care. In this current book I will write down all that I recall about the weight of those burdens to prevent them seeming easy for someone to undertake; and I also advise no one to wish for them who behaves rashly; and let the person who rashly and unjustly desires them fear ever taking them on.

Now I would like this account to ascend in the mind of the reader, just like on a ladder, nearer and nearer at every step, until it is firmly in the uppermost room of the mind that learns it; and therefore I divide it into four sections: one of the parts covers how he may reach that office; the second covers how he should live when he has it; the third covers how he should teach when he has it; the fourth covers how he will wish to recognize his own vices and yet wish not to change them, in case by undertaking [the office of teacher] he should lose his humility, or again in case his life should be different from his ministry, or he should be too presumptuous and severe because of undertaking his office of teacher. But let the fear of his own vices temper it and let him make his teachings acceptable with the examples from his life for those who may not believe his words. And when he does a good deed, let him recall the evil he has done, so that the misery he feels for those evil deeds may temper the joy he felt for the good deeds, to prevent him being puffed up in his mind and swollen with pride in the eyes of the hidden judge and then losing his good deeds through that egotism.

But many are very similar to me in their inexperience, who, though they were never pupils, yet wish to be teachers, and the burden of the office of teacher seems very easy to them because they don't know how huge it is. From the very door of this book, that is from the beginning of this discourse, those who are unwary, who appropriate for themselves the skill of teaching which they never learned, are driven away and rebuked.

Summary of the *Pastoral Care*

Book I of the *Pastoral Care* translates Gregory's account of the qualities of character necessary in those who wish to become teachers: one must want to teach for the right reasons, and be willing to learn how to teach and to behave as one teaches. The pride that can come from having power has to be avoided. The moral defects that affect someone who is not fit to lead are described in terms of a series of physical flaws (so, for example, physical blindness represents lack of spiritual enlightenment).

Book II describes how a pastoral leader must conduct himself in office. He must, for example, be pure of heart, surpass others in his conduct, and teach by example. He must be discreet but willing to admonish if necessary (albeit not too severely). He must show compassion, and combine authority with humility. He must attend to both spiritual matters and worldly occupations; any good works must be done not out of desire for praise but out of love for God. He must detect vices even where they parade as virtues, and reprove appropriately. He should meditate daily on the scriptures.

The focus of Book III is on how teachers need to be discriminating in carrying out their teaching. Taking as its starting point the view that different people require different kinds of teaching, the book identifies a series of contrasting classes of people and outlines the methods to follow in admonishing each. So men are to be admonished more severely than women, and the young are to be admonished more strictly than the old. Other contrasting groups identified here include the poor and the rich, the overly cheerful and overly glum, rulers and subjects, servants and masters, the worldly wise and the foolish, the shameless and the modest, the proud and the fainthearted, the patient and the impatient, the healthy and the unhealthy, the idle and the reckless, the humble and the proud, the peaceful and the quarrelsome, and so on. Teachers are urged to show moderation and discretion in their admonishments.

Book IV turns to the need for the teacher to reflect on his own weaknesses. Teachers should not be too elated if they find that they teach well. In order to avoid pride, teachers must contemplate their mind's frailty and concentrate on what remains to be done.

The Gregorian Epilogue to the *Pastoral Care*

Loca nu, ðu goda wer Iohannes, hu fægerne ond hu wlitigne monnan ic hæbbe atæfred, swa unwlitig writere swa swa ic eom. Ðær ic hæbbe getæht hwelc hierde bion sceal. To ðæm ic wæs gened mid ðinre tælnesse, ðæt ic nu hæbbe manege men gelæd to ðæm stæðe fullfremednesse on ðæm scipe mines modes, ond nu giet hwearfige me self on ðæm yðum minra scylda. 5
Ac ic ðe bidde ðæt ðu me on ðæm scipgebroce ðisses andweardan lifes sum bred geræce ðinra gebeda, ðæt ic mæge on sittan oð ic to londe cume, ond arær me mid ðære honda ðinre geearnunga, forðæm ðe me hæfð gehefegad sio byrðen minra agenra scylda.

The Gregorian Epilogue to the *Pastoral Care*

See now, good man John, how fair and lovely a person I have described, ill-favoured writer as I am. I have shown there what a pastor ought to be. I was compelled by your reproach to lead many people to the shore of perfection in the ship of my mind and I myself am still tossed in the waves of my faults.
5 But I pray you to stretch out to me a plank of your prayers in the shipwreck of this present life so that I can sit on it until I come to land; and lift me up with the hand of your merits because the burden of my own faults has weighed heavily on me.

The Verse Epilogue to the *Pastoral Care*

Ðis is nu se wæterscipe ðe us wereda God
to frofre gehet foldbuendum.
He cwæð ðæt he wolde ðæt on worulde forð
of ðæm innoðum a libbendu
wætru fleowen, ðe wel on hine 5
gelifden under lyfte. Is hit lytel tweo
ðæt ðæs wæterscipes welsprynge is
on hefonrice, ðæt is halig gæst.
Ðonan hine hlodan halge ond gecorene,
siððan hine gierdon ða ðe Gode | herdon 10
ðurh halga bec hider on eorðan
geond manna mod missenlice.
Sume hine weriað on gewitlocan,
wisdomes stream, welerum gehæftað,
ðæt he on unnyt ut ne tofloweð, 15
ac se wæl wunað on weres breostum
ðurh Dryhtnes giefe diop ond stille.
Sume hine lætað ofer landscare
riðum torinnan. Nis ðæt rædlic ðing,
gif swa hlutor wæter, hlud ond undiop, 20
tofloweð æfter feldum oð hit to fenne werð.
Ac hladað iow nu drincan, nu iow Dryhten geaf
ðæt iow Gregorius gegiered hafað
to durum iowrum Dryhtnes welle.
Fylle nu his fætels, se ðe fæstne hider 25
kylle brohte, cume eft hræðe.
Gif her ðegna hwelc ðyrelne kylle
brohte to ðys burnan, bete hine georne,
ðy læs he forsceade scirost wætra,
oððe him lifes drync forloren weorðe. 30

The Verse Epilogue to the *Pastoral Care*

    This, now, is the watercourse that the God of hosts
    promised as a comfort to us, dwellers on earth.
    He said that he wished that living
    waters should always flow in the world
5   from the hearts of those under the sky
    who fully believed in him. There is little doubt
    that the source of the watercourse is
    in the heavenly kingdom, namely the Holy Ghost.
    From there saints and the elect drew it;
10   then those who obeyed God directed it
    by means of holy books here on earth
    in various ways throughout the minds of men.
    Some guard the stream of wisdom
    within their minds, retain it with their lips,
15   so that it does not flow away useless,
    but rather the pool remains deep and still
    in the man's breast through the Lord's grace.
    Some let it run away over the lands
    in streams. It is not a prudent thing
20   if such pure water flows away noisy and shallow
    across the fields until it becomes a marsh.
    But draw yourselves water now to drink, since the Lord has granted you
    that Gregory has directed the Lord's
    well to your doors for you.
25   Let anyone who has brought here a watertight pitcher
    fill his vessel now and come back quickly.
    If any person has brought a leaky pitcher
    here to this stream, let him repair it speedily,
    so as to avoid spilling the clearest of waters
30   or having the drink of life lost to him.

The Old English *Boethius*
(Prose and Prosimetrical Versions)

Prose and Verse Prefaces
Prose and Verse *Vitae*
Epilogue

INTRODUCTION

The Old English *Boethius* survives in two versions, one prose and one alternating prose and verse (or prosimetrical). The prose version is furnished with a prose preface discussing the composition of the Old English work, an introductory account in prose (the Prose *Vita*) describing the historical and biographical circumstances that led to the Latin work, and, at the end of the work, a verse epilogue. The prosimetrical version (now fire-damaged) has the same prose preface, a further short preface in verse discussing the composition of the metrical passages, the historical-biographical account recast in verse (the Verse *Vita*), and no epilogue.

The framing material is all independent of the Latin original, which has no prologue or epilogue. The frame texts have been added at different stages in transmission, ranging from the prose and verse *vitae*, which apparently circulated from the outset with the prose and prosimetrical versions of the work respectively, to the verse epilogue, whose composition may be contemporary or near contemporary with the late manuscript copy (*c.*1100) in which it is preserved.[1] In the case of the prose and verse prefaces, it is possible to be certain only that both were circulating by the mid-tenth century, the date of their earliest surviving copies.

The Work and its Contexts

The main source for the *Boethius* is *De consolatione Philosophiae* (the *Consolation of Philosophy*), written by Anicius Manlius Severinus Boethius in around AD 524, following his exile to Pavia on charges of treason against the king of the Goths and then ruler of Italy, Theoderic. Up to that point in his life Boethius had actively participated in scholarship and politics in Rome, and the reversal in his fortunes seems to have affected

---

[1] Bredehoft (2009), p. 175, dates this epilogue as 'no earlier than the early eleventh century'.

him deeply, prompting him to write what would be his last work. Using his own misery as a starting point, and drawing on the events of his own career, Boethius sets up a dialogue between himself and Philosophia (the female figure of Philosophy) in which he explores the nature of human experience and how an understanding of true happiness and God might ultimately provide consolation in even the most desperate of situations. The work is divided into five books, each made up of alternating prose and verse passages, with the verse usually acting as lyrical commentary on the ideas presented in the prose.

De consolatione Philosophiae does not seem to have circulated widely before the end of the eighth century when it came to the attention of Carolingian scholars. Through the ninth century it enjoyed ever increasing popularity in Carolingian Europe. Copies of the Latin work became more readily available, accompanied by glosses and comments. When the work first became available in Anglo-Saxon England, it is likely to have been in a copy containing both text and commentary, since the *Boethius* shows itself to be well versed in the early medieval commentary tradition.[2] The earliest manuscript evidence for knowledge of and interest in the work in the British Isles is an early glossed manuscript of the Latin work in which a Welsh or Cornish hand from around the end of the ninth century can be identified,[3] and excerpts from the Latin metres copied into the blank spaces of a manuscript of Isidore's *Synonyma* around the year 912, perhaps at Canterbury.[4] From the early decades of the tenth century onwards, the work's importance in study and teaching seems to have been well established in England.

The first version of the *Boethius* was composed in prose throughout. The translator produces a relatively free adaptation of *De consolatione Philosophiae*, recasting Philosophia as Wisdom and Boethius as Mind (Old English *Mod*), and rearranging, condensing, or expanding material at will. The contrast with the technique of close translation adopted in the *Pastoral*

---

[2] For recent discussions, see Godden and Irvine (2009), I.5–8; Papahagi (2009); and Love (2012). An edition of the commentary material is currently in preparation by Malcolm Godden, Rohini Jayatilaka, and Rosalind Love as part of the Oxford-based Boethius in Early Medieval Europe Project.

[3] Love (2012), pp. 121–2 and n. 142.

[4] Godden and Irvine (2009), I.5; Papahagi (2009), n. 30.

Care is striking. It seems likely that the more inventive approach of the *Boethius* reflects an increasing confidence in the use of the vernacular within literary circles by the time this work came to be composed. But the form in which the work circulated may also have influenced the translator's working practices. The commentary material that accompanied Latin copies of the work would have provided the translator with a wealth of information that allowed him to explain and update the work for a contemporary audience. Although no single extant commentary can be identified as the source for the Old English work, the translator has clearly drawn liberally on the material made available by the commentary tradition. A particular fascination with classical mythology and history, and also with natural science, characterizes the translator's approach.

The later version of the *Boethius* alternates verse and prose in a way that reflects more closely the form of the Latin original. For its content, however, it is heavily reliant on the Old English prose version. The sections that correspond to prose sections in the Latin original remain the same in both Old English versions. For the sections that correspond to verse sections in the Latin original, the Old English prose has been versified, creating what have become known as the Old English Metres. The metrical and alliterative requirements of verse mean that the prosimetrical version of the *Boethius* is rather longer than the prose version overall.

The *Boethius* has traditionally been assumed to be composed by King Alfred, largely on the basis of the Prose Preface's claim that Alfred was the author of both the prose and prosimetrical versions. Doubts have been expressed about the reliability of such a claim.[5] The attribution to Alfred may just be a means of adding authority to the production and circulation of a vernacular version of the work. The Verse Preface, in praising Alfred's poetic skills, ostensibly confirms his role in the production of the Metres. Since the composer of the verse gives little sign of being familiar with the original Latin, however, it seems unlikely that the same author, whether Alfred or not, was responsible for both the prose and verse of the *Boethius*.[6]

---

[5] See especially Godden (2007). On the authorship debate, see the General Introduction, pp. 12–14.

[6] For evidence suggesting that the versifier was probably not the original translator, see Godden and Irvine (2009), I.146–50.

The *Boethius* apparently continued to be transmitted in both its prose and prosimetrical versions, possibly with the Latin model of the *opus geminatum* (twinned work) in mind.[7] The late tenth-century author Ælfric drew on a prose version,[8] and the only extant copy of that version, complete with preface, chapter divisions, and chapter list, proves that it was being copied (and corrected, probably by various hands) around 1100. The prosimetrical version, extant now only in a mid-tenth-century copy, seems to have been known to Nicholas Trevet when he wrote his commentary on the Latin work in around 1300.[9]

Manuscripts and Previous Editions

Each of the two versions of the Old English *Boethius* survives in just one manuscript. The prose version is found in:

B   Oxford, Bodleian Library, MS Bodley 180 (s. xi^{ex} / s. xii^{in}).[10]

This manuscript contains the Prose Preface to the *Boethius* and the Epilogue.

The prosimetrical version is found in a badly fire-damaged form in:

C   London, British Library, Cotton MS Otho A. vi, fos. 1–129 (s. x^{med}).[11]

This manuscript contained two prefaces, one in prose and one in verse. The beginning of the work is lost, however, and copies survive only in a later transcription. The manuscript was badly damaged in the Cotton fire of 1731, and some of its text has to be reconstructed from Franciscus Junius' seventeenth-century transcription and collation (see J below).

A fragment of another manuscript (known as the Napier Fragment) was transcribed by Arthur S. Napier towards the end of the nineteenth century, but was subsequently lost.[12] On the basis of its script, Napier dated the fragment as from the first half of the tenth century. It is not possible to tell

---

[7] See Weaver (2016); S. Irvine (2018).
[8] See Godden and Irvine (2009), I.48–9; and Godden (2009b).
[9] See Godden and Irvine (2009), I.212–14.
[10] Ker (1957), no. 305; Gneuss and Lapidge (2014), no. 555.5.
[11] Ker (1957), no. 167; Gneuss and Lapidge (2014), no. 347.
[12] Napier (1887). The Napier fragment (N) is reprinted in Godden and Irvine (2009), I.543–4, and discussed at I.34–41.

whether it belonged to a copy of the prose or prosimetrical version of the work. Its text did not include any of the framing material.

A transcription of B, collated with C and with C's verse sections transcribed in full, made by Franciscus Junius in the seventeenth century, is found in:

J   Oxford, Bodleian Library, MS Junius 12.

This transcription is invaluable for reconstructing the damaged text of C.

The poor condition of one manuscript (C) and the late date of the other (B) make it difficult to be sure about the date and originality of the prefaces attached to them.

The standard edition of the work, which edits and translates the B and C texts separately, is that by Malcolm Godden and Susan Irvine.[13] This supersedes Walter J. Sedgefield's late nineteenth-century edition, which created a prose amalgam of the two texts and relegated the Metres to an appendix.[14] The Epilogue is included in Sedgefield's edition, and also printed separately by Bredehoft.[15] The Metres have been edited separately a number of times, most recently by George Krapp in 1932, by Robinson and Stanley in a facsimile edition in 1991, by Bill Griffiths in 1991 (revised in 1994), and by Wolfgang Obst and Florian Schleburg in 1998.[16]

The Prose Preface to the *Boethius*

The Prose Preface to the *Boethius* writes about King Alfred in the third person, explaining how he composed the work and then asking that those who enjoy reading the book pray for him. Although Alfred's own voice might conceivably be represented in the third person in this preface (just as the Prose Preface to the *Pastoral Care* uses the voice of the king in the third person in its formal opening), other evidence points to a perspective that is distinct from the king's. In the preface the speaker makes much of the

---

[13] Godden and Irvine (2009).   [14] Sedgefield (1899).
[15] Bredehoft (2009), pp. 213–14.
[16] Krapp (1932); Robinson and Stanley (1991); Griffiths (1994); Obst and Schleburg (1998).

obstacles Alfred had to face in his reign, lamenting that the troubles that occurred 'in his days' are 'very hard for us to count'. The speaker seems to be looking back at an era that has ended by the time the preface was composed.

The Prose Preface to the *Boethius* exhibits knowledge of how the verse of the prosimetrical version was produced (that is, by versifying the Old English prose rather than by drawing on the Latin directly), and could have been the work of the versifier or someone close to him. It is curious, however, that this preface, apparently designed for the prosimetrical version, has been attached to a copy of the prose version of the *Boethius*. One possible explanation is that the Prose Preface is a composite piece, consisting of an original preface designed for the prose version which was then interpolated with a passage recording how the verse was composed and by whom. This revised preface, having been adapted for use with a prosimetrical version, then conceivably became attached through an accident in transmission to a copy of the prose version.[17] Such a scenario would mean that although a preface may have accompanied the prose version of the *Boethius* when it was first circulated, that preface may only be partly represented by the Prose Preface to the *Boethius* as it now stands.[18]

The second sentence of the Prose Preface to the *Boethius* recycles a number of words and phrases from the Prose Preface to the *Pastoral Care*. The phrases 'hwilum...word be worde, hwilum andgit of andgite' (sometimes word for word, sometimes sense for sense, lines 2–3), 'angitfullicast gereccan mihte' (could most intelligibly interpret, line 3), and 'mistlicum and manigfealdum woruldbisgum' (many and various worldly cares, line 4) correspond almost verbatim to phrases used in the Preface to the *Pastoral Care*. Although this has sometimes been treated as evidence of shared authorship of the two prefaces, the similarities may in fact be the result of imitation.

---

[17] Discenza (2008), p. 60, suggests alternatively that the preface in its revised form might have been designed to fit both versions at once.

[18] On the problematic nature of the Prose Preface to the *Boethius*, see further, for example, Griffiths (1994), pp. 19–42; Bately (2003), pp. 112–14; Godden (2007), pp. 16–17; and S. Irvine (2018), pp. 13–16.

The writer of the Prose Preface to the *Boethius* is perhaps drawing on the *Pastoral Care* preface as a way of validating his own.

Whether or not Alfred actually had any hand in the composition of the *Boethius*, the Prose Preface's attribution of the work to him is designed to invest it with the textual and political authority implicit in the king's name. This preface also fosters a sense of dialogue between the king and the work's readers (praying to each of those who read the book to pray for him), perhaps reflecting the dialogue form of the work itself. In its emphasis on the troubles which Alfred experienced, and on the extraordinary effort he made to write despite these circumstances, this preface may also be implicitly comparing the king's troubles to those of Boethius, as a way of connecting more closely the translator and the author of the original work. The Prose Preface to the *Boethius* shares a number of its themes with the prose prefaces to the *Dialogues* and the *Pastoral Care*: the relationship between author and authority, the art of translation, and the difficulty in balancing worldly and spiritual occupations.

The Verse Preface to the *Boethius*

The identity of the first-person voice in the Verse Preface to the *Boethius* is uncertain. The plural form *us* in the first line seems to present the speaker as part of the work's audience whom Alfred is addressing. When the first-person pronoun is used again (in line 8), it is in the singular (*ic*) rather than the plural. This *ic* (I) has a number of different possible identities: the supposed author King Alfred (if we assume a move from third-person to first-person voice in the poem, as in the Prose Preface to the Old English *Pastoral Care*); an imagined performer reciting the work to an audience; or the book itself. If the latter, then the poem could be compared to the verse prefaces to the *Pastoral Care* and *Dialogues* in which the book is the speaker (see above pp. 6–7). In the Verse Preface to the *Boethius*, as in the Verse Preface to the *Pastoral Care* (where the book is first *þis ærendgewrit* and later *min/me*), the speaking book may arguably be referred to initially in the third person (*ealdspell*), before being revealed as the speaking voice *ic* later in the poem. James Earl suggests alternatively that *us* and *ealdspell* in line 1 are in apposition to one another, with the plural *us* referring to the Metres ('King Alfred told us, old tales') which in line 8 then speak as a book in the singular.[19] There is no evidence, however, that the Metres in themselves ever constituted a book; rather they seem to have been designed to alternate with prose passages in a prosimetrical version of the Old English *Boethius*.[20]

The ambiguous use of voices in this preface complicates any attempt to identify its author or date of composition. The versifier may have based the claim that Alfred composed the Metres on the account provided by the Prose Preface to the *Boethius*, or on a long-standing tradition of attributing vernacular works to him. The prominence of Alfred's name and title (king of the West Saxons) in the poem is no doubt another aspect of the ambition to invest the work as a whole with the authority implicit in his royal status.

The preface draws attention to its own form through the repetition of words meaning poet ('leoðwyrhta', line 3) or poetry ('leoð' and 'fitte', lines 4 and 9), and through its use of traditional poetic diction ('hæleðum', line 10). It implies that the Metres will be recited out loud to an audience. The verbs 'reahte' (interpreted, explained, line 1), 'meldode' (announced, showed, line 2), and 'spellode' (proclaimed, narrated, line 4) all carry connotations of the spoken word, and the act of speaking is conveyed in 'sprecan' (speak, line 8), 'fon on fitte' (recite in verse, line 9), and 'secgean' (say, line 10).[21] The last line urges the audience to listen ('hliste'). Although it is possible that the Metres were composed with public recitation in mind, it seems more likely that the poet is setting up a fiction of orality that recalls the Old English poetic tradition. The emphasis on the spoken word also looks forward to the fictional context of the work itself which is in the form of a dialogue between Wisdom and Mind.

In the Verse Preface, Alfred is presented as a figure whose verse will provide comfort and advice for the 'selflicne secg' (self-regarding man, line 7). The implied relationship is one of teacher and pupil, similar to that between Wisdom and Mind. The poet perhaps has in mind here comparisons between Alfred and Wisdom, and between the self-regarding man and

---

[19] Earl (1994), p. 91.
[20] O'Brien O'Keeffe (2005), p. 34. See also Thornbury (2014), pp. 21–3.
[21] O'Brien O'Keeffe (2005), pp. 30–1.

Mind. Wisdom, like Alfred, will be seen to interpret *ealdspell* (old stories, line 1) and to reveal *cræft* (skill, line 2).[22] And like the self-regarding man, Mind will succumb to *gilpe* (pride, line 8) when he despairs at the loss of his worldly prosperity, and will crave poetry to avoid *ælinge* (tedium, line 6).[23] Just as Mind chooses to listen to Wisdom, so the contemporary audience, it is implied, should choose to listen to Alfred.

The Prose and Verse *Vitae*

The introductory account of the historical and biographical contexts leading to the composition of the *Consolation of Philosophy* survives in Old English in both prose and metrical versions (the latter a versification of the former). The Prose *Vita* seems to have been composed at the same time as the rest of the *Boethius* and by the same author. It was probably part of the Old English work from the outset. Similarly it is likely that the versifier responsible for the Verse *Vita* was also the author of some or all of the other Metres in the prosimetrical version of the work: Griffith notes that stylistic variations across the Metres 'appear to be generated by theme (e.g. the heroic quality of Metre 1 as against the more philosophical quality of Metre 20)' rather than as the result of more than one versifier at work.[24]

The provision of information about Boethius at the opening of the Old English work has its origin in the genre of the *accessus* (prologue or introduction), the classical and medieval scholarly tradition of providing an introduction to a commentary on a work and its author.[25] The *accessus* characteristically included, or was accompanied by, a *vita* or life of the author. Associated with this tradition are the biographical notes (the so-called *vitae*)

---

[22] Wisdom recounts what is told *on ealdspellum* (in old stories) at Godden and Irvine (2009), I.361 (B Text, ch. 39.89–90). For the link between Wisdom and *cræft*, see, for example, 'wisdom is se hehsta cræft', Godden and Irvine (2009), I.298 (B Text, ch. 27.47).

[23] In chapter 39 of the B Text of the Old English *Boethius*, for example, Wisdom twice mentions Mind's longing for poetry rather than prose: Godden and Irvine (2009), I.361 (chs. 39.108–9 and 39.328–9).

[24] In Godden and Irvine (2009), I.106.

[25] See Copeland (1991), pp. 66–82; Copeland (2016), pp. 151–63; M. Irvine (1994), pp. 121–2; Minnis (1988), pp. 14–15; Quain (1945); Wheeler (2015), pp. 2–24.

that were added by commentators to copies of the Latin *Consolation of Philosophy* from the late ninth century onwards, either on a preliminary leaf or in the margins of the first page.[26] The Old English Prose *Vita* is likely to have drawn on one or more of these Latin *vitae*, though it departs in numerous details from any known version.[27] Its opening passage, for instance, independently mentions the invasion of Italy and sack of Rome by the Visigoths in the early fifth century, yoking it together (unhistorically) with the late fifth-century Ostrogothic invasion under Theoderic. The Verse *Vita* offers a fuller version of events than the prose version, though the kinds of expansion (such as conventional heroic motifs of battle) and the occasional errors in interpretation of the prose (such as the flight of the emperor to the east on the arrival of Rædgota and Alaric) suggest that this was largely due to invention on the versifier's part rather than to consultation of sources beyond the Prose *Vita* itself.[28]

The versifier has used the opportunity offered by the heroic theme to expand on and reshape the prose more drastically than elsewhere. In addition to exploiting general poetic fillers, such as 'mæla gehwilce' (all the time, line 54), he emphasizes the martial aspect of the narrative, incorporating a range of diction and motifs characteristic of Old English heroic verse: the Goths 'sceldas læddon' (brought shields, line 2), for example, and are longing for 'folcgewinnes' (battle, line 10); they are 'sceotend' (warriors, line 11) and 'lindwigende' (shield-bearing soldiers, line 13); Boethius is a 'sincgeofa' (treasure giver, line 50) and a 'hererinc' (warrior, line 71). Other conventions of heroic poetry include the depiction of Boethius as a loyal retainer to his lord: he is 'hlaforde leof' (dear to his lord, line 47).

Also in line with more traditional verse composition, the versifier shows a particular interest in characters' states of mind.[29] A number of mini-narratives are created within the Metre which draw attention to the emotional responses of the participants. Thus, for example, the sack of Rome

---

[26] Godden and Irvine (2009), II.248. For an edition of the *vitae*, see Peiper (1871) and (more recently) Troncarelli (1981), pp. 24–6.

[27] See Godden and Irvine (2009), II.248–57, and (below) the Prose *Vita*, Commentary, lines 1–4, 4–5, 5, 9–10, 23–8.

[28] Godden (2002a), pp. 117–19; Godden and Irvine (2009), II.497–8.

[29] Mize (2013), pp. 155–235.

by Rædgota and Alaric leads into a short vignette recording how the Romans were forced to hand over their treasure and pledge loyalty to the Goths, even though their hearts were firmly with their former ruler who was in exile amongst the Greeks (lines 23–7). The idea that the Romans rejoice at Theoderic's victory (lines 33–41), not realizing till later his heretical beliefs, is also an invention by the versifier. Elsewhere Boethius is imbued with a sense of injustice at the evil behaviour of foreign kings (lines 54–6), and fear of Boethius instils in Theoderic a 'hreoh sefa' (troubled mind, line 71).

The representation of Boethius as an exemplary defender of Christianity against an unrighteous usurper may imply a parallel between him and the ninth-century kings like Alfred who confronted the Danes. An interest in kingship also emerges in the depiction of Theoderic as a king abusing his royal power. The contemporary value placed on kinship and genealogy is reflected in the notion that restoring imperial rule in Rome was justified because the emperor belonged to the kin of their old lords. The combination of virtue and learning that Boethius displays seems close to the image of the ideal 'eloquent ruler' that the Alfredian court was keen to project.[30]

The Epilogue to the *Boethius*

The prose version of the *Boethius* in MS Bodley 180 closes with a prayer which serves as an epilogue to the work. The prayer was not part of the work as originally composed.[31] As Thomas A. Bredehoft has shown, it has the hallmarks of late Old English verse, and was evidently composed in the eleventh century.[32] The prayer has been added by a scribe, either in this copy for the first time or in a recent exemplar of this copy, to provide a closing frame text for a work that did not originally have one.[33] Within its

---

[30] Stanton (2002), pp. 91–100. [31] See, for example, Bately (2003), p. 118.
[32] Bredehoft (2009), pp. 175–9.
[33] Scholarly opinion is divided over whether the hand which wrote the prayer in MS Bodley 180 is the same as or different from the one which copied the main work; see, respectively, Ker (1957), p. 359, and Sedgefield (1899), p. xv.

manuscript context, the first-person speaker of the prayer is probably to be understood as the scribe, who may be seen as responding to a call for prayer made by Wisdom at the end of the work.[34] The prayer may have its roots in the tradition of the scribal colophon,[35] and in this respect may be compared to the verse part of the Epilogue to the Old English *Bede* in Cambridge, Corpus Christi College MS 41 (edited below).

The argument that the prayer is composed in late Old English verse rather than prose is based on the high number of alliterative linkages and the use of the repetitive sequence 'a a a' (now and forever without end, lines 21–2).[36] A number of similarities with the prayer *Min Drihten Leof*, which survives in three eleventh-century manuscripts, have been identified.[37] Echoes of the language of Ælfric and Wulfstan, writers of the late tenth and early eleventh centuries, also occur in the prayer.[38]

Note on the Texts

The texts of the Prose Preface and the Prose *Vita* are based on Oxford, Bodleian Library, MS Bodley 180 [B], fos. 1r and 3v–4r, with collation of substantial variants in London, British Library, Cotton MS Otho A. vi [C], as recorded in the collations transcribed by Junius in Oxford, Bodleian Library, MS Junius 12 [Jc]. The texts of the Verse Preface and the Verse *Vita* are edited from Jc. The text of the Epilogue is based on B, fo. 94r. It is lineated in verse lines following Bredehoft (2009), p. 213, but differs from his text in using modern punctuation and *and* for 7.

The order of the framing texts edited here is not based on any one manuscript but takes account of the range of framing material across the two

---

[34] Godden and Irvine (2009), I.381–2 (B Text, ch. 42.47–50): 'Ac abiddað hine eaðmodlice forþam he is swiðe rummod and swiðe mildheort. Hebbað eower mod to him mid eowrum hondum and biddað þæs þe riht sie and eower þearf sie, forþam he eow nyle wyrnan.' (But pray to him humbly for he is very generous and very merciful. Raise your minds to him with your hands and pray for what is right and necessary for you, for he will not refuse you.)

[35] Bredehoft (2009), pp. 178–9.   [36] Bredehoft (2009), p. 214.

[37] Bredehoft (2009), pp. 209–11, 214.

[38] See the Epilogue to the *Boethius*, Commentary, lines 2 and 13.

manuscripts. The Prose Preface and Verse Preface follow one another, as in the prosimetrical version of the work. The Prose *Vita* and Verse *Vita* are placed sequentially to facilitate comparison of the two alternative versions. The summary of the contents of the main work, and then the Epilogue, follow this collection of prefatory material.

TEXTS AND TRANSLATIONS

The Prose Preface to the *Boethius*

Ælfred kuning wæs wealhstod ðisse bec and hie of boclædene on Englisc wende swa hio nu is gedon. Hwilum he sette word be worde, hwilum andgit of andgite, swa swa he hit þa sweotolost and andgitfullicast gereccan mihte for þam mistlicum and manigfealdum woruldbisgum þe hine oft ægðer ge on mode ge on lichoman bisgodan. Ða bisgu us sint swiþe earfoþrime þe 5 on his dagum on þa ricu becoman þe he underfangen hæfde, and þeah ða he þas boc hæfde geleornode and of Lædene to Engliscum spelle gewende, þa geworhte he hi eft to leoðe swa swa heo nu gedon is; and nu bit and for Godes naman he halsað ælcne þara þe þas boc rædan lyste þæt he for hine gebidde, and him ne wite gif he hit rihtlicor ongite þonne he mihte, forþam 10 þe ælc mon sceal be his andgites mæðe and be his æmettan sprecan þæt he sprecð and don þæt þæt he deþ.

The Prose Preface to the *Boethius*

King Alfred was the translator of this book and turned it from Latin into English as it is now presented. Sometimes he set it down word for word, sometimes sense for sense, so far as he could most clearly and intelligibly interpret it given the many and various worldly cares which often occupied him in both body and mind. The cares which afflicted the kingdoms to which he had succeeded are very difficult for us to count, and yet when he had learned this book and turned it from Latin into English prose, then he produced it again as poetry, just as it is now presented; and he now prays and in God's name entreats each of those who wishes to read this book that he pray for him, and not blame him if he understand it more correctly than he could, because everyone must speak what he speaks and do what he does according to the extent of his understanding and his leisure.

The Verse Preface to the *Boethius*

Ðus Ælfred us   ealdspell reahte,
cyning Westsexna,   cræft meldode,
leoðwyrhta list.   Him wæs lust micel
ðæt he ðiossum leodum   leoð spellode,
monnum myrgen,   mislice cwidas,   5
þy læs ælinge   ut adrife
selflicne secg,   þonne he swelces lyt
gymð for his gilpe.   Ic sceal giet sprecan,
fon on fitte,   folccuðne ræd
hæleðum secgean.   Hliste se þe wille.   10

The Verse Preface to the *Boethius*

Thus Alfred told us ancient stories,
king of the West Saxons, proclaimed his skill,
the poet [proclaimed] his art. He had a great desire
to recite verse to these people,
5   entertainment for men, varied speeches,
lest tedium should drive away
the self-regarding man, when he little heeds
such a thing because of his pride. I must yet speak out,
recite verse, give well-known
10 advice to men. Let him listen who will.

The Prose *Vita* of the *Boethius*

On ðære tide ðe Gotan of Sciððiu mægðe wið Romana rice gewin up ahofon, and mid heora cyningum, Rædgota and Eallerica wæron hatne, Romane burig abræcon and eall Italia rice þæt is betwux þam muntum and Sicilia þam ealonde in anwald gerehton, þa æfter þam foresprecenan cyningum Þeodric feng to þam ilcan rice. Se Ðeodric wæs Amulinga; he was 5 Cristen, þeah he on þam Arrianiscan gedwolan þurhwunode. He gehet Romanum his freondscipe swa þæt hi mostan heora ealdrihta wyrðe beon. Ac he þa gehat swiðe yfele gelæste and swiðe wraðe geendode mid manegum mane; þæt wæs toeacan oðrum unarimedum yflum þæt he Iohannes þone papan het ofslean. 10

Þa wæs sum consul þæt we heretoha hatað, Boetius wæs gehaten, se wæs in boccræftum and on woruldþeawum se rihtwisesta. Se þa ongeat þa manigfealdan yfel þe se cyning Ðeodric wið þam cristenandome and wið þam Romaniscum witum dyde. He þa gemunde þara eðnessa and þara ealdrihta þe hi under þam caserum hæfdon, heora ealdhlafordum. Þa ongan he smea- 15 gan and leornigan on him selfum hu he þæt rice þam unrihtwisan cyninge aferran mihte, and on ryhtgeleaffulra and on rihtwisra anwealde gebringan. Sende þa digellice ærendgewritu to þam kasere to Constentinopolim, þær is Creca heahburg and heora cynestol, forþam se kasere wæs heora ealdhlafordcynnes; bædon hine þæt he him to heora cristendome and to heora 20 ealdrihtum gefultumede.

Þa þæt ongeat se wælhreowa cyning Ðeodric, þa het he hine | gebringan on carcerne and þærinne belucan. Þa hit ða gelomp þæt se arwyrða wer on swa micelre nearanesse becom, þa wæs he swa micle swiðor on his mode gedrefed swa his mod ær swiðor to þam woruldsælþum gewunod was, and 25 he þa nanre frofre beinnan þam carcerne ne gemunde, ac he gefeoll niwol ofdune on þa flor and hine astrehte swiðe unrot, and ormod hine selfne ongan wepan and þus singend cwæð.

The Prose *Vita* of the *Boethius*

At the time when the Goths from Scythia raised war against the kingdom of the Romans, and with their kings called Rædgota and Alaric took by storm the city of the Romans and subjugated the entire kingdom of Italy lying between the mountains and the island of Sicily, then, after the aforementioned kings, Theoderic succeeded to that same kingdom. Theoderic was of the family of the Amulings; he was a Christian, though he persisted in the Arian heresy. He promised his friendship to the Romans so that they could remain entitled to their ancient rights. But he fulfilled those promises very wickedly and concluded very cruelly with many a crime; it was in addition to countless other evils that he ordered the pope John to be killed.

There was then a consul (which we call a leader), called Boethius, who was the most righteous in book learning and worldly virtues. He then perceived the many evils which the king Theoderic carried out against Christianity and the Roman counsellors. He then recalled the privileges and ancient rights that they enjoyed under the emperors, their old rulers. Then he began to mull over and study in his own mind how he could take the kingdom away from that unrighteous king and bring it under the control of orthodox and righteous people. He then secretly sent letters to the emperor at Constantinople, the principal town and royal throne of the Greeks, because the emperor was related to their old lords; they asked him to help them to get back their Christianity and ancient rights.

When the cruel king Theoderic heard of this, he ordered him to be put into prison and locked up in there. When it happened that the honourable man fell into such hardship, then he became all the more greatly distressed in his mind because his mind had been so used to worldly prosperities, and he then could not think of any consolation inside the prison but fell down prostrate on the floor and stretched out in a sorrowful state, and in despair began to weep to himself, and in song spoke as follows.

The Verse *Vita* of the *Boethius*

Hit wæs geara iu   ðætte Gotan eastan
of Sciððia   sceldas læddon,
þreate geþrungon   þeodlond monig,
setton suðweardes   sigeþeoda twa.
Gotene rice   gearmælum weox.   5
Hæfdan him gecynde   cyningas twegen
Rædgod and Aleric;   rice geþungon.
Þa wæs ofer Muntgiop   monig atyhted
Gota gylpes full,   guðe gelysted,
folcgewinnes.   Fana hwearfode   10
scir on sceafte.   Sceotend þohton
Italia   ealla gegongan,
lindwigende.   Hi gelæstan swua
efne from Muntgiop   oð þone mæran wearoð
þær Sicilia   sæstreamum in,   15
eglond micel,   eðel mærsað.

   Ða wæs Romana   rice gewunnen,
abrocen burga cyst;   beadurincum wæs
Rom gerymed.   Rædgot and Aleric
foron on ðæt fæsten;   fleah casere   20
mid þam æþelingum   ut on Crecas.
Ne meahte þa seo wealaf   wige forstandan
Gotan mid guðe.   Giomonna gestrion
sealdon unwillum   eþelweardas,
halige aðas: wæs gehwæðeres waa.   25
Þeah wæs magorinca   mod mid Crecum,
gif hi leodfruman   læstan dorsten.

   Stod þrage on ðam.   Þeod wæs gewunnen
wintra mænigo,   oðþæt wyrd gescraf
þæt þe Ðeodrice   þegnas and eorlas   30
heran sceoldan.   Wæs se heretema
Criste gecnoden,   cyning selfa onfeng
fulluhtþeawum.   Fægnodon ealle

The Verse *Vita* of the *Boethius*

    It was long ago that the Goths brought
shields from Scythia in the east,
violently oppressed many a country,
two victorious nations setting out southwards.
5   The kingdom of the Goths grew year by year.
They had two lawful kings,
Raedgota and Alaric; they flourished in power.
Then many Goths, full of pride,
were enticed over the Alps, longing for war,
10 for battles between armies. The shining banner
fluttered on its staff. The warriors,
shield-bearing soldiers, intended to conquer
all Italy. They did so,
right from the Alps to that famous shore
15 where the large island of Sicily
demarcates its territory with sea currents.
    Then the kingdom of the Romans was conquered,
the finest of cities sacked; Rome was laid open
to the warriors. Raedgota and Alaric
20 went into that stronghold; the emperor fled
with the princes away to the Greeks.
Then the wretched survivors could not withstand the Goths
in warfare, in battle. The guardians of the homeland
reluctantly delivered their ancestors' treasure
25 and sacred promises: there was affliction over both.
Yet the thoughts of the warriors were with the Greeks,
as to whether they would dare to support the leader of the people.
    Things remained thus for a time. The nation stayed conquered
for many years until fate ordained
30 that retainers and noblemen had to
obey Theoderic. That ruler was
committed to Christ; the king himself received
baptism. All the offspring of Roman citizens

Romwara bearn and   him recene to
friðes wilnedon.   He him fæste gehet   35
þæt hy ealdrihta   ælces mosten
wyrðe gewunigen   on þære welegan byrig,
ðenden God wuolde   þæt he Gotena geweald
agan moste.   He þæt eall aleag.
Wæs þæm æþelinge   Arrianes   40
gedwola leofre   þonne Drihtnes æ.
Het Iohannes,   godne papan,
heafde beheawon;   næs ðæt hærlic dæd.
Eac þam wæs unrim   oðres manes
þæt se Gota fremede   godra gehwilcum.   45

   Ða wæs ricra sum   on Romebyrig
ahefen heretoga,   hlaforde leof,
þenden cynestole   Creacas wioldon.
Þæt wæs rihtwis rinc;   næs mid Romwarum
sincgeofa sella   siððan longe.   50
He wæs for weorulde wis,   weorðmynða georn,
beorn boca gleaw;   Boitius
se hæle hatte   se þone hlisan geþah.

   Wæs him on gemynde   mæla gehwilce
yfel and edwit   þæt him elðeodge   55
kyningas cyðdon;   wæs on Creacas hold,
gemunde þara ara   and ealdrihta
þe his eldran mid him   ahton longe,
lufan and lissa.   Angan þa listum ymbe
ðencean þearflice,   hu he ðider meahte   60
Crecas oncerran,   þæt se casere eft
anwald ofer hi   agan moste.
Sende ærendgewrit   ealdhlafordum
degelice,   and hi for Drihtne bæd
ealdum treowum   ðæt hi æft to him   65
comen on þa ceastre,   lete Creca witan
rædan Romwarum,   rihtes wyrðe

        rejoiced and promptly sought
35   peace with him. He promised them firmly
        that they would be permitted to remain
        in possession of all their ancient rights in that wealthy city
        for as long as God wished him to have power
        over the Goths. He failed in fulfilling all that.
40   The heresy of Arius was dearer
        to that prince than God's law.
        He commanded that the good pope John
        should be beheaded; that was not a noble deed.
        In addition to that there were countless other crimes
45   that the Goth committed against all good people.
           Then a certain man amongst the powerful in Rome was
        promoted to consul, one cherished by his lord
        at the time that the Greeks held the throne.
        He was a just man; there was no better treasure-giver
50   amongst the Romans for a long time afterwards.
        He was wise in the ways of the world, eager for honours,
        a man learned in books; Boethius
        was the name of the man who attained that reputation.
           He had in his mind all the time
55   the evil and contempt that the foreign kings
        showed them; he was loyal to the Greeks
        remembering the honours and ancient rights,
        the love and favours, that his ancestors had held
        amongst them for a long time. Then he began cleverly
60   and carefully to consider how he could bring
        back the Greeks so that the emperor might
        have power over them again.
        He secretly sent a letter to his former
        lords, and asked them for the sake of God
65   and their old loyalties that they should return
        to them in that city, and that Greek counsellors should be allowed
        to rule the Romans, and the people allowed

lete þone leodscipe.   Ða þa lare ongeat
Ðeodric Amuling   and þone þegn oferfeng,
heht fæstlice   folcgesiðas 70
healdon þone hererinc.   Wæs him hreoh sefa,
ege from ðam eorle.   He hine inne heht
on carcernes   cluster belucan.
   Þa wæs modsefa   miclum gedrefed
Boetius.   Breac longe ær 75
wlencea under wolcnum;   he þy wyrs meahte
þolian þa þrage   þa hio swa þearl becom.
Wæs þa ormod eorl,   are ne wende,
ne on þam fæstene   frofre gemunde,
ac he neowol astreaht   niðer ofdune 80
feol on þa flore,   fela worda spræc,
forþoht ðearle;   ne wende þonan æfre
cuman of ðæm clammum.   Cleopode to Drihtne
geomran stemne,   gyddode þus.

to have their due rights. Then Theodoric the Amuling
heard about that counsel and seized the official;
he commanded the lords of the people
to guard that warrior firmly. His mind was troubled,
he was fearful because of that nobleman. He commanded him
to be locked in a prison cell.
   Then Boethius' mind was greatly
disturbed. He had enjoyed prosperity under
the skies for a long time before; he found it all the harder
to endure so harsh a time when it came about.
The nobleman was despondent then, did not expect mercy,
nor did he think of any comfort in that prison,
but, stretched out prostrate and face down,
he fell on the floor; spoke many words
in great despair, never expecting to come from there
out of those fetters. He called to the Lord
with a sad voice, singing as follows.

Summary of the *Boethius*

Following the historical introduction, the author turns to his main source. In the first book (chapters 1–6 in the prose version) the Mind of the downcast Boethius is offered comfort by Wisdom. Complaining that the wicked prosper in the world, Mind calls for an explanation of why the justice and order that control the natural world are not imposed on people as well. Wisdom points out that every creature comes from God and that fate has no power independent of God's design. Mind, Wisdom urges, should avoid pride and despair.

Book II (chapters 7–21 in the prose version) emphasizes the need to scorn worldly fortunes because they are false and unstable. Worldly honour and power come under particular scrutiny: they often come to those unworthy of having them, such as Theoderic, Nero, and Tarquin. Nero's crimes are cited to show that power, like all worldly goods, is not intrinsically good, but only insofar as the people who have it are virtuous. Mind explains to Wisdom that he desired power only as a means of ruling his kingdom wisely, and that he aimed to set a good example for his successors. Wisdom rails against people's desire for fame which is trivial in relation to the world as a whole and meaningless in the face of death. Adverse fate, Wisdom argues, is in fact beneficial because it reveals the fragility of earthly prosperity. Wisdom ends by praising God for binding all the conflicting elements in the world so harmoniously.

In Book III (chapters 22–34 in the prose version), Wisdom argues that human pursuit of the false goods of this world (wealth, power, fame, honour, and pleasure) may be misdirected but implicitly indicates the mind's instinctive desire to reach the highest good. Wisdom addresses each of the false goods in turn, demonstrating that none of them confers what it seems to promise. It is, rather, the path to the supreme good that should be sought. This supreme good consists of the gathering of all the goods (power, sufficiency, renown, honour, and joy), whose earthly counterparts people mistakenly pursue, into one indivisible thing, which is God. Wisdom goes on to explain to Mind the irresistible nature of God's power, using examples from both classical mythology and biblical narrative. By way of the story of Orpheus and Eurydice, Wisdom shows the folly of reverting to previous wickedness when one has already repented.

In the fourth book (chapters 36–40 in the prose version) Wisdom takes up the question of why God allows evil to flourish, assuring Mind that the good are always powerful and happy, and the evil powerless and unhappy, even if appearances suggest otherwise. The good, Wisdom argues, receive the reward for their goodness by achieving good, and the evil bring upon themselves their own punishment in achieving evil. By forsaking human virtues, the evil become like beasts even though they keep their human form (this is exemplified through the story of Ulysses and Circe). The wicked need our help not our hatred, says Wisdom, since if they are not punished here they will have eternal punishment. Wisdom shows that providence (the divine intelligence) rules and shapes everything which is carried out by fate (the day-to-day course of events), using the image of the cartwheel to illustrate how all creation revolves around God and is affected in different ways by the workings of fate.

In Book V (chapters 40–2 in the prose version), Wisdom first assures Mind that nothing happens by chance. Tackling then the issue of whether providence or fate is compatible with human freedom, Wisdom argues that both angels and humans have freedom but at different levels, and that God sees everything. Wisdom goes on to address further questions about the compatibility of God's foreknowledge and free will, showing that God's creatures must be free if he is to grant them rewards appropriate to their deeds, and that he leaves certain things undetermined even if they may be harmful. Wisdom then explains about different levels of cognition, presenting a hierarchy which has angels and the wise at the top level, to which all human beings should aspire. Finally Wisdom explains the nature of God's eternity, contrasting it with the human ability to be certain only about present time.

The Epilogue to the *Boethius*

Drihten ælmihtiga God,
wyrhta and wealdend   ealra gesceafta,
ic bidde þe for þinre micelan   mildheortnessan
and for þære halegan   rode tacne
and for Sancta Marian   mægðhade   5
and for Sancte Michaeles   gehyrsumnesse
and for ealra þinra halgana lufan   and heora earnungum
þæt þu me gewissige bet   þonne ic awyrhte to þe,
and gewissa me   to þinum willan
and to minre sawla þearfe   bet þonne ic sylf cunne.   10
And gestaþela min mod to þinum willan   and to minre sawla þearfe,
and gestranga me   wið þæs deofles costnungum,
and afyrra fram me   þa fulan galnysse
and ælce unrihtwisnysse,   and gescylde me
wið minum wiðerwinnum,   gesewenlicum and ungesewenlicum,   15
and tæc me þinne   willan to wyrcenne
þæt ic mæge þe inweardlice lufian   toforon eallum þingum
mid clænum geþance   and mid clænum lichaman,
forþon þe þu eart min sceoppend   and min alesend,
min fultum, min frofer, min trewnes,   and min tohopa.   20
Si þe lof and wylder   nu and a a
a to worulde   buton æghwilcum ende.
Amen.

The Epilogue to the *Boethius*

Lord God Almighty,
creator and ruler of all creatures,
I pray you on account of your great mercy,
and through the sign of the holy cross,
and the virginity of St Mary,
and the obedience of St Michael,
and the love and merits of all your saints,
that you guide me better than I have done towards you;
and guide me according to your will
and my soul's need better than I myself know how to.
And establish my mind to your will and my soul's need,
and strengthen me against the devil's temptations;
and remove from me foul lust
and every unrighteousness; and protect me
from my enemies, visible and invisible;
and teach me to do your will,
so that I may inwardly love you before all things
with pure thought and pure body,
for you are my creator and my redeemer,
my help, my consolation, my trust, and my hope.
Praise and glory be to you now and forever,
world without any end.
Amen.

The Old English *Soliloquies*

Preface

Incipits and Explicits

INTRODUCTION

The *Soliloquies* is furnished with a number of frame texts, all of them independent of the work's Latin source. They consist of a prose preface, and several extended incipits and explicits framing the individual books. The explicit at the end of the final book, which asserts Alfred's role in selecting the content, may refer to the work as a whole. It is not clear if any or all of these pieces were part of the original Old English work or a later addition. The shared themes of the Preface to the *Soliloquies* and the main work, including the importance of learning and the relationship between the earthly and eternal worlds, suggest that the preface-writer knew the work well.

The Work and its Contexts

The *Soliloquies* begins as a relatively free translation of Augustine of Hippo's work *Soliloquia*, written in AD 387, shortly after Augustine converted to Christianity. The Latin work, though it takes the form of a dialogue, is entitled 'soliloquies' (thoughts spoken out loud to oneself) because the two speakers are Augustine and his own reason. It is divided into two books, the first addressing different kinds of knowledge, and the second the immortality of the soul. An intended third book was never completed. The decision to translate the *Soliloquia* into Old English is a curious one, since the work, though circulating widely in Carolingian Europe,[1] seems to have been little known in England in the early medieval period. Like Augustine, the Old English author explores the issue of the human soul's immortality through an inner dialogue between the figures of Augustine and 'Gesceadwisnes' (Reason). Augustine's work, however, is little more than a starting point for the *Soliloquies*, which not only renders its main source very freely but also moves away from it completely soon after

[1] Pratt (2007), p. 314.

Book II begins and adds a third book independently of the *Soliloquia*. For Books II and III, the translator has drawn on a number of different sources, including *De videndo Deo* (*On Seeing God*), also by Augustine, Gregory the Great's homiletic writing, and the *Prognosticon* by Julian of Toledo.[2] Boethius' *De consolatione Philosophiae* may also have been amongst the works consulted, whether in its original or translated form. The fact that the *Soliloquies* shows many points of comparison with the Old English *Boethius*—in form, content, and style—may suggest that the two were written at about the same time (and perhaps by the same author).[3] Like the *Boethius*, the *Soliloquies* has traditionally been attributed to Alfred himself, mainly on the basis of the final explicit and of various linguistic and stylistic correspondences with other works thought to be by Alfred.[4]

The *Soliloquies* has sometimes been linked with a work which Alfred, according to his biographer Asser, called his *Enchiridion*, or handbook. It apparently contained passages from books that had caught Alfred's attention and which he had translated into English.[5] Asser refers to these passages as 'flowers', a conventional image for particularly choice excerpts culled from books, used also in the incipits and explicits of the *Soliloquies* (see further below). The twelfth-century William of Malmesbury claims to have seen the *Enchiridion*; this claim, according to Dorothy Whitelock, may have arisen from a misidentification of a copy of the *Soliloquies* (complete with its allusions to 'flowers' in the incipits and explicits) based on Asser's description.[6] Whitelock's view would explain why William does not otherwise show knowledge of the *Soliloquies*, but does not account for William's description of material in what he understood to be the *Enchiridion* that does not correspond to the text of the *Soliloquies* (or glosses to it).[7] The possibility remains that a handbook linked to Alfred continued to be available as a work in its own right in and beyond his reign. Recently Leslie Lockett has proposed that the translator of the *Soliloquies* 'based much of book 3 on

---

[2] Godden (2001), accessed 28 Nov. 2018; Godden (2003), pp. 189–205; Jayatilaka (2012), pp. 672–3.
[3] Godden and Irvine (2009), I.135–6.
[4] See the General Introduction, p. 14.
[5] Stevenson (1959), ch. 88; translated by Keynes and Lapidge (1983), p. 100.
[6] Whitelock (1966), pp. 71–3, and (1969), pp. 90–1.
[7] Thomson (1999), pp. 103–4, and (2007), pp. 248–9.

a collection of Latin excerpts that he believed, correctly or not, to be the handbook compiled by Alfred himself'.[8]

The *Soliloquies* is a markedly ambitious work for its time, evident in the freedom it takes with its main source and its engagement, in the vernacular, with complex philosophical issues. Though it seems not to have circulated widely—to judge by its apparent invisibility to other writers of the period and by the manuscript evidence (see below)—it is a valuable witness to the intellectual sophistication fostered by the Alfredian literary programme in both authors and audiences alike.

Manuscripts and Previous Editions

The Preface to the *Soliloquies*, along with the work itself, is extant in just one manuscript, London, British Library, Cotton Vitellius A. xv. Within that manuscript it is the first text in what is known as the Southwick Codex (followed there by a translation of the Gospel of Nicodemus, a version of the Dialogues of Solomon and Saturn, and a fragment of a homily on St Quintin), which since the seventeenth century has been joined to the Nowell Codex (home to *Beowulf* amongst other works).[9] The copy of the *Soliloquies* is a late one, written in the mid-twelfth century according to N. R. Ker, perhaps in the southeastern region of England.[10] The only other surviving medieval witness to the work is a copy of two sections of the prayer forming part of Book I of the *Soliloquies*, occurring in a manuscript from the mid-eleventh century, London, British Library, Cotton Tiberius A. iii (fos. 50v–51v).[11]

The manuscript copy of the Preface to the *Soliloquies* begins (on folio 4r) with a large coloured capital on the first word *Gaderode*, suggesting that its scribe viewed the text as complete. It is likely, however, that some material

---

[8] Lockett (2022a), p. 405. See also below the explicit of Book III of the *Soliloquies*, Commentary, lines 1–2.

[9] Ker (1957), no. 215.

[10] For the case for a slightly later date (the third quarter of the twelfth century), see Treharne (2016), pp. 232–5.

[11] Ker (1957), no. 186; Gneuss and Lapidge (2014), no. 363; Szarmach (2005); Szarmach (2015), pp. 228–32.

has been lost before the beginning of the Preface as it now survives, since it seems to begin in the middle of a sentence (see further below). Another coloured initial is found at the top of folio 5r, where the last part of the Preface, a short introduction to the work itself, begins.

The *Soliloquies* has been edited relatively frequently. The three twentieth-century editions, by Henry Hargrove, Wilhelm Endter, and Thomas Carnicelli respectively, have now been superseded by Leslie Lockett's edition and translation of the work, along with its Latin source, in the Dumbarton Oaks Medieval Library series.[12] Her edition takes account of the substantial reordering of the various sections of Book III proposed by Malcolm Godden.[13]

The Preface to the *Soliloquies*

The Preface to the *Soliloquies* uses a first-person voice, but without any indication of who is speaking. This may be the result of damage to the text in the course of transmission. The abrupt opening of the preface, with its lack of a subject pronoun and its use of the adverb *þonne* in a way that suggests a preceding idea or sentence, implies that it is incomplete.[14] It is difficult to know the extent of the loss: Eric Stanley speculates that the preface in its current form might in fact have been a 'second preface, following a more factual first preface',[15] but it is also possible that no more than a few lines have been lost. In any case it seems reasonable to assume that the preface in its original form would have identified its first-person persona. The evidence that we have points towards the voice of Alfred: the preface's images and ideas reflect those of other Alfredian writings (see below), and the explicit of Book III of the work proclaims Alfred's role in producing it. Accepting that the work may be written in Alfred's voice is not of course to claim his authorship, nor even a date of composition within his reign: the most we can say is that this preface seems to fit with a movement, which began in Alfred's lifetime but may well have extended beyond then, to

---

[12] Hargrove (1902); Endter (1922); Carnicelli (1969); Lockett (2022a).
[13] Godden (2003).
[14] Not all scholars would agree; see, for example, Potter (1949), pp. 28–9.
[15] Stanley (1970), p. III; cf. Stanley (1988), pp. 357–8.

associate the king with the composition of a number of high-profile works written in the vernacular.

The Preface to the *Soliloquies* has three parts. In the first (lines 1–21), a narrator, speaking in the first person, records his own wood-gathering and building activities, and urges others to follow suit so as to secure both a comfortable place to live on earth and, in due course, the eternal home. This part ends with a short prayer *sie swa* (may it be so). The second part (lines 22–30), less personal in approach, uses the building metaphor as a starting point for imagining the pleasure of being a tenant living on leased land in the cottage he has built, and in due course earning 'bookland', land held according to privileges specified by a charter.[16] Again it closes with a prayer: *forgife me…* (may he grant me…). The third part (lines 31–5) offers a short description of Augustine's *Soliloquia* on which the work itself is based.

The first part of the preface draws on a number of ideas from the Latin tradition. For the image of wood-gathering in its opening, the author apparently draws on the classical and early medieval *silvae* trope, in which material for literary composition is compared with raw wood intended for building projects.[17] The kind of material that the author had in mind here as a starting point for literary composition is perhaps indicated by the explicit reference later in the preface to three Latin authors—Augustine, Gregory, and Jerome—who, along with 'many other holy fathers', have conveyed God's promise of an eternal home. The preface-writer probably flags up these authors not because of any direct connections they may have to the *Soliloquies* itself, but because they are representative of a broad tradition of drawing on authoritative sources to produce works of Christian wisdom.

In developing the building metaphor, the author may, as Valerie Heuchan suggests, be indebted to the passage in 1 Corinthians 3:9–14, in which Paul, depicted as a wise architect, has laid a foundation for others to build on, and perhaps also to a passage near the end of Aldhelm's preface to his prose *De virginitate* (*On Virginity*) where he announces his intention to write a poetic version of the same work:[18]

---

[16] See the Preface to the *Soliloquies*, Commentary, lines 22–7.
[17] M. Irvine (1994), pp. 435–7. [18] Heuchan (2007).

> I shall try with artistry to adorn the renown of this same chastity, with Christ's cooperation, in the heroic measures of hexameter verse, and, as if the rhetorical foundation-stones were now laid and the walls of prose were built, so I shall—trusting in heavenly support—build a sturdy roof with trochaic slates and dactylic tiles of metre.[19]

For the last part of the Preface to the *Soliloquies*, the writer draws on Augustine's retrospective account of the *Soliloquia* in his work *Retractationes* (*Retractions*):[20]

> I also wrote two books, because of the enthusiasm I had and the love for seeking out, with the help of reason, the truth about those matters which I most wanted to know. I asked myself questions and I replied to myself, as if we were two, reason and I, whereas I was of course just one. As a result I called the work *Soliloquies*.[21]

The passage often appears as a prologue (and occasionally as an epilogue) to Augustine's *Soliloquia* in early manuscripts.[22]

The Preface to the *Soliloquies* is characterized stylistically by its use of extended metaphors whose concrete language is both engaging in its own right and also a pivot on which the spiritual meanings turn.[23] The opening metaphor in which gathering wood represents the process of seeking wisdom is peppered with a barrage of technical terms—*kigclas* (sturdy sticks), *stuþansceaftas* (posts), *lohsceaftas* (tie-beams), *hylfa* (handles), *bohtimbru*

---

[19] Ehwald (1919), p. 321: '...heroicis exametrorum versibus eiusdem praeconium pudicitiae subtiliter comere Christo cooperante conabor et, velut iactis iam rethoricis fundamentis et constructis prosae parietibus, cum tegulis trochaicis et dactilicis metrorum imbricibus firmissimum culmen caelesti confisus suffragio imponam.' Trans. Lapidge and Herren (1979), pp. 130–1.

[20] Godden (2001), accessed 28 Nov. 2018.

[21] Mutzenbecher (1984), pp. 13–14: 'Inter haec scripsi etiam duo uolumina secundum studium meum et amorem, ratione indagandae ueritatis de his rebus quas maxime scire cupiebam, me interrogans mihique respondens, tamquam duo essemus ratio et ego, cum solus essem, unde hoc opus *Soliloquia* nominaui.' Trans. Watson (1990), p. iv.

[22] Godden (2001), accessed 28 Nov. 2018; see also Godden (2009a), p. 115; and Lockett (2022b), pp. 130–1.

[23] Compare the use of concrete images to explain spiritual concepts in other prologues and epilogues, such as the tracking/hunting image in the Prose Preface to the *Pastoral Care*, and the water/watercourse image in the Verse Epilogue to the *Pastoral Care*.

(curved timber), *bolttimbru* (straight timber)[24]—perhaps, as Lockett suggests, designed to confer 'a learned literary flourish' rather than drawn from experience of working with wood.[25] The narrator emphasizes the comfort and aesthetic appeal of a house built with this wood, through which the ultimate goal of an eternal home can be achieved.

The landlord-tenant metaphor in the second part of the preface similarly combines concrete and abstract terminology. The passage begins by evoking the temporal activity of building a dwelling (*cotlyf*, line 23),[26] and of leased land where one can go hunting, fowling, and fishing. Leased land is contrasted with 'bookland', earned *þurh his hlafordes miltse* (through his lord's mercy, line 27). The transitory world serves as a metaphorical parallel to the eternal world, both ultimately in God's control. Here and elsewhere in the preface, the parallels between the two worlds are emphasized through the use of words that resonate in both contexts (such as *ham* 'home', *hlaford* 'lord', and *weliga gifola* 'wealthy benefactor'), and through the insistent repetition of *ægðer (ge)* meaning 'both' (three times in the first section and four in the second).

The themes of this preface echo both the main work and other Alfredian writings. The metaphor of gathering wood emphasizes the importance of learning, particularly in relation to the quest for eternal salvation. This opening part of the preface also emphasizes the role of the teacher, a role taken first by the narrator ('ic lære', I advise, line 7) and then by God ('se þe me lærde', he who taught me, line 12) through the holy fathers. The second part of the preface again sets up a hierarchy of authority, with the tenant dependent on his lord's kindness. Those in authority, the preface suggests, have a responsibility for the welfare, both physical and spiritual, of those they govern.

The gathering of wood and timber may also, as Michael Bintley has suggested, serve more practically as an extended metaphor for the different tools and tasks necessary to build and fortify the towns of the Anglo-Saxon kingdoms.[27] The continuation of the construction metaphor into the second

---

[24] On the difficulty of determining the precise meanings of these words, see Carnicelli (1969), p. 47; Sayers (2008).
[25] Lockett (2022a), p. 370.   [26] On *cotlyf*, see Smith (2012), pp. 126–35.
[27] Bintley (2015), pp. 146–9.

part of the preface may reflect a desire for individuals to contribute towards developing the built environment that underpins a stable society as well as to engage in the pursuit of spiritual wisdom.

The preface throughout shows a particular interest in the relationship between the earthly and eternal worlds. Parallels are drawn between the gathering of wood for building a house and the pursuit of spiritual wisdom, between an earthly dwelling and the eternal home, between temporary loaned land and inheritable bookland, and between a generous landlord and God *se weliga gifola* (the wealthy benefactor, lines 27–8). The eternal world is made apprehensible by being conceived in terms of a temporal one.

The Incipits and Explicits of the *Soliloquies*

Whether the incipits and explicits of the various books of the *Soliloquies* were part of the work as originally circulated or were added in transmission remains uncertain. The allusion to King Alfred in the explicit of Book III has led scholars to credit him with the composition of the work. As Lockett points out, however, he is identified here as a compiler and not as an author.[28]

The incipits and explicits are linked through the linguistic repetition characteristic of their forms (Here begins..., Here ends...). Worthy of particular note is the repeated use of the image of 'blossoms' to refer to the choicest part of a book, which occurs three times in the incipits and explicits of Books I and II. The gathering either of flowers, or honey from flowers, was a standard image for the process of compiling an anthology, or florilegium, of selected passages from great writers of the past.[29] Asser's comparison in his *Life of King Alfred* between a bee flying amongst the flowers and Alfred's literary activity is one example:

> Thereafter during our daily discussions, while searching to this end, as we found other equally pleasing passages the quire grew full, and rightly so:... [the just man,] like the busy bee, wandering far and wide over the

---

[28] Lockett (2022a), p. 404. For the representation of Alfred as compiler, compare below the Preface to the *Laws*.

[29] Gatch (1986), pp. 23–4; M. Irvine (1994), p. 435.

marshes in his quest, eagerly and relentlessly assembles many various flowers of Holy Scripture, with which he crams full the cells of his heart.[30]

The blossom image is not used at the beginning or end of Book III of the *Soliloquies*, but the repeated use of the phrase *cwidas alesan* (to select sayings) seems similarly to reflect a perception of the work as compilatory.

Note on the Texts

The text of the Preface to the *Soliloquies* is edited from London, British Library, Cotton MS Vitellius A. xv, fos. 4r–5v [C]. Readings are supplied from the seventeenth-century transcription of this manuscript by Franciscus Junius in Oxford, Bodleian Library, MS Junius 70 [J], where C is missing. The texts of the incipits and explicits are edited from C, fos. 44r, 53v–54r, 54r, and 59v.

---

[30] Stevenson (1959), ch. 88: 'Ac deinde cotidie inter nos sermocinando, ad haec investigando aliis inventis aeque placabilibus testimoniis, quaternio ille refertus succrevit, nec immerito ... velut apis fertilissima longe lateque gronnios interrogando discurrens, multimodos divinae scripturae flosculos inhianter et incessabiliter congregavit, quis praecordii sui cellulas densatim replevit.' Trans. Keynes and Lapidge (1983), p. 100.

TEXTS AND TRANSLATIONS

The Preface to the *Soliloquies*

Gaderode me þonne kigclas and stuþansceaftas and lohsceaftas, and hylfa to ælcum þara tola þe ic mid wircan cuðe, and bohtimbru and bolttimbru, and, to ælcum þara weorca þe ic wyrcan cuðe, þa wlitegostan treowo be þam dele ðe ic aberan meihte. Ne com ic naþer mid anre byrðene ham þe me ne lyste ealne þane wude ham brengan, gif ic hyne ealne aberan meihte; on ælcum treowo ic geseah hwæthwugu þæs þe ic æt ham beþorfte. Forþam ic lære ælcne ðara þe maga si and manigne wæn hæbbe þæt he menige to þam ilcan wuda þar ic ðas stuðansceaftas cearf. Fetige hym þar ma and gefeðrige hys wænas mid fegrum gerdum, þat he mage windan manigne smicerne wah, and manig ænlic hus settan, and fegerne tun timbrian, | and þær murge and softe mid mæge oneardian ægðer ge wintras ge sumeras, swa swa ic nu ne gyt ne dyde. Ac se þe me lærde, þam se wudu licode, se mæg gedon þæt ic softor eardian mæge ægðer ge on þisum lænan stoclife be þis wæge ða while þe ic on þisse weorulde beo, ge eac on þam ecan hame ðe he us gehaten hefð þurh sanctus Augustinus and sanctus Gregorius and sanctus Ieronimus, and þurh manege oððre halie fædras. Swa ic gelyfe eac þæt he gedo for heora ealra earnunge, ægðer ge þisne weig gelimpfulran gedo þonne he ær þissum wes, ge hure mines modes eagan to þam ongelihte þæt ic mage rihtne weig aredian to þam ecan hame, and to þare ecan are, and to þare ecan reste þe us gehaten is þurh þa | halgan fæderas. Sie swa.

Nis hit nan wundor þeah man swilce ontimber gewirce, and eac on þare utlade and eac on þære bytlinge; ac ælcne man lyst, siððan he ænig cotlyf on his hlafordes læne myd his fultume getimbred hæfð, þæt he hine mote hwilum þaron gerestan, and huntigan, and fuglian, and fiscian, and his on gehwilce wisan to þere lænan tilian, ægþær ge on se ge on lande, oð þone fyrst þe he bocland and æce yrfe þurh his hlafordes miltse geearnige. Swa gedo se weliga gifola, se ðe egðer wilt ge þissa lænena stoclife ge þara ecena hama. Se ðe ægþer gescop and ægðeres wilt, forgife me þæt me to ægðrum onhagige: ge her nytwyrde to beonne, ge huru þider to cumane.

The Preface to the *Soliloquies*

Then I collected sturdy sticks and posts and tie-beams, and handles for each of the tools which I knew how to use, and curved timbers and straight timbers and, for each of the structures which I knew how to make, the most beautiful timbers that I could carry. I never came home with one load with-
5 out wishing to bring home the whole forest if I could have carried it all; in every tree I saw something I needed at home. Therefore I advise each person who is strong and has many wagons to proceed to that same wood where I cut these posts. Let him fetch more there for himself and load his wagons with fine branches so that he can weave many fair walls and construct many
10 excellent houses and build a fine estate, and can dwell therein happily and comfortably in both winters and summers, as I have not yet done. But the one who taught me, to whom the forest was pleasing, he can bring it to pass for me to live more comfortably both in this transient dwelling place along this path while I am in this world, and also in the eternal home which he
15 has promised us through the saints Augustine, Gregory and Jerome, and through many other holy fathers. So I believe indeed he may bring it to pass because of the merits of them all: he may both make this path more comfortable than it was before this, and light up the eyes of my mind so that I can find the right way to the eternal home and to eternal honour, and to the
20 eternal rest which is promised to us through the holy fathers. May it be so.

It is no wonder if a man works with building material in such a way, both in the transporting and constructing of it; but every man finds it pleasing, after he has built a dwelling on his lord's leased land with his help, to be able to rest in it at times, and to hunt, catch birds and go fishing, and to provide
25 for himself in every way on that leased land, both on water and land, until the time that he may earn bookland and eternal inheritance through his lord's mercy. May the wealthy benefactor, who controls both these transient dwelling places and those eternal homes, make it so. He who created and controls both, may he grant me that I am fit for both: to be useful here and
30 especially to arrive there.

| Sanctus Agustinus, Cartaina bisceop, worhte twa bec be his agnum ingeþance; þa bec sint gehatene *Soliloquiorum*, þat is, be hys modis smeaunge and tweounga, hu hys gesceadwisnes answarode hys mode þonne þæt mod ymbe hwæt tweonode, oðþe hit hwæs wilnode to witanne þæs þe hit ær forsweotole ongytan ne meahte.

35

Summary of Book I of the *Soliloquies*

Book I of the *Soliloquies,* much the longest in the work, begins with Augustine pondering on the mortality or immortality of his mind and soul, the nature of God, and what constitutes good and evil actions. His Reason encourages him to find someone who can guide him, to write down what he knows, and to pray, after which Augustine offers a prayer to God. Using metaphors such as a ship and its anchor, and the sun, Reason explains to Augustine that through faith, hope, and reason he can see God with the eyes of his mind. But Augustine has to acknowledge, says Reason, that his desires are still partly rooted in the world: his friends and illness such as toothache, for example, might be a distraction. Wisdom is the highest good, Reason asserts, but cannot be fully attained in this world. Reason proceeds to argue that God is truth, and that adversity is beneficial in the long term.

Saint Augustine, Bishop of Carthage, wrote two books about his own thinking; those books are called the *Soliloquia*, that is, about the reflections and doubts of his mind, how his reason answered his mind when the mind had doubts about something or it wished to know something which it could not understand very clearly before.

Book I Explicit

Her endiað þa blostman þære forman bec.

Book II Incipit

Her onginð seo gadorung þæra blostmena þære æftran bec.

Summary of Book II of the *Soliloquies*

In Book II, Reason affirms to Augustine that the three things he desires, his existence, life, and knowledge, are immortal. At Augustine's continuing uncertainty about the immortality of the human soul, Reason reassures him that the holy fathers were clear on this, suggesting that, just as one trusts one's friends or lord to tell the truth about something one hasn't seen, so one should all the more trust God to speak the truth through his prophets about the immortality of souls. Reason notes that since no creature entirely passes away, it wouldn't make sense if human souls had been made an exception to this. Indeed human souls desire to know about the past and future because they know they are immortal. Augustine, rejoicing at the immortality of souls and of one's intelligence, asks whether the intellect will remain stable after death. Reason promises that he can find the answer to this in the book *De videndo Deo* (*On Seeing God*).

Book I Explicit

Here end the blossoms of the first book.

Book II Incipit

Here begins the gathering of the blossoms of the second book.

Book II Explicit

Hær endiað þa blostman þære æftran bec þe we hatað *Soliloquiorum*.

Book III Incipit

Ða cwæð ic: nu heft þa cwydas geendod þe þu of ðisum twam bocum alese, and næfst me gyt geandweard be ðam þe ic þe nu niehst acsode, þæt wæs be minum gewitte.

Summary of Book III of the *Soliloquies*

Book III begins with Augustine repeating his query about whether or not one's intelligence remains stable after death. Reason confirms that after death the virtuous will remember their friends in this world, citing the story of the wicked rich man and Lazarus to show that even someone in hell remembers his brothers who are still alive. The mind's eye cannot see clearly in this life but, Reason argues, we have to believe what we don't see on the basis of what we can see here. After death we will know everything we want to know, and after Judgement Day we will see and know God fully. Wisdom too will be achieved to the extent that one earlier strove for it. Augustine reiterates that he trusts in the testimonies he has read in holy books, just as he believes the accounts of less authoritative witnesses on matters he knows only by report. One must always, he concludes, pursue greater understanding in this world, and aim for the eternal life.

Book II Explicit

Here end the blossoms of the second book which we call *Soliloquia*.

Book III Incipit

Then I said: Now the sayings have ended which you selected from these two books, and you haven't yet answered for me what I asked you about most recently, which was about my intelligence.

Book III Explicit

Hær endiað þa cwidas þe Ælfred kining alæs of þære bec þe we hatað on [Leden *Soliloquiorum*].

Book III Explicit

Here end the sayings which King Alfred selected from the book which we call in [Latin *Soliloquia*].

The *Laws* of Alfred

Preface

INTRODUCTION

The Preface to the *Laws* of Alfred is the longest prefatory document associated with any Alfredian work. Its combination of a lengthy translation of scriptural material (from the Book of Exodus 20–3 and Acts 15:22–9), an account of the history of law-giving, and a short concluding section outlining the king's aims in producing the work makes it rather different in approach and content from other prefaces. Too often editions and translations of the *Laws* have excluded the large portion of text derived from Mosaic law, belying its significance in the work as a whole.[1] Wormald, noting that the Mosaic Preface occupies over a fifth of the total book, proposed that it might be 'the key of the whole enterprise'.[2] Stefan Jurasinski has called the Mosaic Preface 'an important and underappreciated example of the ninth-century revival of English vernacular prose'.[3]

The Preface to the *Laws* serves to put the process of law-giving in early medieval England into a broad historical and scriptural context that extends back as far as the Mosaic law itself. It asserts the relevance of Mosaic law and its aftermath for the contemporary Christian world of the Anglo-Saxons. It does so by translating a large portion of the Book of Exodus in which the Mosaic law is set down, by yoking together the Mosaic and Christian law-giving traditions, and by recounting how these traditions came to be established amongst the English by way of various synods. It concludes with a statement in Alfred's own voice explaining how and why his law code takes the particular form it does.[4]

This preface, along with the *Prose Psalms*, is an important early example of biblical translation into the vernacular. It gives a fascinating insight into

---

[1] See, for example, Attenborough (1922); Whitelock (1979a); and Keynes and Lapidge (1983). The most recent edition, Jurasinski and Oliver (2021), includes the preface in full.
[2] Wormald (1999), p. 418.   [3] Jurasinski (2012), p. 47.
[4] Explanations of a legislator's motives and techniques are characteristic of prologues found in early Germanic law codes; see Wormald (1977), pp. 105 and 113.

the freedom which even a translator of scriptures felt he had in this period to revise and update for a contemporary audience. The preface frequently updates the tenets of Mosaic law to fit with late ninth-century English customs. As Jurasinski writes, 'Alfred's Prologue is perhaps best seen as a fairly autonomous text which uses Exodus as a mere springboard for its own discussion of matters of interest to the king and his circle'.[5] Some of the changes entail little more than word substitution: Hebrews become Christians, and shekels become shillings. Other changes more substantially or subtly bring the text in line with contemporary norms. In §11, for example, the translator, independently of the biblical source, seems to assume that slaves might be permitted to have some possessions of their own, perhaps on the basis of the situation in ninth-century England,[6] and in §37, the Mosaic stipulation that the gods should not be disparaged becomes instead an injunction against blaspheming the Lord.[7]

The Work and its Contexts

The *Laws* of Alfred consists of a set of statutes combining Alfred's own laws with those of earlier kings. It is not always possible to identify the exact relationship between Alfred's code and the earlier collections, which include those of King Ine (688–726) and of the Kentish kings Æthelberht (d. 616), Hlothhere and Eadric (673–86?), and Wihtred (690–725).[8] Even in the case of Ine's code, which always circulated in tandem with Alfred's, we cannot be sure of the nature and extent of the editing that was required to make it a suitable accompaniment to the latter.[9] In any case, the two, as

---

[5] Jurasinski (2012), p. 58.   [6] See Pelteret (1995), p. 83.

[7] For further examples of the differences between the Mosaic law and its Alfredian rendering, see Liebermann (1908–10); Wormald (1999), p. 421; and the textual commentary in Jurasinski and Oliver (2021).

[8] See Jurasinski and Oliver (2021), ch. 1.

[9] The fact that discrepancies between Alfred's and Ine's codes were allowed to stand, however, is taken by Keynes and Lapidge (1983) as evidence that 'the received text of Ine's code was respected, and was not edited by Alfred to suit his own purposes' (p. 311). Richards (2015) considers that 'the manuscript treatments suggest that Alfred's code with Ine's appendix survives basically as it was first recorded' (p. 283). See further Jurasinski and Oliver (2021), pp. 43–53.

they stand, were clearly seen as two complementary parts of a joint enterprise designed to provide a comprehensive judicial scheme for the Anglo-Saxons in the late ninth century.[10]

The issue of a set of written laws in the name of a king had a long tradition not only in England but also in Europe,[11] and no doubt Anglo-Saxon practice was emulating continental precedent in this regard. In the production of written legislation in the vernacular, however, practice in England differed from that on the Continent, where laws were written in Latin. The *Laws* must have represented an important step in the vision of the king and his advisors to create an English identity defined simultaneously by its geographical and linguistic distinctiveness and by its participation in the widely established traditions of Christian theology and history. Notwithstanding the many opportunities for practical application the *Laws* may have represented, it was also, as Patrick Wormald notes, an 'ideological statement'.[12] Its deeply symbolic role in showcasing Alfred's own political and legal authority should not be underestimated.

Manuscripts and Previous Editions

Of the six extant Old English versions (complete or incomplete) of the *Laws* of Alfred,[13] three contain the work's preface:

E   Cambridge, Corpus Christi College MS 173, fos. 1–56 (s. ix/x–xi²). The Preface to the *Laws* is on fos. 36r–40r and follows after the end of the A version of the *Anglo-Saxon Chronicle*. Its original position was after the annal for 920 (misdated 923), but it was moved, along with the rest of the *Laws*, to after the final annal (for 1070) to avoid a break in the sequence of the continued chronicle. The manuscript was probably written at Winchester.[14]

---

[10] Richards (1986), pp. 173–4.
[11] Wormald (1977); Jurasinski and Oliver (2021), ch. 1.
[12] Wormald (1999), p. 426. On its practical application, see Jurasinski and Oliver (2021), ch. 3.
[13] Two complete manuscripts and four fragments of the *Laws* of Alfred survive. See Richards (1986) and (2015), pp. 284–92, and Jurasinski and Oliver (2021), ch. 4, for detailed discussion of the various manuscripts. Liebermann's sigla are retained here.
[14] Ker (1957), no. 39; Gneuss and Lapidge (2014), no. 52. For discussion of the Winchester association, see Parkes (1976).

G   London, British Library, Cotton MS Nero A. i, fos. 3–57 (s.xi[med]). The Preface to the *Laws* is at fos. 51r–57v (ends imperfectly). The provenance of the manuscript is unknown.[15]

H   Medway Archive and Local Studies Centre, Strood, MS DRc/R1 (formerly Rochester Cathedral Library A. 3. 5), known as the *Textus Roffensis* (s. xii¹), from St Andrew's, Rochester.[16] The Preface to the *Laws* is on fos. 11r–16r. The manuscript was compiled in the time of Ernulf, Bishop of Rochester (1115–24).

Although only three copies of the Preface to the *Laws* survive, the manuscript history of the *Laws* as a whole would suggest that it circulated quite widely in the early medieval period.[17]

The *Laws* of Alfred, including the preface, has been recently edited and translated in full by Stefan Jurasinski and Lisi Oliver.[18] The standard edition of the whole corpus of Anglo-Saxon law codes is the early twentieth-century one by Felix Liebermann, in which the preface was edited in full.[19] The preface was also edited in full (with translation) in an edition of the law codes published in 1840 by Benjamin Thorpe,[20] and in an edition of the *Laws* of Alfred and other law texts (with facing-page German translations) by Karl August Eckhardt in 1958.[21] It has also been edited by Richard J. E. Dammery in his doctoral thesis, edited and translated as an appendix to a study of the *Laws* of Alfred by Todd Preston, and edited and translated separately by Jay Gates.[22] A facsimile edition of the version in E (the manuscript on which this edition is based) by Robin and Flowers was published in 1941.[23]

The Preface to the *Laws* of Alfred

Felix Liebermann, writing in the early twentieth century, opined that the 'whole spirit' of the preface 'agrees far too well with what we know of the

---

[15] Ker (1957), no. 163; Gneuss and Lapidge (2014), no. 340.
[16] Ker (1957), no. 373.   [17] Keynes and Lapidge (1983), p. 304.
[18] Jurasinski and Oliver (2021).   [19] Liebermann (1903–16), I.26–47.
[20] Thorpe (1840), pp. 44–59.   [21] Eckhardt (1958).
[22] Dammery (1990); Preston (2012); Gates (2018).
[23] Flower and Smith (1941). See now also *Parker on the Web* (https://parker.stanford.edu/parker/, accessed 11 Dec. 2018).

character of Alfred to allow us to doubt his sole responsibility for it'.[24] Other more recent scholars such as Janet Bately and Patrick Wormald have agreed that this preface, if not the whole of the *Laws*, is the work of Alfred himself.[25] Malcolm Godden has challenged such a view, arguing that this law code's 'use of the king's voice and claims of his personal role in law collection and the making of edicts is just a standard trope of legal codes throughout Europe in the Middle Ages'.[26]

Scholars generally agree that on historical grounds the *Laws* 'is more likely to date from the 880s or 890s than from the 870s', in other words from the second half of Alfred's reign.[27] Where it fits into the canon of Alfredian works chronologically is more contentious. For Allen Frantzen, for example, it 'represents one of [Alfred's] earlier literary endeavors, perhaps his first'.[28] For Wormald, stylistic similarities with the translation of the *Pastoral Care* suggest that the *Laws* was 'produced early in the king's career as a writer'.[29] Mary P. Richards proposes a date later in the king's literary career, c.895.[30]

The principal aim of the Preface to the *Laws* is to trace the descent of written legislation from Mosaic law to the end of the ninth century. Its material can be divided into four parts, of which the first is much the longest:

1. §§1–48: based on the Mosaic law.
2. §§49–49.6: based on New Testament scriptures.
3. §49.7–8: the history of subsequent synods and their law-giving activity.
4. §§49.9–10: Alfred's own procedure in compiling the *Laws*.[31]

All four parts address in various ways the idea of law-giving and its implications for all sectors of society. The continuity between past and present

---

[24] Liebermann (1908–10), p. 22.

[25] See Bately (1970), p. 453, and (1988), p. 118; Wormald (1999), pp. 272–7. See also Whitelock (1979a), p. 407.

[26] Godden (2007), p. 17.

[27] Keynes and Lapidge (1983), p. 304; see also pp. 38–9 and 163.

[28] Frantzen (1986), p. 11.   [29] Wormald (1999), p. 277.

[30] Richards (2015), p. 282.

[31] In Jurasinski and Oliver (2021), this last section of the preface is edited at the outset of the law code itself.

also informs the preface as a whole. By juxtaposing Mosaic Law and early medieval law, the preface emphasizes the integral relationship between the earliest divine laws and their contemporary equivalents. The precedents of the past convey authority and prestige on the policies of the present.

The first part of the preface is Old Testament in origin.[32] It consists of translated quotations from Mosaic law (the ancient laws of the Hebrews traditionally believed to have been revealed by God to Moses), as conveyed by the Book of Exodus, chapters 20–3. The translations vary in how close they are to their source: in some cases, though not consistently throughout, they offer free adaptations of Mosaic law which may be designed to make the material more relevant to their contemporary audience.

The second part of the preface draws on the New Testament. §49 includes a translation of Christ's statement from the Sermon of the Mount that he had come not to abolish the law but to fulfil it (Matt. 5:17). §§49.3–49.5 translate the letter recording the early church's conciliar decree that freed the Gentiles from a full obligation to Mosaic law (Acts 15:22–9). At the end of §49.6 the Golden Rule (Matt. 7:12) is rendered in its negative form, presumably reflecting its presence in Acts 15:29 in the 'Western' tradition of the New Testament.

Various other sources have been proposed for the preface.[33] The eighth-century Hiberno-Latin work *Liber ex lege Moysi* was proposed as a source by Paul Fournier in 1909,[34] and evidence for its possible influence on the text has recently been explored further by Kristen Carella.[35] The influence of the late antique work *Collatio legum Romanarum et Mosaicarum* was proposed by Wormald as part of a case for connecting Alfred's ideas with those of Archbishop Hincmar of Rheims, though the more recent studies by Carella have found no significant evidence to support such a case.[36]

Penitential texts have also been proposed as sources for various sections of the preface. Audrey Meaney speculated in 2006 that the expanded

---

[32] Biblical citations and quotations are from Weber (1994). The exemplar used by the translator 'seems to have contained a fairly good Vulgate text with few surprises', but cannot be established with more certainty beyond that; see Marsden (1995), p. 402.

[33] For a useful overview, see Jurasinski and Oliver (2021), pp. 61–9.

[34] Fournier (1909), pp. 230–1.   [35] Carella (2005) and (2011).

[36] Wormald (1999), pp. 418–29; Carella (2005) and (2011).

version of Exodus 22:18 in §30, on women who associate with magicians, might be indebted to the *Penitential of Theodore*.³⁷ Stefan Jurasinski has argued, with respect to §13, that the three categories *nedes*, *unwillum*, and *ungewealdes* (out of necessity, unwillingly, by accident), which have been added to the biblical source, 'reflect the taxonomies of lethal violence found in many of the Frankish penitentials that circulated on the Continent (and, perhaps, in England) in the years prior to Alfred's reign'.³⁸ In this section, and elsewhere in other clauses of the preface having to do with violence, Jurasinski suggests, 'it is one's intent that is exculpatory, as is routinely the case in the literature of penance'.³⁹

The last part of the preface takes its cue from the legislative prologue conventional in the law codes of pre-Conquest kings. It may have been influenced in particular by the preface to King Ine's law code, a code known only in the version which circulated in tandem with Alfred's. Ine's royal persona corresponds closely to Alfred's:

> Ic, Ine, mid Godes gife Wesseaxna kyning, mid geðeahte and mid lare Cenredes mines fæder and Heddes mines biscepes and Eorcenwoldes mines biscepes, mid eallum minum ealdormonnum and þæm ieldstan witum minre ðeode and eac micelre gesomnunge Godes ðeowa, wæs smeagende be ðære hælo urra sawla and be ðam staþole ures rices, þætte ryht æw and ryhte cynedomas ðurh ure folc gefæstnode and getrymede wæron, þætte nænig ealdormonna ne us undergeðeodedra æfter þam wære awendende ðas ure domas.

> I, Ine, by God's gift king of the West Saxons, with the advice and instruction of Cenred my father and Hædde my bishop and Eorconwald my bishop, with all my ealdormen and the senior counselors of my people and also a great gathering of God's servants, have been considering the well-being of our souls and the foundation of our kingdom, so that just law and just royal judgments should be established and made strong throughout our folk, so that after this time no ealdorman nor any other subject to us should depart from these our judgments.⁴⁰

---

³⁷ Meaney (2006), pp. 131–3; see also Jurasinski (2010), p. 29, Jurasinski (2015), pp. 56–7, and Oliver (2015), pp. 233–6.
³⁸ Jurasinski (2015), p. 58; cf. Jurasinski (2010), p. 30.   ³⁹ Jurasinski (2015), p. 59.
⁴⁰ Text and translation from Jurasinski and Oliver (2021), pp. 370–1.

Like Ine's, Alfred's preface constructs the king as both a deferential figure who humbly acknowledges the help of his advisers, and a leading player who determines the final legislative output.

Note on the Text

The text of the Preface to the *Laws* of Alfred is based on Cambridge, Corpus Christi College MS 173 [E], fos. 36r–40r. Significant variants in London, British Library, Cotton MS Nero A. i [G] and the *Textus Roffensis* [H] are recorded, along with alterations and emendations in the base text (other than corrections of simple copying errors that the scribe made as he wrote). The conventional paragraph numbering (used by Liebermann and retained in most later editions) is retained in this edition, except that the opening two paragraphs have been numbered as 1 and 1.1 respectively.

TEXT AND TRANSLATION

The Preface to the *Laws* of Alfred

§1 Dryhten wæs sprecende ðas word to Moyse and þus cwæð: Ic eom Dryhten ðin God. Ic ðe ut gelædde of Egipta londe and of hiora ðeowdome.

§1.1 Ne lufa ðu oþre fremde godas ofer me.

§2 Ne minne noman ne cig ðu on idelnesse; forðon þe ðu ne bist unscyldig wið me, gif ðu on idelnesse cigst minne noman.

§3 Gemyne þæt ðu gehalgige þone ræstedæg; wyrceað eow VI dagas and on þam siofoðan restað eow: forðam on VI dagum Crist geworhte heofonas and eorðan, sæs and ealle gesceafta þe on him sint, and hine gereste on þone siofoðan dæg, and forðon Dryhten hine gehalgode.

§4 Ara ðinum fæder and þinre medder, ða þe Dryhten sealde, þæt ðu sie þy leng libbende on eorþan.

§5 Ne sleah ðu.

§6 Ne lige ðu dearnenga.

§7 Ne stala ðu.

§8 Ne sæge ðu lease gewitnesse.

§9 Ne wilna ðu þines nehstan ierfes mid unryhte.

§10 Ne wyrc ðe gyldne godas oððe sylfrene.

§11 Þis sint ða domas þe ðu him settan scealt: Gif hwa gebycgge Cristenne þeow, VI gear ðeowige he; ðy siofoðan beo he frioh orceapunga; mid swelce hrægle he ineode, mid swelce gange he ut. Gif he wif self hæbbe, gange hio ut mid him. Gif se hlaford him þonne wif sealde, sie hio and hire bearn þæs hlafordes. Gif se þeowa þonne | cweðe: 'Nelle ic from minum hlaforde ne from minum wife ne from minum bearne ne from minum ierfe', brenge hine þonne his hlaford to ðære dura þæs temples and þurhþyrlige his eare mid æle, to tacne þæt he sie æfre siððan þeow.

The Preface to the *Laws* of Alfred

§1 The Lord was speaking these words to Moses, saying thus: I am the Lord your God. I led you out of the land of the Egyptians and away from servitude to them.

§1.1 Do not love other strange gods rather than me.

§2 Do not invoke my name in vain; for you will not be guiltless with me if you invoke my name in vain.

§3 Remember to keep the rest-day holy; do your work for six days and rest on the seventh; because Christ made heaven and earth, the seas, and all creatures that are in them, in six days, and rested on the seventh day, and therefore the Lord made it holy.

§4 Honour your father and mother, whom the Lord gave you, so that you may live longer on earth.

§5 Do not kill.

§6 Do not commit adultery.

§7 Do not steal.

§8 Do not give false testimony.

§9 Do not wrongfully desire your neighbour's property.

§10 Do not make gods of silver or gold for yourself.

§11 These are the laws you are to establish for them: If anyone buys a Christian slave, let him [the slave] serve for six years; in the seventh let him be free without payment; let him leave with such garments as he arrived with. If he has a wife of his own, let her leave with him. If, however, the lord gave him the wife, let her and her children be the lord's. If, however, the slave were to say, 'I do not wish to leave my lord, my wife, my children, nor my property', let his lord then bring him to the door of the temple and pierce his ear with an awl, as a sign that he will be a slave ever after.

§12 Ðeah hwa gebycgge his dohtor on þeowenne, ne sie hio ealles swa ðeowu swa oðru mennenu: nage he hie ut on elðeodig folc to bebycganne. Ac gif he hire ne recce, se ðe hie bohte, læte hie freo on elðeodig folc. Gif he ðonne alefe his suna mid to hæmanne, do hiere gyfta: locige þæt hio hæbbe hrægl; and þæt weorð sie hiere mægðhades, þæt is se weotuma, agife he hire þone. Gif he hire þara nan ne do, þonne sie hio frioh.

§13 Se mon se ðe his gewealdes monnan ofslea, swelte se deaðe. Se ðe hine þonne nedes ofsloge oððe unwillum oððe ungewealdes, swelce hine God swa sende on his honda, and he hine ne ymbsyrede, sie he feores wyrðe and folcryhtre bote, gif he friðstowe gesece. Gif hwa ðonne of giernesse and gewealdes ofslea his þone nehstan þurh searwa, aluc ðu hine from minum weofode to þam þæt he deaðe swelte.

§14 Se ðe slea his fæder oððe his modor, se sceal deaðe sweltan.

§15 Se ðe frione forstele and he hine bebycgge, and hit on bestæled sie þæt he hine bereccean ne mæge, swelte se deaðe. Se ðe werge his fæder oððe his modor, swelte se deaðe.

§16 Gif hwa slea | his ðone nehstan mid stane oððe mid fyste, and he þeah ut gongan mæge bi stafe, begite him læce and wyrce his weorc ða hwile þe he self ne mæge.

§17 Se ðe slea his agenne þeowne esne oððe his mennen, and he ne sie idæges dead, ðeah he libbe twa niht oððe ðreo, ne bið he ealles swa scyldig, forþon þe hit wæs his agen fioh. Gif he ðonne sie idæges dead, ðonne sitte sio scyld on him.

§18 Gif hwa on cease eacniende wif gewerde, bete þone æwerdlan, swa him domeras gereccen. Gif hio dead sie, selle sawle wið sawle.

§19 Gif hwa oðrum his eage oðdo, selle his agen fore: toð fore teð, honda wið honda, fet fore fet, bærning for bærninge, wund wið wunde, læl wið læle.

§20 Gif hwa aslea his ðeowe oððe his ðeowenne þæt eage ut and he þonne hie gedo anigge, gefreoge hie for þon. Gif he þonne ðone toð of aslea, do þæt ilce.

§12 If anyone should sell his daughter as a slave, let her not be so entirely a slave as other female slaves are: let him [the one who bought her] not sell her abroad amongst foreign people. But if the man who bought her does not care for her, let her go free amongst foreign people. If, however, he allows his son to have illicit sexual intercourse with her, let him arrange a wedding: let him see that she has clothing; and let him give her the worth of her virginity, that is, the dowry. If he does none of those things for her, then let her be free.

§13 Anyone who kills a man intentionally, let him be put to death. Anyone who kills a man out of necessity or unwillingly or by accident, as God put it into his hands, and he did not ambush him, let him be entitled to life and compensation according to public law, if he should seek sanctuary. If, however, someone kills his neighbour on purpose and intentionally through guile, remove him from my altar so that he may be put to death.

§14 He who strikes his father or mother must be put to death.

§15 He who abducts a free person and sells him, and the charge is laid on him so that he cannot clear himself, let him be put to death. He who curses his father or mother, let him be put to death.

§16 If anyone strikes his neighbour with a stone or his fist, and he [the neighbour] is nevertheless able to go out with a staff, let him [the attacker] fetch a doctor for him and do his work while he himself cannot.

§17 He who strikes his own servant or female slave, and he [the slave] does not die the same day but lives two or three nights, he [the attacker] is not entirely so guilty because it was his own property. If, however, he dies the same day, then let the guilt rest upon him.

§18 If anyone injures a pregnant woman in a quarrel, let him make compensation for the injury as the judges prescribe for him. If she dies, let him give soul for soul.

§19 If anyone puts out another man's eye, let him give his own for it: tooth for tooth, hand for hand, foot for foot, burning for burning, wound for wound, bruise for bruise.

§20 If anyone knocks out his male or female slave's eye and therefore makes them blind in one eye, let him free them for that. And if he knocks out a tooth, let him do the same.

§21 Gif oxa ofhnite wer oððe wif þæt hie dead sien, sie he mid stanum ofworpod, and ne sie his flæsc eten; se hlaford bið unscyldig. Gif se oxa hnitol wære twam dagum ær oððe ðrim, and se hlaford hit wisse and hine inne betynan nolde, and he ðonne wer oððe wif ofsloge, sie he mid stanum ofworpod, and sie se hlaford ofslegen oððe forgolden, swa ðæt witan to ryhte finden. Sunu oððe dohtor gif he ofstinge, ðæs ilcan domes sie he wyrðe. Gif he ðonne ðeow oððe ðeowenne ofstinge, geselle þam hlaforde XXX scillingas | seolfres, and se oxa mid stanum ofworpod.

§22 Gif hwa adelfe wæterpyt oððe betynedne ontyne and hine eft ne betyne, gelde swelc neat swelc ðær on befealle, and hæbbe him ðæt deade.

§23 Gif oxa oðres monnes oxan gewundige, and he þonne dead sie, bebycggen þone oxan and hæbben him þæt weorð gemæne and eac ðæt flæsc swa ðæs deadan. Gif se hlaford þonne wisse þæt se oxa hnitol wære, and hine healdan nolde, selle him oðerne oxan fore and hæbbe him eall ðæt flæsc.

§24 Gif hwa forstele oðres oxan and hine ofslea oððe bebycgge, selle twegen wið and feower sceap wið anum. Gif he næbbe hwæt he selle, sie he self beboht wið ðam fio.

§25 Gif ðeof brece mannes hus nihtes and he weorðe þær ofslegen, ne sie he na mansleges scyldig. Gif he siððan æfter sunnan upgonge þis deð, he bið mansleges scyldig, and he ðonne self swelte, buton he nieddæda wære. Gif mid him cwicum sie funden þæt he ær stæl, be twyfealdum forgielde hit.

§26 Gif hwa gewerde oðres monnes wingeard oððe his æcras oððe his landes awuht, gebete swa hit mon geeahtige.

§27 Gif fyr sie ontended ryt to bærnanne, gebete þone æfwerdelsan se ðæt fyr ontent.

§28 Gif hwa oðfæste his friend fioh, gif he hit self stæle, forgylde be twyfealdum. Gif he nyte hwa hit stæle, geladige hine selfne þæt he ðær nan facn ne gefremede. Gif hit ðonne | cucu feoh wære, and he secgge þæt hit here name oððe hit self acwæle, and gewitnesse hæbbe, ne þearf he þæt geldan. Gif he ðonne gewitnesse næbbe, and he him ne getriewe, swerige he þonne.

§21 If an ox gores a man or woman so that they die, let it be stoned to death, and let its flesh not be eaten; the lord is not liable. If the ox was liable to gore two or three days before and the lord knew it and would not shut it in and then it killed a man or woman, let it be stoned to death; and let the lord be killed or compensation paid, as councillors find right. If it gores a son or daughter, let him be subject to the same judgement. If, however, it gores a male or female slave, let 30 silver shillings be given to their lord, and let the ox be stoned to death.

§22 If anyone digs a waterhole or opens one that is shut up and does not shut it up again, let him pay for whatever animal may fall into it and let him have the dead one.

§23 If an ox wounds another man's ox, and it then dies, let them sell the [live] ox and share the value and also the dead one's flesh. If the lord knew, however, that the ox was liable to gore and would not pen it in, let him give him another ox in compensation and let him have all the flesh.

§24 If anyone steals another man's ox and kills or sells it, let him give two in return for it, and four sheep in return for one. If he does not have what he should give, let him be sold himself in return for the livestock.

§25 If a thief breaks into a man's house at night and is killed there, let the man not be guilty of homicide. If the man does this after sunrise, he is guilty of homicide, and he himself is then to die, unless he acted out of necessity. If what the thief stole is found with him while he is alive, let him pay double its value for it.

§26 If anyone damages another man's vineyard or his fields or any part of his land, let him compensate for it as its value is assessed.

§27 If a fire is kindled to burn rough growth, let him who kindles the fire make amends for the damage.

§28 If anyone entrusts property to his friend, if he steals it himself let him pay double its value in compensation. If he does not know who stole it, let him clear himself from having committed fraud there. If, however, it was livestock and he says that a raiding party took it or it died of itself, and he has a witness, he does not need to pay for it. If he has no witness, however, and he [the owner] does not believe him, then let him [the friend] swear an oath.

§29 Gif hwa fæmnan beswice unbeweddode and hire mid slæpe, forgielde hie and hæbbe hi siððan him to wife. Gif ðære fæmnan fæder hie ðonne sellan nelle, agife he ðæt feoh æfter þam weotuman.

§30 Ða fæmnan þe gewuniað onfon gealdorcræftigan and scinlæcan and wiccan, ne læt þu ða libban.

§31 And se ðe hæme mid netene, swelte se deaðe.

§32 And se ðe godgeldum onsecge ofer God anne, swelte se deaðe.

§33 Utan cumene and elðeodige ne geswenc ðu no, forðon ðe ge wæron giu elðeodige on Egipta londe.

§34 Þa wuduwan and þa stiopcild ne sceððað ge, ne hie nawer deriað. Gif ge þonne elles doð, hie cleopiað to me, and ic gehiere hie and ic eow þonne slea mid minum sweorde, and ic gedo þæt eowru wif beoð wydewan and eowru bearn beoð steopcild.

§35 Gif ðu fioh to borge selle þinum geferan þe mid þe eardian wille, ne niede ðu hine swa swa niedling and ne gehene þu hine mid ðy eacan.

§36 Gif mon næbbe buton anfeald hrægl hine mid to wreonne and to werianne, and he hit to wedde selle, ær sunnan setlgonge sie hit agifen. Gif ðu swa ne dest, þonne cleopað he to me, and ic hine gehiere, forðon ðe ic eom swiðe mildheort.

§37 Ne tæl ðu | ðinne Dryhten, ne ðone hlaford þæs folces ne werge þu.

§38 Þine teoðan sceattas and þine frumripan gongendes and weaxendes agif þu Gode.

§39 Eal ðæt flæsc þæt wildeor læfen, ne eten ge þæt, ac sellað hit hundum.

§40 Leases monnes word ne rec ðu no þæs to gehieranne, ne his domas ne geðafa ðu, ne nane gewitnesse æfter him ne saga ðu.

§41 Ne wend ðu ðe no on þæs folces unræd and unryht gewill on hiora spræce and geclysp ofer ðin ryht, and ðæs unwisestan lare ne him ne geðafa.

§42 Gif ðe becume oðres mannes giemeleas fioh on hond, þeah hit sie ðin feond, gecyðe hit him.

§29 If anyone seduces an unbetrothed virgin and sleeps with her, let him pay her compensation and then have her as his wife. If, however, the virgin's father does not wish to give her, let him [the seducer] pay money corresponding to the dowry.

§30 Do not allow those women to live who are in the habit of receiving magicians, sorceresses, and witches.

§31 And let him who has intercourse with an animal be put to death.

§32 And let him who sacrifices to idols rather than to God alone be put to death.

§33 Do not oppress those who have come from abroad and strangers, because you were formerly strangers in the land of the Egyptians.

§34 Do not harm widows and orphans, nor injure them anywhere. If you do otherwise, they will call out to me, and I will hear them and I will then strike you with my sword, and I will make your wives widows and your children orphans.

§35 If you lend money on security to your companion who wants to dwell with you, do not coerce him like a slave and do not oppress him with interest.

§36 If someone has only a single garment with which to cover and clothe himself, and he gives it as a pledge, let it be given back before sunset. If you do not do so, then he will call to me and I will hear him, for I am very merciful.

§37 Do not rebuke your Lord, nor curse the lord of the people.

§38 Give to God your tithes and your first fruits of livestock and crops.

§39 Do not eat all the flesh that wild animals leave, but give it to dogs.

§40 Do not give credence to the word of a liar, nor consent to his judgements, nor repeat any of his testimony.

§41 Do not turn, against your sense of right, to the people's bad counsel and unjust will in their talk and clamour, and do not agree to the instruction of the most foolish.

§42 If the stray livestock of another man should come into your possession, let him know about it even if he is your enemy.

§43 Dem ðu swiðe emne. Ne dem ðu oðerne dom þam welegan, oðerne ðam earman; ne oðerne þam liofran and oðerne þam laðran ne dem ðu.

§44 Onscuna ðu a leasunga.

§45 Soðfæstne man and unscyldigne ne acwele ðu þone næfre.

§46 Ne onfoh ðu næfre medsceattum, forðon hie ablendað ful oft wisra monna geðoht and hiora word onwendað.

§47 Þam elðeodegan and utan cumenan ne læt ðu no uncuðlice wið hine, ne mid nanum unryhtum þu hine ne drece.

§48 Ne swergen ge næfre under hæðne godas, ne on nanum ðingum ne cleopien ge to him.

§49 Þis sindan ða domas þe se ælmihtega God self sprecende wæs to Moyse and him bebead to healdanne; and siððan se ancenneda Dryhtnes Sunu, ure God, þæt is hælend Crist, on middangeard cwom, he cwæð | ðæt he ne come no ðas bebodu to brecanne ne to forbeodanne, ac mid eallum godum to ecanne; and mildheortnesse and eaðmodnesse he lærde.

§49.1 Ða æfter his ðrowunge, ær þam þe his apostolas tofarene wæron geond ealle eorðan to læranne, and þa giet ða hie ætgædere wæron, monega hæðena ðeoda hie to Gode gecerdon. Þa hie ealle ætsomne wæron, hie sendan ærendwrecan to Antiohhia and to Syrie, Cristes æ to læranne.

§49.2 Þa hie ða ongeaton þæt him ne speow, ða sendon hie ærendgewrit to him. Þis is ðonne þæt ærendgewrit þe ða apostolas sendon ealle to Antiohhia and to Syria and to Cilicia, ða sint nu of hæðenum ðeodum to Criste gecirde:

§49.3 'Ða apostolas and þa eldran broðor hælo eow wyscað; and we eow cyðað þæt we geascodon þæt ure geferan sume mid urum wordum to eow comon, and eow hefigran [wisan budon] to healdanne þonne we him budon, and eow to swiðe gedwealdon mid ðam manigfealdum gebodum, and eowra sawla ma forhwerfdon þonne hie geryhton. Ða gesomnodon we us ymb ðæt, and us eallum gelicode ða þæt we sendon Paulus and Barnaban; ða men wilniað hiora sawla sellan for Dryhtnes naman.

§49.4 Mid him we sendon Iudam and Silam, þæt eow þæt ilce secggen.

§49.5 Þæm halgan gaste wæs geðuht and us, þæt we nane byrðenne on eow settan noldon ofer þæt ðe eow nedðearf wæs to healdanne: þæt is ðonne,

§43 Judge very impartially. Do not give one judgement for the rich and another for the poor, nor give one judgement for someone dearer [to you] and another for someone more hateful.

§44 Always avoid lies.

§45 Never kill a truthful and innocent man.

§46 Never take bribes, for they very often blind the thoughts of wise men and pervert their words.

§47 Do not act in an unkindly manner towards a stranger and someone come from abroad; do not oppress him with any injustices.

§48 Never swear by heathen gods, nor call on them for any reason.

§49 These are the laws that almighty God was himself declaring to Moses and commanded him to keep; and after the Lord's only begotten Son, our God, that is the Saviour Christ, came into the world, he said that he did not come to break these commandments nor to forbid them, but to increase them with all good things; and he taught mercy and humility.

§49.1 Then after his passion, before his apostles were dispersed across the whole earth to teach, and when they were still together, they converted many heathen peoples to God. When they were all together, they sent messengers to Antioch and Syria to teach Christ's law.

§49.2 When they perceived that these were not successful, then they sent a written message to them. This then is the letter that the apostles all sent to Antioch, Syria, and Cilicia, which are now converted from heathen peoples to Christ:

§49.3 'The apostles and the elder brothers wish you health; and we inform you that we have learned that some of our comrades came to you with our words, and bid you hold to a stricter path than we bid them, and too greatly misled you with those many commands, and perverted your souls more than they corrected them. Then we met about that, and were then all pleased to send Paul and Barnabas; those men wish to give their souls for the Lord's name.

§49.4 With them we sent Judas and Silas, so that they might say the same thing to you.

§49.5 It seemed to the Holy Ghost and to us that we did not wish to impose any burden on you beyond what was necessary for you to bear: that

þæt ge forberen þæt ge deofolgeld ne weorðien, ne blod ne ðicggen ne as-
morod, and from | diernum geligerum; and þæt ge willen þæt oðre men
eow ne don, ne doð ge ðæt oþrum monnum.'

§49.6 Of ðissum anum dome, mon mæg geðencean þæt he æghwelcne
on ryht gedemeð; ne ðearf he nanra domboca oþerra. Geðence he þæt he
nanum men ne deme þæt he nolde ðæt he him demde, gif he ðone dom
ofer hine sohte.

§49.7 Siððan ðæt þa gelamp þæt monega ðeoda Cristes geleafan onfengon,
þa wurdon monega seonoðas geond ealne middangeard gegaderode, and eac
swa geond Angelcyn, siððan hie Cristes geleafan onfengon, halegra biscepa
and eac oðerra geðungenra witena. Hie ða gesetton, for ðære mildheort-
nesse þe Crist lærde, æt mæstra hwelcre misdæde þætte ða weoruldhlafordas
moston mid hiora leafan buton synne æt þam forman gylte þære fiohbote
onfon, þe hie ða gesettan; buton æt hlafordsearwe hie nane mildheortnesse
ne dorston gecweðan, forþam ðe God ælmihtig þam nane ne gedemde þe
hine oferhogdon, ne Crist Godes sunu þam nane ne gedemde þe hine to
deaðe sealde, and he bebead þone hlaford lufian swa hine.

§49.8 Hie ða on monegum senoðum monegra menniscra misdæda bote ge-
setton, and on monega senoðbec hie writan, hwær anne dom hwær oþerne.

§49.9 Ic ða Ælfred cyning þas togædere gegaderode and awritan het mon-
ege þara þe ure foregengan heoldon, ða ðe me licodon, and manege þara þe
me ne licodon ic awearp | mid minra witena geðeahte, and on oðre wisan
bebead to healdanne. Forðam ic ne dorste geðristlæcan þara minra awuht
fela on gewrit settan, forðam me wæs uncuð hwæt þæs ðam lician wolde ðe
æfter us wæren. Ac ða ðe ic gemette awðer oððe on Ines dæge mines mæges,
oððe on Offan Mercna cyninges, oððe on Æþelbryhtes þe ærest fulluhte
onfeng on Angelcynne, þa ðe me ryhtoste ðuhton, ic þa heron gegaderode,
and þa oðre forlet.

§49.10 Ic ða Ælfred Westseaxna cyning eallum minum witum þas geeowde,
and hie ða cwædon þæt him þæt licode eallum to healdanne.

is, then, that you refrain from worshipping idols, and from tasting blood or anything strangled, and from illicit sexual intercourse; and whatever you wish that other people not do to you, do not to other people.'

§49.6 From this one law alone, one can be mindful that he judge each man rightly; he does not need any other law-books. Let him be mindful that he judge no man in a way that he would not be judged by him if the man sought judgement over him.

§49.7 Afterwards when it happened that many peoples had accepted the faith of Christ, many synods of holy bishops and also of other distinguished wise men were assembled throughout the whole world, and also throughout all the English people after they had accepted the faith of Christ. They then determined, through the mercy that Christ taught, that at the first offence for almost every misdeed secular lords might with their permission receive without sin monetary compensation, which they then decreed; only for betrayal of one's lord did they dare not declare any mercy, since almighty God granted none to those who despised him, nor did Christ, the Son of God, grant any to him who gave him over to death; and he commanded everyone to love his lord as himself.

§49.8 Then in many synods they established compensations for many human misdeeds, and they wrote them in many synod-books, one law in this place, another in that.

§49.9 Then I, King Alfred, gathered these together, and commanded to be written many of the ones—those that pleased me—that our predecessors observed. And many of those that did not please me I discarded on the advice of my counsellors, and ordered them to be observed in a different way. I dared not presume to put in writing many at all of my own because I did not know what would please those who would come after us. But those that I found either from the time of Ine, my kinsman, or of Offa, king of the Mercians, or of Æthelberht who received baptism first amongst the English people, and that seemed most just to me, those ones I collected in this work, and the others I left out.

§49.10 Then I Alfred, king of the West Saxons, showed these to all my counsellors, and they then said that it pleased them all to observe them.

Summary of the *Laws* of Alfred

The preface leads into the law code proper, which comprises a miscellaneous series of laws relating to such matters as the breaking of oaths and pledges, the church's right to give sanctuary, theft, murder and manslaughter, sexual violence, adultery, damage to another's property, slander, false imprisonment, forcible entry, and affray; it also lists the various compensations due in cases where personal injuries have been inflicted. Alfred's law code circulates with another code identified as that issued by King Ine of Wessex, whose provisions complement the Alfredian ones.

The Old English *Bede*

Preface
Epilogue

INTRODUCTION

For the Old English *Bede* the only extant preface is a translation of the original Latin preface to Bede's *Historia ecclesiastica gentis Anglorum* (*Ecclesiastical History of the English People*).[1] The vernacular version of the preface seems to have been a separate undertaking from the main translation project, however, with a different (probably later) author responsible for its composition.[2] This preface may have replaced one that was already there but no longer survives, or have been added to supply an original lack.

The *Bede* also contains an epilogue, consisting originally of two prose petitions, supplemented in one manuscript by a third petition in verse, the work of a later writer. The tripartite version of the epilogue, extant only in Cambridge, Corpus Christi College MS 41, is edited here.

The Work and its Contexts

The main source for the *Bede* is Bede's ecclesiastical history of the English people which he completed in AD 731, four years before his death. The *Historia ecclesiastica gentis Anglorum* offers an important overview of early English history, particularly in relation to the conversion process. It covers, in five books, the period from Julius Caesar's invasion of Britain (dated by Bede to 60 BC) up to the year the work was completed.[3]

In the monastery at Jarrow, Bede had access to a well stocked library, and was able to draw on a wide range of sources in composing his *Historia*. Orosius and Gildas are amongst the historians furnishing him with material for his earlier chapters. Throughout the work he draws on a large number of

---

[1] For the Latin preface, see Colgrave and Mynors (1969), pp. 2–7.
[2] Waite (2015).
[3] For an outline of the historical events covered by the *Historia*, see the summary of the *Bede* on pp. 180–1.

saints' lives, and he takes account of various papal letters and registers as well as numerous other kinds of documents such as genealogies and annals. He also draws on oral tradition to supplement his other material where no written records are available. The work seems to have grown quickly in popularity through the eighth and ninth centuries, both in England and on the Continent.[4]

The *Bede* was composed in the Mercian dialect some time in the ninth or early tenth centuries, and, like the *Dialogues*, perhaps emerged from a Mercian centre of scholarship such as Worcester.[5] It presents a shortened version of the Latin original, with omissions carefully tailored to ensure that the integrity of the work is retained.[6] Stylistically the translation remains close to the Latin source, retaining many Latinate syntactic constructions. The main author's predilection for word pairs (or doublings) to translate single words in the Latin perhaps shows the influence of the glossing tradition. Ælfric and William of Malmesbury attributed the work to King Alfred, but the Mercian dialect of the translation makes this unlikely.[7] The composition of the work can only certainly be dated to either in or around Alfred's reign.[8]

Manuscripts and Previous Editions

There are five surviving manuscript witnesses to the *Bede*. Two of these copies have lost leaves at the beginning and end, and contain neither preface nor epilogue.[9] The three manuscripts of the *Bede* that serve as witnesses to either its preface or its epilogue, or both, are as follows:

---

[4] See Whitelock (1960); Westgard (2010).
[5] Pioneering work in identifying the dialect as Mercian was done by Miller (1890–8), xxvi–lix; see further Waite (2014).
[6] Whitelock (1962).
[7] For the scholarly context, see Waite (2014) and Rowley (2011), ch. 2.
[8] Waite (2015), p. 32 n. 2. For further discussion of the date of the *Bede*, see Rowley (2011), pp. 36–46.
[9] Oxford, Bodleian Library, Tanner 10 (T), s. ix^{ex}/x^1 (Ker (1957), no. 351; Gneuss and Lapidge (2014), no. 668); and Oxford, Corpus Christi College 279, pt. II (or 279B) (O), s. xi^{in}, (Ker (1957), no. 354; Gneuss and Lapidge (2014), no. 673).

C London, British Library, Cotton MS Otho B. xi (s. x^med and xi¹).[10]
Ca Cambridge, University Library MS Kk. 3. 18 (s. xi²).[11]
B Cambridge, Corpus Christi College MS 41 (s. xi¹).[12]

The preface is extant in full in two of these manuscripts, Ca and B, both from the eleventh century. Variant readings from the earlier mid-tenth-century manuscript C are also available because they were recorded in editions of the *Bede* prepared by Abraham Wheloc and John Smith, and in handwritten collations by Smith, before C was damaged in the Cotton Library fire of 1731.[13]

The two surviving witnesses of the preface are fairly similar textually to one another. The preface as it appears in Ca from the second half of the eleventh century is probably, as Waite notes, 'substantially the same as it had been in the mid tenth century, when it was already attached to the text in C'.[14] Although the version in Ca may be closer than B to the original, this edition bases the text of the preface on B, both because the text has been edited recently elsewhere from Ca, and to accord with the text on which the epilogue is based. B's version of the preface shows relatively few instances of the morphological, lexical, and syntactic revision characteristic of B's text elsewhere.

In both of its extant manuscript copies, the preface is divided into two sections at the same point in the text, with coloured initials marking the beginning of both sections in Ca, and with a gap of one line and capitalized *ic* (I) marking off the second section in B. Since this section break occurs in the middle of a sentence and makes no structural sense, it must reflect a misunderstanding by the scribe who first introduced it.[15]

The two prose petitions of the epilogue are preserved in C, Ca, and B; the verse portion is an addition unique to B. All three witnesses of the prose

---

[10] Ker (1957), no. 180; Gneuss and Lapidge (2014), no. 357.
[11] Ker (1957), no. 23; Gneuss and Lapidge (2014), no. 22.
[12] Ker (1957), no. 32; Gneuss and Lapidge (2014), no. 39.
[13] Wheloc (1643); Smith (1722). Smith's handwritten collations are in a copy of the 1644 reissue of Wheloc's edition in the British Library (shelfmark 698.m.6). A transcript of C was made by Laurence Nowell in 1562 (London, British Library, MS Add. 43703), but this omitted the preface. For a detailed reconsideration of the evidence provided by Wheloc and Smith, see Waite (2015), pp. 42–8.
[14] Waite (2015), p. 55. [15] See Waite (2015), pp. 41–2.

petitions are quite similar to one another. In C these prose prayers, along with the previous autobiographical note and the subsequent copy of the *Anglo-Saxon Chronicle*, were copied in the first quarter of the eleventh century, fifty or more years later than the rest of the work.[16] The text is somewhat fire-damaged and a small portion of it is available only in a separately stored box of fragments.[17] In this edition the text of the epilogue is based on B, the only manuscript to contain the three closing petitions.

The standard edition of the whole of the *Bede* remains the late nineteenth-century one (with a translation) by Thomas Miller;[18] a new edition of the work, also to be published by the Early English Text Society, is in preparation by Greg Waite and Sharon Rowley. The text of the preface (based on Ca), including a full record of variant readings, has recently been printed independently by Waite as an appendix to his article on its authorship and transmission.[19] The tripartite version of the epilogue in B was edited by Fred Robinson, but without collation of the variants of the prose sections in other copies.[20] The verse part of the epilogue in B was edited separately by Elliott Van Kirk Dobbie in the Anglo-Saxon Poetic Records series, by Robinson and Stanley in their facsimile edition, and by Irvine and Godden in the Dumbarton Oaks Medieval Library Series.[21]

The Preface to the *Bede*

The author of the main body of the *Bede* was probably from Mercia, perhaps someone with links to the Alfredian court (since Alfred was known to have had Mercian helpers such as Wærferth, Plegmund, Athelstan, and Werwulf amongst his entourage).[22] As we have seen, however, the writer of the Preface to the *Bede* is someone different from the translator of the

---

[16] Ker (1957), p. 231.

[17] Ker (1957), no. 180, p. 233. The identification of the original location of the fragment that can be identified as belonging to the copy of the epilogue in C was made by Torkar (1981); see especially p. 51.

[18] Miller (1890–8).   [19] Waite (2015), pp. 87–9.   [20] Robinson (1981).

[21] Dobbie (1942), p. 113; Robinson and Stanley (1991); Irvine and Godden (2012), pp. 414–15.

[22] The authorship of the work in relation to its Mercian dialect is discussed by Whitelock (1962), pp. 57–9; Bately (1988); Rowley (2011); and Waite (2014).

rest of the work. The preface, Waite proposes, 'is the product of a writer working some time after the *OE Bede* was completed, possibly in West Saxon circles'.[23] The translator of the preface seems to have been less well trained in Latin than the main *Bede* translator, even if some of his departures from the original can be attributed to factors other than a failure of understanding.[24]

Although the earliest surviving copies of the *Bede* were made at the very end of the ninth or beginning of the tenth century, the preface itself can only be traced to witnesses dating from the mid-tenth to the eleventh centuries.[25] Manuscript evidence cannot therefore be brought to bear in determining how early it might have been composed and attached to the work. Analysis of linguistic and stylistic evidence leads Waite to conclude cautiously that the preface 'appears to be the pastiche of a writer of the first half of the tenth century (if not the end of the ninth) who had some knowledge of the genuine Alfredian Prefaces', but whose dialect was different from that represented in the *Pastoral Care*.[26]

The Preface to the *Bede* has been altered and abridged from Bede's original in the course of its translation into the vernacular.[27] The preface-writer omits, for example, Bede's allusion to the part played by King Ceolwulf in scrutinizing an earlier copy of the work, and revises Bede's passage on how history affects a thoughtful listener or reader (lines 6–11), adding the rhetorical question 'hu wile he wurðan þonne gelæred?' (how then is he to be taught?) to reinforce its message. The kinds of changes this preface makes to the Latin original in vocabulary, syntax, and style are very different overall from those made in the main body of the *Bede*.[28]

The preface follows the structure of its Latin source. The Latin preface develops along conventional rhetorical lines, starting with a salutation expressing the narrator's humility and concluding with the topos of *captatio beneuolentiae* (literally 'seeking out good will').[29] At some stage, however, a copyist or compiler relocated its closing prayer to the end of the *Historia*, where it remained in a group of manuscripts known as C-type,

---

[23] Waite (2015), pp. 31–2.   [24] Waite (2015), p. 84.
[25] See Waite (2015), pp. 39–42.   [26] Waite (2015), p. 85.
[27] See Whitelock (1962), pp. 74–5; Waite (2015), 35–9.
[28] Waite (2015), pp. 57–83.   [29] Kendall (1978), pp. 145–72.

which circulated in Anglo-Saxon England.[30] The lack of the closing prayer in the Old English version of Bede's preface would fit with use by the preface-writer of a C-type manuscript.

The Preface to the *Bede* contains stylistic echoes of the Prose Preface to the *Pastoral Care*. In particular its opening is reminiscent of the opening to the latter:

> Ic Beda, Cristes ðeow and mæssepreost, sende gretan ðone leofustan cining Ceoluulf...(Preface to the *Bede*, lines 1–2);
> Alfred kyning hateð gretan Wærferð biscep his wordum luflice ond freondlice...(Prose Preface to the *Pastoral Care*, lines 1–2)

As Nicole Discenza notes, the translator perhaps 'rendered Bede's sentence as he did because he knew Alfred's letter' and took its style of opening as an appropriate way of establishing authority.[31] Waite has further suggested that the preface-writer's translation of the Latin *lector* (reader) by *leornere* (line 46) may be in imitation of the use of the verb *leornian* with the sense 'to read' (found otherwise mainly in Anglian texts), which occurs in the Preface to the *Pastoral Care* ('ond ða bec ealla be fullan geliornod hæfdon', and had thoroughly learned all the books, lines 37–8) and in the Preface to the *Boethius* ('ða he þas boc hæfde geleornode', when he had learned this book, lines 6–7).[32] The view expressed in the Preface to the *Bede* that it befits a king to teach his people (lines 12–13), in this case a loose translation of the Bedan source itself, is also in keeping with the sentiment of the prose and verse prefaces to the *Pastoral Care*.[33]

The preface makes frequent use of doublings, or word pairs, a stylistic feature that it shares with the rest of the *Bede* and the *Dialogues*, and which is perhaps to be associated with the influence of a similar technique in interlinear glosses to Latin texts.[34] Those which correspond to doublings in the Latin original include 'ðeow and mæssepreost' (line 1); 'to rædenne and...to smeganne' (line 3); 'to writenne and to læranne' (line 4); 'gemende and smeagende' (line 5); 'cwydas and dæda' (lines 5–6); 'fultumiend and lareow'

---

[30] See Lapidge (2008–10), I.civ–cxv; Waite (2015), pp. 55–6.
[31] Discenza (2002), pp. 73. See also Waite (2015), pp. 68–9.
[32] Waite (2015), pp. 66–7.   [33] Klaeber (1902), p. 264.
[34] Bately (1988), p. 133.

(line 15); 'on gewritum oððe on ealdra manna gesegenum' (line 20); 'ymbe Suðseaxe and ymbe Westseaxe' (line 35); 'lif and forðfore' (line 38); 'gewritum oðþe segenum' (line 41); 'wiston and gemundon' (line 47). Those independent of the Latin include 'be Angelðeode and Seaxum' (lines 2–3); 'godne to hergeanne and yfelne to leanne' (lines 9–10); 'gelyfdon and geleornedon' (line 26); 'ærendo and segena' (line 29); 'bidde and halsige' (line 53); 'gemete oðða gehyre' (line 54).

The language of the preface is also strikingly repetitive. The noun '(ge)segene', for example, resonates through the preface in various contexts: 'on gewritum oðða on ealdra manna gesegenum' (line 20); 'of ealdra manna segnum' (line 25); 'þurh Noðhelmes ærendo and segena' (lines 28–9); 'on ealdra manna gewritum oðþe segenum' (lines 40–1); 'mid Isses gesegnum' (line 41); 'ðurh gesegene þæs arweorðan byscpes' (line 43); 'mid gesegenum unrim geleaffulra witena' (line 47); 'þurh swiðe getrywra manna gesegene' (line 52). The past participle 'gelæred' occurs four times within seven lines in the first half of the preface, along with two uses of 'to læranne' in the first half. Other repeated words or phrases include 'gewritum' (lines 20, 36, 41, and 50), 'arweorða' (lines 15, 34, 37, 42, and 43), 'leorningcnihtum' (lines 21 and 26), 'geleornedon' (lines 26, 42, and 45), 'gehireð' (lines 7 and 8), 'ealdra manna' (lines 5, 20, 25, and 41), 'cining-' (lines 1, 12, 27, and 30), 'geacsodon' (lines 38 and 45), 'awrat' (lines 2, 12, and 24), 'ærend-' (lines 29 and 44), 'Cristes geleafan' (lines 25, 31–2, 43, and 46), 'fela' (lines 29 and 35), '(ge)hwylcum' (lines 27 and 30), 'biscop(-)/bysc-' (lines 17, 30, 34, 37, and 43), 'god(-)' (lines 7 and 9), 'yfel(-)' (lines 8 and 10), 'geworden(-)' (lines 28, 40, and 43), 'mannum' (lines 7 and 8), and 'boca/bec' (lines 24 and 49). The amount of lexical repetition may suggest that the preface-writer was more concerned with conveying the content of the original than with stylistic elegance.

The Preface to the *Bede*, like the Latin original, addresses ideas of authority and authoritativeness, evident in the concern with establishing the credentials of the work, and the relationship between past and present, evident in the attention paid to how events of the past may influence the deeds of the present. The vernacular version places more emphasis on the theme of teaching than the Latin does.[35]

---

[35] Molyneaux (2009), pp. 1307–10.

The Epilogue to the *Bede*

The two prose petitions were apparently the work of the main translator of the *Bede*: their translation 'is consistent in style and lexis with the work of the *OE Bede* translator, not with that of the Preface translator'.[36] The first petition translates the prayer Bede placed at the end of his work. This prayer, Fred Robinson notes, 'appears at this point in virtually every non-fragmentary copy of the *History*, both Latin and Old English'.[37] The second petition also derives from Bede's *Historia*, but its original location in the Latin was at the end of Bede's preface. In the C-type group of manuscripts which circulated in Anglo-Saxon England, it was located after the original closing petition, as it is in the Old English version.[38]

The verse petition which supplements the two prose petitions in Cambridge, Corpus Christi College 41, is probably the work of an eleventh-century scribe, who may be either the scribe of the last part of the manuscript in which the poem now survives or the scribe of a previous exemplar. Given the latter possibility, Dobbie's view that 'the date of the writing of the manuscript...may be taken as indicating also the date of the composition of the metrical epilogue' has to be treated with caution.[39] As Fred Robinson acknowledges, however, 'one factor arguing for a later rather than an early date is the absence of the metrical epilogue from any of the other manuscripts of the *History*'.[40]

The epilogue's structure as a series of two (or three) discrete petitions is reflected in the mise-en-page. In C, each of the two prose petitions begins on a new line, with an opening capital letter which extends very slightly into the left margin. In Ca, the beginning of each petition is marked by a red capital, similar to those used to demarcate sections elsewhere in the main body of the text. In B, the scribe has left large spaces (which remained unfilled) for an illuminated capital letter at the beginning of each of the three petitions.[41] The verse petition is also visually differentiated from the prose petitions by being written with red ink ornamented with gold on alternate lines.

---

[36] Waite (2015), p. 56. [37] Robinson (1980), p. 11. [38] See pp. 171–2 above.
[39] Dobbie (1942), p. cxviii. [40] Robinson (1980), p. 25 n. 30.
[41] See also Robinson (1980), pp. 10–11.

The first-person voice of the two prose petitions is clearly Bede's. The identity of the first-person voice in B's verse petition is more ambiguous. The verbal parallels between the opening of this petition and the previous two lead Robinson to argue that the voice here is also to be understood as Bede's.[42] Another possibility is that the first-person voice in this last petition is the scribe's. Richard Gameson interprets the verse part of the epilogue as a scribal colophon (or 'finishing touch').[43] The verse petition draws on tropes associated with the scribal colophon such as begging for the reader's prayers, recording the labour of writing (here in the image of hands in lines 17 and 18), and alluding to the physical book (here in the phrase *þa bredu befo* 'hold the boards', line 15).[44]

All three petitions make a display of humility (in keeping with their petitionary genre). God's authority is acknowledged in them all, and the second and third also acknowledge the power of readers, either to intercede with God or (in the case of the verse petition) to offer support of a more earthly kind. Implicit in all three petitions is the relationship between the act of writing and the attainment of God's grace.

Note on the Texts

The text of the preface is based on Cambridge, Corpus Christi College MS 41 [B], pp. 18–22, with abbreviations silently expanded. Significant variant readings from Cambridge, University Library MS Kk. 3. 18 [Ca] are recorded, along with occasional substantive variants in S (John Smith's handwritten variants) and CWS (variants from C in Smith's and Abraham Wheloc's editions) where they are not witnessed elsewhere.[45]

The text of the epilogue is based on B, pp. 482–4, with abbreviations silently expanded. Significant variant readings for the two prose petitions are recorded from Ca and London, British Library, Cotton MS Otho B. xi [C].

---

[42] Robinson (1980) and (1981).   [43] Gameson (2002), pp. 43–4.
[44] Robinson (1980), pp. 5–8; see also Gameson (2002).
[45] On the witnesses provided by Smith and Wheloc, see p. 169 and n. 13 above.

TEXTS AND TRANSLATIONS

The Preface to the *Bede*

Ic Beda, Cristes ðeow and mæssepreost, sende gretan ðone leofustan cining Ceoluulf. And ic þe sende þæt spell, þæt ic niwan awrat be Angelðeode and Seaxum, þe sylfum to rædenne and on æmettan to smeganne, and eac on ma stowa to writenne and to læranne; and getriwe on þine geornfulnesse, forþon ðu eart swiþe gemende and smeagende ealdra manna cwydas 5 and dæda, and alra swiðust þara mærra manne ure þeode. Forþam ðis gewrit oððe hit god sagaþ be godum mannum, and se ðe hit gehireþ, he onhireð þam; oððe hit yfel sægð be yfelum mannum, and se ðe hit gehireþ, he flyhð þæt and onscunaþ. Forþon hit is god godne to hergeanne and
p. 19 yfelne to leanne, þætte | se geþeo se ðe hit gehire. Gif se oþer nelle, hu 10 wile he wurðan þonne gelæred? For þinre ðearfe and for ðinre þeode ic þis awrat; forðon þe God to cininge geceas, þe gedauenað þine ðeode to læranne. And þæt ðe þy læs tweoge hwæðer þis soð sy, ic cyðe hwanan me þas spell comon.

Ærest me wæs fultumiend and lareow se arweorða abbud Albinus, se wæs 15 wide gefaren and gelæred, and wæs betst gelæred on Angelcynne. Swiþust he me sæde of Ðeodores gemynde, se wæs byscop on Cantwara byrig, and Adrianus abbud, forðon he swiþust wæs mid him gelæred. Eal þæt he on Cantwara mægþe and eac on ðam þeodlandum ðe þær to geþeodde wæron, eal þæt he on gewritum oððe on ealdra manna gesegenum 20 ongeat, oððe fram leorningcnihtum þæs eadegan papan sancte Gregorius, ða he me, eal ða þe gemyndwurðe wæron, þurh Noðhelm ðone æfestan
p. 20 mæssepreost on Lundenbyrig, | oððe hyne to me sende, oððe on stafum awrat and me sende. Fram fruman þissa boca oð þa tiid ðe Angelcynn Cristes geleafan onfengon of ealdra manna segnum oð þas andweardan tiid 25 swiþost we gelyfdon and geleornedon þæt we her writat, and of leorningcnihtum þæs eadegan papan sancte Gregorius, under hwylcum cininge þæt ðonne geworden wæs, þurh Albinus myngunga þæs abbudes and þurh Noðhelmes ærendo and segena. Swiðe fela hi me sædon fram

The Preface to the *Bede*

I Bede, servant of Christ and mass priest, send greetings to the much loved king Ceolwulf. And I am sending you the account I wrote recently about the Angles and Saxons, for you to read yourself and ponder over at leisure, and also for copying and teaching at more religious houses; and I have faith in your dedication because you are very attentive to, and curious about, the sayings and doings of people from the past and especially of all the famous ones amongst our people. For this work either speaks good about good people and whoever hears it imitates that; or it tells evil about evil people and whoever hears it avoids and shuns that. Indeed it is good to praise someone good and reproach someone bad so that the hearer may profit. If the latter resists, how then is he to be taught? I have written this for your benefit and for your people; since God chose you as king, it is fitting for you to teach your people. And to minimize any doubt for you about whether this [account] is accurate, I shall make known where these stories came to me from.

My first helper and teacher was the honourable abbot Albinus, who was widely travelled and had been extensively taught, and was the best educated person amongst the English. He told me especially things from the recollections of Theodore, who had been Bishop of Canterbury, and of Abbot Hadrian, since he had been taught mostly by them. Everything he learned in Kent and also the countries associated with it, everything he learned in the writings or statements of the elderly, or from disciples of the blessed pope St Gregory, all those which were worthy of remembering he sent to me via Nothhelm the devout mass priest in London, either sending him to me in person or writing them down in letters and sending them to me. From the beginning of these books until the time when the English received the faith of Christ, we believed and learned what we write here mostly from the statements of old people, [and from then] up to this present time, from disciples of the blessed pope St Gregory, [with events dated] according to the king they happened under, through Abbot Albinus' recollections and Nothhelm's gehwylcum byscpum, and gehwylcum cininga tidum Eastseaxe and Westseaxe and Eastengle and Norðhymbre þære gife onfengon Cristes geleafan.

Þurh Albinus swiðost ic geþristlæcte þæt ic dorste þis worc onginnan, and eac mid Danielis [...] ðæs arweorþan Wessexena byscpes, se nu git lifiende is. Fela he me sæde ymbe Suðseaxe and ymbe Westseaxe, and eac ymbe Wihtland swiðost he sende on gewritum; and ðurh Cedde þone arweorðan Myrcna bysceop and Ceaddan ymb Myrcna ðeode and Eastseaxena, | ond eac ymbe þara byscpa lif and forðfore we geacsodon fram ðam gebroðrum þæs mynstres ðe hi sylfe astemnedon, þe Læsðinga ea is nemned. Þa ðing þe on Eastenglum gewordene wæron, sume we ða on ealdra manna gewritum oðþe segenum metton, sume we mid Isses gesegnum þæs arweorðan abbudes geleornedon. Ond þætte on Lindesige geworden wæs ymb Cristes geleafan, ðurh gesegene þæs arweorðan byscpes Cynebryhtes and ðurh his ærendgewritu and oðra lifgendra swiðe getrywra, þæt we geleornedon; ond eac þæt we on Norðhymbrum geacsodon ymb Cristes geleafan oþ ðisne andweardan dæg, nales mid anes mannes geþeahte ac mid gesegenum unrim geleaffulra witena, þa ða þing wiston and gemundon, and syððan þæt ic sylf ongeat, ne let ic þæt unwriten. And þæt ic be ðam halegan fæder Cuðberhte wrat, oððe on þisse bec oþþe on oðre, his dæda and his lifes, sume ic ærest nom of þam gewritum þe ic | awriten gemette mid þam broðrum þære ciricean æt Lindesfarene ea, sume, ða þe ic sylf ongitan mihte þurh swiðe getrywra manna gesegene, ic toihte. And þone leornere ic nu eaðmodlice bidde and halsige, gif he hwæt ymbe þis elleshwær on oþere wisan gemete oððe gehyre, þæt he me þæt ne oðwite.

30 reports and statements. They told me very many things as to which bishops [there were], and what the dates of the kings [were when] the East Saxons, West Saxons, East Anglians and Northumbrians received the gift of faith in Christ.

I presumed to embark on this work mainly through Albinus, and also by means of [the encouragement of] Daniel the honourable bishop of the West
35 Saxons who is still alive. He told me many things about the South Saxons and West Saxons; and also about the Isle of Wight [which] he mainly sent in written documents; and through Cedd, the honourable bishop of the Mercians, and Chad about the people of the Mercians and the East Saxons; and we have learnt also about the lives and deaths of the bishops from
40 the brothers of the monastery which they themselves established called Lastingham. Some of the things which happened amongst the East Anglians we found in the writings and statements of elderly people, and some we have learnt from the statements of the honourable abbot Isse. And we learned what happened in Lindsey regarding faith in Christ through what
45 the honourable Bishop Cynebert said and through what he and other very reliable people still living wrote; and also I did not leave unwritten what we learned amongst the Northumbrians about belief in Christ up to this present day, not on the basis of consultation of one person but from the statements of a countless number of faithful witnesses who knew and
50 remembered those things, and what I myself learned later. And some of what I have written about the deeds and life of the holy father Cuthbert, either in this book or another, I first took from the documents I found written by the brothers of the church at Lindisfarne, some things which I myself could ascertain from what very reliable people said, I added. And I now
55 humbly pray to and entreat the reader that if he should find out or hear anything different about this elsewhere, he will not reproach me.

Summary of the *Bede*

The Old English work begins by outlining the geography and the origins of the language and inhabitants of Britain. The starting point for the history itself is Julius Caesar's invasion of Britain. Book I covers events from that point up to AD 605, including the martyrdom of St Alban; the end of Roman rule in Britain in around 410; the attacks by the Picts and Scots; the migration and settlement of the Angles, Saxons, and Jutes in 449, and the conflicts that ensued; the arrival of Augustine, who would become the first Archbishop of Canterbury, and his fellow missionaries in 597. A lengthy question-and-answer section records Pope Gregory's answer to Augustine's questions regarding the ministry in England.

Book II covers events from AD 605 (Bede's date for the death of Pope Gregory) to 633 (the death in battle of King Edwin of Northumbria). It records the work of Augustine and his successors Laurentius, Mellitus, Justus, and Honorius. Much of this book is devoted to the gradual conversion of the Northumbrians, including Edwin, giving due prominence to the role of Bishop Paulinus.

Book III covers the period from AD 633 to 665. The progress of the conversion and the succession of kings and bishops in the various Anglo-Saxon kingdoms are recorded. Much attention is given in the first part of the book to the role of King Oswald of Northumbria who promoted the Christian faith with the help of his bishop Aidan, and at whose tomb miracles occurred. The activities of other prominent religious figures in the various kingdoms, such as Fursey and Cedd, are described.

Book IV begins with the deaths of Archbishop Deusdedit and Erconberht of Kent (664) and covers events to around 687 (the death of St Cuthbert). It records significant battles and their consequences and royal successions. Other prominent figures in this book are Archbishop Theodore and Abbot Adrian, the Mercian bishop Chad, the East Saxon bishop Earconwald and his sister Ethelburga, abbess Etheldreda, abbess Hild, the cowherd and later poet and Abbot Cædmon, and St Cuthbert.

Book V covers the period from around AD 688 to 731 (the death of Archbishop Berhtwald and succession of Tatwine). The book records the religious history of the Anglo-Saxon kingdoms in this period, paying particular attention to the succession and activities of bishops and kings, and to the influential role of such figures as the missionary Willibrord, the visionary hermit and later monk Dryhthelm, and Bishop Wilfrid. Between the end of the historical account and the Epilogue to the *Bede* are a translation of Bede's autobiographical note and the list of his writings.

The Epilogue to the *Bede*

And ic bidde ðe nu goda hælend þæt þu me milde forgeafe swetlice drincan þa word ðines wisdomes þæt þu eac swylce forgyfe þæt ic æt nyhstan to ðe, þam wylle ealles wisdomes, becuman mote symle ætywan beforan þinre ansyne. |

Eac þonne ic eaðmodlice bidde þæt on eallum ðam þe ðis ylce stær tobe- 5
cume ures cynnes to rædenne oððe to gehyrenne, þæt hi for minum untrum-
nessum modes and lichaman gelomlice and geornlice þingian mid ðære
upplican arfæstnesse Godes ælmihtiges and on gehwylcum heora mægðum
þas mede heora edleanes me agyfan þæt ic þe be syndrigum mægðum oððe
þam hyhrum stowum, ða þe ic gemyndelice and þam bigengum þanc- 10
wyrðlice gelyfde geornlice ic tilode to awritenne þæt ic mid eallum þingum
þone westm arfæstre þingunge gemete.

    Bidde ic eac   æghwylcne mann,
    bregorices weard,   þe þas boc ræde
    and þa bredu befo,   fira aldor,   15
    þæt gefyrðrige þone writre   wynsumum cræfte
    þe ðas boc awrat   bam handum twam, |
    þæt he mote manega gyt   mundum synum
    geendigan,   his aldre to willan,
    and him þæs geunne   se ðe ah ealles geweald,   20
    rodera waldend,   þæt he on riht mote
    oð his daga ende   Drihten herigan.
    Amen. Geweorþe þæt.

The Epilogue to the *Bede*

And I now beseech you, good saviour, in that you have graciously granted me to drink sweetly the words of your wisdom, that you likewise grant that I may be allowed to come at last to you, the fount of all wisdom, to appear eternally before your face.

5 Also I humbly beseech that amongst all those to whom this same history of our nation may come—for either reading or hearing—that they will often and strenuously intercede with the mercy on high of almighty God for my weaknesses of mind and body, and that in every province of theirs they will give me this recompense as a reward from them, so that I, who strove
10 assiduously to write down whatever I thought memorable and worthy of the inhabitants' contemplation concerning individual provinces or the more important places, might gain the fruits of pious intercession in all things.

>   I also beseech everyone
>   who reads this book and holds the covers,
> 15 every guardian of a kingdom and lord of men,
>   that he support with his pleasant skill the writer
>   who wrote this book with his two hands,
>   so that he may complete many more
>   with his hands to his lord's will,
> 20 and may he who has power over everything, the ruler of heaven,
>   grant him that he may properly
>   praise the Lord until the end of his days.
>   Amen. So be it.

Textual Notes

The Old English *Dialogues*

The Prose Preface to the Dialogues

Text from CCCC 322 [C], fo. 1r.

The Verse Preface to the Dialogues

Text from O, fo. 1r.
1–2   *Two lines of large capitals, reading respectively* E ÐE ME RÆDAN *and* ÐANCE. HE IN ME FINDAN MÆ *(spacing of words is editorial). Another row of capitals between these two lines is now missing.*
12   Wulfsige] Wulfstan *with* tan *over an erasure, probably of* ige
13   þe] þ *with* e *lost at end of line*
14   wihta] wiht
15   gesceafta] gesc ta *with medial* ea *lost at end of line*
16   þe se] *erasure of one or two letters between* þe *and* se
19   heora] heo *with* ra *missing at end of line*
21   forgyue] forgyu *with* e *missing at end of line*   geo worhte] geworhte
22   geweald] gewe *with* ald *missing at end of line*
27   iorðcyninga] hiorðcyninga

The Gregorian Preface to the Dialogues

Text from O, fos. 1r–3v, with variants from C.
1–4   *Only in* O.
1   Her] *Large decorated initial* h O   æresða] æresð þa O   hlutran] hlutra[ ] O
2   larheowes] larheow O
3   and] a *altered from* o O
5–6   apostolica wer] [ ] wer O, apostolica papa C
6   nama Petrus] C, n[ ]/[ ] O
7   eallum] C, ea[ ] O
8   sanctus Gregorius] C, s[ ]/[ ]gorius O
9   ond þus] C, [ ] O
10–11 Sume...ymbhogena] C, S[ ] dæge [ ]swenced[ ] O
11   for] *em.* ær C, [ ] O
13   þæt þe] þa þing ðe C   ne don] ne C
14   on(2)] in C

186 Textual Notes

16 in] on C
17–18 þa eagan] þam eagum C
20 geswenced] C, ge[ ]nced O
21 se(1)] C, [ ]e O
23 wæs] C, [ ] O
23 gefæra] \ge/færa O, *with* ge *in red*, gefyra C   godcundan] C; god[ ]undan O
25 hefige] hefigum C   cwæð] cwæþ he C   gelomp] gelamp C, ge[ ]omp O
26 ær] C, [ ]r O   gewuna] gewun\a/ O
27 hym to] to him C   dreoge] *em. Hecht* dneoge O, drege C
28 symble] C, symlbe O
29 gecnyssed ond] C, gecnys[ ] O
30 in] on C
32 worldþing þe] C, world[ ] O   we nu] we C
33 buton þa] C, b[ ] O   eac] C, he O
35 eac] C, ic O
36 wite] C, witod O
42 ymbe his] ybe O, ymb his C
44 hwæt ic(1)] hwæt \ic/ O, þæt ic C   Ond] On\d/, *with* d *in red* O
    þæt ic(1)] C, hwæt \ic/ O
46 Petrus] C; Petr[ ] O   þam þe on] þon þe þam CO   þe byð] þæt byð C
47 micles] mycclan C   eom] eom nu C
48 worldle] worulde C
49 þam] C, þom O
50 asworette ic] C, asworette i[c] O
51 ageomorige] geomrige C   gelæteð] gelætað C
52 hit] he C
53 hefigre sy] C, hefigre [ ] O
54 woruldþinga] C, wo[ ]ld- O
57 þæt þonne] þonne C   þæt he] þæt þe he C
58 feor gewiteð] feor gewiteþ C, [ ]teð O
59 æc] ac? O, eac C   gode] godes C, [ ]e O
61 Forþon] for\þon/ *with* þon *in red* O
64 ealle] eallum C
65 þara] þære C
67 þonne ic on eom] *om.* C
69 middangeardes] middaneardes C
70 gif ic] gif \ic/ *with* ic *in different hand?* O   gesceade] asceade C
71 monna naman] namena C
72 ondsware] andsware C, [ ]sware O
74–5 hwæðer eallunga si inæled] hwi þu sy eallinga onæled C
76 lande] C, l[ ]nde O
79 oþþe] C, þe O

The Old English *Dialogues* 187

80   þe ana] þe þa ana C
82   weron] werum C   cyðdon] cyþdon C, cyðd[ ] O
83   wene] C, [ ] O
83–4 ær ðon me þæt spell] ær me spell C
87   recenesse] gerecenysse C
88   swiðe] swa swiþe C
89   hwylc] hulic C
90   gehabbanne] habbanne C
91   bið gemærsod] and gemæred C
92   þa ma] þa þe C, þa O *(see Harting (1937), p. 295)*   inælað] onælað C
     al þa] þa C
93   þonne] *om.* C   gewurðeþ] geweorðeþ C, gewur[ ] O
94   fultum in] fultum on C, f[ ]tum in O
95   foregangendra] C, bysena locendra wera O
96   sylf] C, syl[ ] O
97   swyðor] C, swyðð[ ] O
99   geacsode] acsode C
100 þe þa] C, þ[ ] O
101 witon] C, wi[ ] O
102 no þi þe hig] þæt hi C   gesawon] C, gehyrdon O
103 þæra] C, þ[ ]ra O   eac ic] ic eac C
104 þe þas boc] C, [ ] O
105 ælcum þæra] C, æl[ ]a O
106 þæt þu þæt] þæt þu C
107 an in] and in C
110 onfenge] ne onfengce C   leornode] geleornode C
111 þæt ðæt ic nu secge] þæt ic nu secge þæt C, þæt ic nu secge; Ðæt O

Book I Explicit

Text from O, fo. 30v, with variants from C.
1   Nu] C, [ ]u O   þæs papan] C, þ[ ]apan O
2   ond(1)] 7 C, on O   beneoþan] on þysan oþran leafe C   eac] *om.* C

Book II Incipit

Text from O, fo. 31r, with variants from C.
1–2 Her…gastlican] *In capital letters, coloured and/or decorated, with large initial* h O
1   æftra] C, æft[ ] O   godcundan] *Followed by illegible word or decoration* O
2   burnan] rynelan C
4   toflownesse] toflowendnysse C
5   þoncas] ingeþancas C
6   gyldenmuða] C, gylde[ ]muða O

Book II Explicit

Text from O, fo. 61v, with variants from C.

1   Ond] C, *unclear in O*   haligra] C, halgum O   wera] C, [ ]ra O

Book III Incipit

Text from O, fo. 62r, with variants from C.

1   Her onginneð…flod] *small capitals, decorated with colour, initial* h *missing* O   Her] C, [ ]er O   flod of ðam] C, flo[ ] O   welan se] wylle þe C
2   forð aarn] C, for[ ] O
3   for þæra] C, fo[ ] O   nemniað] C, nemnað O

Book III Explicit

Text from O, fo. 100r, with variants from C.

Book IV Incipit

Text from O, fo. 100r, with variants from C.

1   Her…yþ þare] *In capitals, with large coloured initial* h O
3   mannes] C, mann[ ] O
4   Gregorius] C, Gregor[ ] O   ðus] C, ð[ ] O

The Old English *Pastoral Care*

The Prose Preface to the Pastoral Care

Text from H, fos. 1r–2v, with variants from C, J, and U.

1   *Only in* H. Ðis is seo forespræc hu sanctus Gregorius ðas boc gedihte þe man Pastoralem nemnað JU
2   Wærferð biscep] *only in* H, Wulfsige bisceop U
4   woruldcundra] worul\d/cundra H
6   ærendwrecum] æryndwrytum U
7   hu] CJU, *om.* H
10 ge(3)] ond CJU   ðiowotdomas] þeowdomas U
11 don] CJ, *om.* HU. *Added in* H *in an eleventh-century hand, probably Wulfstan's (see Ker (1957), no. 24a, and Kim (1973), p. 430)*
18 sie] sie ðe C
20 Ond] *om.* CJU   bebiode] beode U
24 lufodon] lufdon U, hæfdon CJ, *added in the margin of* H *by Joscelyn (Kim (1973), p. 431)*
26 ða(2)] *om.* U

28 ðiowa] þeawa U
29 nanwuht] nan þing U
33 Ond] *om.* CJU
34 nu] *om.* U
36 swiðe] *om.* U
37 ealla] *uncertain original reading (altered later to* eallæ*)* H   ealla be fullan] be fullan ealla/-e CJU
38 hie] *om.* U
43 ða(2)] ða ða CJ
44 hie(1)] *om.* U
46 hie(2)] *om.* U
53 to(2)] *om.* U
54 ðone] *om.* U
57 ða(2)] *om.* U   afeallen] oðfeallen CJ
59 mislicum] missenlicum C
61 andgiete] andgi\e/te H
64 ond] *om.* CU
68 nan] *om.* U
70 ealneg] ealne weg U

The Verse Preface to the Pastoral Care

Text from H, fo. 2v, with variants from C, J, T, and U.

1   Þis] *Large decorated initial* þ H
3   iegbuendum] eorðbugendum T, egbugendum U
4   adihtode] adihtnode T
6   Gregorius] *om.* U
8   Forðæm] forðon C, for þæm þe T, forþam U
10 mærðum] merþum T, mærða U
11 min] me TU
13 heht] forþam he het U
14 brengan] bringan T
15 ðorfton] beþorftan TU

The Gregorian Preface to the Pastoral Care

Text from H, fos. 6r–v, with variants from C, J, T, and U.

1   Þu] *large decorated capital* Þ.
2   ond(1)] *om.* U   mid] \mid/ H   min mað] me bediglode T
3   fleon] befleon T
6   hine] hi T   bega] bega a T
7   ondræde he] ondræde he him seþþan T   underfenge] u\n/derfenge H, underfeng T

190　Textual Notes

9   sume] sumere T   near(2)] near byð T
10 leornige] leornigen U   hi(2)] \hi/ H   todæle] todælde T   on(2)] \on/ H
11 ðone] \ðone/ H
12 feorðe is] feorðe JT, feorða C
13 for ðy underfenge] for þære onfenge T
14 oððe(1)(2)] ofþe T   ond] ofþe T
15 for ðy underfenge] and for þære onfenge T
17 gemyne he] gemun hi T
18 worhte] ær worhte T
19 for ðæm] fram þam T
20 ahafen] upahafen T
22 onlice] gelice T
24 ðe] *om.* T
25 his] hire T
26 getælde] getealde T   agniat] onginnaþ T

The Gregorian Epilogue to the Pastoral Care

Text from H, fo. 98r, with variants from C, T, and U.

1   nu ðu] þu nu TU   Iohannes] Iohannes \[ ]fredes cyninges mæssepreost/ T, Ælfredes cynges mæssepreost Iohannes U
2   unwlitig] unwlitigne TU   swa swa] swa C   Ðær] Ðeah TU
3   hierde] se hyrde TU
4   stæðe] stede U
8   hæfð] hæf H

The Verse Epilogue to the Pastoral Care

Text from H, fos. 98r–v, with variants from C.

12 missenlice] *In* H *the* e *is obscured (erasure?)*
16 wæl] wel C
21 *From here in* H *the writing tapers line by line to produce a V-shaped text (illustrated on the front jacket of this book)*
24 welle] wille C

The Old English *Boethius* (Prose and Prosimetrical Versions)

The Prose Preface to the Boethius

Text from B, fo. 1r, with variants from Jc.

1   Ælfred...of] B *has large red initial Æ, with the rest written in majuscule letters over two lines*
4   woruldbisgum] wordum and bisgum B, weoruldbisgum Jc
7   he] *om.* B, he (*in margin*) Jc   hæfde] hæfe B, hæf\d/e Jc
8   þa geworhte he] Jc, and geworhte B
9   for] fo\r/ B
10 ongite] ongit\e/ B

The Verse Preface to the Boethius

Text from Jc, fo. iiib[r]
5   myrgen] r *is oddly formed in Jc and perhaps reads* ri.

The Prose Vita of the Boethius

Text from B, fos. 3v–4r.
2   mid] mið B   Eallerica] *written as* ealle rica B
4   anwald] anwal\d/ B   þa] and þa B
8   gelæste] gelæst B
9   he] \he/ B
11 gehaten] \ge/haten B
17 anwealde] anweald\e/ B
18 digellice] dige\l/lice B
22 gebringan] geb\r/ingan B
23 wer] wæs B
27 flor] l *perhaps altered from* f B

The Verse Vita *of the* Boethius

Text from Jc, fo. 2b[r]
21, 26 Crec–] Grec– Jc
38 Gotena] Godena Jc
56 Creacas] Greacas Jc
66 Creca] Greca Jc
73 carcernes] carcerne Jc

The Epilogue to the Boethius

Text from B, fo. 94r.
10 minre] mire
14 ælce] æl\c/e
19 forþon] fo þon
20 min(4)] mii

The Old English *Soliloquies*

The Preface to the Soliloquies

Text from C, fos. 4r–5v, with readings supplied from J where necessary.

1   Gaderode] G *is a large capital, three lines high, in red ink which is badly corroded*
11   and þær] and þara and þær C
13   eardian mæge] eardian C
14   ic] ie C
15   ecan] he\c/an C   sanctus(1)] scanctus C
16   sanctus] scanctus C
17   gelyfe eac] gely *followed by illegible erasure* C
20   þare(1)] þam C
22   swilce] J, sw… *with corner of page torn away* C
22–3   þare utlade] þa… lade *with corner of page torn away* C, ðære utlade J
26   oð] oð oð C
27–8   weliga gifola] wilega gidfola C
30   huru] \h/uru C
31   Sanctus] *orig. in MS, now obscured (see Lockett (2022a), p. 372)*

Book I Explicit

Text from C, fo. 44r.
1   Her] er, *with two lines of text indented to leave space for large capital* H
    bec] bocum

Book II Incipit

Text from C, fo. 44r.
1   Her] er, *with one line of text indented to leave space for large capital* H
    þæra] þære

Book II Explicit

Text from C, fos. 53v–54r.
1   Hær] ær, *with one line of text indented to leave space for large capital* H

Book III Incipit

Text from C, fo. 54r.
1   Ða] a, *with one line of text indented to leave space for large capital* Ð
    of] on of

Book III Explicit

Text from C, fo. 59v.

1   Hær] ær, *with two lines of text indented to leave space for large capital* H

The *Laws* of Alfred

The Preface to the Laws *of Alfred*

Text from E, fos. 36r–40r, with variants from G and H.

1   Dryhten] ryhten, *with large space left for initial* E
2   forðon þe] forðam H
3   þam] ðone G   sæs] sae G, and sæ H
10 ðe] ðu þe H
11 ðy] ði G, and on þam H   orceapunga] onceapunge; and H   hrægle] reafe H   gange he] ga he G, gange H   to ðære dura þæs temples] æt ðas temples dura G   æle] ale G, ane æle H
12 on þeowenne] to þeowte H   sie hio] sie he G, beo heo H   oðru mennenu] oðer þeowwifman H   bebycgganne] syllanne H   freo] faran freo G, frige H   locige] and locie H   agife he] agyfe H   nan] nanne H
13 se ðe(1)] þe H   monnan] man GH   ofsloge] ofslea H   unwillum] ungewylles H   searwa] syrwunge H
14 se sceal deaðe sweltan] swelte se deaþe H
15 forstele] forsteleþ H   he hine(1)] hine G   hit] hit hym G   mæge] mæg H   his modor] modor G
17 mennen] wifman H   forþon þe] forðam H   fioh] þeow H   ðonne idæges] ðonne he idæges sie G, he þonne byð idæges H
18 cease] ceaste GH   domeras] demeras H   gereccen] getæcan G
19 oðdo] ofdo H   teð] toð GH   wið(1)] for G
20 aslea] ofslea H   anigge] aneage G, anegede H   ðone toð] toð H   ilce] sylfe G
21 ofworpod(1)] oftorfod H   wisse and hine inne] nyste. Gif he hit ðonne wiste and he hine G   ofworpod(2)] ofworpen H   forgolden] se man forgolden H   finden] fyndaþ H   ofstinge(1)] stynge H   ðeow] þeowan H   ðeowenne] ðeowmennen E, ðeowne G, þeowene H   se oxa] se oxa sie G, sy se oxa H   ofworpod(3)] ofworpen H
22 adelfe] delfe G   ontyne] untyne H   swelc(2)] swa H
23 hine healdan] he hyne healdan G
24 wið(1)] *om.* G   næbbe] nite H
25 na] *om.* G   self] *om.* H   forgielde] forgylde he G

194 Textual Notes

26   gewerde] awyrde H
27   ryt] ryht H   æfwerdelsan] æwyrdlan GH   fyr] *om.* H   ontent] ontende G, ontendeþ H
28   geladige] ga ladige G   facn ne gefremede] facen on ne gefremede G, fanc on ne fremede H   oððe] oððe þæt H   gewitnesse(1)] he gewitnesse GH   ne getriewe] getreowe ne sy H
30   gewuniað] gewilniað H   gealdorcræftigan] galdorcræft G   ða libban] hi libban H
31   se(2)] GH; he E
33   no] þa G, ðone H   giu] *om.* H
34   þa(2)] *om.* G   sceððað ge ne hie nawer] sceaððan ge hie nahwer ne ne G, scyþþað and ne hy nawer H   gedo] eow gedo H   beoð(2)] *om.* H
35   swa swa] swa GH   and ne] ne G
36   and to] oððe to GH   cleopað he] clypiað hy H   hine] hy H
38   þine(2)] þinne H   þu] þ *altered from* u E
40   no þæs] na G, þæs H
41   unryht] on unriht H   geclysp] geclæsp G, geclebs H   ðæs] on þæs G ne him] þu H
43   emne] rihte and swiðe emne G, ryhtne dom \and/ H   liofran] leofan H laðran] laðan H
44   ðu a] ða H
46   forðon] forðon þe H   onwendað] awendaþ H
47   hine(1)] ðone G
48   swergen] sweren G   nanum] nænegum G
49   Þis] *large capital* Þ *in* E   healdanne] healdende G   ancenneda] acenneda GH Dryhtnes] godes H   ure God] *om.* H   middangeard] woruld H cwom] becom H   bebodu] word *with* vel bebodu *written above* H ecanne] icanne G, geecenne H
49.2   ða(1)] *om.* H   ðonne] *om.* G   to Syria] Siria G
49.3   broðor] broþra H   wyscað] wyrcað G   wisan budon] *om.* E; wisan budan GH   to swiðe] swyðe H   eallum gelicode ða] ða eallum gelicode G, eallum ða gelicode \þa/ H   men] *om.* H   wilniað hiora sawla] willað hyra saula G, gewilniað hira sawla H   sellan] \to/ syllanne H
49.4   sendon] sendað G, send\on/ H   eow] \hy/ eow H   secggen] secgað G, secgan H
49.5   ðe eow] ðeow G   wæs(2)] is G   is] *om.* E; GH   doð] do H   ge ðæt] G *ends after this*
49.6   Of] E *has decorated capital* O, *preceded in margin by number* I; On H æghwelcne] æghwylcne \dom/ H   gedemeð] \ge/deme H   oþerra] oþera \cepan/ H   he(6)] man H   sohte] soh *written over an erasure* E; ahte H

49.7 onfengon] underfengon H   swa geond Angelcyn] swylce on Anglecynn\e/ H
þe hie ða gesettan] ðe hy ða gesetton, *placed after* hlafordsearwe H   hie(4)]
ðam hy H   nane(2)] nane \mildheortnesse/ H   hine(3)] hine selfne H
49.8 monegra] manega H   monega] manegra H
49.9 Ic] E *has large capital* I, *preceded by gap of one line*   ða(2)] \þara/ H   ða
ðe(2)] þa ða H   awðer] aþær H   fulluhte] *followed by erased* s E; fulluht H
49.10 to healdanne] wel to healdene H

The Old English *Bede*

The Preface to the Bede

Text from B, pp. 18–22, with variants from Ca, S, and CWS.

1   Ic...sende] *Originally blank, filled in by later (early modern) hand* B
2   Ceoluulf] and halettan Ceolwulf Ca
4   getriwe] ic getreowige Ca
6   mærra manne] mærena wera Ca
8   oððe] Ca, oð B
10   gehire] gehitre *with* t *subpuncted* B
10–11   nelle hu wile he wurðan þonne gelæred] nolde hu wurð he elles gelæred Ca
13   þæt ðe þy] þæt ðy Ca   ic cyðe...] B *indicates a new section here by inserting a line gap and using large initials for* ic
17   byscop] bysc *followed by erasure[?]* B
20   he on] he oððe on Ca
22–3   ða þe gemyndwurðe wæron, þurh Noðhelm ðone æfestan mæssepreost on Lundenbyrig] Ca, þæt gemynd þe to cyðanne wæron, onsende þurh Norðhelm ðone ærestan mæssepreost þe on Lundenbyrig wære B
23   on stafum] Ca, mid seaftum B
25   onfengon] onfeng Ca
26   gelydon and geleornedon] geleornodon Ca
    leorningcnihtum] Ca, leorningchintum B
29   Noðhelmes] Ca, Norðhelmes B
30   Eastseaxe] C, Eastseaxena B
31   Westseaxe] Ca, Westseaxena B   Eastengle] Ca, Eastenglena B
    Norðhymbre] Norðhymbra B, Norðanhumbre Ca
33   swiðost] Ca, 7 swiðost B
34   Danielis [...] ðæs *Some text may be missing here* B/Ca
36   Wihtland] Wiht ðæt igland Ca   he sende] he me sende Ca

Textual Notes

37   bysceop and Ceaddan ymb] bysceopes ymb B, bisceop and Ceaddan ymbe Ca
39   ea] Ca, eow B
41   segenum] sægene Ca   gesegnum] gesægene Ca
44   lifgendra] S, licgendra B, lifigendra Ca   getrywra þæt we] getwra þæt we B, getreowra we Ca
45   Norðhymbrum] Norðanhymbra Ca
47   gesegenum] gesægene Ca   þa ða] þa ðe þa Ca
48   And þæt ic] þæt ic Ca
49   on oðre] on oðre bec CWS   his dæda and] þa dæda Ca
50   nom] Ca, manna B
51   Lindesfarene ea] Lindesfarena Ca, Lindesfearona ea CWS
53   halsige] Ca, halsi B   þis elleshwær on oþere] ðis on oðre Ca

The Epilogue to the Bede

Text from B, pp. 482–4, with variants from C and Ca.

1   And] nd *with space left for large capital A* B   goda] duguþa C, dugoþa Ca
2   swylce] fremsum C, fremsumlice Ca
3   wylle] welan C (boxed fragment), willan Ca   symle] and symle C, and symble Ca
3–4   ætywan beforan þinre ansyne] *om.* C, ætywan beforan þinum ansyne Ca
5   Eac] ac *with space left for large capital E* B   ðam] *om.* CCa   tobecume] becyme CCa
6   cynnes] cynn/nes B *(across line-break)*
7   modes and] ge modes ge CCa   mid ðære] mid þa Ca
8   heora mægðum] heora mægðe B, hiora mægþum C, heora mægðum Ca
9   agyfan] agefe C   þe be] CCa, be þe B   oððe] CCa, oð B
10   hyhrum] heorum C, hyrum Ca   gemyndelice] gemyndewyrðe CCa   þancwyrðlice] þoncwyrþe C, þancwyrðe Ca
11   gelyfde] gelyfdon Ca   þingum] *om.* CCa
13   *From here onwards dark brown and red gilt lines alternate.*   Bidde] idde *with space left for large capital B* B
16   wynsumum] wynsum B

Commentary

The Old English *Dialogues*

The Prose Preface to the Dialogues

1 *geofendum Criste*: The present participle and noun here form a dative absolute construction (common in Latin but not in Old English) meaning literally 'Christ granting'. The phrase is perhaps modelled on the equivalent Latin phrase *Deo donante*, common in Anglo-Saxon charters. Whitelock (1979b), p. 90, notes a syntactic parallel in a vernacular charter of 883 which describes Ealdorman Æthelred of Mercia as 'inbryrdendre Godes gife gewelegod and gewlenced mid sume dæle Mercna rices' (by the instigation of God's grace, enriched and honoured with a portion of the Mercian kingdom).

2 *þurh haligra boca gesægene*: The holy books referred to here perhaps include Gregory's *Dialogi* itself (especially its prologue) and Gregory's *Cura pastoralis* (*Pastoral Care*), both of which encourage rulers to maintain a good spiritual and worldly balance in their lives.

3–5 Compare the last part of the Prose Preface to the *Pastoral Care* and the Prose Preface to the *Boethius*, where King Alfred is similarly presented as putting aside earthly concerns in order to spend time on spiritual matters.

6 The reference to *freondum* in the plural may suggest that more than one person contributed to the translation of the work, or at least that the Preface's author wished to convey the impression that it was a communal enterprise.

7 *þas æfterfylgendan lare*: Grammatically this phrase (the direct object of the verb *awriten*) could be either singular or plural.

The Verse Preface to the Dialogues

1 The manuscript text for this line is badly damaged, and has to be reconstructed on the basis of early Middle English glosses visible above where a now missing row of capitals would have been. The reconstruction here follows Yerkes (1980) except that it replaces his *teonð* (which reproduces the form of the gloss) with the more plausible Old English form *tyneð*, which is interpreted as the 3rd pers. pres. sg. form of *tynan* 'to close [a book]' (see also Irvine and Godden (2012), pp. 404 and 423).

198 Commentary

1, 2, 12   *me*: The book itself is the speaker in this Preface. The same technique is used in the Verse Preface to the *Pastoral Care* and (perhaps) the Verse Preface to the *Boethius*. See further the General Introduction above, pp. 6–7.

1   *geðance*: This word may be translated as either 'understanding' or 'thanks'.

12   *Wulfsige*: The manuscript reading *Wulfstan* is the result of an alteration from what was almost certainly *Wulfsige*, presumably referring to Bishop Wulfsige of Sherborne, who conceivably received the book's exemplar from Alfred (line 23) and then himself commissioned a copy. The alteration to Wulfstan may have been made either because the annotator thought that Bishop Wulfstan I of Worcester (Wulfstan the homilist) was responsible for commissioning this copy of the work or because the manuscript was being prepared at the time for the use of Wulfstan II of Worcester (St Wulfstan).

13   *aof*: A unique variant form of *ahof* (pret. sg. of *ahebban*).

14   *walden*: The form without a final *d* is unusual. Dobbie notes other examples in copies of two Kentish poems in British Library, Cotton MS Vespasian D. vi (mainly s. x^{ex}); see his note to line 9 of *The Kentish Hymn* (Dobbie (1942), p. 190).

16   *bideþ*: Although the more usual 3rd pers. pres. sg. form of *biddan* would be *biddeþ*, the variant form *bideþ* is found sporadically elsewhere in the Old English corpus.

20   The line's metrical irregularity (it lacks a half-line) is probably the result of textual corruption.

23   *bysene*: The word here seems to refer primarily to the physical 'exemplar' from which the book has been copied. It may also refer to the examples of spiritual life contained in the book Wulfsige received from Alfred (in which case line 23b can be translated as 'who gave him these examples', or 'who gave him an example of that practice'). Compare the previous uses of the word at lines 3 and 11. The linguistic ambiguity draws attention to the way the book is both material artefact and spiritual guide. See further S. Irvine (2015a), p. 152.

The Gregorian Preface to the Dialogues

1–9   *Her...cwæð*: This introductory passage is independent of Gregory's Latin version. The first sentence (lines 1–4), which appears only in MS O, has parallels with similar sentences introducing Books II–IV, edited as incipits below.

The Old English *Dialogues* 199

2 and 5 *apostolica(n)*: The epithet 'apostolic' refers to the way Gregory's work carries on that of the apostles, perhaps specifically here a reminder to an Anglo-Saxon audience of the impetus he provided for their conversion; see Dekker (2001), p. 37.

10–11 *Sume…ymbhogena*: The idea of being worn down by worldly responsibilities expressed here and later in the Preface is one that is echoed in the prose prefaces to the *Dialogues*, *Pastoral Care*, and *Boethius*.

11 *for*: C's reading *Ær* (where *æ* is curiously a rubricated capital) makes no sense in the context since Gregory is explaining how he is affected by his current papal responsibilities. My emendation assumes that the rubricator has misunderstood what is required here, and that the correct reading is *for* meaning 'on account of'.

18 *eagan minre heortan*: The metaphor is independent of the Latin original, which reads 'ante oculos' (before the eyes); see de Vogüé and Antin (1978–80), II.10.6–7. Wærferth's use of this metaphor to denote inner awareness may have prompted later uses; see M. Wilcox (2006), p. 186.

21 *min sunu Petrus*: Peter is regarded spiritually by Gregory as his son.

22 *mid freondlicre lufan*: The echoes of this phrase in *luflice ond freondlice* near the opening of the Prose Preface to the *Pastoral Care* may suggest that the relationship between Gregory and Peter is envisaged as similar to that between Alfred and Wærferth.

30 *gemyneð*: This verb reflects the use here (and elsewhere in the Gregorian Preface) of the *memoria* topos, a common prefatory convention. Similarities with the Prose Preface to the *Pastoral Care* can be seen in the phrases that Wærferth uses here to outline a process of thought sparked by memory, such as *þonne ic geþence þæt…, me ðinceð…* (44–5); *Ond þonne ic gemune…* (49); and *Ond eac me byð ful oft to gemynde becumen…* (63).

46–53 *Geseoh…ne mæg*: Gregory's concise seafaring metaphor (de Vogüé and Antin (1978–80), II.12.33–6) is expanded and rhetorically heightened by Wærferth, who turns it into two similes, and uses repetition (*on lefan scype/scipe*; *ic eom…mid þam*), word pairs (*asworette ic ond ageomorige*; *se ðoden ond se storm*), and alliteration (e.g. *on lefan scipe neah lond gelæteð*).

85–7 *Ic wolde…þæt þe ne þuhte to hefig, þæt þu ongunne hwæthwega gebrecan in þone wisdom þære recenesse*: Peter, who is Gregory's companion in the study of holy scripture (see line 23 above), here suggests an interruption in that pursuit so that Gregory can provide him with (equally inspiring) examples of virtuous people.

107 *in sumum...andgyte*: The word-for-word/sense-for-sense topos used here has echoes in the prose prefaces to the *Pastoral Care* and *Boethius*.

109 *ceorlisce þeawe*: An example of the use of the topos of *rusticitas* (the unpolished nature of the language of ordinary people).

Book I Explicit

2 *beneoþan*: The word implies this passage was copied from an exemplar in which the second book followed directly afterwards on the same page rather than on a new leaf as in O itself. C, which like O begins Book II on a new page, more aptly has *on þysan oþran leafe* (on this following leaf).

Book II Incipit

1 *yrnet, cymet*: The forms of these verbs in MS C are *yrneð* and *cymð*, in line with the usual inflection *-ð/-þ* for the 3rd pers. pres. sg. in Old English. The inflection *-t* used here in O is normally a non-West Saxon dialectal feature: it occurs commonly in the Kentish Glosses and occasionally in the (Mercian) Vespasian Psalter gloss.

2 *þam halgan gaste forgifendum*: Latinate dative absolute construction.

3 *þa ofergyldan weleras*: On the image of gilded lips, see p. 35 above.

4 *Crysosthomas*: The Greek word for 'golden mouth', and a common epithet for orators, perhaps after John Chrysostom, an early Christian church father (AD 347–407). There was, however, no Greek (nor Roman) tradition of calling Gregory 'golden-mouthed'; see Sims-Williams (1990), pp. 186–7.

5 *se onliht ond geþæned*: *se* is the 3rd pers. pres. subj. sg. of the verb *beon* (MS C has *sy*). The incongruous combination of singular verb and plural subject (*þa þoncas*) may be an example of an author 'committ[ing] himself to a singular verb before formulating the actual grammatical subject' (Mitchell (1987), I.637 (§1523)).

Book II Explicit

1 *þisse, seo þridde*: These forms are feminine because the feminine noun *boc* is understood.

1 *mid haligra wera wundrum*: Although O's reading with *halgum* makes sense ('with the holy miracles of men'), analogy with examples elsewhere in the work suggests that C's reading is correct ('with the miracles of holy men').

Book III Incipit

1 *neorxnawonglican*: Wærferth refers explicitly here to the four rivers flowing out of Paradise (Genesis 2:10–14). For further implications of the four rivers of Paradise, see Dekker (2001), p. 39.
3 *þone Romane… Os Aureum nemniað*: See above the incipit of Book II of the *Dialogues*, Commentary, line 4.

Book IV Incipit

3–4 *sawul… æfter þam gedale þæs lichaman*: The separation of the body and soul was a topic of much interest to authors of the period, who frequently addressed it in both prose (such as in the *Soliloquies* and the *Boethius* as well as numerous homilies) and verse (as in the two Old English *Soul and Body* poems).

The Old English *Pastoral Care*

The Prose Preface to the Pastoral Care

1 That the instruction given here was carried out is attested by the Worcester provenance of various notes and glosses added to the manuscript. Wærferth was Bishop of Worcester from *c*.872 to *c*.915, and translated Gregory's *Dialogi* into Old English. In line 1, a verb of motion is implied after *sceal*; on the lack of an infinitive with 'modal' auxiliaries in Old English, see Mitchell (1987), I.418–21 (§§1000–8).
3 *hate*: This form (cf. *hateð* in the previous line) signals the shift from third to first person, and thus from a formal to more personal tone.
11 *don*: Although the infinitive *don* is not strictly required in this context, the reading of other manuscripts is accepted here since the full use of **sculan* 'to owe' is rare in works associated with Alfred (Schreiber (2003), p. 460).
11 Alfred's own recruitment of scholars from abroad is evidenced in the naming of Grimbald and John later in the preface (line 63).
13 *Swæ clæne hio wæs oðfeallenu*: The antecedent of *hio* is the noun *lar*. The past participle *oðfeallenu* is declined nom. sg. fem. strong, agreeing with the subject. On the decline of learning in England in the decades leading up to Alfred's reign, see the General Introduction, p. 8.
14 *behionan Humbre*: The Humber is a large tidal estuary in the north-east of England.

202 Commentary

23 *witu...for ðisse worulde*: The 'worldly punishments' are probably the Scandinavian invasions to which the English kingdoms had been intermittently subjected over many years. The destruction caused by these invasions is described in the subsequent paragraph.

23 *hit*: The antecedent is *wisdom*. Here, as with *hit* in line 41 below, natural gender is prioritized over grammatical gender (but contrast *hio* in line 13 above).

26 *Đa ic ða ðis eall gemunde*: This phrase (with slight variations) occurs several times in the Preface, acting as a kind of refrain or structuring device.

31 *Swelce hie cwæden*: A different voice (that of previous clerics) is dramatized for rhetorical effect. A similar device is used at line 39 below, where a dialogue is set up between Alfred and himself.

33 *swæð*: The 'track' which can be seen but not followed may be a pun on writing on the page, implying that even if it can be seen it is not necessarily understood. The word *swæð* is also used to denote writing in Exeter Book Riddle 51, line 3 *swaþu* (Krapp and Dobbie (1936), p. 206).

33 On the closure of the hypothetical speech before *Ond forðæm* rather than at the end of the paragraph, see Shippey (1979).

43 *æ*: 'The law' is the law of Moses, traditionally referring to the Pentateuch (the first five books of the Hebrew Bible).

45 *ealle oðre bec*: This probably refers to the other books of the Bible.

48 *suma bec*: This has traditionally been assumed to refer to books such as Gregory's *Cura pastoralis*, whose translation this preface precedes. Anlezark (2017) argues that the phrase refers exclusively to books of the Bible.

56 *hieran hade*: 'A higher order' refers to a higher ecclesiastical order, and possibly also a higher secular office; see Godden (2002b).

61 *hwilum word be worde, hwilum andgit of andgiete*: This reflects a common prefatory trope in the Latin tradition (see the General Introduction). Its use in this preface may perhaps have been prompted specifically by Wærferth's translation of Gregory's Prologue to the *Dialogi*, where the terms *word* and *andgyt* are similarly juxtaposed (see above the Gregorian Preface to the *Dialogues*, line 107).

62–3 *Plegmunde...Assere...Grimbolde...Iohanne*: Plegmund was Archbishop of Canterbury from 890 to 903; Asser was Bishop of St David's and Alfred's biographer; Grimbald came to England from the monastery of St Bertin at St Omer, Flanders, in *c.*886; John came to England from Saxony in northern Germany.

67 *æstel*: The meaning of the word is unknown, but it probably refers to a book-pointer, perhaps similar in form to the Alfred Jewel (now held in the

Ashmolean Museum), and others such as the Bowleaze Cove, Minster Lovell, and Warminster jewels, exquisite decorated gilt objects with sockets that would originally have had wooden sticks or leather strips attached to them. The *æstel* combines imaginatively the ideas of wealth and wisdom that inform the Preface.

67   *mancessa*: A *mancus* was a weight of gold, equivalent in value to 30 silver pence.

70–1   *hie...hie...hio*: The first *hie* (nom. pl.) refers to the book and pointer; the second *hie* (acc. pl. or acc. sg. fem.) refers either to the book and pointer or to the book alone; *hio* (nom. sg. fem.) refers to the book.

The Verse Preface to the Pastoral Care

1   *ærendgewrit*: The work is presumably called a 'letter' or 'message' because the original was addressed by Gregory to a fellow bishop John.

1   *Agustinus*: Augustine of Canterbury led a mission from Rome to Britain in AD 597, thus initiating the process of conversion. The poem seems to imply that a copy of Gregory's *Pastoral Care* (*Cura pastoralis* in Latin) came with him at that time.

6   *Gregorius*: Gregory the Great, Pope Gregory I from 590 to 604, was the author of the *Pastoral Care*, the source for the Old English translation. Gregory is not mentioned by name in the Prose Preface.

11–12 *min...me*: The use of the first-person voice for the book or text is a convention in Old English verse prefaces. See above pp. 64–5, and the General Introduction, pp. 6–7.

14   *bisene*: The word, though much more common in prose than in verse (Discenza (2001), p. 628), is also used three times in the Verse Preface to the *Dialogues*.

14–16 In highlighting the inability of some bishops to read Latin, the Verse Preface offers a different perspective at its close from the Prose Preface, which instead extols the presence of learned bishops nearly everywhere.

The Gregorian Preface to the Pastoral Care

1   *Þu leofusta broður*: Like the Prose Preface preceding it, the Gregorian Preface (as in its Latin source) is conceived as a letter addressed to a specific recipient. No indication is given, however, as to who is addressing whom in the Old English version, which begins immediately after the list of chapter titles in the *Pastoral Care*. The effect is to elide the voices of Alfred and Gregory.

8–10 *Nu ic wilnige…on feower*: Bately (1988), p. 127, notes the changes of detail from the source in this passage, 'with the order of the sentence reversed, Gregory's simile foregrounded, and effective use of alliteration'.

8–9 *suæ suæ on sume hlædre*: The image of the ladder represents an addition by the Old English translator, building on the 'step by step' metaphor of the Latin source (*quibusdam passibus*, Judic et al. (1992), I.124). The suggestion that the treatise should eventually stand firmly on the base of the mind that learns it is also the Old English author's own.

23 *ðyncet*: The 3rd pers. sg. pres. indic. usually ends in *-ð/-þ* in Old English. The ending *-t* is normally a non-West Saxon dialectal feature: it occurs commonly in the Kentish Glosses and occasionally in the (Mercian) Vespasian Psalter gloss. Amongst the manuscripts of the *Pastoral Care*, it occurs only in H (Campbell (1959), p. 301; Schreiber (2003), p. 107).

25–6 *From ðære dura selfre ðisse bec, ðæt is from onginne ðisse spræce*: The Old English author reorders the Latin source to present 'the beginning of this discourse' as a definition of 'the door of this book'.

The Gregorian Epilogue to the Pastoral Care

1 *Iohannes*: The name of the addressee John, referring probably to John, Bishop of Ravenna, is added independently of the Gregorian source here (perhaps from a gloss, though the name is also supplied at the opening of the Latin work). In two manuscripts (T and U), an addition to the text erroneously identifies this John as *Ælfredes cynges mæssepreost*, that is, John, the Old Saxon, who is mentioned in both the Prose Preface and chapter 78 of Asser's *Life of King Alfred* (Stevenson (1959), p. 63; trans. Keynes and Lapidge (1983), p. 93; Schreiber (2003), p. 622). The voice here seems to have been interpreted as Alfred's rather than Gregory's, 'not unreasonably given the invisibility of Gregory as author so far' (Godden (2011), p. 465).

4–5 Gregory's comparison between the conflicts created through an earthly existence and a journey on a ship being buffeted round on a turbulent sea is a conventional topos (Curtius (1953), p. 130). The *scip modes* (ship of the mind) metaphor is independently added in the Old English, drawing perhaps on its use in the prologue to Gregory's *Dialogi* and its Old English version; see M. Wilcox (2006), p. 193.

The Verse Epilogue to the Pastoral Care

1–8 Cf. John 7:38–9 (which quotes then comments on Christ's words): '"He who believes in me, as the scripture said, rivers of living water will flow from his breast." This however he said concerning the spirit.'

13–14 The idea of guarding wisdom with one's lips is expressed in similar terms in the Old English *Metrical Psalms* 140:4: 'þæt on welerum wisdom healde' (to guard wisdom on my lips) (O'Neill (2016), p. 572).

23 *Gregorius*: The association between Gregory and the stream of wisdom recalls the extended incipits of the four books of the *Dialogues* (Godden (2011), pp. 467–88).

24 *to durum iowrum*: The image of doors as an entry point for wisdom recalls the last sentence of the Gregorian Preface to the *Pastoral Care*, where the author explains that 'the very door of this book' is 'the beginning of this discourse' (lines 25–6), itself an adaptation of the Latin 'loquutionis nostrae ianua' (the door of our discourse) in the Gregorian source (Judic et al. (1992), I.126).

25–30 These lines were probably inspired by John 4:7–26, the story of the meeting between a Samaritan woman and Christ at Jacob's well. This is acknowledged by a tenth-century annotator of MS Hatton 20, who cites John 4:13–14 in a note following the epilogue in that copy.

The Old English *Boethius* (Prose and Prosimetrical Versions)

The Prose Preface to the Boethius

2–4 On the overlaps in wording here with the Prose Preface to the *Pastoral Care*, lines 59, 61, and 65, see above pp. 94–5. On the trope of 'word for word' and 'sense for sense', and the afflictions endured by Alfred, see the General Introduction, p. 6 and n. 18, and p. 8 respectively.

6 *on þa ricu*: The use of plural forms in this phrase probably reflects the way in which Alfred, initially king of Wessex alone, acquired during his reign control of all of England outside the Danelaw. In the Prose Preface to the *Pastoral Care* Alfred uses the singular form of *rice* (*ða ða ic to rice feng* 'when I succeeded to the kingdom', line 18), referring specifically to Wessex.

8 *swa swa heo nu gedon is*: This repeats a phrase used earlier in the Prose Preface (line 2). The first time it is used, the phrase 'as it is now done' refers to a prose version of the work; the second time it seems to refer to a version containing poetry (incongruous since the Prose Preface occurs in a manuscript containing only the prose version of the work). On the possibility that the sentence in the Preface referring to the versification is a later interpolation, see above p. 94.

10 The ambiguous pronouns can be understood to mean: 'and not blame him [Alfred] if he [the reader] understand it more correctly than he [Alfred] could'.

The Verse Preface to the Boethius

1   *us*: This first-person plural pronoun probably refers to the audience listening to the work.

1   *ealdspell*: Grammatically this noun could be either singular or plural.

2   *cræft*: This word carries a rich resonance from its wide range of meanings in the *Boethius* and elsewhere in the Alfredian writings, encompassing skill, strength, and virtue: see Clemoes (1992); Discenza (1997) and (2005), ch. 4.

3   *leoðwyrhta*: nominative singular, in apposition to *cyning*.

4   *leoð spellode*: The phrase is a curious one, since elsewhere in the *Boethius* a distinction is maintained between reciting verse (for which the verb *singan* is used) and speaking prose (for which the verb *spellian* is used). The use of *leoð* with *spellian* may indicate that the versifier was not the author of the prose version of the *Boethius*. See also S. Irvine (2015a), p. 163, and (2018), pp. 7–8 and n. 20.

5   *mislice cwidas*: This ambiguous phrase perhaps alludes to the different discourses of prose and verse (Frantzen (2003), p. 134), and if so would represent an acknowledgement on the poet's part of the prosimetrical nature of the work that follows.

6   *ælinge*: This is the only use of this word as a noun in the Old English corpus (it appears three times elsewhere as an adjective). See *DOE* 'ælenge' (noun); O'Brien O'Keeffe (2005), pp. 31–4; and Discenza (2008), p. 76 n. 61.

8   *ic*: The voice of the Preface shifts here into the first-person singular. This may be the voice of the book; other possibilities are the supposed author Alfred, or someone imagined to be reciting the poetry to an audience. See further pp. 95–6 above.

The Prose Vita *of the* Boethius

1–4   *On ðære tide…in anwald gerehton*: The connection made here between Rædgota (Radagaisus) and Alaric by the Old English author is independent of the extant Latin *vitae* and is historically unfounded. The two were leaders of quite distinct Gothic armies: Radagaisus was defeated in battle and killed in AD 406; Alaric, though he invaded Italy at around the same time, succeeded in sacking Rome in 409 but died in further fighting a year or so later. A tradition that the two commanders were allies against Rome, which also seems to be reflected in the Old English *Orosius*, may have been circulating at the time.

1   *Gotan of Sciððiu mægðe*: The Goths were a nomadic people who had settled in various places including Scythia, an area that covered Central Asia and parts of Eastern Europe.

4–5 *æfter þam foresprecenan cyningum Þeodric feng to þam ilcan rice*: The invasion of Italy by the Ostrogothic leader Theoderic in AD 488 is also erroneously presented by the Old English author as linked to these earlier invasions. Theoderic went on to rule Italy until his death in 526.

5 *Amulinga*: This refers to the descent which Theoderic claimed from a legendary king of the Goths called Amal. The information is independent of the extant Latin *vitae*.

6 *on þam Arrianiscan gedwolan*: The Goths' belief in the heretical doctrine of the third-century priest Arius, who denied that Christ and God were of the same substance, distinguished them from the orthodoxy of Rome.

9–10 *he Iohannes þone papan het ofslean*: Although there is a tradition that Pope John died after being imprisoned by Theoderic, the report that he ordered him to be killed seems to be independent from the *vitae* and other sources.

11 *sum consul þæt we heretoha hatað*: Boethius's consulship, which he held in AD 510, was considerably earlier than the crisis that led to his exile and death. The Old English author is probably following the Latin *vitae*, since they too highlight his role as consul (presumably because it was wrongly viewed as a long-term rather than one-year office) instead of the more important post of Master of the Offices which he held from 522 or 523 onwards.

15–17 *Þa ongan he smeagan…aferran mihte*: Like the Latin *vitae*, but unlike Boethius himself, the Old English author unambiguously implicates Boethius in the plot to overthrow Theoderic, attributing to him motives which would have had positive resonances for an Anglo-Saxon audience (the restoration of a former dynastic line of rulers). The idea of mulling something over in one's mind also foreshadows the dialogue between Mind and Wisdom that follows.

23–8 *Þa hit ða gelomp…þus singend cwæð*: This passage describing Boethius' sorrow and despair does not correspond to anything in the *vitae*, and is apparently inferred from what follows (which is a rendering of the opening metre of *De consolatione Philosophiae*).

The Verse Vita *of the* Boethius

7 (and 19) *Rædgod and Aleric*: On the historical inaccuracy of merging the two leaders and their armies, see the Prose *Vita*, Commentary, lines 1–4.

13 *swua*: The spelling *wu* for *w*, uncommon in Old English, recurs in *wuolde* (line 38).

20 *fleah casere*: The emperor referred to here is Honorius, who was in fact based in Ravenna at this time. The versifier seems to have inferred Honorius' flight from Rome (wrongly) from the prose version; see Godden (2002a).

27 *gif hi leodfruman læstan dorsten*: The pronoun *hi* refers to the Greeks, whom the warriors hope will support the leader of the people (*leodfruman*), that is, the emperor who fled from Rome.

29 *wintra*: The noun *winter* (genitive plural *wintra*), literally 'winter', is often used to denote the period of one year in Old English.

42–3 *Het Iohannes, godne papan, | heafde beheawon*: The detail that Pope John was beheaded may be an imaginative interpretation of the prose source by the versifier, though an unknown source cannot be ruled out.

69 *Ðeodric Amuling*: Unlike the prose, the verse postpones identifying Theoderic as an Amuling (descendant of Amal) until near the end of the account, perhaps because it was a detail the versifier either did not understand or considered relatively tangential.

83 *Cleopode to Drihtne*: The detail that Boethius directs his song to the Lord is the versifier's own, and points to a greater degree of Christianisation than in the prose.

The Epilogue to the Boethius

2 *wyrhta and wealdend ealra gesceafta*: The phrase is characteristic of Wulfstan and perhaps derives from his writings; on this parallel and the one with Ælfric noted below, see Bredehoft (2009), pp. 175–8.

13 *fulan galnysse*: This collocation is otherwise found only in Ælfric's works.

21–2 The unusual threefold repetition of *a* (always) is here lineated across two lines for the purposes of alliterative linkage; see Bredehoft (2009), p. 214.

The Old English *Soliloquies*

The Preface to the Soliloquies

1–21 The Preface presents an extended metaphor of gathering wood from the forest to build houses to describe the process of gathering excerpts from Latin authors to construct one's own literary works (see above p. 125 for its link to the *silvae* tradition). The metaphor alludes to the grammatical idea of *compilatio* (M. Irvine (1994), pp. 435–7); the choice of this metaphor rather than the more standard image of gathering flowers (which is used elsewhere in the *Soliloquies*) or a bee gathering honey from flowers may, as Gatch suggests, reflect the author's focus here on the use to which the materials are put rather than the act of gathering itself (Gatch (1986), pp. 207–8). For the image of building used as a metaphor for spiritual improvement, compare 'wisdom timbran' and 'timbrian þæt hus his modes' in the *Boethius* (Godden and Irvine (2009), I.264 (B Text, chs. 12.6 and 12.16)), and 'timbran eaðmodnesse' in the *Pastoral Care* (Sweet (1871), p. 443.30); see further S. Irvine (2005), pp. 179–80; for other analogues, see Treschow (2007), pp. 260–1.

1 Despite the presence of an ornamental capital 'G' on *Gaderode*, the use of *þonne* in the opening phrase would seem to indicate that some material is missing at the beginning of the Preface.

2 *tola*: Compare the *Boethius* where, in another sustained metaphor, tools are used to denote the resources which a king needs to rule with: Godden and Irvine (2009), I.277–8 (B Text, ch. 17.1–25).

3–8 *treowo, wude, treowo, wuda*. Compare the account of Hercules's defeat of the Hydra in the *Boethius*, where an ingenious use of wood indicates a sharp intellect: Godden and Irvine (2009), I.361 (B Text, ch. 39.89–98); S. Irvine (2003), p. 176.

4 *naþer*: Since 'neither' doesn't fit well with the context here, the word (abbreviated in the manuscript) is conceivably an error for *nahwær* 'never'.

4–6 *ham*: The word is repeated three times, and perhaps emphasized further through the pattern of juxtaposing it with words beginning with 'b': *byrðene ham, ham brengan*, and *ham beþorfte*. These allusions to an earthly home anticipate the idea of an eternal home, expressed three times later in this preface (twice in the singular, *þam ecan hame*, and once in the plural, *þara ecena hama*).

11 *þær...mid mæge oneardian*: The word *mid* can be construed either as an adverb, linked to *þær* and meaning 'amongst those, therein', with *mæge* as the present subjunctive singular of the verb *magan* 'may', or as a preposition, with *mæge* as the dative singular of the noun *mæg* 'wife' or 'kinsman'. The former interpretation is preferred here.

15–16 By citing the names of the saints Augustine, Gregory, and Jerome, the Old English author brings to bear their implicit authority as Fathers of the Church on his own literary enterprise. The main source for this work is Augustine's *Soliloquia*; other sources include Augustine's *De videndo Deo* (*On Seeing God*), and writings by Gregory, Boethius, and Julian of Toledo (see p. 122 above).

18 *modes eagan*: A similar metaphor is used in the Gregorian Preface to the *Dialogues* (*þa eagan minre heortan*, lines 17–18), where it is independent of the Latin source. The idea of 'the eyes of the mind' recurs in a number of Alfredian works; see M. Wilcox (2006).

22–30 No source has been identified for the landlord-tenant metaphor used here.

22–7 The author brings to bear a distinction between *lænland* (loan-land) and *bocland* (bookland). *Bocland* is 'land held by charter in hereditary possession' (see *DOE* 'bocland'), as opposed to *lænland* or *folcland* (land held in unchartered tenure). See also Keynes and Lapidge (1983), pp. 308–9 nn. 23–4; Williams (2014), pp. 282–3. The distinction develops the contrast between transient and eternal dwellings introduced earlier in the preface.

28 *gifola* (benefactor): This word is a *hapax legomenon* (see *DOE* 'gyfola, gifola') and was perhaps unfamiliar to the scribe who mistakenly writes *gidfola*. The related adjective *gifol* (generous), also rare, is used only in works associated with Alfred (twice in the *Pastoral Care* and once in the *Boethius*) except for one Kentish gloss; see *DOE* 'gyfol, gifol', and Smith (2012), p. 133.

30 *nytwyrde* (useful): The word reflects a common theme of Alfredian writings. It recurs elsewhere in this work and also in the *Pastoral Care* (twelve times) and in the *Boethius* (four times). See Heuchan (2007), p. 10.

31 *twa bec*: The third book added in the Old English version is not mentioned here.

33 *hu hys gesceadwisnes answarode hys mode*: The preface anticipates here a dialogue between Augustine's reason (*gesceadwisnes*) and his mind (*mod*); the latter is called A(u)gustinus and *ic* within the dialogue itself. In the *Boethius*, the figure of Wisdom (*wisdom*) is sometimes referred to as Reason (*gesceadwisnes*). The two works present their dialogues in similar ways: in both, Reason (or Wisdom) answers Mind, puts its doubts to rest, and explains things it does not understand.

Book I Explicit

1 The *blostma* (blossom, flower) image, used in this explicit and in the incipits of Books II and III, was a traditional metaphor for gathering excerpts from great writers of the past. See further the section on the incipits and explicits in the Introduction above.

Book III Incipit

1 *nu heft þa*: emended by earlier editors to '[þu] hef[s]t þa' (as in Carnicelli (1969), p. 92). This emendation seems dubious, given the odd phrasing of 'you have ended the sayings'. If left unemended, the passage resembles an incipit (with 'heft' perhaps a spelling of 3rd pers. pres. sg. *hefð*, used in error for the plural form). It has lexical overlaps with incipits and explicits elsewhere in the work, particularly with the final explicit ('cwydas', 'geendod',

'bocum', and 'alese'). It seems possible that this material originated at some stage as an incipit, and that the current wording, including the initial '[Ð]a cwæð ic', may be linked in some way to the generally chaotic state of Book III.

Book III Explicit

1–2 This reconstruction of the final explicit follows Kiernan (1996), p. 114, and Godden (2003), pp. 187–8. Other recent reconstructions include that adopted by Carnicelli (1969): 'þe we hatað on [Ledene *de uidendo deo* and on Englisc *be godes ansyne*]' (based on the prominent mention of the work *De videndo Deo* towards the end of Book II), and that used in Lockett (2022a), pp. 302–3: 'þe we hatað on leden *Liber manualis* oððe *Enchiridion*, þæt ys on englisc *Handboc*' ([from the book] that we call in Latin *Liber manualis* or *Enchiridion*, which is *Handbook* in English). Lockett's reconstruction is based on the presentation of Alfred in the final explicit as a compiler who 'selected' the sayings, which, she suggests, opens up the possibility that the translator was someone else who thought he was translating the handbook of excerpts that Alfred compiled known as *Enchiridion* (see pp. 122–3 above). Since Book III seems, however, to be designed as a continuation of the first two books—it maintains the dialogue between Augustine and Reason, for example—the simpler conjecture that this explicit refers to the work as a whole rather than just Book III is accepted here.

The *Laws* of Alfred

The Preface to the Laws *of Alfred*

1   Based on Exod. 20:1–2.
1.1 Based on Exod. 20:3. §§1–10 correspond to the ten commandments.
2   Based on Exod. 20:7. The preposition *wið* here means 'to, towards'.
3   Based on Exod. 20:8, 20:9, 20:11.
4   Based on Exod. 20:12.
5   Based on Exod. 20:13.
6   Based on Exod. 20:14. The literal meaning of the text is 'Do not lie secretly'.
7   Based on Exod. 20:15.
8   Based on Exod. 20:16.
9   Based on Exod. 20:17.
10   Based on Exod. 20:23.

11 Based on Exod. 21:2–6. The adaptation of the phrase 'servum hebraeum' (Hebrew servant) in Exod. 21:2 to *Cristenne þeow* (Christian slave) makes the Old English text more relevant to its contemporary readers.

12 Based on Exod. 21:7–11. In this section the Old English text seems to be altered from its source to bring the Mosaic law closer to the norms of late ninth-century England in relation to the question of marriage between free persons and slaves, particularly in its statement that the woman, when purchased by a free man, is 'not as much of a slave as other slaves', and in more overtly designating her as the recipient of the dowry than in the source. See further Jurasinski (2012).

12 *Ðeah hwa gebycgge his dohtor on þeowenne*: In keeping with its biblical source, this clause is translated here as 'If anyone should sell his daughter as a slave'. Although *gebicgan/gebycgan* normally means 'to buy' in Old English, it does occur elsewhere with the meaning 'to sell' (see *DOE* 'gebicgan' B.1. and B.2.). For an alternative translation as 'Though anyone should buy his [the slave's] daughter in servitude', see Jurasinski (2012), pp. 57–8; Jurasinski and Oliver (2021), p. 235.

12 *on elðeodig folc*: This repeated phrase renders 'populo...alieno' (Exod. 21:8), and is usually interpreted as referring to a 'foreign people' (see, for example, *DOE* 'elþeodig'), with the implication that the woman is not to be sold abroad or to people from abroad, but may be let free amongst such people. Pelteret (1995) notes that the repetition is 'puzzling, since Ine, §11 had prohibited the sale of anyone across the sea and the release of a free-born slave to a foreign people has no sanction in Exodus 21:8' (p. 83), and suggests that it may have been accidental. Jurasinski (2012), pp. 62–3, suggests that *folc* carries the meaning of household here, and the prohibition is on selling her to another household: the other use of *elðeodige* in the Preface to the *Laws* of Alfred, however, pairs it with *utan cumene* (see §33). In psalters it can be used with the sense of 'Gentiles, heathens' (*DOE* 'elþeodig' 2.a.i.), and the word may carry some of that resonance in the context of the Mosaic law too.

12 *do hiere gyfta*: For the sense 'arrange a wedding', see *DOE* 'gyft, gift' 3a.i.a.

13 Based on Exod. 21:12–14. The outline of three kinds of unintentional homicide (necessary, unwilling, and unwitting) is independent of the biblical source; see further p. 149 above.

13 *swelte se deaðe*: This recurring phrase, rendered as 'let him be put to death', literally translates as 'may he die / let him die by death' (*swelte* pres. subj. sg.; *deaðe* instr. sg.), itself a close translation of the Vulgate's *morte moriatur* (let him die by means of death).

14 Based on Exod. 21:15.
15 Based on Exod. 21:16–17. The Mosaic law is qualified to specify that only someone 'convicted' for such an abduction should be put to death.
16 Based on Exod. 21:18–19. The Old English version seems to require a more active input by the perpetrator, who must himself obtain a doctor for the victim and carry out his work for him until he is able to do it himself. See further Jurasinski and Oliver (2021), p. 239.
17 Based on Exod. 21:20–1. There are a number of changes from the source (Jurasinski (2010), pp. 35–8). The stipulation that the blow must be from a rod is omitted. The period during which the perpetrator is guilty of the victim's death is extended from immediately (implied by *in manibus eius*, 'in his hands') to any time on the same day. The phrase 'let the guilt rest on him' (referring to the perpetrator) only implies rather than specifies that he will be punished. The time after which the perpetrator is considered not to be guilty is increased from one/two days to two/three days. Finally, where the Mosaic law pronounces as guiltless the perpetrator whose victim does not die for two or three days, the Old English code leaves his status more ambiguous: he is 'not entirely so guilty' as he would have been if death had been the same day. Jurasinski (2015), p. 58, notes that, unlike in Exodus, 'it is the interior condition of the master that is at issue in this text'.
18 Based on Exod. 21:22–3. Note that the role of the woman's husband in imposing any punishment is omitted in the *Laws*.
19 Based on Exod. 21:24–5. The forms of the nouns make it difficult to determine whether the Old English writer has in mind singular or plural, and accusative or dative cases.
20 Based on Exod. 21:26–7.
21 Based on Exod. 21:28–32. The use of *scillingas* rather than 'shekels' makes the text more applicable to early medieval England. Liebermann (1908–10), p. 29, calls this 'a thoughtless English adaptation, as introducing a price far too low'.
22 Based on Exod. 21:33–4.
23 Based on Exod. 21:35–6.
24 Based on Exod. 22:1. The second sentence relating to those with nothing to give is moved here from Exod. 22:3. On the possibility that the *Liber ex lege Moysi* was also a source, see Jurasinski and Oliver (2021), p. 247.
25 Based on Exod. 22:2–4. Alfred's code restricts the time frame for the burglary to night-time, and inserts a get-out clause in cases of self-defence ('buton he nieddæda wære'). On the implications of these changes for the

possible sources of Alfred's code, see Wormald (1999), pp. 419–20; Carella (2005), pp. 94–7.

26 Based on Exod. 22:5.

27 Based on Exod. 22:6. BT translates *ryt* as 'rough growth on land (?)'. This meaning implies (in line with the Vulgate) that amends must be made for any crops the fire damages in the course of burning the stubble. The reading *ryht* in MS H, accepted by Thorpe, seems less convincing: it would presumably imply that although a fire were kindled to burn on a straight course it might deviate from that course and damage crops in doing so. Lambarde's reading *ryp* (reaping, harvest) is similarly unpersuasive; for a summary of 'the Lambarde problem' (the contentious debate over whether Lambarde had access to a now lost manuscript or manuscripts for his 1568 edition), see Wormald (1999), pp. 260–2.

28 Based on Exod. 22:7–14. On the 'marked differences' between the Old English and the Latin original here, see Wormald (1999), p. 420; Jurasinski and Oliver (2021), p. 251.

29 Based on Exod. 22:16–17.

30 Based on Exod. 22:18. On this expansion of the Latin original, see pp. 148–9 above.

31 Based on Exod. 22:19.

32 Based on Exod. 22:20.

33 Based on Exod. 22:21.

34 Based on Exod. 22:22–3.

35 Based on Exod. 22:25.

36 Based on Exod. 22:26–7.

37 Based on Exod. 22:28.

38 Based on Exod. 22:29–30.

38 *teoðan sceattas* (tithes): The phrase refers to the one-tenth of annual income that had to be paid as a tax to the church.

38 *frumripan gongendes and weaxendes*: The literal meaning is 'first fruits of [anything] walking and [anything] growing'; *DOE* 'gangan' I.1.c.iv. translates it as 'first fruits of livestock and crops'.

39 Based on Exod. 22:31.

40 Based on Exod. 23:1.

41 Based on Exod. 23:2.

42 Based on Exod. 23:4.

43 Based on Exod. 23:6. The Latin source is expanded considerably for purposes of clarity.

44 Based on Exod. 23:7.

45 Based on Exod. 23:7.
46 Based on Exod. 23:8.
47 Based on Exod. 23:9.
48 Based on Exod. 23:13.
49 The text here links the Mosaic laws to the New Testament, through a rendering of Christ's statement from the Sermon of the Mount that he had come not to abolish the law but to fulfil it (Matt. 5:17). On the possibility that 'mid eallum godum' might refer to the 'bebodu' (commandments), meaning that Christ intended to fulfil the law by adding new laws implicit in the Mosaic laws, see Jurasinski and Oliver (2021), p. 263.
49.1 Based on Acts 15:22.
49.2 Based on Acts 15:23.
49.3–5 These sections render into Old English the letter sent by the apostles to the Gentiles of Antioch, Syria, and Cilicia (Acts 15:23–9). Christ's Golden Rule (Matt. 7:12) is introduced in its negative form at the end of §49.5, where it derives from Acts 15:29 in the Western text of the New Testament (Keynes and Lapidge (1983), p. 163).
49.6 In this section the Golden Rule is discussed in the context of law-giving.
49.7–8 The Preface to the *Laws* here surveys the history of law-giving from the early Christian period onwards, through synods (ecclesiastical assemblies) held world-wide, including in England. Past precedents of law-giving are used as a way of investing Alfred's law code with unimpeachable authority.
49.7 The account of synods in the first sentence of this paragraph may, as Keynes and Lapidge suggest, be influenced by the letter of Fulco, Archbishop of Rheims, to King Alfred: see Keynes and Lapidge (1983), p. 305, and, for a translation of the relevant passage of the letter, p. 184.
49.7 *swa hine*: The phrasing here is ambiguous; it seems to mean either that everyone should love his lord as he loves Christ, or that everyone should love his lord as much as he loves himself (compare the injunction in Matt. 22:39 that one should love one's neighbour as much as oneself). The latter is more plausible; see further Jurasinski and Oliver (2021), p. 271.
49.9–10 The first-person voice of the king invests the *Laws* with royal authority, on top of the religious and historical authority conveyed hitherto. The statement that Alfred 'þas togædere gegaderode' recalls the opening of the Preface to the *Soliloquies*, and the mention of collaboration with advisers is reminiscent of the Prose Preface to the *Pastoral Care*.
49.9 Of the three sets of laws which Alfred mentions consulting by name (Ine's, Offa's, and Æthelberht's), Ine's survives in the form in which it is appended to Alfred's, and Æthelberht's survives independently. Offa's

216 Commentary

code does not survive as an independent document. On possible links between the laws of Offa and a capitulary incorporated in the report of legates to Pope Hadrian about their activities in England in AD 786 (known as the Legatine Capitulary), see Wormald (1977), p. 112 n. 40, (1991), (1999), pp. 106–7; Keynes and Lapidge (1983), pp. 305–6; and Jurasinski and Oliver (2021), pp. 276–8.

49.9 *Forðam...forðam*: A correlative clause in which the first *forðam* does not need to be translated and the second can be translated as 'because'.

The Old English *Bede*

The Preface to the Bede

1 *sende gretan* (sent to be greeted): The construction with *sendan* followed by an infinitive in a passive accusative-infinitive construction is highly unusual in Old English (Waite (2015), p. 68). It is possible that it represents an attempt by the author of the preface to emulate the opening of the Prose Preface to the *Pastoral Care*, with *sende* replacing the more usual *hate* 'command' to take account of Bede's subordinate relationship to the king. Ca presents a variant reading in its addition of 'and halettan' (and [sent] to be saluted) before 'Ceolwulf'. Although this may have been part of the original text of the preface, it is also possible, as suggested by Frederick Klaeber (1902), p. 262, and the Smiths (in their 1722 edition) respectively, that it was either a later addition or a misrendering of a form *hæleþan* (heroic) derived from the noun *hæleþ*. See also Waite (2015), pp. 48 and 68.

2 *Ceoluulf*: King of Northumbria for most of the period from AD 729 to 737. He abdicated in 737 and entered the monastery at Lindisfarne.

2–3 *be Angelðeode and Seaxum*: The Angles and Saxons were two of the Germanic peoples who migrated to Britain and became the Anglo-Saxons.

4 *stowa* (religious houses): Although the word *stow* can mean 'place' in a general sense, the context here suggests it refers more specifically to religious houses or monasteries. The mention of *stowa* is an addition to the source.

4 *and to læranne*: This reference to teaching is an addition to the source.

7–8 *se ðe hit gehireþ, he onhireð þam* (whoever hears it imitates that): The idea of imitation may be reflected in the similar sound of the two verbs *gehireþ* and *onhireð*.

10 *Gif se oþer nelle* (If the latter [the hearer] resists): The author emphasizes here the need for an audience to engage fully with the material if they are to benefit from it. The preface-writer's awareness of reluctant readers,

which is independent of the Latin source, recalls the Verse Preface to the *Boethius*.

11–13 See above p. 172 on the echoes of other Alfredian prefaces here and elsewhere in this preface.

15 *Albinus*: Abbot of St Augustine's Abbey, Canterbury, from *c.* AD 709 until his death in 732.

17–18 *Ðeodores* and *Adrianus*: Theodore was Archbishop of Canterbury from AD 668 to 690; Hadrian was Abbot of St Augustine's Abbey, Canterbury, from *c.*670 to 710. The school they established in Canterbury became a renowned centre of learning. Waite (2015), p. 69, argues that when Bede wrote that Albinus was educated under Theodore and Hadrian, the preface-writer misinterpreted this as meaning that Albinus gave Bede information *about* Theodore and Hadrian. Higham (2006), p. 29, interprets it as a deliberate change designed to emphasize the importance of Theodore and Hadrian.

19–20 *eac on ðam þeodlandum ðe þær to geþeodde wæron* (and in the countries that were associated with it): The idea of association may be reflected in the repetition of *þ* and *d* in *þeodlandum* and *geþeodde*.

21 *fram leorningcnihtum*: Misinterpretation of the Latin original leads the preface-writer to state that Albinus obtained information from, rather than about, disciples of Gregory (Waite (2015), p. 70).

22–3 The divergence between B and Ca is probably the result of scribal confusion at some point in transmission. Ca's version offers the more plausible reading. B's more convoluted version probably represents a later attempt to make sense of a corrupt exemplar.

22 and 29 Nothhelm was appointed Archbishop of Canterbury in AD 735; he died in 739.

23 *stafum*: B's reading *seaftum*, emended here, suggests that the scribe was unfamiliar with the word *stæf* meaning 'letter' or, in the plural, 'writing', since *mid seaftum* makes no sense (unless the scribe was thinking of the word *sceaft* 'pole, shaft', interpreted as a writing implement). The other use of *stæf* elsewhere in Ca is similarly mangled in B:

> Ca and þa stafas mid him awritenne hæfde
> B and þa stanas mid him hæfde

See also Klaeber (1902), pp. 264–5; Grant (1989).

24 *þissa boca* (of these books): The preface-writer refers here to the five books that make up the work (the book-divisions are indicated in the Old English as well as in the Latin).

218 Commentary

34 *mid Danielis [...] ðæs arweorþan Wessexena byscpes*: The use of the genitive case after *mid* would be very unusual and may indicate the omission of one or more words after *mid*. Miller's proposed *myngunge* 'exhortation' (cf. line 28 of this preface) is reflected in the translation offered in this edition. Daniel was Bishop of Winchester from AD 705 to 744.

36–7 Cedd (*c.*620–64) was a Northumbrian monk and bishop who evangelized amongst the Mercians and East Saxons. His brother Cadd (d. 672), after holding the abbacy of several monasteries, became bishop of the Northumbrians, then of the Mercians and people of Lindsey (see comment on line 42 below). The copy of the preface in B refers only to *Cedde* and is clearly corrupt at this point: perhaps the scribe was confused by the similarity of the names *Cedde* and *Ceadda*.

41 *Isses*: Isse (Latin Esi) is an otherwise unknown abbot.

42 *Lindesige*: A kingdom south of the Humber estuary which became absorbed into Northumbria in the seventh century.

51 On the emendation to *Lindesfarene [ea]*, see Waite (2015), pp. 63–4.

52–4 The preface (like its Latin source) here uses the modesty topos characteristic of the prefatory tradition.

The Epilogue to the Bede

1–12 The two prose petitions are written in the voice of Bede. On the location of the second petition in the Latin source, see p. 174 above.

13 *ic*: In the verse petition the first-person voice may be either the scribe's or, as suggested by Robinson (1980 and 1981), a continuation of Bede's from the previous petitions. See also p. 175 above.

13–15 The epithets *bregorices weard* and *fira aldor* are construed here as being in apposition to *æghwylcne mann*. Grammatically (though less plausibly in the context), they could refer instead to an addressee. See Robinson (1981), p. 16 n. 24.

13a, 15a, and 16a These three half-lines are all metrically deficient. Robinson (1981), p. 11, speculates from these occasional lapses that 'the poet was a man familiar with vernacular verse and somewhat knowledgeable about it but not very practiced in it'.

15 *þa bredu*: The book is depicted as being in its finished state within board covers.

16 *wynsumum*: The manuscript reading *wynsum* for dat. pl. *wynsumum* is an example of the scribal error known as haplography (the omission of repeated letters). See Robinson (1981), p. 18 n. 26b.

17–18 *bam handum twam…mundum synum*: These phrases probably allude to scribal writing technique (rather than implying ambidexterity on the part of the scribe). A scribe needed to use both hands for writing: one held the quill and the other held the penknife required to keep the page still and sharpen the quill. The repeated reference to hands may be designed to emphasize a traditional link between the activity of writing and the articulation of divine teaching; see Robinson (1980), pp. 15–16, and Robinson (1981), pp. 18–19 n. 27.

19 *his aldre to willan*: The noun *aldor* could refer here to either a secular lord or the Lord (or both).

Glossary and List of Proper Names

List of Proper Names: The proper names are glossed separately at the end of the main glossary. The same principles are followed as for the main glossary.

Sigla for the Old English Texts:

GDPPr	Prose Preface to the *Dialogues*
GDVPr	Verse Preface to the *Dialogues*
GDGPr	Gregorian Preface to the *Dialogues*
GDEx1	Explicit to Book I of the *Dialogues*
GDIn2	Incipit to Book II of the *Dialogues*
GDEx2	Explicit to Book II of the *Dialogues*
GDIn3	Incipit to Book III of the *Dialogues*
GDEx3	Explicit to Book III of the *Dialogues*
GDIn4	Incipit to Book IV of the *Dialogues*
PCPPr	Prose Preface to the *Pastoral Care*
PCVPr	Verse Preface to the *Pastoral Care*
PCGPr	Gregorian Preface to the *Pastoral Care*
PCGEp	Gregorian Epilogue to the *Pastoral Care*
PCVEp	Epilogue to the *Pastoral Care*
BoPPr	Prose Preface to the *Boethius*
BoVPr	Verse Preface to the *Boethius*
BoPVi	Prose *Vita* to the *Boethius*
BoVVi	Verse *Vita* to the *Boethius*
BoEp	Epilogue to the *Boethius*
SoPr	Preface to the *Soliloquies*
SoEx1	Explicit to Book I of the *Soliloquies*
SoIn2	Incipit to Book II of the *Soliloquies*
SoEx2	Explicit to Book II of the *Soliloquies*
SoIn3	Incipit to Book III of the *Soliloquies*
SoEx3	Explicit to Book III of the *Soliloquies*
LwPr	Preface to the *Laws* of Alfred
BdPr	Bedan Preface to the *Bede*
BdPEp	Prose Epilogue to the *Bede*
BdVEp	Verse Epilogue to the *Bede*

Headwords: An alphabetical arrangement is used, with proper names listed separately at the end. The letter **æ** comes after **a** and **þ** comes after **t** (**þ** rather than **ð** is always used in headwords). The prefix **ge-** has been disregarded in the ordering. Headwords which occur in the texts are used wherever possible. The gender of nouns is given after the headword: where the gender of a noun is unclear from the instances in the texts and the dictionaries record variation, the possibilities are given in the form m./n., etc. Nouns are strong unless stated otherwise. The class of verbs is given after the headword: an arabic numeral indicates a strong verb, a roman numeral a weak one.

Citations of examples, grammatical forms, and variant spellings: Where fewer than ten examples are found, all are normally cited. Otherwise, except where the citation of all forms may be of particular interest, four examples are normally supplied from a range of texts, concluding with 'etc.'. Where emended forms are cited, they are placed in square brackets. All forms of words are given. The order of citations follows the order of the texts in this edition. Citations are by line number except for LwPr whose citations are by section number.

Abbreviations: After the headword, nouns are indicated by m., f., or n. for masculine, feminine, or neuter; nouns are strong unless specified as wk. for weak; verbs are indicated by vb 1–7 for strong verbs classes 1–7, vb I–III for weak verbs classes I–III, anom.vb for anomalous verbs, pret.pres.vb for preterite present verbs; adjectives are indicated by adj.; pronouns are indicated by pron.; adverbs are indicated by adv.; prepositions are indicated by prep.; conjunctions are indicated by conj.; numerals are indicated by num. Where a word takes a particular case, w. is used for with. An impersonal verb is indicated by impers.; the transitive or intransitive use of a verb is indicated by trans. or intrans.

In citing forms, case, number, and gender (or combinations thereof) are shown as, for example, asm. for accusative singular masculine, gs. for genitive singular; where any confusion is possible fuller forms (nom., acc., gen., dat., and instr.) are used. Indeclinable forms are indicated by indecl. All forms of adjectives are recorded; comparative and superlative forms of adjectives and adverbs are shown by comp. and superl. Verbal forms are indicative unless stated otherwise; the infinitive is indicated by infin., the inflected infinitive by infl.infin., the present tense by pres., the preterite tense by pret., the subjunctive mood by subj., the imperative mood by imp., the present participle by pres.pt., the past participle by pp. The singular is indicated by s. and the plural by p.; the numbers 1–3 indicate 1st, 2nd, and

Glossary and List of Proper Names 223

3rd person (person marked only where necessary). A reflexive use of the verb is indicated by refl.

a adv. *always, ever.* GDVPr.5, GDGPr.55, PCVEp.4, LwPr.44. **a. a. a.** *forever.* BoEp.21–2
aarn see **ayrnan**
abbod m. *abbot.* ns. **abbud** BdPr.15, 18; gs. **abbodes** GDEx1.4, **abbudes** BdPr.28, 42
aberan vb 4. *to carry (away).* infin. SoPr.4, 5
ablendan vb I. *to blind.* pres.p. **ablendað** LwPr.46
abrecan vb 4. *to take by storm, sack.* pret.p. **abræcon** BoPVi.3; pp. **abrocen** BoVVi.18
abysgian vb II. *to busy, bother.* infin. GDGPr.68
ac conj. *but.* GDGPr.70, PCPPr.33, BoPVi.7, SoPr.12, etc. **æc** GDGPr.59. as introductory particle **ac la** *oh, so* GDGPr.25
acsian vb II. *to ask.* pret.s. **acsode** SoIn3.2
geacsian vb II. *to learn by asking, discover.* pret.s. **geacsode** GDGPr.99, 106; pret.p. **geascodon** LwPr.49.3, **geacsodon** BdPr.38, 45; pres.pt. dsm. **acsiendum** GDGPr.85
acwelan vb 4. *to die, kill.* imp.s. **acwele** LwPr.45; pret.subj.s. **acwæle** LwPr.28
adelfan vb 3. *to dig.* pres.subj.s. **adelfe** LwPr.22
adihtian vb II. *to compose (a text).* pret.s. **adihtode** PCVPr.4
adrifan vb I. *to drive away.* pres.3s. **adrifeð** GDGPr.52; pres.subj.s. **adrife** BoVPr.6; pp. npm. **adrifene** PCGPr.26
afeallan vb 7. *to fall away, decay.* pp. **afeallen** PCPPr.57
afylan vb I. *to pollute.* pp. **afyled** GDGPr.40
afyrran vb I. *to remove, take away.* infin. **aferran** BoPVi.17; imp.s. **afyrre** BoEp.13
agan pret.pres.vb. *to have, possess, hold.* infin. BoVVi.39, 62; pres.3s. **ah** GDVPr.22, BdVEp.20; pret.p. **ahton** BoVVi.58
agen adj. *own.* nsn. LwPr.17; asm. **agenne** LwPr.17; asf. **agne** GDGPr.42; asn. PCPPr.30, 38, 44, 46, 47, LwPr.19; gsn. **agenes** GDGPr.59; dsf. **agenre** GDGPr.17; dsn. **agnum** SoPr.31; apm. **agene** PCGPr.12; gp. **agenra** PCGPr.15, PCGEp.9
ageomrian vb II. *to groan.* pres.1s. **ageomorige** GDGPr.51
agnian vb II. *to appropriate, acquire.* pres.p. **agniat** PCGPr.26
agyfan vb 5. *to give (back), bestow.* imp.s. **agif** LwPr.38; pres.subj.s. **agife** LwPr.12, 29; pres.subj.p. BdPEp.9; pp. **agifen** LwPr.36
ah see **agan**
ahebban vb 6. *to raise, lift up, exalt, promote.* pret.s. **aof** GDVPr.13; pret.p. **ahofon** BoPVi.1; pp. **ahafen** PCGPr.20, **ahefen** BoVVi.47
aht pron. (w.g.). *anything.* GDGPr.25
ahton see **agan**
al see **eall**
aldor m. *lord. king.* as. BdVEp.15; gs.[or ds.?] **aldre** BdVEp.19

aldorlicnes f. *authority*. gs. **aldorlicnesse** GDGPr.101
alefan vb I. *to allow, let*. pres.subj.s. **alefe** LwPr.12
aleogan vb 2. *to leave unfulfilled*. pret.s. **aleag** BoVVi.39
alesan vb 5. *to select*. pret.2s. **alese** SoIn3.1; pret.3s. **alæs** SoEx3.1
alesend m. *redeemer*. ns. BoEp.19
alne, alra see **eall**
alucan vb 2. *to remove, exclude*. imp.s. **aluc** LwPr.13
amen used as concluding formula. BoEp.23, BdVEp.23
an num.pron.adj. *a, one*. nsm. GDVPr.15, GDGPr.81, PCPPr.66, PCGPr.11; asm. **anne** PCPPr.17, LwPr.32, 49.8, **ænne** PCPPr.24, asf. **ane** PCPPr.66; asn. **an** PCPPr.15; gsm. **anes** BdPr.46; dsm. **anum** LwPr.24, 49.6; dsf. **anre** SoPr.4. after noun or pron. *alone*. nsm. **ana** GDGPr.16, 80; asn. **an** GDGPr.107
ancenned adj. *only begotten*. nsm. **ancenneda** LwPr.49
and, ond conj. *and*. GDPPr.2, GDVPr.5, GDGPr.3, PCPPr.2, etc.
andgit n. *meaning, sense*. as. PCPPr.61; BoPPr.2, **andgyt** GDGPr.107; gs. **andgites** BoPPr.11; ds. **andgite** BoPPr.3, **andgiete** PCPPr.61, **andgyte** GDGPr.107
andgitfullice adv. *intelligibly*. superl. **andgitfullicost** PCPPr.65, **andgitfullicast** BoPPr.3
andweard adj. *present, current*. asm. **andweardan** BdPr.46; asf. **andweardan** GDGPr.64, BdPr.25; gsn. **andweardan** PCGEp.6; dsf. **andweardan** PCGPr.4
andwyrdan vb I (w.d.). *to answer*. pret.s. **andwyrde** PCPPr.39; pp. **geandweard** SoIn3.2
anfeald adj. *single*. asn. LwPr.36
anforlætan vb 7. *to abandon, lose*. pret.s. **anforlet** GDGPr.44
angan see **onginnan**
anige adj. *blind in one eye*. apm. **anigge** LwPr.20
animan vb 4. *to take*. infin. GDGPr.104, 108
anlepe adj. *single*. asm. **anlepne** PCPPr.17
answarode see **ondswarian**
ansyn f. *face, sight*. ds. **ansyne** BdPEp.4. *state or quality (of repose)*. ds. **onsyne** GDGPr.39
anw(e)ald(e) see **onweald**
aof see **ahebban**
apostol m. *apostle*. np. **apostolas** LwPr.49.1, 49.2, 49.3; gp. **apostola** GDGPr.103
apostolic adj. *apostolic, papal*. nsm. **apostolica** GDGPr.5, gsm. **apostolican** GDGPr.2, GDIn2.3, GDEx3.1
ar f. *honour, glory, mercy*. gs. **are** BoVVi.78; ds. **are** SoPr.20; gp. **ara** BoVVi.57
arædan vb I. *to read*. infin. PCPPr.54, 58
aræran vb I. *to lift up*. imp.s. **arær** PCGEp.8
areccean vb I. *to translate, interpret*. infin. PCPPr.15, 65

aredian vb II. *to find (the way)*. infin. SoPr.19
arfæst adj. *pious*. gsf. **arfæstre** BdPEp.12
arfæstnes f. *mercy*. ds. **arfæstnesse** BdPEp.8
arian vb II (w.d.). *to honour*. imp.s. **ara** LwPr.4
Arrianisc adj. *Arian*. dsm. **Arrianiscan** BoPVi.6
arwurþe adj. *honourable*. nsm. **arweorða** BdPr.15, **arwyrða** BoPVi.23; asm. **arweorðan** BdPr.37; gsm. **arweorþan** BdPr.34, 42, 43; gp. **arwurðra** GDGPr.100, 111
ascinan vb 1. *to be bright, illustrious*. pret.p. **ascinon** GDGPr.74
geascodon see **geacsian**
ascung f. *question*. as. **ascunge** GDGPr.72
asecgan vb III. *to tell*. pres.1s. **asecge** GDGPr.80
aslean vb 6. *to remove by striking*. **aslean ut** *to knock out*. pres.subj.s. **aslea** LwPr.20. **of aslean** *to knock out*. pres.subj.s. **aslea** LwPr.20
asmorian vb II. *to choke, suffocate*. pp. asn. (used as noun) **asmorod** *thing killed by strangulation* LwPr.49.5
aspringan vb 3. *to gush (up), issue (forth)*. infin. GDGPr.3; pres.s. **aspringeð** GDIn4.1
asteman vb I. *to establish, found*. pret.p. **astemnedon** BdPr.39
astreccan vb I. *to stretch out*. pret.s. **astrehte** BoPVi.27; pp. **astreaht** BoVVi.80
asworettan vb I. *to sigh*. pres.1s. **asworette** GDGPr.50
atæfran vb I. *to depict, describe*. pp. **atæfred** PCGEp.2. [*DOE* 'atyfran, atefran']
ateon vb 2. *to remove*. infin. GDGPr.104
ateorian vb II. *to run out*. pres.subj.s. **ateorige** GDGPr.84
atyhtan vb I. *to entice*. pp. **atyhted** BoVVi.8
aþ m. *oath, promise*. ap. **aðas** BoVVi.25
aþindan vb 3. *to swell*. pp. **aðunden** PCGPr.20
awendan vb I. *to translate*. pret.s. **awende** PCPPr.65, PCVPr.12
aweorpan vb 3. *to discard*. pret.s. **awearp** LwPr.49.9
awritan vb 1. *to write (down)*. infin. GDVPr.12, LwPr.49.9; infl.infin. **awritenne** BdPEp.11; pres.1s. **awrite** PCGPr.4; pres.subj.p. **awriten** GDPPr.7; pret.s. **awrat** BdPr.2, 12, 24, BdVEp.17; pp. **awriten** GDEx3.3, BdPr.50; pp. npf. **awritene** PCPPr.30
awþer conj. with **oþþe** . . . **oþþe** *either...or*. LwPr.49.9
awuht n. *anything*. as. LwPr.26. adv. *at all*. LwPr. 49.9
awyrcan vb I. *to act (in certain way towards someone* (dat.)*)*. pret.s. **awyrhte** BoEp.8
ayrnan vb 3. *to flow, issue (forth)*. pret.s. **aarn** GDIn3.2

æ f. *law, testament*. ns. PCPPr.43, BoVVi.41; as. LwPr.49.1
æc see **ac**
æce see **ece**
æcer m. *field*. ap. **æcras** LwPr.26

226 Glossary and List of Proper Names

æfæst adj. *pious, devout.* asm. **æfestan** BdPr.22; gsm. **æfæstan** GDEx11.4
æfre adv. *ever.* GDGPr.74, PCPPr.40, PCGPr.7, BoVVi.82, LwPr.11
æft see **eft**
æfter prep.w.d. *after, across, according to, corresponding to.* GDGPr.39, GDEx2.1, GDIn4.3, PCVEp.21, BoPVi.4, LwPr.25, 29, 40, 49.1, 49.9
æfterfylgan vb I. *to follow.* pres.pt. (used as adj.) *following.* dsf. **æfterfyligendan** GDIn4.5; asf./apf. **æfterfylgendan** GDPPr.7
æfterspyrigean vb I (w.d.). *to follow, pursue.* infin. PCPPr.33
æftra adj. *second.* nsm. GDIn2.1; nsf. **æftere** GDEx11.2; gsf. **æftran** SoIn2.1, SoEx2.1
æfwerdelsa wk.m. *damage.* as. **æfwerdelsan** LwPr.27
æghwylc pron. and adj. *each one, every.* asm. **æghwylcne** BdVEp.13, **æghwelcne** LwPr.49.6. **buton æghwilcum** *without any.* BoEp.22
ægþer pron. *each, both.* as. SoPr.29; gsn. **ægðeres** SoPr.29; dsn. **ægðrum** SoPr.29. conj. **ægþer ge . . . ge (eac)** *both...and.* PCPPr.4, 7, 9, 10, 34, BoPPr.4, SoPr.11, 13, 17. **ægþær ge . . . ge** SoPr.26. **egðer ge . . . ge** SoPr.28
æl m. *awl.* ds. **æle** LwPr.11
ælc pron. *each, each one.* adj. *each, every.* nsm. BoPPr.11; asm. **ælcne** BoPPr.9, SoPr.23; asf. **ælce** BoEp.14; gsn. **ælces** BoVVi.36; dsm. **ælcum** PCPPr.66; dsf. **ælcere** GDGPr.104, **ælcre** PCPPr.66; dsn. **ælcum** GDGPr.105, SoPr.2, 3, 6
ælinge m./f./n. *tedium.* ns. BoVPr.6
ælmihtig adj. *almighty.* nsm. GDGPr.68, LwPr.49.7, **ællmihtig** GDVPr.20, **ælmihtega** LwPr.49, **ælmihtiga** BoEp.1; gsm. **ælmihtiges** BdPEp.8; dsm. **ælmihtegum** PCPPr.18
æltowe adj. *sound.* nsm. GDVPr.9
geæmetigan vb II. *to free, disengage.* pres.subj.s. **geæmetige** PCPPr.21
æm(et)ta wk.m. *leisure.* ds. **æmettan**. BoPPr.11, BdPr.3. [*DOE* 'æmta']
ænig adj. *any.* asm. (as pron.) **ænigne** GDVPr.27, PCPPr.18; asf. **ænige** GDGPr.98; asn. SoPr.23; gp. **ænigra** GDGPr.74
ænlic adj. *peerless, excellent.* asn. SoPr.10
ænne see **an**
ær prep.w.d. *before.* PCPPr.57, SoPr.18, LwPr.36. **ær þam þe** conj. *before.* PCPPr.26, LwPr.49.1, **ær ðon** GDGPr.83
ær adv. *before, previously.* GDGPr.14, PCPPr.31, BoPVi.25, SoPr.34, etc. For **sið oððe ær** see **siþ**
æran see **ærra**
ærcebiscop m. *archbishop.* ds. **ærcebiscepe** PCPPr.62
ærende n. *report.* ap. **ærendo** BdPr.29
ærendwreca wk.m. *messenger.* ap. **ærendwrecan** LwPr.49.1; dp. **ærendwrecum** PCPPr.6
ærendgewrit n. *written message, letter.* ns. LwPr.49.2; as. PCPPr.15, PCVPr.1, BoVVi.63, LwPr.49.2; ap. **ærendgewritu** BoPVi.18, BdPr.44

ærest adv. *first*. GDGPr.8, 57, PCPPr.43, LwPr.49.9, BdPr.15, 50
ærest(a) adj. *first*. nsm. æresða GDGPr.1. æt ærestan *first, to begin with*. GDGPr.5
ærgenemned adj. *aforementioned*. nsm. ærgenemda GDIn4.4
ærra adj. *previous, earlier, preceding*. gsn. æran GDGPr.50; dp. ærran GDIn3.5
æspring m./n. *spring, fountain*. gs. æspringes GDIn2.2
æstel m. *book-marker, a pointer for keeping one's place while reading*. ns. PCPPr.67, as. PCPPr.68
æt prep.w.d. *at, in, for, from*. GDGPr.5, PCPPr.62, SoPr.6, LwPr.49.7, etc. For æt ham, see ham. For æt nyhstan see neah
ætgædere adv. *together*. LwPr.49.1
ætsomne adv. *together*. LwPr.49.1
ætywan vb I. *to show, reveal*. pret.s. ætywde GDGPr.16. *to appear*. infin. BdPEp.3
æþele adj. *noble, famous, magnificent*. gsm. æþelan GDIn4.1.
æþeling m. *prince, nobleman*. ds. æþelinge BoVVi.40; dp. æþelingum BoVVi.21.
æwerdla wk.m. *injury*. as. æwerdlan LwPr.18.

bam see begen.
bæc n. *back*. In on bæc *behind*. GDGPr.30-1.
bæftan adv. *after*. In her bæftan *immediately after (this), hereafter*. GDGPr.71.
bærnan vb I. *to burn*. infl.infin. bærnanne LwPr.27
bærning f. *burning*. as.[for bærninge?] LwPr.19, ds. bærninge LwPr.19
be prep.w.d./i. *by, concerning, about, according to*. GDPPr.7, GDGPr.6, GDEx1.3, PCPPr.17, etc.; bi PCVPr.14, LwPr.16
be adv. *thereby, from (it)*. bi PCPPr.72
beadurinc m. *warrior*. dp. beadurincum BoVVi.18
beahgifa wk.m. *treasure-giver*. ds. beahgifan GDVPr.23
bearn n. *son, child, offspring*. as. GDVPr.6; ds. bearne LwPr.11; np. BoVVi.34, LwPr.11, 34
bebeodan vb 2 (w.d. of person). *to command, order*. pres.1s. bebiode PCPPr.67; pret.s. bebead LwPr.49, 49.7, 49.9
bebod n. *command, commandment*. ap. bebodu LwPr.49
bebycgan vb I. *to sell*. infl.infin. bebycganne LwPr.12; pres.subj.s. bebycgge LwPr.15, 24; pres.subj.p. bebycggen LwPr.23; pp. beboht LwPr.24
bec see boc
becom(-) see becuman
becuman vb 4. *to come, befall*. infin. BdPEp.3; pres.3s. becymeð GDGPr.94; pres. subj.s. becume PCGPr.11, LwPr.42; pret.s. becom BoPVi.24, BoVVi.77; pret.p. becomon PCPPr.23, becoman BoPPr.6; pp. becumen GDGPr.63
gebed n. *prayer*. gp. gebeda PCGEp.7
befæstan vb I. *to apply*. infin. PCPPr.22; pres.subj.s. befæste PCPPr.22. *to commend, make acceptable*. pres.subj.s. befæste PCGPr.16

befeallan vb 7. *to fall*. pres.subj.s. **befealle** LwPr.22
befeolan vb 3 (w.d.). *to apply to*. infin. PCPPr.53
befon vb 7. *to hold*. pres.subj.s. **befo** BdVEp.15
beforan prep.w.a./d. *before, in front of*. GDGPr.17, PCGPr.19, BdPEp.3. as adv. GDGPr.61
began anom.vb. *to conduct oneself, behave* (reflex.). pres.subj.s. **bega** PCGPr.6
begen adj. *both*. dp. **bam** BdVEp.17
begietan vb 5. *to obtain, gain, acquire*. infin. PCPPr.12, **begytan** GDVPr.8; pres. subj.s. **begite** LwPr.16; pret.s. **begeat** GDVPr.16; pret.p. **begeaton** PCPPr.32
begiondan prep.w.d. *beyond*. PCPPr.16
behabban vb III. *to confine*. pp. **behæfd** GDGPr.34
beheawan vb 7. *to cut off*. infin. **beheawon** BoVVi.43
behionan prep.w.d. *on this side of*. PCPPr.14
beinnan prep.w.d. *within, inside*. BoPVi.26
belucan vb 2. *to lock up*. infin. BoPVi.23, BoVVi.73
beneoþan adv. *below*. GDExi.2
beodan vb 2. *to command*. pret.p. **budon** LwPr.49.3(x2)
beon anom.vb. *to be*. infin. BoPVi.7, **bion** PCGPr.13, PCGEp.3; infl.infin. **beonne** PCGPr.23, SoPr.30; pres.1s. **beo** GDGPr.54, SoPr.14, **eom** GDGPr.47, 48 67, PCGEp.2, LwPr.1, 36; pres.2s. **eart** BoEp.19, BdPr.5, **bist** LwPr.2; pres.3s. **is** GDPPr.3, GDGPr.14, GDExi.1, PCPPr.52, etc., **ys** GDGPr.13, 28; **bið** GDGPr.91, 95, GDIn4.5, PCPPr.66, LwPr.17, 21, 25; **byð** GDVPr.5, 9, GDGPr.16, 46(x2), 56, 63, 90, 97; pres.p. **beoð** GDGPr.12, LwPr.34(x2), **sint** PCGPr.26, BoPPr.5, SoPr.32, LwPr.3, 11, 49.2, **siendon** GDVPr.19, PCPPr.70, **sindon** PCPPr.22, **sindan** LwPr.49; pres.subj.s. **se** GDIn2.5, **si** GDGPr.75, BoEp.21, SoPr.7, **sie** PCPPr.18, PCGPr.14, SoPr.21, LwPr.4, etc., **sy** GDGPr.53, BdPr.13, **sig** GDGPr.97, **beo** LwPr.11; pres.subj.p. **sien** PCPPr.49, 53, 69, LwPr.21; pret.s. **wæs** GDGPr.6, GDIn2.6, PCPPr.57, PCGEp.3, etc., **wes** SoPr.18; pret.p. **wæron** GDGPr.71, PCPPr.5, BoPVi.2, LwPr.33, etc.; pret.subj.s. **wære** GDGPr.34, PCPPr.27, 42, LwPr.21, 23, 25, 28; pret.subj.p. **wæren** PCPPr 25, 70, LwPr.49.9. **beon on** *to be worth*. pres.3s. **bið** PCPPr.67. With neg. pres.3s. **nis** PCVEp.19, SoPr.22; pret.s. **næs** BoVVi.43, 49; pret.p. **næron** GDGPr.79, PCPPr.30; pret. subj.p. **næren** PCPPr.16, PCGPr.23
beorn m. *warrior, man*. ns. BoVVi.52
bereccan vb I. *to clear, exculpate*. infin. **bereccean** LwPr.15
bestælan vb I. *to lay a charge (on)*. pp. **bestæled** LwPr.15
beswican vb 1. *to seduce*. pres.subj.s. **beswice** LwPr.29
bet compar.adv. *better*. GDGPr.70, BoEp.8, 10
(ge)betan vb I. *to repair, mend, make compensation for*. pres.subj.s. **(ge)bete** PCVEp.28, LwPr.18, 26, 27
betera adj. (compar. of **god**). *better*. nsn. **betre** PCPPr.48; asf. **beteran** GDGPr.98

betest adj. (superl. of **god**). *best*. nsm. PCVPr.9
betst superl.adv. *best, the most*. BdPr.16
betwih prep.w.a. *amongst*. GDPPr.8
betwix, betwux prep.w.a. *between, amongst*. GDPPr.4, BoPVi.3
betynan vb I. *to close, shut*. infin. LwPr.21; pres.subj.s. **betyne** LwPr.22; pp. asm. (used as noun) **betynedne** LwPr.22
beþurfan pret.pres.vb (w.g.). *to need*. pret.s. **beþorfte** SoPr.6
bi see **be**
(ge)biddan vb 5. *to pray, ask*. pres.1s. **bidde** PCGEp.6, BoEp.3, BdPr.53, BdPEp.1, 5, BdVEp.13; pres.3s. **bideþ** GDVPr.16, **bit** BoPPr.8; pres.subj.s. **bidde** GDVPr.18, **gebidde** BoPPr.10; pret.s. **bæd** BoVVi.64; pret.p. **bædon** BoPVi.20
gebigan vb I. *to turn, bend*. pres.subj.p. **gebigen**. GDPPr.5
bigenga wk.m. *inhabitant*. dp. **bigengum** BdPEp.10
bindan vb 3. *to bind*. pp. **gebunden** GDGPr.21
bion see **beon**
bisceop m. *bishop*. ns. GDVPr.12, 16, SoPr.31, **biscep** PCPPr.71, **byscop** BdPr.17; as. **bysceop** BdPr.37, **biscep** PCPPr.2; gs. **bisceopes** GDIn3.2, **byscpes** BdPr.34, 43; ds. **biscepe** PCPPr.63; np. **biscepas** PCPPr.69; gp. **biscepa** LwPr.49.7, **byscpa** BdPr.38; dp. **biscepum** PCVPr.14, **byscpum** BdPr.30
bisceoplic adj. *episcopal, befitting a bishop*. gsm. **biscoplican** GDGPr.12; gsf. **bisceoplican** GDGPr.38
biscepstol m. *bishopric, episcopal see*. ds. **biscepstole** PCPPr.66
bisen, bysen f. *example, exemplar*. as. **bisene** GDVPr.11, **bysene** GDVPr.23; ds. **biesene** GDVPr.3, **bisene** GDGPr.3, PCVPr.14, **bysene** GDVPr.7, 75, 100; np. **bysene** GDVPr.92; dp. **bysenum** GDVPr.94, **bisenum** PCGPr.16
bisgian vb II. *to occupy, busy*. pret.p. **bisgodan** BoPPr.5
bisgu f. *occupation, trouble, affair*. np. **bisgu** BoPPr.5; dp. **bisgum** PCPPr.59, **bysegum** GDGPr.38
bit see **biddan**
blinnan vb 3. *to come to an end*. pres.3s. **blinneð** GDGPr.83
blis f. *bliss*. ns. GDVPr.6
blod n. *blood*. as. LwPr.49.5
blostm, blostma wk.m. *blossom, flower*. np. **blostman** SoEx1.1, SoEx2.1; gp. **blostmena** SoIn2.1
boc f. *book*. ns. GDVPr.11, GDEx1.1, 2, GDEx3.1, 2, PCPPr.1; as. GDVPr.16, GDGPr.104, PCPPr.60, 68, BoPPr.7, 9, BdVEp.14, 17; gs. **bec** PCGPr.25, BoPPr.1, [SoEx1.1], SoIn2.1, SoEx2.1; ds. **bec** GDIn4.5, PCPPr.68, PCGPr.4, SoEx3.1, BdPr.49; np. **bec** SoPr.32; ap. **bec** PCPPr.37, 45, 48, PCVEp.11, SoPr.31; gp. **boca** GDPPr.2, PCPPr.28, 29, BoVVi.52, BdPr.24; dp. **bocum** GDPPr.6, GDIn3.5, SoIn3.1
boccræft m. *book learning*. dp. **boccræftum** BoPVi.12
bocland n. *'bookland', land held by charter in hereditary possession*. as. SoPr.27

boclæden n. *written Latin.* ds. **boclædene** BoPPr.1
gebod n. *command.* dp. **gebodum** LwPr.49.3
bohtimber n. *curved timber.* ap. **bohtimbru** SoPr.2
bolttimber n. *straight timber.* ap. **bolttimbru** SoPr.2
borg m. *loan, (as) security.* ds. **borge** LwPr.35
bot f. *remedy, compensation.* gs. **bote** LwPr.13; ap. **bote** LwPr.49.8
breac see **brucan**
(ge)brecan vb 4. *to break.* infl.infin. **brecanne** LwPr.49. *to break into.* pres.subj.s. **brece** LwPr.25. In **gebrecan in** *to interrupt, break into.* infin. GDGPr.87
bred n. *board (of a book-cover).* ap. **bredu** BdVEp.15. *plank.* as. PCGEp.7
bregorice n. *kingdom.* gs. **bregorices** BdVEp.14
brengan vb I. *to bring, produce.* infin. PCVPr.14, SoPr.5; pres.subj.s. **brenge** LwPr.11; pret.s. **brohte** PCVPr.2; pret.subj.s. PCVEp.26, 28
breost n./m. *breast.* as. **breosð** GDGPr.2; gp. **breosta** GDIn2.6; dp. (with sg. meaning) **breostum** PCVEp.16
gebringan vb I. *to bring.* infin. BoPVi.17, 22
broþor m. *brother.* ns. **broður** PCGPr.1; np. LwPr.49.3; dp. **broðrum** BdPr.51, **gebroðrum** BdPr.39
brucan vb II (w.g.). *to use, benefit from.* pret.s. **breac** BoVVi.75
brytta wk.m. *giver.* In **sinces brytta** *treasure-giver.* ns. GDVPr.24
gebunden see **bindan**
burg f. *stronghold, dwelling, city.* as. **burig** BoPVi.3; ds. **byrig** BoVVi.37, BdPr.17 (**Cantwara byrig**, *Canterbury*); gp. **burga** BoVVi.18; dp. **burgum** GDVPr.6
burna wk.m., **burne** wk.f. *stream, spring.* gs. **burnan** GDGPr.1, GDIn4.1; ds. **burnan** GDIn2.2, PCVEp.28
buton prep.w.d. *without.* GDGPr.42, BoEp.22, LwPr.49.7. prep.w.a. in **nab-ban butan** *not to have (anything) but, to have only.* LwPr.36. conj. *except, only.* GDGPr.33, LwPr.49.7. *unless* (w.subj.) PCPPr.71, LwPr.25
gebycgan vb I. *to buy, sell.* pres.subj.s. **gebycgge** LwPr.11, 12; pret.s. **bohte** LwPr.12
byrig see **burg**
byrþen f. *load, burden.* ns. PCGPr.24, PCGEp.9; as./ap. **byrðenne** PCGPr.3, LwPr.49.5; ds. **byrðene** SoPr.4; gp. **byrðenna** PCGPr.3
bysc(e)op see **bisceop**
bysegum see **bysgu**
bysen(-) see **bisen**
bysgung f. *activity, labour.* gs. **bysgunge** GDGPr.30
bytling f. *(act of) building.* ds. **bytlinge** SoPr.23

carcern n. *prison.* gs. **carcernes** [BoVVi.73]; ds. **carcerne** BoPVi.23, 26
casere m. *emperor, caesar.* ns. BoVVi.20, 61, **kasere** BoPVi.19; ds. **kasere** BoPVi.18; dp. **caserum** BoPVi.15
cearf see **ceorfan**

ceas f. *quarrel*. ds. **cease** LwPr.18
ceaster f. *city*. as. **ceastre** BoVVi.66
cempa wk.m. *champion, warrior*. ns. PCVPr.4
ceorfan vb 3. *to cut down*. pret.s. **cearf** SoPr.8
ceorlisc adj. *unrefined*. dsm. **ceorlisce** GDGPr.109
(ge)ceosan vb 2. *to choose*. pret.s. **geceas** BdPr.12; pp. npm. (used as noun) **gecorene** PCVEp.9; dp. **gecorenum** GDGPr.81
cidan vb I. *to chide*. pret.2s. **ciddesð** PCGPr.2
gecierran vb I. *to turn, convert*. pret.p. **gecerdon** LwPr.49.1; pp. npm. **gecirde** LwPr.49.2
cigan vb I. *to call, invoke*. imp.s. **cig** LwPr.2; pres.2s. **cigst** LwPr.2
cining(-) see **cyning**
cirice wk.f. *church*. gs. **ciricean** BdPr.51; np. **ciricean** PCPPr.27
clamm m. *chain, fetter*. dp. **clammum** BoVVi.83
clæne adj. *clean, pure*. gsf. **clænan** GDGPr.1; dsm. **clænum** BoEp.18; dsn. **clænum** BoEp.18.
clæne adv. *entirely*. PCPPr.13
cleopian vb II. *to call, call out* (intrans.). pres.3s. **cleopað** LwPr.36; pres.p. **cleopiað** LwPr.34; pres.subj.p. **cleopien** LwPr.48; pret.s. **cleopode** BoVVi.83
cluster n. *cell, prison*. as. BoVVi.73
geclysp ?. *clamour, outcry*. as. LwPr.41. [*DOE* 'geclips']
gecnawan vb 7. *to understand*. infin. GDIn4.2, PCPPr.50
cnodan vb 7. *to be committed (to)*. pp. **gecnoden** BoVVi.32
cnyssan vb I. *to batter, buffet*. pp. **gecnyssed** GDGPr.29, **gecnysed** GDGPr.48
com see **cuman**
consul m. *consul*. ns. BoPVi.11
gecoplice adv. *suitably*. GDGPr.110
costnung f. *temptation*. dp. **costnungum** BoEp.12
cotlyf n. *cottage, dwelling*. as. SoPr.23
cræft m. *skill*. as. PCGPr.26, BoVPr.2; ds. **cræfte** BdVEp.16
Cristen adj. *Christian*. nsm. BoPVi.5; asm. **Cristenne** LwPr.11; npm. **Cristne** PCPPr.25; npf. **Cristna** PCPPr.47
cristendom m. *Christianity*. ds. **cristendome** BoPVi.20, **cristenandome** BoPVi.13
cucu see **cwic**
cuman vb 4. *to come*. infin. BoVVi.83; infl.infin. **cumane** SoPr.30; pres.3s. **cymeð** GDGPr.87, **cymet** GDIn2.1; pres.subj.s. **cume** PCGEp.7, PCVEp.26; pret.s. **com** GDGPr.20, PCPPr.3, **cwom** LwPr.49; pret.p. **comon** GDGPr.17, LwPr.49.3, BdPr.14; pret.subj.s. **come** LwPr.49; pret.subj.p. **comen** BoVVi.66; pp. dsm. **cumenan** LwPr.47; apm. **cumene** LwPr.33
cunnan pret.pres.vb. *to know, know how to*. pres.1s. **cunne** BoEp.10; pres.p. **cunnon** PCPPr.33, PCGPr.24; pres.subj.p. **cunnen** PCPPr.54; pret.s. **cuðe** SoPr.2, 3; pret.p. **cuðon** PCPPr.42, 58, PCVPr.16; pret.subj.p. **cuðen** PCPPr.14

cuþ adj. *known, familiar*. nsn. GDGPr.101

cweþan vb 5. *to say*. pres.subj.s. **cweðe** LwPr.11; pret.s. **cwæð** GDGPr.9, GDIn2.7, PCPPr.39, PCVEp.3, etc.; pret.p. **cwædon** LwPr.49.10; pret.subj.p. **cwæden** PCPPr.31

gecweþan vb 5. *to speak, declare*. infin. LwPr.49.7; pres.pt. **cweþende** GDIn3.5

cwic, cucu adj. *living, alive*. dsm. **cwicum** LwPr.25. In **cucu feoh** *livestock*. nsn. LwPr.28

cwide m. *speech, saying*. np. **cwidas** SoEx3.1, **cwydas** SoIn3.1; ap. **cwidas** BoVPr.5, **cwydas** BdPr.5

cymet, cymeþ see **cuman**

gecynde adj. *natural, lawful, rightful*. apm. BoVVi.6

cynehad m. *kingship*. gs. **cynehades** GDPPr.1

cynerice n. *kingdom*. gs. **kynerices** PCPPr.59

cynestol m. *royal throne*. ns. BoPVi.19; ds. **cynestole** BoVVi.48

cyning m. *king*. ns. BoVPr.2, BoPVi.13, 22, BoVVi.32, LwPr.49.9, 49.10, **kining** SoEx3.1, **kuning** BoPPr.1, **kyning** PCPPr.2, PCVPr.11; as. **cining** BdPr.1; gs. **cyninges** LwPr.49.9; ds. **cyninge** BoPVi.16, **cininge** BdPr.12, 27; np. **kyningas** PCPPr.5, BoVVi.56; ap. **cyningas** BoVVi.6; gp. **cyninga** GDVPr.25, **cininga** BdPr.30; dp. **cyningum** BoPVi.2, 4

cynn n. *people, nation*. gs. **cynnes** BdPEp.6

cyst f. *best*. ns. BoVVi.18

(ge)cyþan vb I. *to make known, inform, reveal*. infin. PCPPr.3 (with passive meaning *to be made known*); imp.s. **gecyðe** LwPr.42; pres.1s. **cyðe** BdPr.13, **gecyðe** GDGPr.70, 105; pres.p. **cyðað** LwPr.49.3; pret.p. **cyðdon** GDGPr.82, BoVVi.56

gedafenian vb II (w.d.). *to be fitting or appropriate*. pres.s. **gedauenað** BdPr.12

dæd f. *deed*. ns. BoVVi.43; ap. **dæde** GDGPr.68, **dæda** BdPr.6; gp. **dæda** GDGPr.40, BdPr.50

dæg m. *day*. ns. GDGPr.83; as. LwPr.3, BdPr.46; ds. **dæge** GDGPr.10, LwPr.49.9; ap. **dagas** LwPr.3; gp. **daga** GDGPr.27, BdVEp.22; dp. **dagum** BoPPr.6, LwPr.3, 21

dæl m. *part, portion*. as. PCPPr.38, 47; gp. **dæla** PCGPr.11. **be þam dele ðe** conj. *to the extent that*. SoPr.3–4

deacon(e) see **diacon**

dead adj. *dead*. nsm. LwPr.17(x2), 23; nsf. LwPr.18; asn. **deade** LwPr.22; gsm. **deadan** LwPr.23; np. LwPr.21

dearnenga adv. *secretly*. LwPr.6. [*DOE* 'dyrnunga']

deaþ m. *death*. as. GDGPr.35; ds. **deaðe** LwPr.49.7. For **deaðe** (is.) in **deaðe sweltan** *to be put to death*, see **sweltan**

degelice see **digellice**

dele see **dæl**

dema wk.m. *judge.* gs. **deman** PCGPr.20
(ge)deman vb I. *to judge, adjudge, pass judgement on.* imp.s. **dem** LwPr.43(x3); pres.3s. **gedemeð** LwPr.49.6; pres.subj.s. **deme** LwPr.49.6; pret.s. **gedemde** LwPr.49.7(x2); pret.subj.s. **demde** LwPr.49.6
deofol m. or n. *devil.* gs. **deofles** BoEp.12
deofolgeld n. *idol.* ap. LwPr.49.5
derian vb I/II. *to injure, harm.* imp.p. **deriað** LwPr.34
deþ see **don**
diacon m. *deacon.* ns. **deacon** GDGPr.21; gs. **diacones** GDEx1.2, GDEx3.2; ds. **deacone** GDGPr.6
dierne adj. *secret, hidden.* dp. **diernum** LwPr.49.5
digellice adv. *secretly.* BoPVi.18. **degelice** BoVVi.64
digle adj. *secret, secluded.* asf. **diglan** GDGPr.45, gsm. **dieglan** PCGPr.20; dsf. **diglan** GDGPr.14. comp. dsn **digolran** GDGPr.67
digolnes f. *seclusion, secluded place.* ds. **digolnesse** GDGPr.16
diop adj. *deep.* nsm. PCVEp.17
dohtor f. *daughter.* as. LwPr.12, 21
dom m. *law, decree, judgement.* as. **dom** LwPr.43, 49.6, 49.8; gs. **domes** LwPr.21; ds. **dome** LwPr.49.6; np. **domas** LwPr.11, 49; ap. **domas** LwPr.40
domboc f. *book of law, law-code.* gp. **domboca** LwPr.49.6
domere m. *judge.* np. **domeras** LwPr.18
(ge)don anom. vb. *to do, make, take.* infin. GDGPr.13, [PCPPr.11], PCPPr.56 (*bring*), BoPPr.12; imp.p. **doð** LwPr.49.5; pres.2s. **dest** LwPr.36; pres.3s. **deþ** BoPPr.12, LwPr.25; pres.p. **doð** GDGPr.13, LwPr.34; pres.subj.s. **do** PCPPr.68, LwPr.12(x2), 20, **gedo** SoPr.18, 27, LwPr.20; pres.subj.p. **don** LwPr.49.5; pret.s. **dyde** GDIn3.5, BoPVi.14, SoPr.12; pp. npn. **gedonan** (*performed, committed*) GDGPr.18. *to cause, bring to pass.* infin. SoPr.13; pres.1s. **gedo** LwPr.34; pres.subj.s. **do** PCPPr.20, **gedo** SoPr.17; pres.subj.p. **gedon** PCPPr.50; pp. **gedon** BoPPr.2, 8
dorst- see **durran**
dreccean vb I. *to afflict, oppress.* pres.subj.s. (or imp.s.?) **drece** LwPr.47
(ge)drefan vb I. *to afflict, trouble, disturb.* pp. **gedrefed** GDGPr.29, 54, BoPVi.25, BoVVi.74
gedrefedness f. *affliction, tribulation.* ap. **gedrefednesse** GDPPr.9; dp. **gedrefednessum** GDGPr.48
dreogan vb 2. *to suffer.* pres.1s. **dreoge** GDGPr.27, 44
drihten m. *lord, the Lord.* ns. BoEp.1, **dryhten** PCVEp.22, LwPr.1(x2), 3, 4; as. LwPr.37, BdVEp.22; gs. **drihtnes** BoVVi.41, **dryhtnes** PCVPr.4, PCVEp.17, 24, LwPr.49, 49.3; ds. **drihtne** BoVVi.64, 83
drincan vb 3. *to drink.* infin. GDIn4.2, PCVEp.22, BdPEp.1
drohtnian vb II. *to engage, spend life (in).* pres.p. **drohtniað** GDGPr.32

drync m. *drink*. ns. PCVEp.30
durran pret.pres.vb. *to dare*. pret.s. **dorste** LwPr.49.9, BdPr.33; pret.p. **dorston** LwPr.49.7; pret.subj.p. **dorsten** BoVVi.27
duru f. *door*. ds. **dura** PCGPr.25, LwPr.11; dp. **durum** PCVEp.24
dust n. *dust*. ds. **duste** GDGPr.40
gedwellan vb I. *to lead astray, mislead*. pret.p. **gedwealdon** LwPr.49.3
gedwola wk.m. *error, heresy*. ns. BoVVi.41; ds. **gedwolan** BoPVi.6
dyde see **don**

eac adv. *also*. GDGPr.33, GDEx1.2, PCPPr.24, PCGPr.5, etc.; prep.w.d. *in addition to*. BoVVi.44. **eac swa** *likewise, also*. GDVPr.23, LwPr.49.7. **eac swylce** *likewise, also*. BdPEp.2
eaca wk.m. *increase*. ds. **eacan** GDGPr.29, 63. *interest*. is. **eacan** LwPr.35
eacnian vb II. *to flourish*. pres.pt. (used as adj.) *pregnant*. asn. **eacniende** LwPr.18
eadig adj. *blessed*. nsm. **eadiga** GDGPr.8, **eadega** GDGPr.5; gsm. **eadigan** GDEx1.3, **eadegan** GDIn2.3, BdPr.21, 27
eage wk.n. *eye*. as. LwPr.19, 20; ap. **eagan** GDGPr.18, SoPr.18; dp. **eagum** GDVPr.7, PCGPr.20
geeahtian vb II. *to appraise, assess the value*. pres.subj.s. **geeahtige**. LwPr.26
eala interj. *oh!* GDGPr.27, 80
eald adj. *old, senior*. nsf. GDGPr.28; gp. **ealdra** BdPr.5, 20, 25, 41; dp. **ealdum** BoVVi.65. comp. npm. **eldran** LwPr.49.3
ealdhlaford m. *former lord*. dp. **ealdhlafordum** BoPVi.15, BoVVi.63
ealdhlafordcynn n. *kin of the old lords*. BoPVi.19
ealdian vb II. *to grow old, decay*. pret.p. **ealdedon** GDGPr.67
ealdriht n. *ancient right*. gp. **ealdrihta** BoPVi.7, 14, BoVVi.36, 57; dp. **ealdrihtum** BoPVi.21
ealdspell n. *ancient story*. as./ap. BoVPr.1
eall adj. *all*. nsf. **eall** PCPPr.51; nsn. **eall** PCPPr.27, **eal** GDGPr.16, LwPr.39; asm. **ealne** SoPr.5(x2), LwPr.49.7, **alne** GDVPr.13; asf. **ealle** PCPPr.44, LwPr.49.1; asn. **eall** PCPPr.26, 27, 36, BoPVi.3, BoVVi.39, LwPr.23; gsm. **ealles** BdPEp.3; gsn. **ealles** GDVPr.22; dsn. **ealle** GDGPr.64; npm. **ealle** PCPPr.50, LwPr.49.1, 49.2; npf. **ealla** PCPPr.47, **al** GDGPr.92; npn. **ealle** BoVVi.33, **eall** GDGPr.18; apm. **ealle** PCPPr.10, **ealla** BoVVi.12; apf. **ealla** PCPPr.37, 46, **ealle** PCPPr.45, LwPr.3; apn. **eal** GDGPr.31, BdPr.22, **eall** GDGPr.32; gp. **ealra** GDVPr.25, BoEp.2, 7, SoPr.17, **eallra** GDVPr.15, **alra** BdPr.6; dp. **eallum** GDGPr.3, PCPPr.49, BoEp.17, LwPr.49, etc. as noun. n. *everything*. as. PCGPr.4, BdPr.18, 20; gs. **ealles** BdVEp.20
ealles adv. *entirely*. LwPr.12, 17
eallunga adv. *entirely*. GDGPr.75
ealneg adv. *always*. PCPPr.70

Glossary and List of Proper Names   235

ealond   see eglond
eardian   vb II. *to live.* infin. SoPr.13, LwPr.35
eare   wk.n. *ear.* as. LwPr.11
earfoþrime   adj. *hard to count.* npf. earfoþrimu BoPPr.5
earm   adj. *poor, wretched.* dsm. earman LwPr.43
geearnian   vb II. *to earn.* pres.subj.s. geearnige SoPr.27
(ge)earnung   f. *merit.* ap. earnunge SoPr.17; gp. geearnunga PCGEp.8; dp. earnungum BoEp.7
eastan   adv. *from the east.* BoVVi.1
eaþe   adv. *easily.* GDVPr.4, PCPPr.50
eaþmod   adj. *humble.* dsn. eaðmode PCGPr.2
eaþmodian   vb II. *to humble.* pp. geeaðmodad GDGPr.97
eaþmodlice   adv. *humbly.* BdPr.53, BdPEp.5
eaþmodnes   f. *humility.* as. eaðmodnesse PCGPr.13, LwPr.49
Ebriscgeðiode   n. *the Hebrew language.* ds. PCPPr.43
ecan   vb I. *to increase.* infl.infin. ecanne LwPr.49
ece   adj. *eternal.* msn. GDVPr.15; asn. æce SoPr.27; dsm. ecan SoPr.15, 19; dsf. ecan SoPr.20(x2); gp. ecena SoPr.28
edlean   n. *reward, payment.* as. GDGPr.37; gs. edleanes BdPEp.9
edwit   n. *scorn, insult, contempt.* ns. BoVVi.55
efne   adv. *even, right.* BoVVi.14. *evenly, impartially.* emne LwPr.43
eft   adv. *back, again.* PCPPr.39, 43, 45, PCGPr.14, PCVEp.26, BoPPr.8, BoVVi.61, LwPr.22. æft BoVVi.65
ege   m. *fear.* ns. PCGPr.15, BoVVi.72
eglond   n. *island.* ns. BoVVi.16; ds. ealonde BoPVi.4
egþer   see ægþer
eldran   wk.mp. *elders, ancestors.* np. BoVVi.58
eldran   (comp. adj.) see eald
elles   adv. *else, otherwise.* GDGPr.33, LwPr.34
elleshwær   adv. *elsewhere.* BdPr.54
elþeodig   adj. *foreign* (often as noun). asn. LwPr.12 (x2); dsm. elðeodegan LwPr.47; npm. elðeodge BoVVi.55, elðeodige LwPr.33; apm. elðeodige LwPr.33
emb(e-)   see ymb(e-)
emne   see efne
emtan   see æm(et)ta
ende   m. *end.* as. BdVEp.22; ds. BoEp.22
endian   vb II. *to end.* pret.s. endað GDEx3.1; pret.p. endiað SoEx1.1, SoEx2.1, SoEx3.1
geendian   vb II. *to end, conclude.* infin. geendigan BdVEp.19; pret.s. geendode BoPVi.8; pp. geendad GDEx1.1, geendod SoIn3.1
Englisc   adj. *English.* asn. PCPPr.54, 58; dsn. Engliscum BoPPr.7. as noun n. *the English language.* as. PCPPr.15(x2), 60(x2), 65, PCVPr.11, BoPPr.1

eom see **beon**
eorl m. *man, nobleman.* ns. BoVVi.78; ds. **eorle** BoVVi.72; np. **eorlas** BoVVi.30
eorþe wk.f. *earth.* as. **eorðan** LwPr.3, 4, 49.1; ds. **eorþan** PCVEp.11
eorþlic adj. *earthly.* apf. **eorðlice** GDGPr.68, **eorþlican** GDPPr.4, 9; gp. **eorðlicra** GDGPr.40
geeowan vb I. *to show.* pret.s. **geeowde** LwPr.49.10
eower poss.adj. *your.* npn. **eowru** LwPr.34(x2); gp. **eowra** LwPr.49.3; dp. **iowrum** PCVEp.24
esne m. *servant.* as. LwPr.17
etan vb 5. *to eat.* pres.subj.p. **eten** LwPr.39; pp. **eten** LwPr.21
eþel m. *homeland, territory.* as. PCPPr.8, BoVVi.16; gs. **eðles** GDGPr.93
eþelweard m. *defender or guardian of the homeland.* np. **eþelweardas** BoVVi.24
eþnes f. *privilege, comfort.* gp. **eðnessa** BoPVi.14

facn n. *deceit, fraud.* as. LwPr.28
fana wk.m. *banner.* ns. BoVVi.10
faran vb 6. *to go, travel* (intrans.). pres.s. **farað** GDIn4.3; pret.p. **foron** BoVVi.20; pp. **gefaren** BdPr.16
fæder m. *father.* ns. LwPr.29; as. LwPr.14, 15; gs. GDGPr.2; ds. BdPr.49, LwPr.4; ap. **fædras** SoPr.16, **fæderas** SoPr.21; gp. **fædera** GDGPr.95
fæger adj. *fair, fine, pleasant.* asm. **fægerne** PCGEp.1, **fegerne** SoPr.10; dsf. **fægerre** GDGPr.39; gp. **fægran** GDIn3.3; dp. **fegrum** SoPr.9
fægnian vb II. *to rejoice.* pret.p. **fægnodon** BoVVi.33
fæmne wk.f. *woman, virgin.* as.gs. **fæmnan** LwPr.29(x2); ap. **fæmnan** LwPr.30
gefæra see **gefera**
fæst adj. *fast, watertight.* asm. **fæstne** PCVEp.25
fæste adv. *firmly.* BoVVi.35
fæsten n. *place of confinement, prison.* as. BoVVi.20; ds. **fæstene** BoVVi.79
fæstlice adv. *firmly.* PCGPr.9, BoVVi.70
fætels m. *vessel, container.* as. PCVEp.25
gefea wk.m. *joy.* as. **gefean** PCGPr.19
feawe pl.adj. *few.* npm. PCPPr.25, **feawa** PCPPr.14, 16
(ge)feallan vb 7. *to fall.* pret.s. **feol** BoVVi.81, **gefeoll** BoPVi.26
fegerne, fegrum see **fæger**
fela indecl.adj. and pron. with noun usually in gen. *many, much.* BoVVi.81, LwPr.49.9, BdPr.29, 35. **feola** GDVPr.2
feld m. *open country, field.* dp. **feldum** PCVEp.21
fenn n. *fen, marsh.* ds. **fenne** PCVEp.21
feoh n. *property, money, livestock.* ns. LwPr.28 (in **cucu feoh** *livestock*), **fioh** LwPr.17, 42; as. LwPr.29, **fioh** LwPr.28, 35; ds. **fio** LwPr.24

feond m. *enemy*. ns. LwPr.42
feor adv. *far*. GDGPr.52, 58, 61
feorh n. *life*. gs. **feores** LwPr.13
feorþa adj. *fourth*. nsm. **feorðe** PCGPr.12; nsf. **feorðe** GDEx3.2, GDIn4.1
feower num. *four*. PCGPr.10, LwPr.24
gefera wk.m. *companion, comrade*. ns. **gefæra** GDGPr.23; ds. **geferan** LwPr.35; np. **geferan** LwPr.49.3
feran vb I. *to go, travel*. infin. GDGPr.4
fetian vb II. *to fetch*. pres.subj.s. **fetige** SoPr.8
gefeþrian vb II. *to load (a wagon)*. pres.subj.s. **gefeðrige** SoPr.9
fifteg num. *fifty*. dp. **fiftegum** PCPPr.67
findan vb 3. *to find*. infin. GDVPr.2; infl.infin. **findenne** GDGPr.90; pres.subj.p. **finden** LwPr.21; pp. **funden** GDGPr.91, PCPPr.43, LwPr.25
fio(h) see **feoh**
fiohbot f. *compensation in money*. gs. **fiohbote** LwPr.49.7
fiorm f. *benefit, use*. as. **fiorme** PCPPr.29
firas mp. *men, mankind*. gp. **fira** BdVEp.15
first m. *time, period*. as. PCPPr.54, **fyrst** SoPr.26
fiscian vb II. *to go fishing*. infin. SoPr.25
fitt f. *poem, verse*. as. **fitte** BoVPr.9
flæsc n. *flesh*. ns.as. LwPr.21, 23(x2), 39
fleon vb 2. *to flee, avoid, escape*. infin. PCGPr.3; pres.3s. **flyhð** BdPr.9; pret.s. **fleah** BoVVi.20
flod m. *current*. ns. GDIn3.1; ds. **flode** GDIn3.4
flor f. *floor*. as. BoPVr.27, **flore** BoVVi.81
flowan vb 7. *to flow*. pret.subj.p. **fleowen** PCVEp.5
folc n. *people, nation*. as. LwPr.12(x2); gs. **folces** PCPPr.6, LwPr.37, 41
folccuþ adj. *well-known*. asm. **folccuðne** BoVPr.9
folcryht adj. *by public law*. gsf. **folcryhte** LwPr.13
folcgesiþ m. *lord of the people*. ap. **folcgesiðas** BoVVi.70
folcgewinn n. *battle between armies*. gs. **folcgewinnes** BoVVi.10
foldbuend m. *earthdweller*. dp. **foldbuendum** PCVEp.2
folgoþ m. *position, office*. as. PCGPr.11; gs. **folgoðes** GDGPr.12
fon vb 7. *to seize*. In **fon on** *to undertake, engage in*. infin. BoVPr.9. In **fon to** *to succeed to*. pret.s. **feng** PCPPr.18, BoPVi.5
for prep.w.d./a. *because of, on account of, in respect of*. GDGPr.11, GDIn3.3, PCGPr.13, BoPPr.4, etc.
forbærnan vb I. *to burn (up)*. pp. **forbærned** PCPPr.27
forbeodan vb 2. *to forbid*. infl.infin. **forbeodanne** LwPr.49
forberan vb 4. *to refrain (from)*. pres.subj.p. **forberen** LwPr.49.5

for(e) prep.w.d. *in compensation for.* LwPr.19(x3)

fore adv. *before (in time), beforehand.* GDVPr.26; PCVPr.3. *in compensation* LwPr.19, 23

foregangan vb 7. *to precede.* pres.pt. (used as noun) *predecessor.* gp. **foregangendra** GDGPr.95

foregenga wk.m. *predecessor.* np. **foregengan** LwPr.49.9

foresprecen adj. *aforementioned.* dp. **foresprecenan** BoPVi.4

forgifan vb 5. *to grant, give.* pres.subj.s. **forgife** SoPr.29, **forgyfe** BdPEp.2; pret.2s. **forgeafe** BdPEp.1; pret.3s. **forgeaf** GDVPr.23; pres.pt. dsm. **forgifendum** GDIn2.2; pp. **forgifen** GDPPr.3. *to forgive.* pres.subj.s. **forgyue** GDVPr.21

forgitan vb 5. *to forget.* pres.3s. **forgiteð** GDGPr.59

forgyldan vb 3. *to redeem by payment, pay compensation.* pres.subj.s. **forgielde** LwPr.25, 29, **forgylde** LwPr.28; pp. **forgolden** LwPr.21

forhergian vb II. *to ravage, plunder.* pp. **forhergod** PCPPr.27

forhogian vb II. *to despise.* pret.s. **forhogode** GDGPr.31

forhwerfan vb I. *to pervert, overthrow.* pret.p. **forhwerfdon** LwPr.49.3

forhwon adv. *why.* GDGPr.26

forlætan vb 7. *to leave out, omit.* pres.subj.s. **forlæte** PCGPr.13; pret.s. **forlet** LwPr.49.9. *to abandon, let go.* pret.s. **forlet** GDGPr.56; pret.p. **forleton** PCPPr.41; pp. **forlæten** PCPPr.34

forleosan vb 2. *to lose.* pres.3s. **forleoseð** GDGPr.57; pres.subj.s. **forleose** PCGPr.21; pret.s. **forleas** GDGPr.45, 58, 59; pp. **forloren** PCVEp.30

forma adj. *first.* nsf. **forme** GDEx1.1; gsf. **forman** SoEx1.1; dsm. **forman** LwPr.49.7

foron see **faran**

forsceadan vb 7. *to spill (water).* pres.subj.s. **forsceade** PCVEp.29

forstandan vb 6. *to understand, withstand.* infin. BoVVi.22; pret.s. **forstod** PCPPr.64

forstelan vb 4. *to steal.* pres.subj.s. **forstele** LwPr.15, 24

forsweotole adv. *very clearly.* SoPr.34

forswigian vb II. *to pass over in silence.* pp. npn. **forswigode** GDGPr.78

forþ adv. *henceforth, onwards, continually.* GDGPr.3, GDIn3.2, PCVEp.3

forþam adv. *therefore, indeed.* GDGPr.108, SoPr.7, BdPr.6, **forþan** GDPPr.5, **forðæm** PCVPr.8, **forðon** GDGPr.5, 8, 56, [61], 95, PCPPr.20, LwPr.3, BdPr.9. conj. *because* GDGPr.87, BoPVi.19, LwPr.3, **forðæm** PCVPr.15, **forþon** GDGPr.15, PCGPr.2, LwPr.46, BdPr.5, 12, 18. Also w. **þe**. BoPPr.10, LwPr.49.7, **forðæm** PCPPr.29, 30, PCGEp.8, **forþon** PCGPr.24, BoEp.19, LwPr.2, 17, 33, 36. correlative **forðæm** ... **forðæm** ... *therefore...because.* PCPPr.33–4, LwPr.49.9

forþbringan vb 3. *to bring forth, produce.* pp. **forðbroht** GDGPr.109

forþencan vb I. *to despair.* pp. **forþoht** *in despair.* BoVVi.82

forþfor f. *death.* as. **forðfore** BdPr.38

forþy adv. *therefore*. PCPPr.48, 70, PCGPr.10
fot m. *foot*. as. **fet** [for **fot**?] LwPr.19; ds. **fet** LwPr.19
fram see **from**
gefræge adj. *famous, renowned*. superl. nsm. **gefrægost** PCVPr.10
gefrægn see **gefrignan**
gefrætwian vb II. *to adorn*. pp. nsf. **gefrætewudu** GDEx3.2
fremde adj. *strange*. apm. LwPr.1.1
(ge)fremman vb I. *to do, perform*. pret.s. **(ge)fremede** BoVVi.45, LwPr.28
fremsumlice adv. *kindly*. PCGPr.1
freo see **frio(h)**
gefreogan vb II. *to free*. pres.subj.s. **gefreoge** LwPr.20
freond m. *friend, kinsman*. ns. GDGPr.14; ds. **friend** LwPr.28; dp. **freondum** GDPPr.6
freondlic adj. *friendly*. dsf. **freondlicre** GDGPr.22
freondlice adv. *in a friendly way, affectionately*. PCPPr.2, PCGPr.1
freondscipe m. *friendship*. as. BoPVi.7
gefrignan vb 3. *to learn of, find out, ask about*. pret.s. **gefrægn** GDGPr.110; pret.subj.s. **gefrugne** GDVPr.52
frio(h) adj. *free*. nsm. LwPr.11; nsf. LwPr.12; asm. **frione** LwPr.15; asf. **freo** LwPr.12; gp. **friora** PCPPr.52
friþ m. or n. *peace*. gs. **friðes** BoVVi.35
friþstow f. *sanctuary*. as. **friþstowe** LwPr.13
frofor f. *comfort, consolation*. ns. **frofer** BoEp.20; gs. **frofre** BoPVi.26, BoVVi.79; ds. **frofre** PCVEp.2
from prep.w.d. *from, by*. GDGPr.22, PCPPr.68, PCGPr.25, BoVVi.14, etc., **fram** GDGPr.67, 104, BoEp.13, BdPr.21, 24, 29, 38
fruma wk.m. *beginning*. ds. **fruman** GDGPr.57, BdPr.24
frumripa wk.m. (only in pl.). *first fruits*. ap. **frumripan** LwPr.38
frymþ f. *beginning*. ds. **frymðe** GDGPr.22
fuglian vb II. *to catch birds*. infin. SoPr.25
ful adj. *foul*. asf. **fulan** BoEp.13
ful adv. *very*. GDVPr.4, GDGPr.12, 63, 92, LwPr.46
fulgan anom.vb (w.d.). *to carry out*. pres.3s. **fulgað** GDVPr.11
full adj. *full*. nsm. BoVVi.9. as adv. in **be fullan** *thoroughly*. PCPPr.37
fullfremednes f. *perfection*. gs. **fullfremednesse** PCGEp.4
fulluht m. *baptism*. gs. **fulluhte** (for **fulluhtes**) LwPr.49.9
fulluhtþeaw m. *(rite of) baptism*. dp. **fulluhtþeawum** BoVVi.33
fulmedeme adj. *fully perfect*. dp. **fulmedemum** GDGPr.80
fulneah adv. *very nearly, almost*. GDGPr.35
fultum m. *help*. ns. GDGPr.94, BoEp.20; ds. **fultume** PCPPr.51, SoPr.24
(ge)fultumian vb I/II (w.d.). *to help*. pret.subj.s. **gefultumede** BoPVi.21

fultumiend m. *helper*. ns. BdPr.15
funden see **findan**
furþum adv. *even*. PCPPr.15, 17
furþur adv. *further*. PCPPr.55. **furðor** PCPPr.55
fyllan vb I. *to fill*. pres.subj.s. **fylle** PCVEp.25; pp. npf. **gefylda** PCPPr.28
fyr n. *fire*. ns. LwPr.27; as. LwPr.27
fyrst see **first**
gefyrþrian vb II. *to support, promote*. pres.subj.s. **gefyrðrige** BdVEp.16
fyst f. *fist*. ds. **fyste** LwPr.16

(ge)gaderian vb II. *to gather, collect*. pret.s. **(ge)gaderode** SoPr.1, LwPr.49.9(x2); pp. npm. **gegaderode** LwPr.49.7
gadorung f. *gathering, collection*. ns. SoIn2.1
galnes f. *lust*. as. **galnysse** BoEp.13
gan anom.vb. *to go*. pres.3s. **gæð** GDIn2.2
gangan vb 7. *to go*. infin. **gongan** LwPr.16; pres.subj.s. **gange** LwPr.11(x2); pres. pt. **gangende** *walking, living, moving (of cattle)*, in **frumripan gongendes** *first fruits of livestock*. LwPr.38. [*DOE* 'gangan' I.1.c.iv.]
gast m. *spirit*. In **se halga gast** *the Holy Ghost*. ns. **gæst** PCVEp.8; ds. **gaste** GDIn2.2, LwPr.49.5
gastlic adj. *spiritual*. gsn. **gastlices** GDVPr.3, GDIn2.2 (or gsm.); dsn. **gastlican** GDPPr.5
gæst see **gast**
gealdorcræftiga wk.m. *magician*. ap. **gealdorcræftigan** LwPr.30
gear n. *year*. ap. LwPr.11
geara adv. *long ago*. **geara iu** BoVVi.1
gearmælum adv. *year by year*. BoVVi.5
gearolice adv. *readily, clearly*. GDPPr.2
geld- see **gyldan**
gemende see **gyman**
geo adv. *formerly, previously*. GDVPr.21. **iu** PCPPr.4, BoVVi.1 (see **geara**). **giu** PCPPr.37, LwPr.33
geofendum see **giefan**
geogoþhad m. *youth*. gs. **geogoþhades** GDGPr.22
geomor adj. *sad, miserable*. dsf. **geomran** BoVVi.84
geond prep.w.a. *through, throughout*. PCVEp.12, LwPr.49.1, 49.7(x2). **giond** PCPPr.4, 5, 27, 37, 57
geondwadan vb 6. *to know thoroughly, explore*. pret.s. **gindwod** PCVPr.6
georn adj. *eager*. nsm. BoVVi.51; npm. **giorne** PCPPr.9
georne adv. *speedily, zealously, intently*. GDGPr.43, PCVEp.28
geornfulnes f. *eagerness, dedication*. as. **geornfulnesse** BdPr.4

geornlice adv. *eagerly, assiduously.* BdPEp.7, 11
gerd f. *branch, stick.* dp. **gerdum** SoPr.9 [*DOE* 'gyrd']
giefan vb 5. *to give.* pret.s. **geaf** PCVEp.22; pres.pt. dsm. **geofendum** GDPPr.1
giefu f. *gift.* as. **giefe** PCVEp.17. gs. **gife** BdPr.31; ds. **gyfe** GDIn3.3
giemeleas adj. *stray.* nsn. LwPr.42
giemen f. *care.* gs. **giemenne** PCGPr.3
giernnes f. *eagerness.* In **of giernesse** *on purpose.* LwPr.13. [*DOE* 'geornnes, gyrnnes']
gierwan vb I. *to direct (a stream of water).* pret.p. **gierdon** PCVEp.10; pp. **gegiered** PCVEp.23
giet see **gyt**
gif conj. *if.* GDGPr.70, PCPPr.48, BoVVi.27, SoPr.5, etc.; **gyf** GDGPr.15
gife see **giefu**
gifola wk.m. *benefactor.* ns. [SoPr.28]
gilp m. *pride, arrogance.* ds. **gilpe** BoVPr.8
gindwod see **geondwadan**
gioguþ f. *young people.* ns. PCPPr.51
giomonn m. *man of old, ancestor.* gp. **giomonna** BoVVi.23
giond see **geond**
giorne see **georn**
giu see **geo**
gleaw adj. *wise, learned.* nsm. BoVVi.52
gleawmod adj. *wise, prudent.* nsm. PCVPr.6
glengan vb I. *to adorn.* pp. **geglenged** GDEx2.2
gnornung f. *grief, grieving.* ns. GDGPr.27; as. **gnornunge** GDGPr.26; ds. **gnornunge** GDGPr.14
God m. *God.* ns. GDPPr.3, PCPPr.22, BoVVi.38, LwPr.13, etc.; as. LwPr.32; gs. **Godes** GDPPr.6, GDVPr.6, GDGPr.7, PCPPr.28, 51, 67, BoPPr.9, LwPr.49.7, BdPEp.8; ds. **Gode** PCPPr.6, 11, 18, 69, PCVEp.10, LwPr.38, 49.1
god m. *god* (other than God). ap. **godas** LwPr.1.1, 10, 48
god n. *good.* as. GDGPr.57, **gode** GDGPr.59 (or ap.); ap. BdPr.7; gp. **godena** PCPPr.36; dp. **godum** LwPr.49
god adj. *good.* nsm. **goda** PCGEp.1, BdPEp.1; nsn. BdPr.9, **gode** GDGPr.89; asm. **godne** BoVVi.42, BdPr.9; asn. PCGPr.17; npm. **gode** GDGPr.76; apn. **godan** PCGPr.21; gp. **godre** GDVPr.3, **godra** GDGPr.88, 92, 95, BoVVi.45; dp. **godum** GDGPr.82, 86, BdPr.7, **godan** PCGPr.19
godcund adj. *divine, ecclesiastical.* gsf. **godcundan** GDGPr.23, GDIn2.1; dsn. **godcundan** GDPPr.5; npm. **godcundan** PCPPr.9; gp. **godcundra** PCPPr.4
godgeld n. *idol.* dp. **godgeldum** LwPr.32
godspel n. *gospel.* as. GDGPr.102
gongan see **gangan**

gegongan vb 7. *to conquer.* infin. BoVVi.12
gretan vb I. *to greet.* infin. (used with passive meaning *to be greeted*). PCPPr.2, BdPr.1
guþ f. *war, battle.* gs.ds. **guðe** BoVVi.9, 23
gyddian vb II. *to sing, recite.* pret.s. **gyddode** BoVVi.84
gyf see **gif**
gyfe see **giefu**
gyft f. *gift.* In **gyfta don** *to arrange a wedding* [*DOE* **gyft, gift** 3a.i.a]. ap. **gyfta** LwPr.12
gyldan vb 3. *to pay.* infin. **geldan** LwPr.28; pres.subj.s. **gelde** LwPr.22
gylden adj. *golden.* asm. **gyldenan** GDIn3.2; apm. **gyldne** LwPr.10
gyldenmuþa adj. *golden-mouthed.* nsm. GDIn2.6
gylp m. *boasting, pride.* gs. **gylpes** BoVVi.9
gylt m. *sin, guilt, offence.* ds. **gylte** LwPr.49.7; ap. **gyltas** GDVPr.21
gyman vb I (w.g.). *to heed.* pres.3s. **gymð** BoVPr.8; pres.pt. (used as adj.) *attentive (to)* (w.a.). nsm. **gemende** BdPr.5
gyt adv. *yet.* GDGPr.53, SoPr.12, SoIn3.2, BdVEp.18. **giet** PCPPr.33, PCGEp.5, BoVPr.8, LwPr.49.1. **git** BdPr.34

habban vb III. *to have, possess.* infin. PCPPr.13, 71; infl.infin. **gehabbanne** GDGPr.90; pres.1s. **habbe** GDPPr.1, **hæbbe** PCGEp.2(x2), 4; pres.2s. **hafast** GDVPr.17, GDGPr.26; pres.3s. **hæfð** PCGEp.8, SoPr.24, **hefð** SoPr.15, ?**heft** SoIn3.1; **hafað** GDPPr.3, PCVEp.23; pres.p. **habbað** PCPPr.19, 34, 51; pres. subj.s. **hæbbe** PCGPr.18, SoPr.7, LwPr.11, 12, 22, 23, 28, 29; pres.subj.p. **hæbben** PCPPr.52, LwPr.23; pret.s. **hæfde** GDGPr.57, 61, PCPPr.64, PCGPr.19, BoPPr.6, 7; pret.p. **hæfdon** PCPPr.6, 38, BoPVi.15, **hæfdan** BoVVi.6; pp. **gehæfd** GDGPr.91
had m. *order, office.* ds. **hade** PCPPr.56; np. **hadas** PCPPr.9; gp. **hada** PCPPr.4. *person.* dp. **hadum** GDGPr.108
halga wk.m. *saint.* gp. **halgana** BoEp.7
halgian vb II. *to make or keep holy.* pres.subj.s. **halgige** LwPr.3; pret.s. **gehalgode** LwPr.3
halig adj. *holy.* nsm. PCVEp.8; asm. **halegan** GDGPr.2; gsm. **haligan** GDIn3.2; gsf. **halgan** GDGPr.100, **halegan** BoEp.4; gsn. **halgan** GDGPr.23; dsm. **halgan** GDIn2.2, LwPr.49.5, **halegan** BdPr.49; npm. **halge** PCVEp.9; apm. **halige** BoVVi.25, **halie** SoPr.16, **halgan** SoPr.20; apf. **halga** PCVEp.11; gp. **haligra** GDPPr.2, GDPPr.7, GDVPr.10, GDGPr.7, GDEx2.1, GDIn3.4, **halegra** LwPr.49.7; dp. **halgum** GDVPr.18
halsian vb II. *to entreat.* pres.1s. **halsige** BdPr.53; pres.3s. **halsað** BoPPr.9
ham m. *home.* ds. **hame** SoPr.15, 19, GDVPr.5; gp. **hama** SoPr.28. locative (ending-less) used as adv. after verb of motion SoPr.4, 5. **æt ham** *at home* SoPr.6

hand f. *hand.* ns. GDGPr.109; as. **honda** LwPr.19; ds. **honda** PCGEp.8, LwPr.19; ap. **honda** LwPr.13; dp. **handum** GDVPr.17, BdVEp.17. **on hond** *into the possession of* (w.d.). LwPr.42

gehat n. *promise.* ap. BoPVi.8

hatan vb 7. *to order, command.* pres.3s. **hateð** PCPPr.2; pret.s. **het** GDVPr.12, BoPVi.10, 22, BoVVi.42, LwPr.49.9, **heht** PCVPr.13, BoVVi.70, 72. *to name, call.* pres.p. **hatað** BoPVi.11, SoEx2.1, SoEx3.1; pp. **haten** GDIn2.4, **gehaten** BoPVi.11; pp. npm. **hatne** BoPVi.2; npf. **gehatene** SoPr.32; passive **hatte** *is called, was called.* BoVVi.53

gehatan vb 7. *to promise.* pret.s. **gehet** PCVEp.2, BoPVi.6, BoVVi.35; pp. **gehaten** SoPr.15, 20

hatte see **hatan**

hæbbe see **habban**

(ge)hæfd(-) see **habban**.

gehæftan vb I. *to retain, keep captive.* pres.p. **gehæftað** PCVEp.14

hæfþ see **habban**

hæle m. *man.* ns. BoVVi.53

hælend m. *Saviour.* ns. LwPr.49, BdPEp.1

hæleþ m. *man.* dp. **hæleðum** BoVPr.10

hælo f. *health, salvation.* as. LwPr.49.3

hæman vb I. *to have illicit sexual intercourse.* infl.infin. **hæmanne** LwPr.12; pres. subj.s. **hæme** LwPr.31

hær see **her**

hærlic adj. *noble.* nsf. BoVVi.43

hæþen adj. *heathen.* apm. **hæðne** LwPr.48; apf. **hæðena** LwPr.49.1; dp. **hæðenum** LwPr.49.2

he m., **heo** f., **hit** n., **hi** pl. pers.pron.3. *he, she, it, they.* nsm. GDVPr.2, GDGPr.15, GDIn3.4, PCVPr.8, etc.; nsf. **heo** GDGPr.28(x2), BoPPr.8, **hio** PCPPr.13, PCGPr.9, BoPPr.2, BoVVi.77, etc.; nsn. **hit** GDGPr.10, PCPPr.26, PCVEp.21, BoVVi.1, etc., **hyt** GDGPr.26, 30(x2), 31, 38; asm. **hine** GDVPr.2, PCGPr.6, PCVEp.5, BoPVi.20, etc., **hiene** PCPPr.22, **hyne** SoPr.5, BdPr.23; asf. **hie** PCPPr.12(x2), 44, BoPPr.1, LwPr.12, **hi** PCGPr.10, BoPPr.8; asn. **hit** GDGPr.41, PCPPr.23, PCGPr.15, BoPPr.3, etc., **hyt** GDGPr.16; gsm. **his** GDEx1.2, PCPPr.2, PCVPr.12, BoPVi.7, etc., **hys** GDGPr.6, 15(x2), 22, SoPr.9, 32, 33(x2); gsf. **hire** LwPr.11, 12, **hiere** LwPr.12; gsn. **his** GDGPr.30, 36, 43, PCGPr.4, etc., **hys** GDGPr.39; dsm. **him** GDVPr.18, GDGPr.9, PCPPr.71, PCVEp.30, etc., **hym** GDGPr.27, SoPr.8; dsf. **hiere** LwPr.12, **hire** LwPr.12(x2); dsn. **him** PCPPr.33; npm. **hi** GDPPr.6, GDGPr.67, 102, PCVPr.15, **hie** PCPPr.7, 10, 11, LwPr.21, etc., **hig** GDGPr.102(x2), **hy** BoVVi.36; npf. **hi** PCGPr.4; npn. **hig** GDGPr.18, 78, 79; apm. **hi** BoVVi.62, 64, **hie** LwPr.34, **hig** GDGPr.68; apf. **hi** PCGPr.6; gp. **heora** GDVPr.19, GDGPr.66, GDEx2.2, BoPVi.2, etc., **hiora** GDVPr.7, 11, GDEx1.1, 3,

PCPPr.7, LwPr.1, etc., **hira** GDGPr.67, PCGPr.5, 13; dp. **him** GDGPr.77, PCPPr.8, BoPVi.20, BoVVi.6, etc.
heafod n. *head.* ds. **heafde** BoVVi.43
heah adj. *exalted, important.* comp. dp. **hyhrum** BdPEp.10
heahburg f. *principal town.* ns. BoPVi.19
healdan vb 7. *to keep, observe.* infin. **healdon** BoVVi.71; infl.infin. **healdanne** LwPr.49, 49.3, 49.5, 49.9, 49.10; pret.p. **heoldon** LwPr.49.9, **hioldon** (*occupied*) PCPPr.31. *to keep charge of, pen in.* infin. LwPr.23
gehealdan vb 7. *to maintain.* pret.p. **gehioldon** PCPPr.8
heaness f. *height, high place.* as. **heanesse** GDPPr.3, **heanesse** GDGPr.65
hefig adj. *heavy, strict, burdensome.* nsm. GDGPr.86; dsn. **hefige** GDGPr.25; comp. nsn. **hefigre** GDGPr.45, 53; asf. **hefigran** LwPr.49.3
hefigian vb II. *to weigh heavy on.* pp. **gehefegad** PCGEp.8
hefignes f. *weight.* as. **hefignesse** PCGPr.3
heft, hefþ see **habban**
heht see **hatan**
help f. *help.* as. **helpe** GDVPr.18; ds. **helpe** GDVPr.10
gehenan vb I. *to oppress, afflict.* pres.subj.s. **gehene** LwPr.35
heofon m. *heaven.* ap. **heofonas** LwPr.3
heofonlic adj. *heavenly.* gsm. **heofonlican** GDGPr.93; gsn. **heofonlican** GDGPr.35; dsn. **heofonlican** GDVPr.5; apn. **heofonlican** GDPPr.9, GDGPr.33
heofonrice n. *heavenly kingdom.* ds. **hefonrice** PCVEp.8
heora see **he**
heorte wk.f. *heart.* gs. **heortan** GDGPr.18, 25
her adv. *here.* GDGPr.1, GDEx1.2, PCPPr.32, BdPr.26, etc.; **hær** SoEx2.1, SoEx3.1. For **her bæftan** see **bæftan**
heran vb I (w.d.). *to obey.* infin. BoVVi.31; pret.p. **herdon** PCVEp.10
heræfter adv. *hereafter, below.* GDEx3.2
here m. *raiding party.* ns. LwPr.28
hererinc m. *warrior, hero.* as. BoVVi.71
heretema wk.m. *ruler.* ns. BoVVi.31
heretoha wk.m. *general, leader (referring to Roman consul).* ns. BoPVi.11, **heretoga** BoVVi.47
herian vb I/II. *to praise.* infin. **herigan** BdVEp.22; infl.infin. **hergeanne** BdPr.9
heron adv. *herein, in this (book/work).* GDVPr.19, LwPr.49.9
het see **hatan**
hi see **he**
gehicgan vb III. *to think about, reflect on.* pres.1s. **gehicge** GDGPr.43; pres.subj.s. **gehicge** GDPPr.9
hider adv. *to here, hither.* PCVEp.11, 25. **hieder** PCPPr.12
hie, hiene, hiere see **he**

Glossary and List of Proper Names 245

gehier- see **(ge)hyran**
hierde m. *shepherd*. ns. PCGEp.3
hierra adj. (compar. of **heah**). *higher*. dsm. **hieran** PCPPr.56
hiersumedon see **hyrsumian**
him see **he**
hio(ra) see **he**
hirdelic adj. *pastoral*. gsf. **hirdelecan** PCGPr.3
hire see **he**
gehire(þ) see **gehyran**
his, hit see **he**
hiwcuþlice adv. *intimately*. GDGPr.22
hladan vb 6. *to draw water*. imp.p. **hladað** PCVEp.22; pret.p. **hlodan** PCVEp.9
hlaford m. *lord*. ns. LwPr.11(x2), 21(x3), 23; as. LwPr.37, 49.7; gs. **hlafordes** SoPr.24, 27, LwPr.11; ds. **hlaforde** BoVVi.47, LwPr.11, 21
hlafordsearu f. *betrayal of a lord*. ds. **hlafordsearwe** LwPr.49.7
hlæder f. *ladder*. as. **hlædre** PCGPr.9
hlisa wk.m. *reputation, fame*. as. **hlisan** BoVVi.53
hlistan vb I. *to listen*. pres.subj.s. **hliste** BoVPr.10
hlud adj. *loud, noisy*. nsn. PCVEp.20
hlut(t)or adj. *clear, pure*. nsn. PCVEp.20; gsf. **hlutran** GDGPr.1, **hluttran** GDIn4.1
hnitol adj. *liable to gore or toss*. nsm. LwPr.21, 23
hold adj. *loyal*. nsm. BoVVi.56
honda see **hand**
hord n. *hoard*. as. PCVPr.7
hrægl n. *garment*. as. LwPr.12, 36; ds. **hrægle** LwPr.11
hræþe adv. *quickly*. PCVEp.26
hreoh adj. *troubled*. nsm. BoVVi.71
hreohnes f. *turbulence*. gs. **hreohnesse** GDGPr.49
hu adv. (interrog.direct or indirect). *how*. GDGPr.5, PCPPr.5, BoPVi.16, BoVVi.60, etc.
hund m. *dog*. dp. **hundum** LwPr.39
huntigan vb II. *to hunt*. infin. SoPr.25
huru adv. *indeed, especially*. SoPr.30. **hure** SoPr.18
hus n. *house*. as. SoPr.10, LwPr.25
hwa m.f., **hwæt** n. interrog.pron. *who, what*. nsn. GDGPr.44(x2), LwPr.49.9. indef.pron. *someone, something*. nsm. PCPPr.72, LwPr.11, 12, 13, etc.; asn. SoPr.34, LwPr.24, BdPr.53; gsn. **hwæs** SoPr.34; dsm. **hwæm** PCGPr.4
hwanan adv. *from where*. BdPr.13
hwær adv. *somewhere* PCPPr.71. In **hwær ... hwær** *in this place...in that*. LwPr.49.8

hwæthwugu pron. *something.* SoPr.6, **hwæthwega** GDGPr.97. adv. *somewhat, a little.* **hwæthwega** GDGPr.85, 87

hwæþer conj. *whether.* GDGPr.73, 74, 78, BdPr.13

hwæþere adv. *however.* In þonne . . . **hwæþere** *however.* GDGPr.76–7

gehwæþeres adv. *in both respects.* BoVVi.25

hwearfian vb II. *to move, flutter* (intrans.). pret.s. **hwearfode** BoVVi.10. *to be tossed* (w. reflex. obj. in acc.). pres.1s. **hwearfige** PCGEp.5

hwelc interrog.pron. and adj. *what, what kind of, which.* nsm. PCGEp.3; nsn. **hwylc** GDGPr.30, 89; dsm. **hwilcum** GDGPr.105, **hwylcum** BdPr.27; npm. **hwelce** PCPPr.3; npn. **hwelc** PCPPr.23; dp. **gehwylcum** BdPr.30(x2)

(ge)hwelc, (ge)hwilc pron. *each one.* asn. PCVPr.12; gsf. **gehwelcre** GDVPr.14; dsm. **gehwilcum** BoVVi.45; ism. **gehwylce** GDGPr.28; isn. **gehwilce** BoVVi.54. adj. *each, every, any.* nsm. PCVEp.27; dsf. **gehwilce** SoPr.25; dp. **gehwylcum** BdPEp.8

hwil f. *time, space of time.* **ða hwile ðe** conj. *while* PCPPr.53, LwPr.16. **ða while þe** SoPr.14

gehwilc(-) see **gehwelc**

hwilum adv. *at times, sometimes, occasionally.* GDPPr.9, PCPPr.61(x2), BoPPr.2(x2), SoPr.24. **hwilon** GDPPr.4

gehwylc(-) see **gehwelc**

gehwyrfan vb I. *to turn.* pres.3s. **gehwyrfeð** GDGPr.43

hyhrum see **heah**

hyht m. *hope, bliss.* ns. GDVPr.5

hylf n. *handle.* ap. **hylfa** SoPr.1

hyne see **he**

(ge)hyran vb I. *to hear.* infin. GDGPr.5; infl.infin. **gehyrenne** BdPEp.6, **gehieranne** LwPr.40; pres.1s. **gehiere** LwPr.34, 36; pres.3s. **gehireþ** BdPr.7, 8; pres. subj.s. **gehyre** BdPr.54, **gehire** BdPr.10; pret.p. **gehyrdon** GDGPr.103; pret. subj.s. **hyrde** GDVPr.26; pp. **gehyred** GDPPr.2; pp. (used as noun) *listener.* gsm. **geheredan** GDGPr.94

hyrsumian vb II. *to obey.* pret.p. **hiersumedon** PCPPr.6

hyrsumnes f. *obedience.* ds. **hyrsumnesse** BoEp.6

hys see **he**

hyþ f. *harbour.* as. **hyðe** GDGPr.55; gs. **hyðe** GDGPr.62

ic pers.pron.1. *I, me, we, us.* ns. **ic** GDPPr.1, GDGPr.10, PCPPr.16, PCGPr.2, etc.; as. **me** GDVPr.1, GDGPr.82, PCVPr.12, PCGPr.1, etc.; gs. **min** PCVPr.11, PCGPr.2; ds. **me** GDGPr.16, PCPPr.3, PCGPr.22, BoEp.13, etc.; np. **we** GDPPr.4, GDGPr.5, PCPPr.12, BoPVi.11, etc., **wæ** GDGPr.13; dp. **us** GDGPr.13, PCPPr.23, PCVEp.1, BoPPr.5, etc.

idæges adv. *on the same day.* LwPr.17(x2)

idelnes f. *idleness.* In **on idelnesse** *in vain.* LwPr.2(x2)

iegbuend m. *island-dweller*. dp. **iegbuendum** PCVPr.3
ieldran wk.m.pl. *ancestors*. np. PCPPr.31
ierfe n. *property*. gs **ierfes** LwPr.9; ds. **ierfe** LwPr.11
ilca pron. and adj. *same*. nsm. GDIn2.6; nsn. **ylce** BdPEp.5; asn. **ilce** LwPr.20, 49.4; gsm. **ilcan** GDIn2.4, LwPr.21; dsm. **ilcan** BoPVi.5, SoPr.8; gp. **ylcena** GDEx3.3
in prep.w.d. *in, on*. GDVPr.2, GDGPr.12, BoPVi.12, BoVVi.15, etc.; w.a. *into*. In **in anwald gereccan** *subjugated* BoPVi.4. In **gebrecan in** *to interrupt* GDGPr.87
inælan vb I. *to inflame*. pres.p. **inælað** GDGPr.92; pp. **inæled** GDGPr.75
ingan anom.vb. *to arrive, enter*. pret.s. **ineode** LwPr.11
ingehygd f. *understanding, perception*. as. GDVPr.9
ingong m. *entrance, beginning*. as. GDGPr.36
innanbordes adv. *at home, within (their) borders*. PCPPr.7
inne adv. *within, inside*. BoVVi.72, LwPr.21
innoþ m. *the inside (of the body), heart*. dp. **innoðum** PCVEp.4
intinga wk.m. *cause*. as. **intingan** GDGPr.104
ingeþanc n. *mind, thinking, intention*. as. **ingeðonc** PCGPr.8; ds. **ingeþance** SoPr.32, **ingeðonce** PCGPr.2
inweardlice adv. *inwardly*. BoEp.17
iorþcyning m. *earthly king*. gp. **iorðcyninga** GDVPr.27
iow see **þu**
iowrum see **eower**
is see **beon**
iu see **geo**

kasere see **casere**
kigcel m. *sturdy stick, prop*. ap. **kigclas** SoPr.1. [*DOE* 'cycgel']
kining see **cyning**
kylle m. *leather bottle, pitcher*. as. PCVEp.26, 27
kynerices see **cynerice**
kuning, kyning see **cyning**

la interj. *oh!* GDGPr.25, 85
geladian vb II. *to clear, vindicate*. pres.subj.s. **geladige** LwPr.28
gelamp see **gelimpan**
land n. *land*. as. **lond** GDGPr.53, PCPPr.12; gs. **landes** LwPr.26; ds. **lande** GDGPr.76, SoPr.26, **londe** GDGPr.51, PCPPr.42, PCGEp.7, LwPr.1, 33
landscaru f. *a share or portion of land*. as. (or ds. or ap?) **landscare** PCVEp.18
lar f. *teaching, instruction*. ns. PCPPr.40, 57; as. **lare** PCPPr.10, 11, BoVVi.68, LwPr.41; as./ap. **lare** GDPPr.7, PCGPr.16; gs. **lare** GDGPr.24; ds. **lare** GDGPr.3, 7; np. **lare** GDGPr.93
lareow m. *teacher*. ns. GDIn4.4, BdPr.15; gs. **lareowes** GDIn4.2, **larheowes** GDGPr.2; np. **lareowas** PCGPr.23; gp. **lareowa** PCPPr.19

lareowdom m. *the office of a teacher*. gs. **lareowdomes** PCGPr.15, 24, 27

laþ adj. *hateful, hated*. comp. dsm. **laðran** LwPr.43

læce m. *doctor*. as. LwPr.16

(ge)lædan vb I. *to lead, bring*. pret.s. **gelædde** LwPr.1; pret.p. **læddon** BoVVi.2; pp. **gelæd** PCGEp.4

Læden n. *the Latin language*. as. PCPPr.60, [Leden SoEx3.2]; ds. **Lædene** PCPPr.15, BoPPr.7

Lædenspræc f. *Latin language*. as. **Lædenspræce** PCVPr.16

Lædengeþiode n. *the Latin language*. as. PCPPr.55; gs. **Lædengeðiodes** PCPPr.57

læfan vb I. *to leave, bequeath*. pres.subj.p. **læfen** LwPr.39; pret.p. **læfdon** PCPPr.32, **lefdon** PCPPr.24

læl f. *bruise, weal*. ns.(?) LwPr.19; as./ds. LwPr.19

læn n. *loan*. ds. **læne** PCPPr.71

læn f. *leased land*. ds. **læne** SoPr.24, **lænan** SoPr.26

læne adj. *transient, temporary*. dsn. **lænan** SoPr.13; gp. **lænena** SoPr.28

læran vb I. *to advise, instruct, teach*. infin. PCPPr.55; infl.infin. **læranne** LwPr.49.1(x2), BdPr.4, 13; pres.1s. **lære** PCGPr.5, SoPr.7; pres.subj.s. **lære** PCPPr.54, PCGPr.12; pret.s. **lærde** SoPr.12, LwPr.49, 49.7; pp. **gelæred** BdPr.11, 16(x2), 18; pp. npm. **gelærede** (*learned*) PCPPr.69

læs adv. (comp. of **lytle**). *less*. In **þy læs** conj. *lest, to prevent, in case*. PCGPr.4, 13, 19, PCVEp.29, BoVPr.6, BdPr.13

læst adj. (superl. of **lytel**). *least, smallest*. asf. **læste** PCVPr.16

læstan vb I (w.d.). *to support, follow*. infin. BoVVi.27

gelæstan vb I. *to accomplish, fulfil*. pret.s. **gelæste** [BoPVi.8]; pret.p. **gelæstan** BoVVi.13

lætan vb 7. *to let, allow, leave*. imp.s. **læt** LwPr.30; pres.p. **lætað** PCVEp.18; pres. subj.s. **læte** LwPr.12; pret.s. **let** BdPr.48, **læt** GDGPr.31; pret.p. **læton** GDGPr.62; pret.subj.s. **lete** BoVVi.66, 68. *to act (towards), treat*. imp.s. **læt** LwPr.47

gelætan vb 7. *(of a ship's movement) to shape a course*. pres.3s. **gelæteð** GDGPr.51

leafa wk.m. *leave, permission*. ds. **leafan** LwPr.49.7

geleafa wk.m. *faith, belief*. as. **geleafan** LwPr.49.7(x2), BdPr.43, 46; gs. **geleafan** BdPr.25, 32

geleafful adj. *faithful*. gp. **geleaffulra** GDIn2.5, BdPr.47; dp. **geleaffullum** GDGPr.82

lean vb 6. *to reproach*. infl.infin. **leanne** BdPr.10

leas adj. *false*. asf. **lease** LwPr.8; gsn. **leases** LwPr.40

leasung f. *falsehood, lie*. ap. **leasunga** LwPr.44

lef adj. *frail*. dsn. **lefan** GDGPr.46, 51

lefdon see **læfan**

leng see **longe**

leode mp. *people*. dp. **leodum** BoVPr.4

Glossary and List of Proper Names   249

leodfruma wk.m. *leader of the people*. as. **leodfruman** BoVVi.27
leodscipe m. *people*. as. BoVVi.68
leof adj. *beloved, dear, cherished*. nsm. BoVVi.47; comp. nsm. **leofre** BoVVi.41; dsm. **liofran** LwPr.43; superl. nsm. **leofosta** GDGPr.21, **leofusta** PCGPr.1; asm. **leofustan** BdPr.1
leoht adj. *light, easy*. nsn. PCGPr.24; npf. **leohte** PCGPr.5
leornere m. *reader*. as. BdPr.53; gs. **leorneres** PCGPr.8
(ge)leornian vb II. *to learn*. infin. **leornigan** BoPVi.16; pres.subj.s. **leornige** PCGPr.10; pret.s. **leornode** GDGPr.110, **geliornode** PCPPr.62, **geleornade** GDGPr.83; pret.p. **geliornodon** PCPPr.44, 45, **geleornodon** PCGPr.27, **geleornedon** GDGPr.102, BdPr.26, 42, 45; pp. **geliornod** PCPPr.37, 64; pp. asf. **geleornode** BoPPr.7
leorningcniht m. *pupil, disciple*. np. **leorningcnihtas** PCGPr.23; dp. **leorningcnihtum** BdPr.21, 26
leoþ n. *poetry, verse*. as. BoVPr.4; ds. **leoðe** BoPPr.8
geleoþian vb II. *to relax, calm*. pres.subj.p. **geleoðigen** GDPPr.4
leoþwyrhta wk.m. *poet*. ns. BoVPr.3
let(e) see **lætan**
libban vb III. *to live*. infin. LwPr.30; pres.subj.s. **libbe** PCGPr.11, LwPr.17; pres. pt. **libbende** LwPr.4, **lifiende** BdPr.35, pres.pt. npn. **libbendu** PCVEp.4; gp. **lifgendra** BdPr.44
gelice adv. *alike, equally*. GDGPr.36, 51. superl. **gelicost** GDGPr.46
licgan vb 5. *to lie*. imp.s. **lige** LwPr.6; pres.1s. **licge** GDGPr.66
lichoma wk.m. *body*. gs. **lichaman** GDIn4.4, BdPEp.7, **lichomon** GDGPr.34; ds. **lichoman** BoPPr.5, **lichaman** BoEp.18, **lichomon** GDGPr.34
(ge)lician vb II (w.d.). *to please, be pleasing to*. infin. LwPr.49.9; pret.s. **licode** SoPr.13, LwPr.49.10, **gelicode** LwPr.49.3; pret.p. **licodon** LwPr.49.9(x2), **gelicedon** GDGPr.66
geliefan vb I. *to believe*. pres.1s. **geliefe** PCPPr.20, **gelyfe** SoPr.17; pres.3s. **geliefeð** GDVPr.10; pres.subj.p. **geliefen** PCGPr.17; pret.p. **gelyfde** BdPEp.11; pret.p. **gelyfdon** BdPr.26; pret.subj.p. **gelifden** PCVEp.6
lif n. *life*. ns. GDGPr.64, PCGPr.14; as. BdPr.38; gs. **lifes** GDVPr.3, GDGPr.35, 36, 50, 96, PCGPr.16, PCGEp.6, PCVEp.30, BdPr.50, **liues** GDGPr.4; ds. **life** GDGPr.7, 67; np. GDGPr.74
lifi(g)end- see **libban**
lige see **licgan**
geliger n. *sexual intercourse*. dp. **geligerum** LwPr.49.5
gelimpan vb 3. *to happen, occur*. With subject ðæt. pret.s. **gelamp** LwPr.49.7. With subject **hit** or noun subject. pret.s. **gelomp** BoPVi.23, GDGPr. 25, **gelamp** GDGPr.10
gelimpful adj. *comfortable*. comp. *more comfortable*. asm. **gelimpfulran** SoPr.18
lindwigend m. *shield-bearing soldier*. np. **lindwigende** BoVVi.13

liofran see **leof**
geliorn- see **geleornian**
liornung f. *learning*. as. **liornunga** PCPPr.10, 53
liss f. *favour, kindness*. gp. **lissa** BoVVi.59
list m. *art, skill*. as. BoVPr.3. dp. **listum** as adv. *cleverly*. BoVVi.59
liþan vb I. *to sail*. pres.p. **liðað** GDGPr.61
locian vb II. *to look, see, observe*. imp.s. **loca** PCGEp.1; pres.subj.s. **locige** LwPr.12; pres.pt. **lociende** GDGPr.24
loc n. *enclosure*. ap. **locu** GDGPr.34
lof n. or m. *praise*. ns. BoEp.21
lohsceaft m. *stave, tie-beam*. ap. **lohsceaftas** SoPr.1
gelomlice adv. *often, frequently*. BdPEp.7
lond(-) see **land**
longe adv. *long, for a long time*. GDGPr.20, PCPPr.69, BoVVi.50, 58, 75. comp. **leng**. LwPr.4
lufian vb II. *to love*. infin. BoEp.17, LwPr.49.7; imp.s. **lufa** LwPr.1.1; pres.p. **lufiað** GDGPr.8; pret.s. **lufade** GDGPr.36; pret.p. **lufodon** PCPPr.24(x2), 31
luflice adv. *lovingly, affectionately*. PCPPr.2
lufu str. and wk.f. *love*. as. **lufe** GDPPr.8; gs. **lufan** BoVVi.59; ds. **lufan** GDGPr.22, 93, 96, BoEp.7
lust m. *desire*. ns. BoVPr.3
gelyf(d)- see **geliefan**
lyft f. *sky*. ds. **lyfte** PCVEp.6
lystan vb I (impers.w.a./d. of person and w.g. of thing). *to please*. pres.3s. **lyst** SoPr.23, **lysteð** GDVPr.2, GDGPr.4, GDIn4.2; pres.subj.s. **lyste** BoPPr.9; pret. subj.s. **lyste** SoPr.5
gelystan vb I (w.g. of thing). *to fill with longing for*. pret.s. **gelyste** GDGPr.13; pp. **gelysted** BoVVi.9
lyt adv. *little*. BoVPr.7
lytel adj. *little*. nsm. PCVEp.6; asf. **lytle** PCPPr.29

ma indecl. noun (w.g.). *more*. PCPPr.42; PCVPr.13; SoPr.9; BdPr.4; as adv. (comp. of **micle**) *more, rather*. GDGPr.92, LwPr.49.3
maga adj. *strong*. nsm. SoPr.7
magan pret.pres.vb. *to be able, may*. pres.1/3s. **mæg** GDVPr.2, GDGPr.15, PCPPr.17, SoPr.13, etc.; pres.p. **magon** GDGPr.5, 89, 90, GDIn4.2, PCPPr.51; pres.subj.s. **mæge** PCPPr.21, 22, PCGEp.7, BoEp.17, SoPr.11, [13], LwPr.15, 16(x2), **mage** SoPr.9, 19; pres.subj.p. **mægen** PCPPr.50, 53, 54; pret.s. **meihte** SoPr.4, 6, **meahte** PCPPr.65, PCVPr.15, BoVVi.22, 60, 76, SoPr.35, **mihte** BoPPr.3, 10, BoPVi.17, BdPr.52; pret.p. **meahton** PCPPr.30
magorinc m. *man, warrior*. gp. **magorinca** BoVVi.26

man indefinite pron. *one*. ns. PCPPr.11, SoPr.22, **mon** GDGPr.15, PCPPr.32, 55(x2), LwPr.26, 49.6
man n. *evil, crime*. gs. **manes** BoVVi.44; ds. **mane** BoPVi.9
man see also **man(n)**
geman see **gemunan**
mancess m. *mancus (gold coin worth 30 silver pence)*. gp. **mancessa** PCPPr.67
manig adj. *many*. nsm. **monig** BoVVi.8; asm. **manigne** SoPr.7, 10; asn. SoPr.10, **monig** PCVPr.5, BoVVi.3; dsn. **manegum** BoPVi.8; npm. **monige** GDGPr.66, 92, PCPPr.16, 58, PCGPr.22, **monega** LwPr.49.7; npf. **monega** LwPr.49.7; apm. **manege** PCGEp.4, SoPr.16, LwPr.49.9, **monege** LwPr.49.9; apf. **manega** BdVEp.18, **monega** LwPr.49.1, 49.8; gp. **monigra** GDGPr.41, **monegra** LwPr.49.8; dp. **monegum** LwPr.49.8
manigfeald adj. *many, numerous*. apn **manigfealdan** BoPVi.12; dp. **manigfealdum** PCPPr.59, BoPPr.4, **manigfealdum** LwPr.49.3, **monigfealdum** GDEx1.3
man(n) m. *person, man*. ns. **mon** GDVPr.8, PCPPr.68, BoPPr.11, LwPr.26, 36, **monn** GDGPr.60, 81; as. **man** SoPr.23, LwPr.45; **mann** BdVEp.13; gs. **mannes** GDIn4.3, LwPr.25, 42, BdPr.46, **monnes** GDGPr.56, LwPr.23, 26, 40; np. **men** LwPr.49.3, 49.5, **menn** GDGPr.92, PCPPr.40; ap. **men** PCGEp.4; gp. **monna** GDGPr.42, 64, 71, 74, GDIn3.4, PCPPr.52, PCVPr.10, **manna** GDPPr.7, GDGPr.7, 39, 41, PCVEp.12, BdPr.5, 20, 25, 41, 52, **manne** BdPr.6; dp. **monnum** GDGPr.98, PCPPr.24, 49, BoVPr.5, LwPr.49.5, **mannum** GDGPr.36, BdPr.7, 8
manna wk.m. *man*. as. **monnan** PCGEp.1, LwPr.13
manncynn n. *mankind*. gs. **monncynnes** PCVPr.8
manslege m. *homicide*. gs. **mansleges** LwPr.25(x2)
mara adj. (compar. of **micel**). *greater*. nsm. PCPPr.41; asf. **maran** GDGPr.26
maþ see **miþan**
maþm m. *treasure*. gp. **maðma** PCPPr.28
mæg m. *kinsman*. gs. **mæges** LwPr.49.9
mæg, mæge(n) see **magan**
mægen n. *virtue, virtuous deed*. ns. GDGPr.90, 91; np. **mægenu** GDGPr.77; gp. **mægna** GDGPr.89; dp. **mægnum** GDGPr.74. *power, extent*. as. PCGPr.24
mægþ f. *nation, province, country*. ds. **mægðe**. BoPVi.1, BdPr.19; dp. **mægðum** BdPEp.[8], 9
mægþhad m. *virginity*. gs. **mægðhades** LwPr.12; ds. **mægðhade** BoEp.5
mæl n. *time, occasion*. gp. **mæla** BoVVi.54
gemæne adj. *in common, together*. npm. LwPr.23
mænigo f. *multitude*. as.(?) BoVVi.29
mære adj. *great, famous, renowned*. asm. **mæran** BoVVi.14; gp. **mærra** BdPr.6
mærnyss f. *distinction, glory*. ds. **mærnysse** GDPPr.1

mærsian vb II. *to bound, demarcate.* pres.3s. **mærsað** BoVVi.16. *to make known, transmit.* pp. **gemærsod** GDGPr.91

mærþu f. *glory, glorious deed.* dp. **mærðum** PCVPr.10

mæssepreost m. *mass priest.* ns. BdPr.1; as. BdPr.23; ds. **mæssepreoste** PCPPr.64, **mæssepriste** PCPPr.63

mæst adj. (superl. of **micel**). *largest, most, very great.* nsf. **mæste** GDPPr.3; gp. **mæstra** LwPr.49.7. as noun (w.g.) PCVPr.8

mæst adv. (superl. of **micle**). *most, the most.* GDGPr.15

mæþ f. *measure, extent.* ds. **mæðe** BoPPr.11

me see **ic**

meahte, meahton see **magan**

mearcian vb II. *to record, inscribe.* pp. npn. **gemearcude** GDVPr.19

mearcung f. *marking out.* ds. **mearcunge** GDGPr.71

med f. *reward, meed.* as. **mede** GDGPr.37, BdPEp.9

medder see **modor**

medmare adv. (comp. of **medmicel**). *more briefly.* GDGPr.43

medsceatt m. *bribe.* dp. **medsceattum** LwPr.46

meldian vb II. *to proclaim, declare.* pret.s. **meldode** BoVPr.2

men(n) see **man(n)**

mengeo f. *multitude.* ns. PCPPr.28

menian vb I. *to direct one's course, proceed.* pres.subj.s. **menige** SoPr.8

mennen n. *female slave.* as. LwPr.17; np. **mennenu** LwPr.12

mennisc adj. *human.* gp. **menniscra** LwPr.49.8

gemet n. *extent, measure.* In **þy gemete þe** *in the same way as.* GDIn4.3.

(ge)metan vb I. *to meet, find, gain.* pres.subj.s. **gemete** BdPr.54, BdPEp.12; pret.s. **gemette** LwPr.49.9, BdPr.51; pret.p. **metton** BdPr.41

gemetgian vb II. *to moderate, temper.* pres.subj.s. **gemetgige** PCGPr.15, 18

micel adj. *great, large.* nsm. BoVPr.3; nsf. PCPPr.28; nsn. BoVVi.16; asf. **micle** GDPPr.3; gsm. **micles** GDGPr.47; dsf. **micelre** BoPVi.24, **micelan** BoEp.3

micelnes f. *magnitude, greatness.* gs. **micelnesse** PCGPr.25

micle adv. *much, greatly.* GDGPr.53, BoPVi.24

miclum adv. *much, greatly.* BoVVi.74

mid prep.w.d. *with, amongst.* GDGPr.10, GDIn2.4, PCPPr.35, BoPVi.2, etc. **myd** SoPr.24

middangeard m. *world.* as. LwPr.49, 49.7; gs. **middangeardes** GDGPr.69

mihte see **magan**

milde adv. *kindly, graciously.* BdPEp.1

mildheort adj. *merciful.* nsm. LwPr.36

mildheortnes f. *mercy.* as. **mildheortnesse** LwPr.49, 49.7; ds. **mildheortnessan** BoEp.3, **mildheortnesse** LwPr.49.7

milts f. *mercy.* as. **miltse** SoPr.27

min poss.adj. *my*. nsm. **min** GDGPr.21(x2), 23, BoEp.19(x2); nsf. **min** BoEp.20(x2); nsn. GDGPr.29; asm. **minne** LwPr.2(x2); asn. **min** BoEp.11; gsm. **mines** LwPr.49.9; gsf. **minre** GDGPr.18, 25, BoEp.10, 11; gsn. **mines** GDGPr.49, 50, 64, PCGEp.5, SoPr.18; dsm. **minum** PCPPr.62(x2), 63(x2), LwPr.11; dsf. **minre** GDGPr.17; dsn. **minum** GDPPr.8, PCPPr.66, SoIn3.3, LwPr.11(x3), 13, 34; gp. **minra** PCGEp.5, 9, LwPr.49.9(x2); dp. **minum** GDPPr.6, BoEp.15, BdPEp.6, LwPr.49.10

misdæd f. *misdeed*. ds. **misdæde** LwPr.49.7; gp. **misdæda** LwPr.49.8

mislic adj. *varied, various*. apm. **mislice** BoVPr.5; dp. **mislicum** PCPPr.59, **mistlicum** BoPPr.4

mislician vb II. *to displease*. pret.s. **mislicode** GDGPr.17

missenlice adv. *in various ways*. PCVEp.12

miþan vb I (w.g.). *to hide*. pret.s. **mað** PCGPr.2

mod n. *mind, heart, spirit*. ns. GDGPr.29, 58, BoPVi.25, BoVVi.26, SoPr.33; as. BoEp.11; gs. **modes** GDGPr.49, 68, PCGPr.10, PCGEp.5, SoPr.18, BdPEp.7, **modis** SoPr.32; ds. **mode** GDPPr.8, GDGPr.64, 94, PCPPr.35, PCGPr.20, BoPPr.5, BoPVi.24, SoPr.33; ap. **mod** GDPPr.4 (or sg.), PCVEp.12 (or sg.)

modor f. *mother*. as. LwPr.14, 15; ds. **medder** LwPr.4

modsefa wk.m. *mind*. ns. BoVVi.74

modgeþanc m. *mind, thoughts*. ns. GDVPr.8; np. **modgeþancas** GDGPr.56

modwelig adj. *wealthy in mind*. superl. nsm. **modwelegost** PCVPr.10

mon(-) see **man(n)/manna**

monig(-) see **manig(-)**

most- see **motan**

motan pret.pres.vb. *to be allowed to, may*. pres.p. **motan** GDVPr.7; pres.subj.s. **mote** SoPr.24, BdPEp.3, BdVEp.18, 21; pret.p. **moston** LwPr.49.7; pret.subj.s. **moste** BoVVi.39, 62; pret.subj.p. **mostan** BoPVi.7, **mosten** BoVVi.36

gemunan pret.pres.vb (w.g.). *to remember*. pres.1s. **geman** PCGPr.4; pret.s. **gemunde** PCPPr.26(x2), 36, 43, 57, BoPVi.14, 26, BoVVi.57, 79; pret.p. **gemundon** BdPr.47

mund f. *hand*. dp. **mundum** BdVEp.18

gemune see **gemynan**

munt m. *mountain*. dp. **muntum** BoPVi.3

murge adv. *happily, pleasantly*. SoPr.11

muþ m. *mouth*. as. GDIn3.2; ds. **muðe** GDGPr.103, GDIn4.1

myd see **mid**

gemynan vb I. *to remember*. imp.s. **gemyne** LwPr.3; pres.1s. **gemune** GDGPr.49; pres.3s. **gemyneð** GDGPr.30, 58, 60; pres.subj.s. **gemyne** PCGPr.17

gemynd n. and f. *mind, memory, memorial, recollection*. as. PCPPr.3; ds. **gemynde** GDGPr.63, 88, BoVVi.54, BdPr.17; np. GDVPr.19

gemyndelic adj. *memorable*. apn. **gemyndelice** BdPEp.10

gemyndwurðe adj. *worthy of remembering*. apn. BdPr.22

mynegung f. *exhortation, recollection.* as./ap. **mynegunge** GDPPr.8, **myngunga** BdPr.28

mynster n. *minster, church, monastery.* gs. **mynstres** BdPr.39; ds. **mynstre** GDGPr.14, 30, 50, 56, PCPPr.68

myrgen n. *entertainment.* as. BoVPr.5

na see **no**

nabban vb III ('ne habban'). *not to have, have not.* pres.2s. **næfst** SoIn3.2; pres. subj.s. **næbbe** LwPr.24, 28, 36

nagan pret.pres.vb ('ne agan'). *not to have.* pres.subj.s. **nage** LwPr.12

nalæs adv. *not, not at all.* GDGPr.102. **nales** BdPr.46

nama wk.m. *name.* ns. GDGPr.6; as.ds. **naman** PCPPr.24, 67, BoPPr.9, LwPr.49.3. **noman** LwPr.2(x2); ap. **naman** GDGPr.71

nan adj. *none, no.* nsm. PCPPr.68, PCGPr.5; nsn. SoPr.22; asm. **nænne** PCPPr.38; asf. **nane** LwPr.40, 49.5, 49.7(x3); asn. **nan** LwPr.12, 28; gsf. **nanre** BoPVi.26; dsm. **nanum** LwPr.49.6; dsf. **nanre** PCPPr.53; gp. **nanra** LwPr.49.6; dp. **nanum** LwPr.47, 48

nanwuht pron. *nothing.* PCPPr.29

naþer adv. *neither.* With meaning *never* (error for **nahwær**?). SoPr.4

nawer adv. ('nahwær'). *nowhere, in no place.* **nawer** LwPr.34

næbbe see **nabban**

næfre adv. *never.* PCGPr.22, LwPr.45, 46, 48

næfst see **nabban**.

nænig adj. *not any.* asn. GDGPr.53; npn. **nænige** GDGPr.77

nænne see **nan**

næren, næron see **beon**

ne negative particle. *not.* GDGPr.13, PCPPr.17, PCGPr.5, PCVEp.15, etc. as conj. *nor.* LwPr.34, 37, 40, 43, 47, 48. **ne eac** *nor even.* PCPPr.24

neah adv. *near.* GDGPr.51. comp. **near** PCGPr.9(x2). superl. **niehst** *last, most recently.* SoIn3.2. In **æt nehstan** *at last, in the end.* GDGPr.52, 60, 61. **æt nyhstan** BdPEp.2

nearanes f. *difficulty, strait.* ds. **nearanesse** BoPVi.24

neat n. *animal, beast.* as. LwPr.22

nedan vb I. *to compel, coerce.* pres.subj.s. **niede** LwPr.35; pp. **genyded** GDGPr.12, **gened** PCGEp.3

nedes adv. *of necessity.* LwPr.13

nedþearf adj. *necessary.* nsn. LwPr.49.5

nedþearf f. *need.* as./ds. **nedþearfe** GDGPr.41

nehsta wk.m. *neighbour.* as./gs. **nehstan** LwPr.9, 13, 16

nehstan see also **neah**

nelle see **nyllan**

nemnan vb I. *to name, call.* pres.p. **nemniað** GDIn3.3; pp. **(ge)nemned** PCPPr.60, BdPr.40
neorxnawonglic adj. *paradisal, of Paradise.* dsm. **neorxnawonglican** GDIn3.1
neowol adj. *prostrate.* nsm. BoVVi.80, **niwol** BoPVi.26
netene see **nyten**
niede see **nedan**
niedbeþearf adj. *necessary.* superl. npf. **niedbeðearfosta** PCPPr.49
nieddæda m. *someone acting out of necessity.* ns. LwPr.25
niedling m. *slave.* as. LwPr.35
niehst see **neah**
niht f. *night.* ap. LwPr.17
nihtes adv. *by night.* LwPr.25
niman vb 4. *to take.* pres.1s. **nime** GDGPr.107; pret.s. **nom** BdPr.50; pret.subj.s. **name** LwPr.28
nis see **beon**
nitan pret.pres.vb ('ne witan'). *not to know.* pres.1s. **nat** GDGPr.74; pres.p. **nyton** GDGPr.78; pres.subj.s. **nyte** LwPr.28
niþer adv. *down, downwards.* BoVVi.80
niwan adv. *recently.* BdPr.2
niwe adj. *new.* nsf. GDGPr.28; gsn. **niwes** GDGPr.26
niwnes f. *newness, novelty.* ds. **niwnesse** GDGPr.68
niwol see **neowol**
no adv. *by no means, not at all.* GDGPr.60, 62, 102, 109, GDIn4.3, LwPr.33, 41, 47, 49. **na** PCGPr.27, LwPr.25
genoh adv. *quite, enough.* GDGPr.13, 43
noht indef.pron. *nothing.* GDGPr.33. adv. *not at all.* GDGPr.73, 76, 88, PCPPr.16
nohwæþer conj. *neither.* In **nohwæðer ne . . . ne** *neither...nor* PCPPr.23–4
nold- see **nyllan**
nom see **niman**
noman see **nama**
norþ adv. *north.* PCVPr.13
notu f. *employment.* ds. **note** PCPPr.54
nu adv. *now.* GDVPr.17, GDGPr.5, PCPPr.12, PCVEp.1, etc. conj. *now that.* PCVEp.22
genyded see **nedan**
nyhstan see **neah**
nyllan anom.vb ('ne willan'). *to be unwilling, will not.* pres.1s. **nelle** LwPr.11; pres.subj.s. **nelle** LwPr.29, BdPr.10; pret.s. **nolde** GDGPr.68; pret.p. **noldon** PCPPr.35, 38, LwPr.49.5; pret.subj.s. **nolde** LwPr.21, 23, 49.6
nyte, nyton see **nitan**
nyten, neten n. *animal.* ds. **netene** LwPr.31; gp. **nytena** GDIn4.3

nytwyrde adj. *useful.* nsm. **nytwyrde** SoPr.30
nyþerlic adj. *lowly.* dp. **nyþerlican** GDGPr.66
of prep.w.d. *from.* GDGPr.56, GDIn2.1, PCPPr.15, BoPPr.7, etc.
ofdune adv. *down.* BoPVi.27, BoVVi.80
ofer prep.w.a./d. *over, beyond, contrary to, rather than.* PCVPr.2, PCVEp.18, BoVVi.8, BoVVi.62, LwPr.1.1, 32, 41, 49.5, 49.6
ofergylden adj. *gilded.* apm. **ofergyldan** (for **ofergyld(e)nan**?) GDIn2.3
oferfon vb 7. *to seize.* pret.s. **oferfeng** BoVVi.69
oferhlifian vb II. *to tower over, rise above.* pret.s. **oferhlifade** GDGPr.32
oferhogian vb II. *to despise.* pret.p. **oferhogdon**. LwPr.49.7
ofermetto f. *pride.* dp. **ofermettum** PCGPr.20
oferstigan vb 1. *to rise above.* pret.s. **oferstah** GDGPr.33
ofhnitan vb 1. *to gore.* pres.subj.s. **ofhnite** LwPr.21
ofslean vb 6. *to kill.* infin. BoPVi.10; pres.subj.s. **ofslea** LwPr.13(x2), 24; pret.subj.s. **ofsloge** LwPr.13, 21; pp. **ofslegen** LwPr.21, 25
ofstingan vb 3. *to gore.* pres.subj.s. **ofstinge** LwPr.21(x2)
oft adv. *often.* GDPPr.2, GDGPr.12, 63, 94, PCPPr.3, BoPPr.4, LwPr.46. superl. **oftost** PCPPr.21
ofweorpan vb 3. *to kill by throwing (e.g. stone).* pp. **ofworpod** LwPr.21(x3)
on prep.w.a./d. *on, in, into, onto, amongst, towards, concerning.* GDGPr.4, GDIn3.3, PCGPr.4, BoPVi.12, etc.
onbærnan vb I. *to kindle.* pp. **onbærned** GDGPr.95
ongebrengan vb I. *to inflict (something) on.* pret.p. **ongebrohton** GDGPr.19
oncerran vb I. *to turn, bring back.* infin. BoVVi.61
oncnawan vb 7. *to know, learn.* infin. GDGPr.90; pret.s. **oncnew** GDGPr.73, **oncneow** GDGPr.83
ond see **and**
ondrædan vb 7. *to fear.* pres.subj.s. **ondræde** PCGPr.7
ondswarian vb II (w.d.). *to answer.* pret.s. **ondswarode** GDGPr.80, 99, **answarode** SoPr.33
ondswaru f. *answer.* as. **ondsware** GDGPr.72
oneardian vb II. *to dwell, inhabit.* infin. SoPr.11
onfon vb 7 (often w.g.). *to receive, accept.* infin. LwPr.30, 49.7; imp.s. **onfoh** LwPr.46 (w.d.); pret.s. **onfeng** BoVVi.32 (w.d.), LwPr.49.9; pret.p. **onfengon** LwPr.49.7(x2), BdPr.25, 31; pret.subj.s. **onfenge** GDPr.110
ongeat see **ongytan**
ongemang prep.w.d. *amongst.* PCPPr.59
ongin n. *beginning.* ds. **onginne** PCGPr.25
onginnan vb 3. *to begin.* infin. BdPr.33; pres.3s.**onginneð** GDEx1.2, GDIn3.1, GDEx3.2, **ongynneð** GDGPr.1, GDEx2.1, **onginð** SoIn2.1; pret.s. **ongan** PCPPr.58, BoPVi.15, 28, **angan** BoVVi.59; pret.subj.s. **ongunne** GDGPr.86

ongytan vb 5. *to understand, perceive, realise, learn, hear of.* infin. GDGPr.89, SoPr.35, **ongietan** PCGPr.12, **ongiotan** PCPPr.29, **ongitan** BdPr.52; pres.3s. **ongyteð** GDGPr.98; pres.subj.s. **ongite** BoPPr.10; pret.s. **ongeat** GDGPr.81, BoPVi.12, 22, BoVVi.68, BdPr.21, 48; pret.p. **ongeaton** LwPr.49.2; pp. **ongyten** GDPPr.2
onhagian vb II (impers.). *to be feasible, to be fitting.* pres.subj.s. **onhagige** SoPr.29
onhirian vb II (w.d.). *to imitate.* pres.3s. **onhireð** BdPr.8
onlic adj. *similar.* npm. **onlice** PCGPr.22
on(ge)lihtan vb I. *to illuminate, light up.* pres.subj.s. **ongelihte** SoPr.19; pp. **onliht** GDIn2.5
onlutan vb 2. *to bend, stoop.* infin. PCPPr.35
onscunian vb II. *to shun, avoid.* imp.s. **onscuna** LwPr.44; pres.3s. **onscunað** BdPr.9
onsecgan vb III. *to sacrifice (to).* pres.subj.s. **onsecge** LwPr.32
onsendan vb I. *to send.* infin. PCPPr.66
onstal m. *supply.* as. PCPPr.18
onstyrian vb I/II. *to afflict.* pp. **onstyred** GDGPr.47
onsyne see **ansyn**
ontendan vb I. *to kindle.* pres.3s. **ontent** LwPr.27; pp. **ontended** LwPr.27
ontihtan vb I. *to inspire.* pp. **ontihted** GDGPr.75
ontimber n. *(building) material.* as. SoPr.22. [*DOE* 'antimber']
ontynan vb I. *to open up.* pres.subj.s. **ontyne** LwPr.22
onweald m. *power, authority, control.* as. PCPPr.7, **onwald** PCPPr.6, **anwald** BoPVi.4 (**in anwald gerehton** *subjugated*), BoVVi.62; ds. **anwealde** BoPVi.17
onwendan vb I. *to change, pervert.* pres.p. **onwendað** LwPr.46
openlice adv. *plainly, clearly.* GDGPr.16
orceapunga adv. *without payment.* LwPr.11
ordfruma wk.m. *source.* ds. **ordfruman** GDGPr.106
ormod adj. *despondent, despairing.* nsm. BoPVi.27, BoVVi.78
oþ prep.w.a. *until.* GDGPr.78, PCPPr.54, BoVVi.14, SoPr.26, BdPr.24, 25, 46, BdVEp.22
oþ conj. *until.* PCGEp.7
oþdon anom.vb. *to put out.* pres.subj.s. **oþdo** LwPr.19
oþer adj. and pron. *other, another, second.* nsm. PCGPr.11; asm. **oþerne** LwPr.23, 49.8; asf. **oðre** PCPPr.72; gsm. **oðres** LwPr.23, 24, 26, 42; gsn. **oðres** BoVVi.44; dsm. **oðrum** LwPr.19; dsf. **oðerre** PCPPr.53, **oðre** BdPr.49, LwPr.49.9, **oþere** BdPr.54; npm. **oðre** LwPr.49.5; npf. **oðra** PCPPr.47; apm. LwPr.1.1, 49.9, **oððre** SoPr.16; apf. **oðre** PCPPr.45; apn. **oðru** GDGPr.59; gp. **oþer(r)a** GDGPr.41, GDIn4.3, LwPr.49.6, 49.7, **oðra** BdPr.44; dp. **oþrum** GDGPr.98, PCPPr.24, 59, BoPVi.9, LwPr.49.5. *latter.* nsm. BdPr.10. **oþer** . . . **oþer** *one...another.* LwPr.43(x2)
oþfæstan vb I. *to commit, entrust.* pres.subj.s. **oðfæste** LwPr.28. *to set (to a task).* pp. npm. **oðfæste** PCPPr.53

oþfeallan vb 7. *to decline.* infin. PCPPr.40; pp. nsf. **oðfeallenu** PCPPr.13
oþþæt conj. *until.* GDGPr.59, PCGPr.9, BoVVi.29
oþþe conj. *or.* GDGPr.79, PCPPr.15, PCVEp.30, LwPr.10, etc. In **oþþe . . . oþþe** *either...or* GDVPr.26–7, GDGPr.77–8, PCGPr.14, LwPr.13, etc.
oþwitan vb 1. *to reproach, blame.* pres.subj.s. **oðwite** BdPr.54
oxa wk.m. *ox.* ns. LwPr.21(x3), 23(x2); as. **oxan** LwPr.23(x3), 24

papa wk.m. *pope.* ns. PCVPr.5; as. **papan** BoPVi.10, BoVVi.42; gs. **papan** GDGPr.2, GDEx1.1, GDIn3.2, BdPr.21, 27

geræcan vb I. *to stretch out, extend.* pres.subj.s. **geræce** PCGEp.7
ræd m. *advice, counsel.* as. BoVPr.9
rædan vb I. *to read.* infin. GDVPr.1, BoPPr.9; infl.infin. **rædenne** BdPr.3, BdPEp.6; pres.p. **rædað** GDGPr.104; pres.subj.s. **ræde** BdVEp.14. *to rule, govern* (w.d.). infin. BoVVi.67
rædlic adj. *advisable, prudent.* nsn. PCVEp.19
ræfnian vb II. *to suffer.* pres.1s. **ræfnige** GDGPr.45
ræstedæg m. *rest-day.* as. LwPr.3
ræste see **rest**
reccan vb I (w.g.). *to care (for, about).* imp.s. **rec** LwPr.40; pres.subj.s. **recce** LwPr.12
(ge)reccan vb I. *to narrate, tell, interpret.* infin. BoPPr.3; pret.s. **reahte** BoVPr.1; pres.pt. **reccende** GDIn4.5. *to direct, prescribe.* pres.subj.p. **gereccen** LwPr.18; pret.p. **gerehton** BoPVi.4 (**in anwald gerehton,** *subjugated*)
recceleas adj. *careless.* npm. **reccelease** PCPPr.40
recene adv. *at once, quickly.* BoVVi.34
(ge)recenes f. *(scriptural) exposition.* gs. **recenesse** GDGPr.87; ds. **gerecenesse** GDGPr.89
rest f. *rest.* as. **resðe** GDVPr.22; gs. **ræste** GDGPr.39; ds. **reste** SoPr.20
(ge)restan vb I. *to rest, remain.* infin. SoPr.25; imp.p. **restað** LwPr.3; pret.s. **gereste** LwPr.3
rice n. *kingdom, power.* ns. BoVVi.5, 17; as. BoPVi.3, 16; gs. **rices** GDVPr.22; ds. **rice** PCPPr.18, 66, BoPVi.1, 5, BoVVi.7; ap. **ricu** BoPPr.6
rice adj. *powerful.* gp. **ricra** BoVVi.46
riht adj. *right, proper, just.* asm. **rihtne** SoPr.19; dsn. **rihtum** GDVPr.1. on **riht/ryht** *rightly, properly.* LwPr.49.6, BdVEp.21. superl. npm. **ryhtoste** LwPr.49.9
riht n. *law, justice, what is right.* as. **ryht** LwPr.41; gs. **rihtes** BoVVi.67; ds. **rihte** GDPPr.5, **ryhte** LwPr.21
gerihtan vb I. *to direct, correct.* pret.p. **geryhton** LwPr.49.3
rihtgeleaffull adj. *right-believing, orthodox.* gp. **ryhtgeleaffulra** BoPVi.17
rihtlice adv. *rightly, correctly.* comp. **rihtlicor** BoPPr.10

Glossary and List of Proper Names 259

rihtspell n. *true doctrine*. as. **ryhtspell** PCVPr.5
rihtwis adj. *just, righteous*. nsm. BoVVi.49; gp. **rihtwisra** BoPVi.17; superl. nsm. **rihtwisesta** BoPVi.12
rinc m. *man*. ns. BoVVi.49
riþ m. *(small) stream*. dp. **riðum** PCVEp.19
rod f. *cross*. gs. **rode** BoEp.4
rodor m. *sky, heaven* (in pl.). gp. **rodera** BdVEp.21, **rodra** PCVPr.9
Romanisc adj. *Roman*. dp. **Romaniscum** BoPVi.14
geruxl n. *clamour, disturbance*. dp. **geruxlum** GDGPr.10. [*DOE* 'gehruxl']
(ge)ryht- see **(ge)riht-**
ryman vb I. *to extend*. pret.p. **rymdon** PCPPr.8
geryman vb I. *to open up*. pp. **gerymed** BoVVi.19
ryt m./f./n.? *rough growth*. as. LwPr.27

saga(þ) see **secgan**
same see **swa**
sancta, sanctus, *saint*. ns. GDGPr.6, 8, GDIn4.4; as. SoPr.15(x2), 16; gs. **sancte** GDExi.4, GDIn2.3, GDIn3.2, GDEx3.1, BoEp.6, BdPr.21, 27, **sanctus** GDGPr.2, **sancta** BoEp.5
sar n. *sorrow, pain*. as. GDGPr.18; gs. **sares** GDGPr.15, 64; ds. **sare** GDGPr.25
sawl f. *soul*. ns. **sawul** GDIn4.3, as. **sawle** LwPr.18(x2); gs. **sawla** BoEp.10, 11; ap. **sawla** LwPr.49.3(x2)
sæ, se f. and m. *sea*. as. GDGPr.52, PCVPr.2; gs. **sæs** GDGPr.47; ds. SoPr.26; ap. **sæs** LwPr.3
sæd-, sæge see **secgan**
(ge)sægen f. *saying, statement, account*. as./ap. **gesægene** GDPPr.2, **gesegene** BdPr.43, 52; ds. **(ge)sægene** GDGPr.91, 99, 111; ap. **segena** BdPr.29; dp. **(ge)segenum** BdPr.20, 41, 47, **(ge)segnum** BdPr.25, 41
sægþ see **secgan**
gesæliglic adj. *happy, blessed*. npf. **gesæliglica** PCPPr.5
sæstream m. *sea current*. dp. **sæstreamum** BoVVi.15
gesceadan vb 7. *to arrange, distinguish*. pres.1s. **gesceade** GDGPr.70
gesceadwisnes f. *reason*. ns. SoPr.33
sceaft m. *staff*. ds. **sceafte** BoVVi.11
gesceaft f. *creature*. ap. **gesceafta** LwPr.3; gp. **gesceafta** GDVPr.15, BoEp.2
sceal(t) see **sculan**
sceap n. *sheep*. ap. LwPr.24
sceatt m. *property, goods*. ap. **sceattas** LwPr.38 (**teoðan sceattas** *tithes*)
sceawian vb II. *to look at, contemplate*. pres.1s. **sceawige** GDGPr.65; pres.2s. **sceawast** GDVPr.17
sceawung f. *contemplation*. ds. **sceawunge** GDGPr.35

sceld m. *shield.* ap. **sceldas** BoVVi.2
sceolden, -on, sceolon see **sculan**
sceoppend see **scyppend**
sceotend m. *warrior.* np. BoVVi.11
sceþþan vb I. *to harm, injure.* imp.p. **sceððað** LwPr.34
scilling m. *shilling.* ap. **scillingas** LwPr.21
scinlæce wk.f. *sorceress.* ap. **scinlæcan** LwPr.30
scip n. *ship.* ds. **scipe** GDGPr.51, PCGEp.4, **scype** GDGPr.46, 49
scipgebroc n. *shipwreck.* ds. **scipgebroce** PCGEp.6
scir adj. *clear, bright, shining.* nsm. BoVVi.11. superl. asn. **scirost** PCVEp.29
scir f. *office.* gs. **scire** GDGPr.38
scoldon see **sculan**
gescop see **gescyppan**
gescrifan vb I. *to ordain, decree.* pret.s. **gescraf** BoVVi.29
sculan pret.pres.vb. *must, ought.* pres.3s. **sceal.** PCPPr.1, PCGEp.3, BoPPr.11, LwPr.14; pres.2s. **scealt** LwPr.11; pres.p. **sceolon** GDGPr.13; pret.p. **sceoldon** PCPPr.12, 13, **scoldon** PCPPr.11, **sceoldan** BoVVi.31; pret.subj.p. **sceolden** PCPPr.40
scyld f. *fault, guilt, sin.* ns. LwPr.17; gp. **scylda** PCGEp.5, 9
gescyldan vb I. *to shield, protect.* imp.s. **gescylde** BoEp.14
scyldig adj. *guilty.* nsm. LwPr.17, 25(x2)
scype see **scip**
gescyppan vb 6. *to create.* pret.s. **gescop** SoPr.29
scyppend m. *creator.* ns. **sceoppend** BoEp.19; ds. **scyppende** GDGPr.67
scyrpan vb I. *to sharpen, strengthen.* pp. **gescyrped** GDPPr.8
se m., **seo** f., **þæt** n. dem.pron. and def.art. *that one, that, the.* nsm. **se** GDGPr.1, GDIn2.1, PCPPr.71, BoPVi.5, etc.; nsf. **seo** GDPPr.3, GDGPr.14, GDEx1.2, BoVVi.22, etc., **sio** GDEx1.1, PCPPr.40, PCGPr.18, PCGEp.9, etc.; nsn. **þæt** GDGPr.29, BoPVi.9, BoVVi.43, SoPr.33, etc.; asm. **þone** GDGPr.2, GDIn3.1, PCPPr.6, BoVVi.14, etc., **þane** SoPr.5; asf. **þa** GDGPr.45, GDIn2.4, PCPPr.59, 68, etc.; asn. **þæt** GDGPr.102, PCPPr.49, BoPVi.16, BoVVi.20, etc., **þætte** BdPr.42; gsm. **þæs** GDGPr.2, GDIn2.3, PCGEp.8, LwPr.11, etc., **ðas** GDVPr.23; gsf. **þære** GDGPr.1, 14, GDIn2.1, BoEp.4, etc., **þare** GDIn4.1; gsn. **þæs** GDGPr.23, 34, PCPPr.6, LwPr.11, etc.; dsm. **þam** GDVPr.5, GDGPr.6, GDIn3.3, BoVVi.72, etc., **þæm** GDIn2.2, PCGPr.10, BoVVi.40, LwPr.49.5, etc.; dsf. **þære** GDGPr.22, PCPPr.68, BoVVi.37, SoPr.23, etc., **þare** GDIn4.2, SoPr.20, **þere** SoPr.26; dsn. **þam** GDPPr.5(x2), BoPVi.4, 5, etc., **þæm** PCPPr.35, 68, PCGEp.4(x2), etc.; ism. **þy** LwPr.35; isn. **þi** GDGPr.40, 45, 97, 102, etc., **þy** GDGPr.43, GDIn4.3, PCGPr.13, LwPr.11, etc., **þon** GDIn4.4; often w. compar., *the, by that.* GDGPr.97, PCPPr.41, BoVVi.76, LwPr.4, etc.; np.(all genders) **þa** GDGPr.18, GDIn2.5, PCPPr.9, LwPr.49.3, etc.; ap.(all genders) **þa** GDGPr.33,

GDIn2.3, BoPPr.6, BoPVi.12, etc.; gp. **þara** GDGPr.65, GDEx3.3, PCPPr.29, PCGPr.3, etc., **þæra** GDGPr.75, 103, 105, GDIn3.3, **þære** SoIn2.1; dp. **þam** GDGPr.4, BoPVi.3, BoVVi.21, LwPr.49.3, etc., **þæm** PCGPr.18, 19, PCGEp.5, BoVVi.83, etc. **þæs** adv. *to that extent, so.* GDGPr.97

se see **sæ**; also see **beon**
geseah see **geseon**
sealde see **sellan**
sealt adj. *salt, salty.* asm. **sealtne** PCVPr.2
searoþonc m. *clever thought, ingenuity.* gp. **searoðonca** PCVPr.7
searu n. *cunning, trick, guile.* ap. **searwa** LwPr.13
secan vb I. *to seek.* pres.subj.s. **gesece** LwPr.13; pret.s. **sohte** GDPPr.5, PCPPr.12; pret. subj. s. **sohte** LwPr.49.6
secg m. *man.* as. BoVPr.7
secgan vb III. *to say, tell.* infin. GDVPr.26, **secgean** BoVPr.10; imp.s. **sæge** LwPr.8, **saga** LwPr.40; pres.1s. **secge** GDGPr.100, 106, 111; pres.3s. **sagað** GDVPr.11, BdPr.7, **sægð** BdPr.8; pres.subj.s. **secgge** LwPr.28; pres.subj.p. **secggen** LwPr.49.4; pret.s. **sæde** BdPr.17, 35; pret.2s. **sægdest** GDGPr.85; pret.p. **sædon** BdPr.29; pp. **gesægd** GDGPr.71
gesegen-, segnum see **(ge)sægen**
sefa m. *heart, mind.* ns. BoVVi.71; gs. PCVPr.7
selest adj. (superl. of **god**). *best.* nsm. **selesða** GDVPr.24
self pron. *himself, herself, etc.* nsm. PCGEp.5, LwPr.11, 16, 24, 25, 28, 49, **sylf** GDGPr.66, 81, BoEp.10, BdPr.48, 52, **selfa** BoVVi.32; nsn. LwPr.28, **sylf** GDGPr.96; asm. **selfne** BoPVi.27, LwPr.28, **sylfne** GDGPr.83; asn. **sylf** GDGPr.16, 41; gsm. **sielfes** GDVPr.7, **sylfes** GDGPr.43; dsm. **selfum** PCPPr.39, BoPVi.16, **sylfum** GDGPr.9, BdPr.3; dsf. **selfre** PCGPr.25; npm.apn. **selfe** PCPPr.23, **sylf** GDGPr.34, **sylfe** BdPr.39
selflic adj. *self-regarding.* asm. **selflicne** BoVPr.7
selflice n. *egotism.* as. PCGPr.21
sella adj. (comp. of **god**). *better.* nsm. BoVVi.50
(ge)sellan vb I. *to give, give up.* infin. LwPr.29, 49.3; imp.p. **sellað** LwPr.39; pres.subj.s. **selle** LwPr.18, 19, 23, 24(x2), 35, 36, **geselle** LwPr.21; pret.s. **sealde** PCPPr.22, LwPr.4, 49.7; pret.p. **sealdon** BoVVi.24; pret.subj.s. **sealde** LwPr.11
sendan vb I. *to send.* infin. PCVPr.15; pres.1s. **sende** BdPr.1, 2; pret.s. **sende** PCVPr.13, BoPVi.18, BoVVi.63, BdPr.23, 24, 36; pret.p. **sendan** LwPr.49.1, **sendon** LwPr.49.2(x2), 49.3, 49.4; pret.subj.p. **sende** LwPr.13
seolfor n. *silver.* gs. **seolfres** LwPr.21
geseon vb 5. *to see.* infin. GDVPr.7, GDGPr.53, 55, **gesion** PCPPr.33; imp.s. **geseoh** GDGPr.46; pres.p. **geseoð** GDGPr.62; pret.s. **geseah** GDGPr.24, PCPPr.26, SoPr.6; pret.p. **gesawon** GDGPr.102
seonoþ m. *synod.* np. **seonoðas** LwPr.49.7; dp. **senoðum** LwPr.49.8

seonoþboc f. *synod-book.* ap. **senoðbec** LwPr.49.8
setlgong m. *setting (of sun).* ds. **setlgonge** LwPr.36
(ge)settan vb I. *to construct, establish, set down, set out, impose.* infin. SoPr.10, LwPr.11, 49.5, 49.9; pret.s. **sette** BoPPr.2; pret.p. **setton** BoVVi.4, **gesetton** LwPr.49.7, 49.8, **gesettan** LwPr.49.7
gesewenlic adj. *visible.* dp. **gesewenlicum** BoEp.15
sibb f. *peace.* as. **sibbe** PCPPr.7
si(e) see **beon**
sielf- see **self**
sigeþeod f. *victorious nation.* np. **sigeþeoda** BoVVi.4
sinc n. *treasure.* gs. **sinces** GDVPr.24
sincgeofa wk.m. *treasure-giver, lord.* ns. BoVVi.50
sien, siendon see **beon**
sindan, sint see **beon**
singan vb 3. *to sing.* pres.pt. **singend.** BoPVi.28
sio see **se**
siodu m. *morality.* as. **siodo** PCPPr.7
siofoþa adj. *seventh.* asm. **siofoþan** LwPr.3; dsm. **siofoþan** LwPr.3; isn. **siofoþan** LwPr.11
gesion see **geseon**
sittan vb 5. *to sit.* infin. PCGEp.7; pret.s. **sæt** GDGPr.20. *to be placed, rest.* pres. subj.s. **sitte** LwPr.17
siþ adv. *late.* In **sið oððe ær** *ever.* GDVPr.26
siþþan adv. *afterwards, later.* PCPPr.55, PCVPr.11, PCVEp.10, BoVVi.50, LwPr.11, 25, 29, **syððan** BdPr.48. conj. *after.* PCPPr.45, 64, SoPr.23, LwPr.49, 49.7(x2)
slæpan vb I. *to sleep, lie with.* pres.subj.s. **slæpe** LwPr.29
slean vb 6. *to strike, beat, kill.* imp.s. **sleah** LwPr.5; pres.1s. **slea** LwPr.34; pres.subj.s. **slea** LwPr.14, 16, 17; pp. **slegen** GDGPr.54
smeagan vb II. *to ponder, consider, examine.* infin. BoPVi.15; infl.infin. **smeganne** BdPr.3; pres.pt. (used as adj.) *curious (about)* (w.a.). nsm. **smeagende** BdPr.5
smeaung f. *reflection, investigation, study.* ds. **smeaunge** GDGPr.23, SoPr.32
smicer adj. *beautiful, fair.* asm. **smicerne** SoPr.10
snyttro f. *wisdom, intelligence.* as. PCVPr.7
softe adv. *comfortably.* SoPr.11. comp. **softor** *more comfortably.* SoPr.13
sohte see **secan**
solor m. *uppermost room.* ds. **solore** PCGPr.10
gesomnian vb II. *to meet, assemble.* pret.p. **gesomnodon** LwPr.49.3
sona adv. *straightaway.* PCPPr.39
sorg f. *sorrow, grief.* as. **sorge** GDGPr.19
soþ adj. *true.* nsn. BdPr.13
soþfæst adj. *truthful.* asm. **soðfæstne** LwPr.45

Glossary and List of Proper Names 263

sped f. *means, opportunity.* ap. **speda** PCPPr.52
spell n. *narrative, prose, tale, account, story.* ns. GDGPr.84; as. BdPr.2; ds. **spelle** BoPPr.7; np. BdPr.14; gp. **spella** GDGPr.105
spellian vb II. *to speak, recite.* pret.subj.s. **spellode** BoVPr.4
spor n. *track, trail.* ds. **spore** PCPPr.35
spowan vb 7 (impers.w.d.). *to succeed.* pret.s. **speow** PCPPr.8, LwPr.49.2
spræc f. *speech, talk, discourse.* ns. PCGPr.8; as. LwPr.41; gs. **spræce** GDIn2.1, PCGPr.26
gespræc n. *speech, conversation.* gs. **gespræces** GDEx1.3, **gespreces** GDEx1.1, GDEx3.1; ds. **gespræce** GDEx2.2; dp. **gesprecum** GDEx3.3
sprecan vb 5. *to speak, say, tell.* infin. BoPPr.11, BoVPr.8; pres.1s. **sprece** GDGPr.70; pres.3s. **sprecð** BoPPr.12; pret.s. **spræc** GDGPr.6, 61, BoVVi.81; pres.pt. **sprecende** GDGPr.9, GDIn2.6, GDIn3.4, GDIn4.5, LwPr.1, 49
stalian vb II. *to steal.* imp.s. **stala** LwPr.7
stan m. *stone, rock.* ds. **stane** LwPr.16; dp. **stanum** LwPr.21(x3)
(ge)standan vb 6. *to stand, remain.* pres.subj.s. **gestonde** PCGPr.9; pret.s. **stod** BoVVi.28; pret.p. **stodon** PCPPr.28
gestaþelian vb II. *to establish, confirm.* imp.s. **gestaþela** BoEp.11
stæf m. *stick, staf.* ds. **stafe** LwPr.16. *letter (of alphabet).* dp. **stafum** [BdPr.23]
stæpmælum adv. *step by step, gradually.* PCGPr.9
stær n. *history.* ns. BdPEp.5
stæþ n. *shore.* ds. **stæþe** PCGEp.4
stelan vb 4. *to steal.* pret.s. **stæl** LwPr.25; pret.subj.s. **stæle** LwPr.28(x2)
stemn f. *voice.* ds. **stemne** BoVVi.84
steopcild n. *orphan.* np. LwPr.34; ap. **stiopcild** LwPr.34
(ge)stigan vb 1. *to climb, ascend.* infin. GDVPr.4; pres.subj.s. **stigge** PCGPr.8
stille adj. *calm, still.* nsm. PCVEp.17
stilnes f. *peace.* as. **stilnesse** GDGPr.62, PCPPr.51
stiopcild see **steopcild**
stiþ adj. *severe.* nsm. PCGPr.14
stoclif n. *dwelling place.* ds. **stoclife** SoPr.14; gp. **stoclife** SoPr.28
gestonde see **(ge)standan**
storm m. *storm.* ns. GDGPr.52; dp. **stormum** GDGPr.48
stow f. *(monastic) place.* as. **stowe** GDGPr.45; ds. **stowe** GDGPr.14, PCPPr.70; ap. **stowa** PCPPr.31; gp. **stowa** BdPr.4; dp. **stowum** BdPEp.10
gestrangian vb II. *to strengthen.* imp.s. **gestranga** BoEp.12
stream m. *river, stream.* ns. GDGPr.1, GDIn2.1; as. PCVEp.14; gs. **streames** GDIn2.5
gestrienan vb I. *to gain, win.* pret.s. **gestriende** PCVPr.8
gestrion n. *treasure.* as. BoVVi.23
strong adj. *strong.* gsf. **strongan** GDGPr.49

stuþansceaft f. *post.* ap. stuþansceaftas SoPr.1, 8
suiþe see swiþe
sum adj. and pron. *one, some, a certain.* nsm. BoPVi.11, BoVVi.46; asm. sumne PCPPr.47; asf. sume PCGPr.9; asn. PCGEp.6; dsm. sume GDGPr.10; npm. sume PCVPr.15, PCVEp.13, 18, LwPr.49.3; apf. suma PCPPr.48; apn. sume BdPr.40, 41, 50, 51; gp. sumra GDGPr.11, sumera GDGPr.64; dp. sumum GDGPr.107(x2)
sumer m. *summer.* ap. sumeras SoPr.12
sunne wk.f. *sun.* gs. sunnan LwPr.25, 36
sunu m. *son.* ns. GDGPr.21, LwPr.49, 49.7; as. LwPr.21, suna LwPr.12
suþ adv. *south.* PCVPr.13
suþan adv. *(from the) south.* PCPPr.17, PCVPr.2
suþweardes adv. *southwards.* BoVVi.4
swa adv. *thus, so.* GDPPr.3, GDGPr.39, BoPVi.24, BoVVi.77, etc., swæ PCPPr.13, 16, 20, 21, etc. (PCPPr only), swua BoVVi.13. swæ same *likewise.* PCPPr.45. swa þæt *in such a way that.* BoPVi.7. correlative swa . . . swa (swa) *as...as.* GDGPr.52, PCGEp.2, BoPVi.24-5. as part of rel. pron. swa hwæt swa *whatever.* GDGPr.16. conj. *as, just as.* GDVPr.11, GDGPr.102, PCVP.3, LwPr.26, etc. swa swa *just as.* BoPPr.3, 8, SoPr.12, LwPr.35. swæ swæ PCPPr.61, 64, 69. suæ suæ PCGPr.8-9. For swa þeah see þeah
swæþ n. *track.* as. PCPPr.33
swelc, swilc adj. *such a.* dsn. swelce LwPr.11(x2). pron. *such.* gsn. swelces BoVPr.7; gp. swelcra PCVPr.13. swelc . . . swelc *such...as.* LwPr.22
swelce conj. *as if, like.* PCPPr.31, LwPr.13, swylce GDGPr.36
swelce adv. *also, likewise, in such a way.* swylce GDGPr.56, 59, swilce SoPr.22. eac swylce *also, likewise.* BdPEp.2
sweltan vb 3. *to die.* pres.subj.s. swelte LwPr.25. In deaðe sweltan *to be put to death.* infin. LwPr.14; pres.subj.s. swelte LwPr.13(x2), 15(x2), 31, 32
geswencan vb I. *to afflict, oppress, trouble.* imp.s. geswenc LwPr.33; pp. geswenced GDGPr.10, 20, 24, 47
sweord n. *sword.* ds. sweorde LwPr.34
sweotol adv. *clearly.* superl. sweotolost BoPPr.3
sweotollice adv. *clearly.* GDGPr.17
swerian vb I.? *to swear an oath.* pres.subj.s. swerige LwPr.28. swerian under *to swear by.* pres.subj.p. swergen LwPr.48
swetlice adv. *sweetly, pleasantly.* BdPEp.1
swigian vb II. *to be silent.* pres.pt. swigende GDGPr.20
swilc(-) see swelc(-)
swiþe adv. *very, greatly.* GDGPr.10, PCPPr.3, BoPPr.5, BoPVi.8, etc., swyðe GDGPr.20, suiðe PCGPr.1(x2), 22, 24. swiðe swiðe *very much.* PCPPr.36. comp. swiþor *more, more greatly.* BoPVi.24, 25. þæs þi swyðor *so much the more* GDGPr.97. superl. swiðust *most, especially.* BdPr.6, 16, 18, swiþost BdPr.26, 33, 36

swua see **swa**
swylce see **swelce**
sy see **beon**
sylf(-) see **self**
sylfren adj. *(made of) silver*. apm. **sylfrene** LwPr.10
symle adv. *always*. BdPEp.3; **symble** GDGPr.15, 23, 28(x2), 44, 97
syn poss.adj. *his*. dp. **synum** BdVEp.18(?)
synderlice adv. *individually*. GDGPr.108
syndrig adj. *separate, individual*. dp. **syndrigum** BdPEp.9
synn f. *sin*. ds. **synne** LwPr.49.7
syþþan see **siþþan**

tacn n. *sign*. ds. **tacne** BoEp.4, LwPr.11
tæcan vb I. *to teach, show*. imp.s. **tæc** BoEp.16; pp. **getæht** PCGEp.2
tælan vb I. *to rebuke*. imp.s. **tæl** LwPr.37; pret.2s. **tældesð** PCGPr.1; pp. npm. **getælde** PCGPr.26
tælnes f. *reproach*. ds. **tælnesse** PCGEp.3
templ n. *temple*. gs. **temples** LwPr.11
teon vb 2. *to draw, pull*. pp. **getogen** GDGPr.21
teoþa adj. *tenth*. apm. **teoðan** LwPr.38 (**teoðan sceattas** *tithes*)
tid f. *time*. as. **tiid** BdPr.24, 26; ds. **tide** BoPVi.1; np. **tida** PCPPr.5; dp. **tidum** (*dates*) BdPr.30
getihtan vb I. *to urge, persuade*. pres.p. **getihtað** GDGPr.92
tilian vb II. *to strive*. pret.s. **tilode** BdPEp.11. *to take care of, provide for* (w.g.). infin. SoPr.26
timbrian vb II. *to build*. infin. SoPr.11; pp. **getimbred** SoPr.24
to prep.w.d. *to, for, as, in, at*. GDPPr.5, GDVPr.16, PCPPr.18, BoPVi.18, etc. With infl.infin. GDGPr.90, PCPPr.49, BoEp.16, SoPr.30, etc. **to þam** (or **þon**) . . . **þæt** conj. *so that, to the extent that*. GDIn2.4, PCPPr.21, PCGEp.3, SoPr.19, LwPr.13
to adv. *too*. GDGPr.86, PCPPr.14(x2), LwPr.49.3
tobecuman vb 4. *to come to, reach*. pres.subj.sg. **tobecume** BdPEp.5
todælan vb I. *to divide*. pres.1s. **todæle** PCGPr.10; pres.3s. **todæleð** GDGPr.41
toeacan prep.w.d. *in addition to, as well as*. BoPVi.9
tofaran vb 6. *to disperse, scatter*. pp. npm. **tofarene** LwPr.49.1
toflowan vb 7. *to flow apart, disperse*. pres.3s. **tofloweð** PCVEp.15, 21
toflownes f. *flow, flowing*. as. **toflownesse** GDIn2.4
toforon prep.w.d. *before*. BoEp.17
togædere adv. *together*. LwPr.49.9
getogen see **teon**
tohopa wk.m. *hope*. ns. BoEp.20

toican vb I. *to add*. pret.s. **toihte** BdPr.52
tol n. *tool*. gp. **tola** SoPr.2
torinnan vb 3. *to run away*. infin. PCVEp.19
tostregdan vb I(?). *to disperse*. pres.3s. **tostregdeð** GDGPr.40
toþ m. *tooth*. as. LwPr.19; ds. **teð** LwPr.19
toweard adj. *future, coming*. gsn. **toweardan** GDGPr.96
treow n. *tree*. ds. **treowo** SoPr.6; ap. **treowo** SoPr.3
treow f. *faith, loyalty*. dp. **treowum** BoVVi.65
getreowe adj. *true, loyal, reliable*. gp. **getrywra** BdPr.44, 52; dp. **getreowum** GDPPr.6
treownes f. *trust*. ns. **trewnes** BoEp.20
getriwian vb II. *to trust, believe*. pres.1s. **getriwe** BdPr.4; pres.subj.s. **getriewe** LwPr.28
getrymian vb II. *to strengthen*. pp. **getrymed** GDEx2.2
trymnes f. *edification*. ns. GDGPr.88
getrywra see **getreowe**
tuegra see **twa, twegen**
tun m. *estate*. as. SoPr.10
twa, twegen num. *two*. nom. BoVVi.4; acc. BoVVi.6, SoPr.31, LwPr.17, 24; gen. **twegea** GDEx2.2, **tuegra** GDEx1.1; dat. **twam** SoIn3.1, LwPr.21, BdVEp.17
tweo m. *doubt*. ns. PCVEp.6; ds. **tweon** GDGPr.42
tweogan vb I. *to doubt*. pres.1s. **tweoge** GDGPr.76; pres.subj.s. **tweoge** BdPr.13
tweonian vb II. *to doubt*. pret.s. **tweonode** SoPr.34
tweoung f. *doubt*. gs. **tweounge** GDGPr.105; ds. **tweounga** SoPr.33
twyfeald adj. *twofold, double*. nsm. GDGPr.94. In **be twyfealdum** *in double*. LwPr.25, 28
tynan vb I. *to close (a book)*. pres.3s. **tyneð** GDVPr.1

þa adv. *then*. GDGPr.13, PCPPr.8, BoPVi.11, BoVVi.17, etc. conj. **þa (þa)** *when*. GDGPr.56, PCPPr.18, 23, LwPr.49.1, etc. Correlative **þa (þa) ... þa ...** *when...then....* PCPPr.26, BoPPr.6, BoPVi.22, LwPr.49.2, etc.
þa pron. see **se**
geþafian vb II. *to consent to, agree to*. imp.s. **geðafa** LwPr.40, 41
geþah see **(ge)þicgan**
geþanc n. *thought, intention, understanding*. ds. **geðance** GDVPr.1, BoEp.18
þancwyrþlic adj. *deserving thanks, worthy*. apn. **þancwyrðlice** BdPEp.10
þar see **þær**
þara see **se**
þaron see **þæron**
þam, þæm see **se**
þat see **þæt**

geþæf adj. *not wishing for change.* nsm. PCGPr.13
þænian vb II. *to serve.* pp. geþæned GDIn2.5. [BT 'þegnian']
þær adv. *there.* GDGPr.17, PCPPr.69, PCGEp.2, SoPr.11, etc., þar SoPr.8. þær (þær) conj. *where.* PCPPr.22, BoPVi.18, BoVVi.15, þar GDVPr.5, SoPr.8
þærinne adv. *inside that place.* BoPVi.23
þære see se
þæron adv. *in that place, therein.* PCGPr.11, 12. þaron SoPr.25
þæs pron. see se and þes
þæt conj. *that, so that.* GDPPr.4, GDVPr.4, GDGPr.10, PCPPr.3, etc. þat SoPr.9, 32, þætte GDPPr.2, GDGPr.77, PCPPr.16, BoVVi.1, etc. ðette PCGPr.18. þæt þe BoVVi.30
þæt pron. see se
þe indecl. relative particle *who, which, that.* GDPPr.3, GDGPr.4, PCPPr.5, BoPVi.13, etc. þæ GDGPr.99. *when* BoPVi.1
þe pron. see þu
þeah adv. *nevertheless, yet.* PCPPr.58, PCGPr.23, BoPPr.6, BoVVi.26, LwPr.16. swa þeah *however* GDGPr.57. conj. *although.* GDGPr.96, BoPVi.6, SoPr.22, LwPr.12, 17, 42. þeah þe GDGPr.34, PCGPr.22
geþeaht n. *consultation, counsel.* ds. geþeahte LwPr.49.9; BdPr.46
þearf f. *need, benefit.* ns. GDPPr.4; ds. þearfe GDGPr.43, BoEp.10, 11, BdPr.11
þearfa wk.m. *a needy or poor person.* ns. GDVPr.13
þearflice adv. *seriously, carefully.* BoVVi.60
þearl adj. *severe, harsh.* nsf. BoVVi.77
þearle adv. *severely, excessively.* BoVVi.82
þeaw m. *custom, manner, practice.* ds. þeawe GDGPr.109; ap. ðeawas PCPPr.25; dp. þeawum GDPPr.7, GDGPr.7, GDIn3.4
þegn m. *thane, retainer, man.* as. BoVVi.69; np. þegnas BoVVi.30; gp. ðegna PCVEp.27
þencean vb I. *to think (of), intend, consider.* infin. GDGPr.33, 42, BoVVi.60; pres.3s. ðencð GDVPr.1; pret.p. þohton BoVVi.11
geþencean vb I. *to think (of), consider, devise.* infin. GDGPr.15, 55, PCPPr.17, LwPr.49.6; imp.s. geðenc PCPPr.22; pres.1s. geþence GDGPr.44, 65; pres. subj.s. geðence LwPr.49.6
þenden conj. *as long as, while.* BoVVi.38, 48
þenung f. *religious service.* ap. ðeninga PCPPr.14. *ministry.* ap. ðenunga PCGPr.14
þeod f. *people, nation.* ns. BoVVi.28; as. þeode BdPr.12, 37; gs. þeode BdPr.6; ds. ðeode BdPr.11; np. ðeoda LwPr.49.7, ðioda PCPPr.47; ap. ðeoda LwPr.49.1; dp. ðeodum LwPr.49.2
þeodan vb I. *to associate.* pp. geþeoded GDGPr.63 (geþeoded to eacan *exacerbated*), pp. npn. geþeodde BdPr.20

geþeode n. *language.* as. geðiode PCPPr.30, 38, 44, 46, 47, 50; gp. geðeoda PCPPr.42

þeodlond n. *country.* as. BoVVi.3; dp. þeodlandum BdPr.19

þeof m. *thief.* ns. LwPr.25

geþeon vb 3. *to flourish, profit.* pres.subj.s. geþeo BdPr.10; pret.p. geþungon BoVVi.7; pp. gp. geðungenra (*virtuous, distinguished*) LwPr.49.7

þeow m. *servant, slave.* ns. GDVPr.13, LwPr.11, BdPr.1; as. LwPr.11, 21; ds. ðeowe LwPr.20; gp. ðiowa PCPPr.28

þeow adj. *servile, serving, like a slave.* nsf. ðeowu LwPr.12; asm. þeowne LwPr.17

þeowa wk.m. *slave.* ns. LwPr.11

þeowdom m. *servitude.* ds. ðeowdome LwPr.1

þeowen f. *a female slave.* as.ds. þeowenne LwPr.12, 20, [21]

þeowian vb II. *to serve.* pres.subj.s. ðeowige LwPr.11

þes m., þeos f., þis n. dem.pron. and adj. *this.* nsm. þes GDGPr.83, þæs GDIn4.4; nsf. þeos PCPPr.1, PCGPr.8; nsn. þis GDGPr.45, PCVEp.1, BdPr.6, 13, BdPEp.5; asm. þisne SoPr.17, BdPr.46; asf. þas GDVPr.16, GDGPr.64, BoPPr.7, BdPr.25, etc.; asn. þis GDGPr.78, PCPPr.26, 36, PCVPr.1, LwPr.25, BdPr.12, 33; 53; gsm. þises GDGPr.11, 69; gsf. ðisse GDGPr.38, 48, PCGPr.25(x2), BoPPr.1; gsn. ðisses PCPPr.59, PCGEp.6; dsm. þis SoPr.14, ðys PCVEp.28; ðissum LwPr.49.6; dsf. þisse GDEx2.1, GDIn4.5, PCPPr.23, PCGPr.4, SoPr.14, BdPr.49; dsn. þisum, þissum GDGPr.76, PCPPr.57, SoPr.13, 18; npn. þas BdPr.14; apf. þas GDPPr.4, PCPPr.31, SoPr.8; apn. þas GDGPr.31, LwPr.1; gp. þissa PCPPr.21, SoPr.28, BdPr.24, þisra GDGPr.54; dp. þeossum GDVPr.18, þissum GDIn4.5, ðiossum, BoVPr.4, þisum GDGPr.9, 66, GDIn2.6, SoIn3.1

(ge)þicgan vb 5. *to eat, taste, partake (of).* pres.subj.p. ðicggen LwPr.49.5. *to attain.* pret.s. geþah BoVVi.53

þider adv. *there, to that place.* BoVVi.60, SoPr.30

þin poss.adj. *your.* nsm. LwPr.1, 42; asm. þinne BoEp.16, LwPr.37; asf. þine BdPr.4, 11; gsm. þines LwPr.9, BdPEp.2; dsm. þinum BoEp.9, 11, LwPr.4, 35; dsf. þinre PCGEp.3, BoEp.3, LwPr.11, BdPr.11(x2), BdPEp.3; apm. þine LwPr.38(x2); gp. þinra PCGEp.7, BoEp.7, ðinre PCGEp.8; dp. þinum GDVPr.17

þinc- see þyncan

þing n. *thing.* ns. PCVEp.19; ap. GDGPr.31, 59, BdPr.40, 47; gp. þinga GDGPr.77; dp. þingum GDGPr.66, BoEp.17, LwPr.48, BdPEp.11

þingian vb II. *to intercede.* pres.subj.p. BdPEp.7

þingung f. *intercession.* gs. þingunge BdPEp.12

geþiode see geþeode

þiowa see þeow

þiowotdom m. *service.* ap. ðiowotdomas PCPPr.10

þis(-) see þes

þoden m. *violent wind.* ns. GDGPr.52

geþoht m. *thought.* as. LwPr.46
þohton see þencean
þolian vb II. *to suffer, endure.* infin. BoVVi.77
þonan adv. *from there, thence.* PCVEp.9, BoVVi.82
þonc m. *thanks.* ns. PCPPr.18, 69. *thought.* np. þoncas GDIn2.5
þone pron. see se
þonne adv. *then, therefore.* GDGPr.52, PCGPr.21, SoPr.1, LwPr.11, etc. conj. *when.* GDGPr.42, 61, 65, 97, PCGPr.17, BoVPr.7, SoPr.33. correlative þonne . . . þonne *when…then.* GDGPr.40, 49, 54, 57
þonne conj.w.comp. *than.* GDGPr.26, 67, 93, BoPPr.10, BoVVi.41, BoEp.8, 10, SoPr.18
þrag f. *time.* as. þrage BoVVi.77; ds. þrage (*for a time*) BoVVi.28
þreat m. *violence.* ds. þreate BoVVi.3
þreo num. *three.* LwPr.17; dp. ðrim LwPr.21
þridda adj. *third.* nsm. GDIn3.1, PCGPr.12; nsf. þridde GDEx2.1, GDEx3.1
geþringan vb 3. *to oppress.* pret.p. geþrungon BoVVi.3
þriste adj. *presumptuous.* nsm. PCGPr.14
geþristlæcan vb I. *to presume.* infin. LwPr.49.9; pret.s. geþristlæcte BdPr.33
þrowian vb II. *to suffer.* pres.3s. þrowað GDGPr.38
þrowung f. *passion, suffering.* ds. ðrowunge LwPr.49.1
þrym m. *glory, majesty.* as. GDVPr.13
þu, ge pers.pron. *you.* ns. þu GDVPr.17, GDGPr.26, PCPPr.20, PCGPr.1, etc.; as. þe PCPPr.20, BoEp.17; ds. þe GDGPr.25, PCPPr.3, BoEp.21, LwPr.35, etc.; np. ge LwPr.33, 34(x2), 39, etc. (all in LwPr); ap. eow LwPr.3(x2), 34, 49.3, iow PCVEp.22; dp. eow LwPr.49.3(x4), 49.4, 49.5(x3), iow PCPPr.48, PCVEp.22, 23
(ge)þuht(-) see þyncan
geþungon see geþeon
þurfan pret.pres.vb (w.g.). *to need.* pres.3s. ðearf LwPr.28, 49.6; pret.p. ðorfton PCVPr.15
þurh prep.w.a. *through.* GDGPr.1, 68, GDIn2.3, PCPPr.32, PCVPr.7, etc.
þurhþyrlian vb II. *to pierce.* pres.subj.s. þurhþyrlige LwPr.11
þurhwunian vb II. *to remain, continue, persist.* pret.s. þurhwunode BoPVi.6
þus adv. *thus, so, in this way.* GDGPr.9, 25, GDIn2.7, GDIn3.5, GDIn4.5, BoVPr.1, BoPVi.28, BoVVi.84, LwPr.1
geþwærlic adj. *compatible.* nsf. geþwærlicu GDGPr.88
þy see se
þyncan vb I (impers.w.d.). *to seem.* pres.3s. ðyncð PCPPr.48(x2), þinceð GDGPr.35, 45, 53, 70, ðyncet PCGPr.23; pres.subj.p. ðyncen PCGPr.5; pret.p. ðuhton LwPr.49.9; pret.subj.s. þuhte GDGPr.86. pp. geðuht (in wæs geþuht *seemed*) LwPr.49.5
þyrel adj. *leaky.* asm. ðyrelne PCVEp.27
þyrstan vb I (impers.w.d. of thing). *to feel thirsty.* pres.s. þyrsteð GDIn4.2

unarimed adj. *countless*. dp. **unarimedum** BoPVi.9
unbeweddod adj. *not betrothed*. asf. **unbeweddode** LwPr.29
uncuþ adj. *unknown*. nsn. PCPPr.69, LwPr.49.9
uncuþlice adv. *in an unkindly manner*. LwPr.47
under prep.w.a./d. *under*. PCVEp.6, BoPVi.15, BoVVi.76, BdPr.27. For **swerian under**, see **swerian**
underfeng m. *undertaking, acceptance*. ds. **underfenge** GDGPr.11, PCGPr.13, 15
underfon vb 7. *to receive, succeed to, undertake*. infl.infin. **underfonne** PCGPr.5; pret.subj.s. **underfenge** PCGPr.7; pp. **underfangen** BoPPr.6
understondan vb 6. *to understand, make sense of*. infin. PCPPr.14
undiop adj. *shallow*. nsn. PCVEp.20
uneaþe adv. *with difficulty*. GDGPr.55
uneþnes f. *anxiety, stress*. dp. **uneðnessum** GDGPr.11
ungelærednes f. *lack of instruction, inexperience*. ds. **ungelærednesse** PCGPr.22
ungelic adj. *unlike, dissimilar, different*. nsf. GDGPr.88; nsn. PCGPr.14
unmæte adj. *huge*. dp. **unmætum** GDGPr.54
geunnan pret.pres.vb (w.g.). *to grant*. pres.subj.s. **geunne** BdVEp.20
unnyt n. *uselessness, idleness*. as. PCVEp.15
unræd m. *bad counsel*. as. LwPr.41
unriht adj. *unjust, wrong*. asn. **unryht** LwPr.41
unriht n. *injustice, wrong*. gs. **unrihtes** GDGPr.15; ds. **unryhte** LwPr.9; np. **unriht** GDGPr.18; dp. **unryhtum** LwPr.47
unrihtlice adv. *unjustly*. **unryhtlice** PCGPr.6
unrihtwis adj. *unjust, unrighteous*. dsm. **unrihtwisan** BoPVi.16
unrihtwisnes f. *unrighteousness*. as. **unrihtwisnysse** BoEp.14
unrim n. *countless number*. ns. BoVVi.44; gs. BdPr.47
unrot adj. *unhappy, sorrowful*. nsm. BoPVi.27
unrotnes f. *misery*. ns. PCGPr.18
unryht(-) see **unriht(-)**
unscyldig adj. *without guilt, innocent*. nsm. LwPr.2, 21; asm. **unscyldigne** LwPr.45
ungeselig adj. *unhappy*. nsn. **ungeselige** GDGPr.29
ungesewenlic adj. *invisible*. dp. **ungesewenlicum** BoEp.15
untrumnes f. *illness, weakness*. dp. **untrumnessum** BdPEp.6
untweogendlice adv. *unhesitatingly*. GDGPr.100
unþeaw m. *vice*. ap. **unðeawas** PCGPr.12; gp. **unðeawa** PCGPr.16
unwar adj. *unwary*. npm. **unwaran** PCGPr.26
unwærlice adv. *rashly*. PCGPr.6(x2)
ungewealdes adv. *unintentionally, by accident*. LwPr.13
unwillum adv. *unwillingly, reluctantly*. BoVVi.24, LwPr.13
unwis adj. *foolish*. superl. gsm. **unwisestan** LwPr.41
unwlitig adj. *unlovely*. nsm. PCGEp.2

unwriten adj. *unwritten.* asn. BdPr.48
upgong m. *rising (of sun).* ds. **upgonge** LwPr.25
up(p) adv. *up.* GDVPr.4, GDGPr.3, GDIn2.1, BoVi.1. For **cymeð** . . . **upp** see **cuman**
upplic adj. *on high.* dsf. **upplican** BdPEp.8
ure poss.adj. *our.* nsm. LwPr.49; gsm. **ures** GDGPr.2; gsf. BdPr.6; gsn. **ures** BdPEp.6; dsn. PCPPr.35; npm. PCPPr.31, LwPr.49.3, 49.9; apn. GDPPr.4; gp. **ura** GDGPr.95; dp. **urum** LwPr.49.3
us see **ic**
ut adv. *out, away, outward, abroad.* PCPPr.8, PCVEp.15, BoVPr.6, BoVVi.21, etc.
utan adv. *from abroad.* LwPr.33, 47
utanbordes adv. *from abroad.* PCPPr.11
ute adv. *outside, abroad.* PCPPr.12
utlad f. *carrying away, transporting.* ds. **utlade** [SoPr.23]

waa m. *woe, affliction.* ns. BoVVi.25
wah m. *wall.* as. SoPr.10
walden(d) see **wealdend**
wæge see **weg**
wæl m. *pool, deep water (of a stream).* ns. PCVEp.16
wælhreow adj. *cruel, blood-thirsty.* nsm. **wælhreowa** BoPVi.22
wæn m. *wagon.* as. SoPr.7; ap. **wænas** SoPr.9
wære(n), wæron see **beon**
wæs see **beon**
wæter n. *water.* ns. PCVEp.20; np. **wætru** PCVEp.5; gp. **wætra** PCVEp.29
wæterpyt m. *water-hole.* as. LwPr.22
wæterscipe m. *watercourse, pool of water.* ns. PCVEp.1; gs. **wæterscipes** PCVEp.7
we see **ic**
wealaf f. *survivors (of misfortune).* ns. BoVVi.22
geweald n. *control, power, rule.* as. GDVPr.22, BoVVi.38, BdVEp.20. (his) **gewealdes** *intentionally.* LwPr.13(x2)
wealdan vb 7 (w.g./d.). *to control.* pres.3s. **wilt** SoPr.28, 29; pret.p. **wioldon** BoVVi.48
wealdend m. *ruler, lord.* ns. BoEp.2, **waldend** BdVEp.21, **walden** GDVPr.14
wealhstod m. *translator.* ns. BoPPr.1; ap. **wealhstodas** PCPPr.46
weard m. *guardian.* as. BdVEp.14; ds. **wearde** PCVPr.9
wearoþ m. *shore.* as. BoVVi.14
weaxan vb 7. *to grow, increase.* pret.s. **weox** BoVVi.5; pres.pt. **weaxende** in **frumripan** . . . **weaxendes** *first fruits…of crops.* LwPr.38
wed n. *pledge.* ds. **wedde** LwPr.36
weg m. *way, path.* as. GDGPr.4, **weig** SoPr.17, 19; ds. **wæge** SoPr.14

wel adv. *well, fully*. PCPPr.54, PCVEp.5

wela wk.m. *wealth*. as. **welan** PCPPr.32, 34

welan see **wella**

weler m. *lip*. ap. **weleras** GDIn2.3; dp. **welerum** PCVEp.14

welhwær adv. *nearly everywhere*. PCPPr.70

welig adj. *wealthy, rich*. asm. **weliga** [SoPr.27]; dsm. dsf. **welegan** BoVVi.37, LwPr.43

wella wk.m. *spring, stream*. ds. **welan** GDIn3.1

welle m. *spring, stream, well*. as. PCVEp.24. See also **wylle**

welsprynge m. *source (of water)*. ns. PCVEp.7

wenan vb I (w.g.). *to think, expect*. pres.1s. **wene** GDGPr.76, 83, PCPPr.16; pres. subj.s. **wene** GDGPr.96; pret.s. **wende** BoVVi.78, 82; pret.p. **wendon** PCPPr.39

wendan vb I. *to translate*. infin. PCPPr.38, 60; pres.subj.p. **wenden** PCPPr.50; pret.s. **wende** BoPPr.2; pret.p. **wendon** PCPPr.44, 46, 48; pp. asf. **gewende** BoPPr.7. *to turn*. imp.s. **wend** LwPr.41.

weofod n. *altar*. ds. **weofode** LwPr.13

weorc n. *work, job, deed*. as. PCGPr.17, LwPr.16, **worc** BdPr.33; ap. PCGPr.21; dp. **weorcum** PCGPr.18, 19. *structure*. gp. **weorca** SoPr.3

weorþ n. *worth, value*. ns. LwPr.12, as. LwPr.23

(ge)weorþan vb 3. *to become, happen, perform*. infin. PCPPr.40, **wurðan** BdPr.11; pres.3s. **gewurðeð** GDGPr.60, 93; pres.subj.s. **geweorþe** BdVEp.23, **weorðe** PCVEp.30, LwPr.25; pret.p. **wurdon** LwPr.49.7; pp. **geworden** BdPr.28, 43; pp. npn. **gewordene** GDGPr.78, 79, BdPr.40. In **weorþan to** *to become*. pres.3s. **werð** PCVEp.21

weorþian vb II. *to honour, exalt, worship*. pres.subj.p. **weorðien** LwPr.49.5; pp. **geweorðod** GDPPr.1

weorþmynd f. *honour*. gp. **weorðmynða** BoVVi.51

weoruld f. *world*. as. **world** GDGPr.65; gs. **worldle** GDGPr.48; ds. **weorulde** BoVVi.51, SoPr.14, **worulde** PCPPr.23, PCVEp.3, BoEp.22

weoruldbisgu f. *worldly care*. dp. **woruldbisgum** BoPPr.4

weoruldcund adj. *secular*. gp. **woruldcundra** PCPPr.4

weoruldhlaford m. *secular lord*. np. **weoruldhlafordas** LwPr.49.7

weoruldlic adj. *worldly*. gp. **woruldlicra** GDGPr.11, **worldlicra** GDGPr.39

weoruldsælþ f. *worldly blessing or prosperity*. dp. **woruldsælþum** BoPVi.25

weoruldscir f. *worldly affair, worldly office*. dp. **worldscirum** GDGPr.12

weoruldþeaw m. *worldly virtue*. dp. **woruldþeawum** BoPVi.12

weoruld(ge)þing n. *worldly matter, secular affair*. ap. **worldþing** GDGPr.32; gp. **worldgeþingða** GDPPr.3, **woruldþinga** GDGPr.54, PCPPr.21

weotuma wk.m. *dowry*. ns. LwPr.12; ds. **weotuman** LwPr.29

wepan vb 7. *to weep*. infin. BoPVi.28

wer m. *man*. ns. GDGPr.6, PCGEp.1; as. LwPr.21(x2); gs. **weres** GDEx1.3, GDIn2.3, GDEx3.1, PCVEp.16; np. **weras** GDGPr.76; gp. **wera** GDGPr.93, 100, GDEx2.1; dp. **werum** GDGPr.81, 86, **weron** GDGPr.82

werdan vb I. *to injure, damage*. pres.subj.s. **gewerde** LwPr.18, 26
wergan wk I. *to curse*. imp.s. **werge** LwPr.37; pres.subj.s. **werge** LwPr.15
werian vb I. *to defend, guard*. pres.p. **weriað** PCVEp.13. *to clothe*. infl.infin. **werianne** LwPr.36
werod n. *troop, host*. gp. **wereda** PCVEp.1
werþ see **(ge)weorðan**
wes see **beon**
westm m. *fruit*. as. BdPEp.12
while see **hwil**
wicca wk.f. *witch*. ap. **wiccan** LwPr.30
wide adv. *widely*. BdPr.16
wif n. *woman, wife*. as. LwPr.11(x2), 18, 21(x2); ds. **wife** LwPr.11, 29; np. **wif** LwPr.34
wig n. *war, warfare*. ds. **wige** PCPPr.9, BoVVi.22
wiht f. *creature*. gp. **wihta** GDVPr.14
wildior n. *wild animal*. np. **wildeor** LwPr.39
gewill n. *will, desire*. as. LwPr.41
willa wk.m. *will, desire, pleasure, delight*. as. **willan** GDGPr.8, BoEp.16; ds. **willan** BoEp.9, 11, BdVEp.19
willan anom.vb. *to wish, want*. pres.1s. **wille** GDGPr.103, 106, PCPPr.66; pres.3s. **wile** BdPr.11, **wyle** GDGPr.42; pres.subj.s. **wille** PCPPr.20, 55, 56, 71, PCGPr.13, BoVPr.10, LwPr.35; pres.subj.p. **willen** LwPr.49.5; pret.s. **wolde** GDGPr.85, PCPPr.70, PCGPr.2, PCVEp.3, LwPr.49.9, **wuolde** BoVVi.38; pret.p. **woldon** PCPPr.41; pret.subj.s. **wolde** GDGPr.108
wilnian vb II (w.g. of thing and **to** w.d. of person asked). *to desire, wish, ask for*. imp.s. **wilna** LwPr.9; pres.1s. **wilnige** PCPPr.8; pres.p. **wilniað** PCPPr.23, LwPr.49.3; pres.subj.s. **wilnie** PCPPr.5, **gewilnige** PCGPr.6; pret.s. **wilnode** SoPr.34, **wilnade** GDPPr.6; pret.p. **wilnedon** BoVVi.35
wilnung f. *desire*. In **for ðære wilnunga** *deliberately*. PCPPr.40–1
wilt see **wealdan**
windan vb 3. *to weave*. infin. SoPr.9
wingeard m. *vineyard*. as. LwPr.26
gewin(n) n. *conflict, struggle, war*. as. BoPVi.1; gs. **gewinnes** GDGPr.37; dp. **gewinnum** GDGPr.69
gewinnan vb 3. *to conquer*. pp. **gewunnen** BoVVi.17, 28
winter m. *winter*. ap. **wintras** SoPr.11; gp. **wintra** BoVVi.29
wioldon see **wealdan**
wiotona see **wita**
(ge)wirc- see **wyrcan**
wis adj. *wise*. nsm. BoVVi.51; apm. **wise** PCPPr.46
gewis adj. *certain, sure*. nsn. GDGPr.13
wisdom m. *wisdom*. as. GDGPr.87, PCPPr.11, 21, 32, 34, 41; gs. **wisdomes** PCVEp.14, BdPEp.2, 3; ds. **wisdome** PCPPr.9

wise wk.f. *way, path, role, behaviour.* as. **wisan** GDGPr.41, 98, [LwPr.49.3]; ds. **wisan** GDGPr.17, SoPr.26, LwPr.49.9, BdPr.54; ap. **wisan** GDGPr.99

wislic adj. *wise.* dp. **wislicum** GDEx3.3

wisse see **witan**

gewissian vb II. *to guide, direct.* imp.s. **gewissa** BoEp.9; pres.subj.s. **gewissige** BoEp.8

wiston see **witan** pret.pres.vb

gewit (gewitt-) n. *reason, intelligence.* ds. **gewitte** SoIn3.3

wita wk.m. *wise man, counsellor.* np. **witan** LwPr.21; ap. **witan** BoVVi.66; gp. **witena** GDGPr.111, GDEx3.3, LwPr.49.7, 49.9, **wiotona** PCPPr.36; dp. **witum** BoPVi.14, LwPr.49.10. *witness.* gp. **witena** BdPr.47

witan pret.pres.vb. *to know.* infl.infin. **witanne** SoPr.34, **wiotonne** PCPPr.49; pres.p. **witon** GDGPr.101; pres.subj.s. **wite** GDGPr.106; pret.p. **wiston** PCPPr.29, BdPr.47; pret.subj.s. **wisse** LwPr.21, 23

witan vb 1. *to blame, accuse.* pres.subj.s. **wite** BoPPr.10

gewitan vb 1. *to depart.* pres.3s. **gewiteð** GDGPr.58; pret.s. **gewat** GDGPr.56

wite n. *punishment, torment.* as. GDGPr.36; np. **witu** PCPPr.23

gewitendlic adj. *transitory.* apn. **gewitendlican** GDGPr.31

gewitloca wk.m. *mind.* ds. **witlocan** PCVEp.13

gewitnes f. *witness, testimony.* as. **gewitnesse** LwPr.8, 28(x2), 40

witodlice adv. *certainly, indeed.* GDGPr.20, 42, 89

wiþ prep.w.a./g./d. *against, in opposition to.* BoPVi.1, 13(x2), BoEp.12, 15. *with, towards.* LwPr.2, 47. *in exchange for.* LwPr.18, 19(x3), 24(x3)

wiþerwinna wk.m. *enemy.* dp. **wiðerwinnum** BoEp.15

wiþmetenes f. *comparison.* ds. **wiðmetenesse** GDGPr.75, 95

wlenco f. *riches, prosperity, distinction.* gp. **wlencea** BoVVi.76

wlitig adj. *beautiful, lovely.* asm. **wlitigne** PCGEp.1. superl. apn. **wlitegostan** SoPr.3

wolcen n. *cloud, sky.* dp. **wolcnum** BoVVi.76

wold(-) see **willan**

word n. *word, speech.* as. PCPPr.61, BoPPr.2, LwPr.40; gs. **wordes** (*scripture*) GDGPr.23; ds. **worde** PCPPr.61, BoPPr.2; ap. GDGPr.107, 108, LwPr.1, 46, BdPEp.2; gp. **worda** GDIn3.3, PCVPr.12, BoVVi.81; dp. **wordum** GDGPr.9, GDIn2.6, GDEx3.3, GDIn4.5, PCPPr.2, PCGPr.16, LwPr.49.3

geworden(-) see **(ge)weorþan**

(ge)worhte see **(ge)wyrcan**

wor(u)ld- see **weoruld-**

wraþe adv. *cruelly, terribly.* BoPVi.8

wreon vb 1/2. *to cover.* infl.infin. **wreonne** LwPr.36

gewrit n. *writing, (written) document.* ns. GDGPr.110, BdPr.7; as. PCPPr.54, 58, LwPr.49.9; dp. **gewritum** BdPr.20, 36, 41, 50

writan vb I. *to write, write a copy.* infl.infin. **writenne** BdPr.4; pres.1s. **write** GDGPr.105; pres.p. **writat** BdPr.26; pres.subj.s. **write** PCPPr.72; pret.s. **wrat** BdPr.49; pret.p. **writon** GDGPr.101, **writan** LwPr.49.8; pres.pt. gsm. (used as noun) **writendan** (*the one writing*) GDGPr.110

writere m. *writer, scribe.* ns. PCGEp.2; as. **writre** BdVEp.16; dp. **writerum** PCVPr.12

wudu m. *wood, forest.* ns. SoPr.12; as. **wude** SoPr.5; ds. **wuda** SoPr.8

wuduwe wk.f. *widow.* np. **wydewan** LwPr.34; ap. **wuduwan** LwPr.34

wuldor n. *glory.* ns. **wylder** BoEp.21

gewuna wk.m. *custom, habit.* ns. GDGPr.26; ds. **gewunan** GDGPr.28

wund f. *wound.* ns. LwPr.19; as. **wunde** LwPr.19; ds. **wunde** GDGPr.30, LwPr.19

gewundian vb II. *to wound.* pres.subj.s. **gewundige** LwPr.23

wundor n. *wonder, miracle.* ns. SoPr.22; np. **wundru** GDGPr.77; gp. **wundra** GDGPr.91; dp. **wundrum** GDPPr.7, GDGPr.74, GDEx1.3, GDEx2.1, GDIn3.4

wundrian vb II. *to wonder (at).* pret.s. **wundrade** PCPPr.36

wunian vb II. *to remain, dwell.* pres.3s. **wunað** PCVEp.16; pret.s. **wunode** GDGPr.50

gewunian vb II. *to remain, be accustomed (to), to be in the habit of.* infin. **gewunigen** BoVVi.37; pres.p. **gewuniað** LwPr.30; pret.s. **gewunode** GDGPr.32; pret.p. **gewunedon** GDGPr.18; pp. **gewunod** BoPVi.25

gewunnen see **gewinnan**

wuolde see **willan**

wurdon see **(ge)weorþan**

(ge)wurþ- see **(ge)weorþan**

wydewan see **wuduwe**

wylder see **wuldor**

wylle m. *well, fount (of wisdom).* ds. BdPEp.3

wyn f. *joy.* ns. GDVPr.5

wynsum adj. *kindly, pleasant.* dsm. **wynsumum** [BdVEp.16]

(ge)wyrcan vb I. *to work, do, make, produce.* infin. **wyrcan** SoPr.3, **wircan** SoPr.2; infl.infin. **wyrcenne** BoEp.16; imp.s. **wyrc** LwPr.10; imp.p. **wyrceað** LwPr.3; pres.p. **wyrceað** GDGPr.8; pres.subj.s. **wyrce** PCGPr.17, LwPr.16, **gewirce** SoPr.22; pret.s. **(ge)worhte** GDVPr.21, PCGPr.18, BoPPr.8, SoPr.31, LwPr.3

wyrd f. *fate.* ns. BoVVi.29

wyrhta wk.m. ns. *maker, creator.* BoEp.2

wyrs adv. (comp. of **yfele**). *(the) worse.* BoVVi.76

wyrþe adj. (w.g.). *in possession of, entitled to, subject to.* nsm. LwPr.13, 21; npm. BoPVi.7, BoVVi.37, 67

wyscan vb I. *to wish.* pres.p. **wyscað** LwPr.49.3

yfel n. *evil (thing), ill, harm.* ns. BoVVi.55; gs. **yfeles** PCGPr.17; ap. BoPVi.13, BdPr.8

yfel adj. *evil, wicked.* asm. **yfelne** BdPr.10; dp. **yfelum** BdPr.8, **yflan** PCGPr.18
yfele adv. *wickedly, badly.* BoPVi.8
yfelic adj. *wretched, poor.* nsm. GDGPr.81
ylc- see **ilca**
ymbe prep.w.a. *about, concerning.* GDGPr.42, BoVVi.59, SoPr.34, BdPr.35(x2), 36, 38, 53, **ymb** GDGPr.59, PCPPr.10(x3), LwPr.49.3, BdPr.37, 43, 45, **embe** GDGPr.41, 70
ymbhigdu f. *care, anxiety.* ap. **ymbhigdo** GDPPr.4
ymbhoga wk.m. *care, anxiety, trouble.* ap. **embehogan** GDGPr.38; gp. **ymbhogena** GDGPr.11
ymbsyrwan vb I. *to deliberate about, ambush.* pret.subj.s. **ymbsyrede** LwPr.13
yrfe n. *inheritance.* as. SoPr.27
yrnan vb 3. *to run, flow.* infin. GDGPr.3; pres.3s. **yrnet** GDIn2.1
yþ f. *wave.* ns. GDIn4.1; dp. **yþum** GDGPr.47, 54, PCGEp.5

List of Proper Names

Adrianus *Hadrian, abbot of monastery of St Peter and St Paul (later known as St Augustine's) outside Canterbury.* gs.? BdPr.18
Agustinus *St Augustine of Canterbury.* ns. PCVPr.1
Agustinus *St Augustine of Hippo.* ns. SoPr.31; as. **Augustinus** SoPr.15
Albinus *Albinus, abbot, successor to Hadrian.* ns. BdPr.15; as. BdPr.33; gs. BdPr.28
Aleric see **Eallerica**
Amuling *descendant of the Amal line.* ns. BoVVi.69; gp. **Amulinga** BoPVi.5
Angelcyn(n) n. *the English people, England.* ns. (or np.?) BdPr.24; as. PCPPr.4, 5, 27, 37, 58, LwPr.49.7; ds. **Angelcynne** PCPPr.13, 52, LwPr.49.9, BdPr.16
Angelþeod *the English people, the Angles.* ds. **Angelðeode** BdPr.2
Antiohhia *Antiochia.* ds. LwPr.49.1, 49.2
Arrianus *the heretic Arius.* gs. **Arrianes** BoVVi.40
Asser *Asser, Welsh scholar, became Bishop of Sherborne, King Alfred's biographer.* ds. **Assere** PCPPr.62
Augustinus see **Agustinus**

Ælfred *King Alfred the Great.* ns. GDPPr.1, PCPPr.2, PCVPr.11, BoPPr.1, BoVPr.1, SoEx3.1, LwPr.49.9, 49.10, **Ælfryd** GDVPr.25
Æthelbryht *Æthelbryht, king of Kent.* gs. **Æthelbryhtes** LwPr.49.9

Barnabas *Barnabas.* as. **Barnaban** LwPr.49.3
Beda *Bede.* ns. BdPr.1
Benedictus *Benedict, saint.* gs. **Benedictes** GDEx1.4
Boetius *Boethius.* ns. BoPVi.11, **Boitius** BoVVi.52; gs. **Boetius** BoVVi.75

Glossary and List of Proper Names 277

Cantware fp. *the people of Kent.* gp. **Cantwara** BdPr.17, 19
Cartaina *Carthage.* gs. SoPr.31
Ceadda *Chad, Mercian bishop.* as. **Ceaddan** BdPr.37
Cedde *Cedd, Mercian bishop.* as. BdPr.36
Ceoluulf *Ceolwulf, king of Northumbria.* as. BdPr.2
Cilicia *Cilicia.* ds. LwPr.49.2
Constentinopolim *Constantinople.* ds. BoPVi.18
Creacas mp. *the Greeks.* np. PCPPr.44, BoVVi.48; ap. BoVVi.56, **Crecas** BoVVi.21, 61; gp. **Creca** BoPVi.19, BoVVi.66; dp. **Crecum** BoVVi.26; **Grecum** GDIn2.4
Crist *Christ.* ns. LwPr.3, 49, 49.7(x2); gs. **Cristes** LwPr.49.1, 49.7(x2), BdPr.1, 25, 31, 43, 46; ds. **Criste** GDPPr.1, BoVVi.32, LwPr.49.2
Crysosthomas *Chrysostom ('golden mouth', referring to Gregory).* GDIn2.4
Cuþbyrht *Cuthbert, bishop.* ds. **Cuðberhte** BdPr.49
Cynebyrht *Cynebyrht, Bishop of Lindsey.* gs. **Cynebryhtes** BdPr.44

Daniel *Daniel, Bishop of Winchester.* gs. **Danielis** BdPr.34

Eallerica *the Gothic king Alaric.* ns. BoPVi.2, **Aleric** BoVVi.19; as. **Aleric** BoVVi.7
Eastengle mp. *the East Anglians.* np. BdPr.31; dp. **Eastenglum** BdPr.40
Eastseaxe mp. *the East Saxons.* np. BdPr.30; gp. **Eastseaxena** BdPr.38
Egipte mp. *the Egyptians.* gp. **Egipta** LwPr.1, 33
Engle mp. *the English.* dp. **Englum** GDVPr.25

Gota wk.m. *Goth.* ns. BoVVi.9, 45; np. **Gotan.** BoPVi.1, BoVVi.1; ap. **Gotan** BoVVi.23; gp. **Gotene** BoVVi.5, **Gotena** BoVVi.38
Grecum see **Creacas**
Gregorius *Gregory, saint.* ns. GDGPr.6, 8, 80, 99, etc., GDIn2.6, GDIn4.4, PCVPr.6, PCVEp.23; as. SoPr.16; gs. **Gregories** GDIn2.4, GDEx3.1, **Gregorius** GDGPr.3, GDEx1.1, GDIn3.2, BdPr.21, 27
Grimbold *Grimbold, Frankish priest and scholar.* ds. **Grimbolde** PCPPr.63

Hierdeboc f. *Shepherd Book (referring to the 'Cura pastoralis').* as. PCPPr.61
Humbre *the river Humber.* ds. **Humbre** PCPPr.14, 16

Ieronimus *Jerome, saint.* as. SoPr.16
Ine *Ine, king of the West Saxons.* gs. **Ines** LwPr.49.9
Iohannes *John, continental Saxon, became abbot of Athelney in Somerset.* ds. **Iohanne** PCPPr.63
Iohannes *John, Bishop of Ravenna.* ns. PCGEp.1
Iohannes *Pope John I.* as. BoPVi.9, BoVVi.42
Isse *Isse, abbot.* gs. **Isses** BdPr.41
Italia mp. *the Italians.* ap. BoVVi.12; gp. BoPVi.3
Iudas *Judas.* as. **Iudam** LwPr.49.4

Lædenware mp. *the Romans*. np. PCPPr.45
Læsþinga ea *Lastingham*. as.? BdPr.39
Lindesfarene ea *Lindisfarne*. ds. BdPr.51
Lindesige *Lindsey*. ds. BdPr.42
Longbeardas mp. *the Lombards*. dp. **Longbeardum** GDGPr.73
Lucas *Luke, evangelist*. ns. GDGPr.101
Lundenbyrig *the city of London*. ds. BdPr.23

Marcus *Mark, evangelist*. ns. GDGPr.101
Maria *Mary, saint*. gs. **Marian** BoEp.5
Merce mp. *the Mercians*. gp. **Mercna** LwPr.49.9, **Myrcna** BdPr.37(x2)
Michael *Michael, saint*. gs. **Michaeles** BoEp.6
Moyses *Moses*. ds. **Moyse** LwPr.1, 49
Muntgiop m. *the Alps, 'Mountains of Jove'*. as. BoVVi.8; ds. BoVVi.14
Myrcna see **Merce**

Norþanhymbre mp. *the Northumbrians*. np. **Norðhymbre** BdPr.31; dp. **Norðhymbrum** BdPr.45
Noþhelm *Nothhelm, Archbishop of Canterbury*. as. BdPr.22; gs. **Noðhelmes** BdPr.29

Offa *Offa, king of Mercia*. gs. **Offan** LwPr.49.9
Os Aureum *Golden Mouth (referring to Gregory)*. as. GDIn3.3

Paulus *Paul, apostle*. as. LwPr.49.3; gs. **Paules** GDGPr.103
Petrus *Peter, apostle*. gs. **Petres** GDGPr.103
Petrus *Peter, deacon*. ns. GDGPr.6, 21, 27, 46, 73, 80, 85, 106; gs. **Petres** GDEx1.2, GDEx3.2
Plegmund *Plegmund, Mercian scholar, became Archbishop of Canterbury*. ds. **Plegmunde** PCPPr.62

Rædgota *the Gothic king Rædgota (Radagaisus)*. ns. BoPVi.2, **Rædgot** BoVVi.19; as. **Rædgod** BoVVi.7
Rom f. *Rome*. ns. BoVVi.19; gs. **Rome** PCVPr.5
Romane mp. *the Romans*. np. GDIn3.3; gp. **Romana** BoPVi.1, BoVVi.17, **Romane** BoPVi.3; dp. **Romanum** BoPVi.6
Romebyrig *the city of Rome*. ds. BoVVi.46
Romwara fp. *the Romans*. gp. PCVPr.9, BoVVi.34; dp. **Romwarum** BoVVi.49, 67

Sciþþia f. *Scythia*. gs./ds.? **Sciþþiu** BoPVi.1; ds. BoVVi.2
Seaxe mp. *the Saxons*. dp. **Seaxum** BdPr.3
Sicilia *the island of Sicily*. ns. BoVVi.15; ds. BoPVi.3

Silas *Silas*. as. **Silam** LwPr.49.4
Soliloquia np. *Soliloquies*. gp. **Soliloquiorum** SoPr.32, SoEx2.1, [SoEx3.2]
Suþseaxe mp. *the South Saxons*. ap. BdPr.35
Syria *Syria*. ds. LwPr.49.2, **Syrie** LwPr.49.1

Temese *the Thames*. ds. PCPPr.17

Þeodore *Theodore, Archbishop of Canterbury*. gs. **Ðeodores** BdPr.17
Þeodric *the Gothic king Theoderic*. ns. BoPVi.5(x2), 13, 22, BoVVi.69; ds. **Ðeodrice** BoVVi.30

Wærferþ *Wærferth, Bishop of Worcester*. PCPPr.2
Westseaxe mp. *the West Saxons*. np. BdPr.31; ap. BdPr.35; gp. **Westsexna** BoVPr.2, **Westseaxna** LwPr.49.10, **Wessexena** BdPr.34
Wihtland *Wight (Isle of)*. as. BdPr.36
Wiogora ceaster f. *Worcester*. ds. **Wiogora ceastre** PCPPr.1
Wulfsige *Wulfsige, Bishop of Sherborne*. GDVPr.12 (**Wulfstan** *in manuscript*)

Bibliography

This bibliography includes only items cited in this edition.

Primary Sources

Anlezark, Daniel (ed. and trans.). 2009. *The Old English Dialogues of Solomon and Saturn*. Anglo-Saxon Texts 7 (Cambridge: D. S. Brewer).

Attenborough, F. L. (ed. and trans.). 1922. *The Laws of the Earliest English Kings* (Cambridge: Cambridge University Press; reprinted New York: Russell & Russell, 1963).

Baker, Peter (ed.). 2000. *The Anglo-Saxon Chronicle: A Collaborative Edition*. Vol. 8: *MS F* (Cambridge: D. S. Brewer).

Bately, Janet M. (ed.). 1986. *The Anglo-Saxon Chronicle: A Collaborative Edition*. Vol. 3: *MS A* (Cambridge: D. S. Brewer).

Campbell, A. (ed.). 1962. *The Chronicle of Æthelweard* (London: Nelson).

Carlson, Ingvar (ed.). 1975–8. *The Pastoral Care Edited from British Museum MS Cotton Otho B.ii*. 2 vols. Stockholm Studies in English 34 and 48 (Stockholm: Almqvist & Wiksell International).

Carnicelli, Thomas A. (ed.). 1969. *King Alfred's Version of St. Augustine's* Soliloquies (Cambridge, MA: Harvard University Press).

Colgrave, Bertram (ed.). 1968. *The Earliest Life of Gregory the Great* (Lawrence: University of Kansas Press).

Colgrave, Bertram, and R. A. B. Mynors (eds. and trans.). 1969. *Bede's Ecclesiastical History of the English People*. Oxford Medieval Texts (Oxford: Clarendon Press).

Cubbin, G. P. (ed.). 1996. *The Anglo-Saxon Chronicle: A Collaborative Edition*. Vol. 6: *MS D* (Cambridge: D. S. Brewer).

Curry, James Joseph Mark. 1966. *Alcuin,* De Ratione Animae*: A Text with Introduction, Critical Apparatus, and Translation* (PhD diss., Cornell University).

Dammery, Richard J. E. 1990. 'The Law-Code of King Alfred the Great'. 2 vols (PhD diss., University of Cambridge).

Dobbie, Elliott Van Kirk (ed.). 1942. *The Anglo-Saxon Minor Poems*. Anglo-Saxon Poetic Records 6 (New York: Columbia University Press, and London: Routledge and Kegan Paul).

Eckhardt, Karl August (ed.). 1958. *Leges Anglo-Saxonum 601–925* (Göttingen: Musterschmidt).

Ehwald, Rudolf (ed.). 1919. *Aldhelmi Opera*. Monumenta Germaniae Historica, Auctores Antiquissimi 15 (Berlin: Weidmann).

Endter, Wilhelm (ed.). 1922. *König Alfreds des Grossen Bearbeitung der Soliloquien des Augustinus*. Bibliothek der angelsächsischen Prosa 11 (Hamburg: Henri Grand).

Flower, Robin, and Hugh Smith (eds). 1941. *The Parker Chronicle and Laws (Corpus Christi College, Cambridge, MS. 173): A Facsimile*. Early English Text Society o.s. 208 (London: Oxford University Press, reprinted 1973).

Fulk, R. D. (ed. and trans.). 2021. *The Old English Pastoral Care*. Dumbarton Oaks Medieval Library (Cambridge, MA, and London: Harvard University Press).

Gates, Jay (ed. and trans.). 2018. 'Prologue to the Laws of King Alfred: An Edition and Translation for Students'. *The Heroic Age: A Journal of Early Medieval Northwestern Europe* 18, https://www.heroicage.org/issues/18/gates.php.

Godden, Malcolm (ed. and trans.). 2016. *The Old English History of the World: An Anglo-Saxon Rewriting of Orosius*. Dumbarton Oaks Medieval Library (Cambridge, MA, and London: Harvard University Press).

Godden, Malcolm, and Susan Irvine (eds). 2009. *The Old English Boethius: An Edition of the Old English Versions of Boethius's* De Consolatione Philosophiae. 2 vols (Oxford: Oxford University Press).

Griffiths, Bill (ed.). 1991. *Alfred's Metres of Boethius*. Anglo-Saxon Books (Pinner: Anglo-Saxon Books; rev. ed. 1994).

Hargrove, Henry Lee (ed.). 1902. *King Alfred's Old English Version of Saint Augustine's Soliloquies*. Yale Studies in English 13 (New York: Henry Holt and Co.).

Hecht, Hans (ed.). 1900. *Bischof Wærferths von Worcester Übersetzung der Dialoge Gregors des Grossen*. Bibliothek der angelsächsischen Prosa 5 (Leipzig: Georg H. Wigand).

Irvine, Susan (ed.). 2004. *The Anglo-Saxon Chronicle: A Collaborative Edition*. Vol. 7: *MS E* (Cambridge: D. S. Brewer).

Irvine, Susan, and Malcolm Godden (eds and trans.), with Mark Griffith and Rohini Jayatilaka. 2012. *The Old English Boethius with Verse Prologues and Epilogues Associated with King Alfred*. Dumbarton Oaks Medieval Library (Cambridge, MA, and London: Harvard University Press).

Jones, Christopher A. (ed. and trans.). 2012. *Old English Shorter Poems*. Vol. I: *Religious and Didactic*. Dumbarton Oaks Medieval Library (Cambridge, MA, and London: Harvard University Press).

Judic, Bruno, Floribert Rommel, and Charles Morel (eds). 1992. *Grégoire le Grand, Règle Pastorale*. 2 vols. Sources Chrétiennes 381–2 (Paris: Les Éditions du Cerf).

Jurasinski, Stefan, and Lisi Oliver (eds). 2021. *The Laws of Alfred: The* Domboc *and the Making of Anglo-Saxon Law*. Studies in Legal History (Cambridge: Cambridge University Press).

Ker, N. R. (ed.). 1956. *The Pastoral Care. King Alfred's Translation of St Gregory's Regula Pastoralis, MS. Hatton 20 in the Bodleian Library at Oxford, MS. Cotton Tiberius B. XI. in the British Museum, MS. Anhang 19 in the Landesbibliothek at*

Kassel. Early English Manuscripts in Facsimile 6 (Copenhagen: Rosenkilde and Bagger).

Keynes, Simon, and Michael Lapidge (trans.). 1983. *Alfred the Great: Asser's Life of King Alfred and Other Contemporary Sources* (Harmondsworth: Penguin).

Klaeber, Fr. 1902/1904. 'Zur altenglischen Bedaübersetzung'. *Anglia* 25: pp. 257–315; 27: pp. 243–82, 399–435.

Krapp, George Philip (ed.). 1932. *The Paris Psalter and the Meters of Boethius*. Anglo-Saxon Poetic Records 5 (New York: Columbia University Press).

Krapp, George Philip, and Elliott Van Kirk Dobbie (eds). 1936. *The Exeter Book*. Anglo-Saxon Poetic Records 3 (London: Routledge and Kegan Paul).

Lapidge, Michael (ed.), and Paolo Chiesa (trans.). 2008–10. *Beda: Storia degli inglesi (Historia ecclesiastica gentis Anglorum)*. 2 vols (Rome: Fondazione Lorenzo Valla; Milan: A. Mondadori).

Lapidge, Michael, and Michael Herren (trans.). 1979. *Aldhelm: The Prose Works* (Cambridge: The Boydell Press).

Liebermann, Felix (ed.). 1903–16. *Die Gesetze der Angelsachsen*. 3 vols (Halle: M. Niemeyer).

Lockett, Leslie (ed. and trans.). 2022a. *Augustine's Soliloquies in Old English and Latin*. Dumbarton Oaks Medieval Library (Cambridge, MA, and London: Harvard University Press).

Miller, Thomas (ed.). 1890–8. *The Old English Version of Bede's Ecclesiastical History of the English People*. 2 vols. Early English Text Society o.s. 95–6 and 110–11 (London: Oxford University Press).

Mutzenbecher, Almut (ed.). 1984. Augustine, *Retractionum Libri II*. Corpus Christianorum Series Latina 57 (Turnhout: Brepols).

Mynors, R. A. B., R. M. Thomson, and M. Winterbottom (eds). 1998–9. *William of Malmesbury, Gesta Regum Anglorum*. 2 vols. Oxford Medieval Texts (Oxford: Clarendon Press).

New, Melvyn (ed.). 1996. *The Florida Edition of the Works of Laurence Sterne*. Vol. 4: *The Sermons* (Gainesville: University Press of Florida).

O'Brien O'Keeffe, Katherine (ed.). 2001. *The Anglo-Saxon Chronicle: A Collaborative Edition*. Vol. 5: *MS C* (Cambridge: D. S. Brewer).

Obst, Wolfgang, and Florian Schleburg (eds). 1998. *Lieder aus König Alfreds Trostbuch: die Stabreimverse der altenglischen Boethius-Übertragung* (Heidelberg: C. Winter).

O'Neill, Patrick P. (ed.). 2001. *King Alfred's Old English Prose Translation of the First Fifty Psalms* (Cambridge, MA: The Medieval Academy of America).

O'Neill, Patrick P. (ed. and trans.). 2016. *Old English Psalms*. Dumbarton Oaks Medieval Library 42 (Cambridge, MA: Harvard University Press).

Peiper, Rudolf (ed.). 1871. *Anicii Manlii Severini Boetii Philosophiae consolationis libri quinque: accedunt eiusdem atque incertorum opuscula sacra* (Leipzig: Teubner).

Preston, Todd (ed. and trans.). 2012. *King Alfred's Book of Laws: A Study of the Domboc and its Influence on English Identity* (Jefferson, NC: McFarland and Co.).

Rauer, Christine (ed. and trans.). 2013. *The Old English Martyrology: Edition, Translation and Commentary* (Cambridge: D. S. Brewer).

Robinson, Fred, and E. G. Stanley (eds). 1991. *Old English Verse Texts from Many Sources: A Comprehensive Collection*. Early English Manuscripts in Facsimile 23 (Copenhagen: Rosenkilde and Bagger).

Schreiber, Carolin (ed.). 2003. *King Alfred's Old English Translation of Pope Gregory the Great's* Regula Pastoralis *and its Cultural Context: A Study and Partial Edition According to All Surviving Manuscripts Based on Cambridge, Corpus Christi College 12*. Texte und Untersuchungen zur Englischen Philologie 25 (Frankfurt-am-Main: Peter Lang).

Sedgefield, Walter John (ed.). 1899. *King Alfred's Old English Version of Boethius De Consolatione Philosophiae* (Oxford: Clarendon Press).

Smith, John (ed.). 1722. *Historiæ Ecclesiasticæ Gentis Anglorum libri Quinque...* (Cambridge: John Smith).

Stevenson, William Henry (ed.). 1959. *Asser's Life of King Alfred, together with the Annals of Saint Neots, erroneously ascribed to Asser* (Oxford: Clarendon Press, 1904), reissued with an introduction by Dorothy Whitelock (Oxford: Clarendon Press).

Sweet, Henry (ed.). 1871. *King Alfred's West Saxon Version of Gregory's Pastoral Care*, Early English Text Society o.s. 45 (London: Oxford University Press; repr. 1958).

Sweet, Henry, and Dorothy Whitelock (eds). 1967. *Sweet's Anglo-Saxon Reader in Prose and Verse*. 15th ed. (Oxford: Oxford University Press).

Thorpe, B. (ed. and trans.). 1840. *Ancient Laws and Institutes of England* (London: Eyre and Spottiswoode).

Vogüé, Adalbert de, and Paul Antin (eds). 1978–80. *Grégoire le Grand, Dialogues*, 3 vols. Sources Chrétiennes 259–61 (Paris: Les Éditions du Cerf).

Watson, Gerard (trans.). 1990. *Saint Augustine, Soliloquies and Immortality of the Soul* (Warminster: Aris & Phillips).

Weber, Robert (ed.). 1994. *Biblia Sacra iuxta Vulgatam Versionem*. 4th ed. (Stuttgart: Deutsche Bibelgesellschaft).

Wheloc, Abraham (ed.). 1643. *Historiæ Ecclesiasticæ Gentis Anglorum Libri V. A venerabili Beda Presbytero scripti...* (Cambridge: Roger Daniel).

Whitelock, Dorothy (ed.). 1979a. *English Historical Documents c. 500–1042*. 2nd ed. (London: Eyre Methuen, and New York: Oxford University Press).

Wilcox, Jonathan (ed.). 1994. *Ælfric's Prefaces* (Durham: Durham Medieval Texts).

Wright, C. E. (ed.), with appendix by Randolph Quirk. 1955. *Bald's Leechbook (British Museum Royal MS 12 D. xvii)*. Early English Manuscripts in Facsimile 5 (Copenhagen: Rosenkilde and Bagger).

Yerkes, David. 1980. 'The Full Text of the Metrical Preface to Wærferth's Translation of Gregory [Hecht 2.1–17]'. *Speculum* 55: pp. 505–13.

Secondary Sources

Anlezark, Daniel. 2017. 'Which Books are "Most Necessary" to Know? The Old English Pastoral Care Preface and King Alfred's Educational Reform'. *English Studies* 98.8 (2017): pp. 759–80.

Anlezark, Daniel. 2021. 'Drawing Alfredian Waters: The Old English *Metrical Epilogue* to the *Pastoral Care*, Boethian *Metre* 20, and *Solomon and Saturn II*'. In *Meanings of Water in Early Medieval England*, ed. Carolyn Twomey and Daniel Anlezark. Studies in the Early Middle Ages 47 (Turnhout: Brepols), pp. 241–66.

Bately, Janet M. 1970. 'King Alfred and the Old English Translation of Orosius'. *Anglia* 88: pp. 433–60.

Bately, Janet M. 1988. 'Old English Prose Before and During the Reign of Alfred'. *Anglo-Saxon England* 17: pp. 93–138.

Bately, Janet. 2002. 'Book Divisions and Chapter Headings in the Translations of the Alfredian Period'. In *Early Medieval English Texts and Interpretations: Studies Presented to Donald G. Scragg*, ed. Elaine Treharne and Susan Rosser. Medieval and Renaissance Texts and Studies (Tempe, Arizona: Arizona Center for Medieval and Renaissance Studies), pp. 151–66.

Bately, Janet. 2003. 'The Alfredian Canon Revisited: One Hundred Years On'. In *Alfred the Great: Papers from the Eleventh-Century Conferences*, ed. Timothy Reuter (Aldershot, Hants.: Ashgate), pp. 107–20.

Bately, Janet. 2009. 'Did King Alfred Actually Translate Anything? The Integrity of the Alfredian Canon Revisited'. *Medium Ævum* 78: 189–209.

Bately, Janet M. 2015. 'Alfred as Author and Translator'. In *A Companion to Alfred the Great*, ed. Nicole Guenther Discenza and Paul E. Szarmach. Brill's Companions to the Christian Tradition 58 (Leiden and Boston: Brill), pp. 113–42.

Bintley, Michael D. J. 2015. *Trees in the Religions of Early Medieval England* (Woodbridge: The Boydell Press).

Bostock, J. Knight. 1976. *A Handbook on Old High German Literature*. 2nd ed., revised by K. C. King and D. R. McLintock (Oxford: Clarendon Press).

Bredehoft, Thomas A. 2009. *Authors, Audiences, and Old English Verse* (Toronto, Buffalo, London: University of Toronto Press).

Brown, Michelle P., and Carol A. Farr (eds). 2001. *Mercia: An Anglo-Saxon Kingdom in Europe* (London and New York: Leicester University Press).

Campbell, A. 1959. *Old English Grammar* (Oxford: Clarendon Press).

Carella, Bryan. 2005. 'The Source of the Prologue to the Laws of Alfred', *Peritia* 19: pp. 91–118.

Carella, Bryan. 2011. 'Evidence for Hiberno-Latin Thought in the Prologue to the Laws of Alfred'. *Studies in Philology* 108: pp. 1–26.

Clemoes, Peter. 1992. 'King Alfred's Debt to Vernacular Poetry: the Evidence of *ellen* and *cræft*'. In *Words, Texts and Manuscripts: Studies in Anglo-Saxon Culture Presented to Helmut Gneuss on the Occasion of his Sixty-fifth Birthday*, ed. Michael Korhammer with the assistance of Karl Reichl and Hans Sauer (Cambridge: D. S. Brewer), pp. 213–38.

Copeland, Rita. 1991. *Rhetoric, Hermeneutics, and Translation in the Middle Ages: Academic Traditions and Vernacular Texts* (Cambridge: Cambridge University Press).

Copeland, Rita. 2016. 'Academic Prologues to Authors'. In *The Oxford History of Classical Reception in English Literature. I. (1800–1558)*, ed. Rita Copeland (Oxford: Oxford University Press), pp. 151–66.

Cross, J. E. 1969. 'The Metrical Epilogue to the Old English Version of Gregory's *Cura Pastoralis*'. *Neuphilologische Mitteilungen* 70: pp. 381–6.

Curtius, Ernst Robert. 1953. *European Literature and the Latin Middle Ages*. Trans. W. R. Trask (London and Henley: Routledge and Kegan Paul).

Dance, Richard. 2004. 'Sound, Fury and Signifiers; or Wulfstan's Language'. In *Wulfstan, Archbishop of York: The Proceedings of the Second Alcuin Conference*, ed. Matthew Townend. Studies in the Early Middle Ages 10 (Turnhout: Brepols), pp. 29–61.

Dearnley, Elizabeth. 2016. *Translators and their Prologues in Medieval England*. Bristol Studies in Medieval Cultures (Woodbridge: D. S. Brewer).

Dekker, Kees. 2001. 'King Alfred's Translation of Gregory's *Dialogi*: Tales for the Unlearned?'. In *Rome and the North: The Early Reception of Gregory the Great in Germanic Europe*, ed. Rolf H. Bremmer Jr, Kees Dekker, and David F. Johnson (Paris: Peeters), pp. 27–50.

Discenza, Nicole Guenther. 1997. 'Power, Skill, and Virtue in the Old English *Boethius*'. *Anglo-Saxon England* 26: pp. 81–108.

Discenza, Nicole Guenther. 1998. '"Wise wealhstodas": The Prologue to Sirach as a Model for Alfred's Preface to the *Pastoral Care*'. *Journal of English and Germanic Philology* 97: pp. 488–99.

Discenza, Nicole Guenther. 2001. 'Alfred's Verse Preface to the *Pastoral Care* and the Chain of Authority'. *Neophilologus* 85: pp. 625–33.

Discenza, Nicole Guenther. 2002. 'The Old English *Bede* and the Construction of Anglo-Saxon Authority'. *Anglo-Saxon England* 31: pp. 69–80.

Discenza, Nicole Guenther. 2005. *The King's English: Strategies of Translation in the Old English* Boethius (Albany: State University of New York Press).

Discenza, Nicole Guenther. 2008. 'Alfred the Great and the Anonymous Prose Proem to the *Boethius*'. *Journal of English and Germanic Philology* 107: pp. 57–76.

Discenza, Nicole Guenther, and Paul E. Szarmach. 2015. 'Appendix: Annotated Bibliography on the Authorship Issue'. In their *A Companion to Alfred the Great*. Brill's Companions to the Christian Tradition 58 (Leiden and Boston: Brill), pp. 397–415.

Earl, James W. 1994. 'King Alfred's Talking Poems'. *Pacific Coast Philology* 24 (1989): pp. 49–61. Reprinted in revised form in his *Thinking about* Beowulf (Stanford: Stanford University Press), pp. 87–99.

Evans, Ruth. 1999. 'An Afterword on the Prologue'. In *The Idea of the Vernacular: An Anthology of Middle English Literary Theory, 1280–1520*, ed. Jocelyn Wogan-Browne, Nicholas Watson, Andrew Taylor, and Ruth Evans. Exeter Medieval Texts and Studies (Exeter: University of Exeter Press, and Pennsylvania: Pennsylvania State University Press), pp. 371–8.

Fournier, Paul. 1909. 'Le *Liber ex lege Moysi* et les tendances bibliques du droit canonique irlandais'. *Revue Celtique* 30: pp. 221–34.

Frantzen, Allen J. 1986. *King Alfred*. Twayne's English Authors Series 425 (Boston: Twayne Publishers, a division of G. K. Hall & Co.).

Frantzen, Allen J. 2003. 'The Form and Function of the Preface in the Poetry and Prose of Alfred's Reign'. In *Alfred the Great: Papers from the Eleventh-Century Conferences*, ed. Timothy Reuter (Aldershot, Hants.: Ashgate), pp. 121–36.

Franzen, Christine. 1991. *The Tremulous Hand of Worcester: A Study of Old English in the Thirteenth Century* (Oxford: Oxford University Press).

Fulk, R. D. 2012. 'Anglian Features in Late West Saxon'. In *Analysing Older English*, ed. David Denison, Ricardo Bermúdez-Otero, Chris McCully, and Emma Moore (Cambridge: Cambridge University Press), pp. 63–74.

Galloway, Andrew. 2005. 'Middle English Prologues'. In *Readings in Medieval Texts: Interpreting Old and Middle English Literature*, ed. David Johnson and Elaine Treharne (Oxford: Oxford University Press), pp. 288–305.

Gameson, Richard. 2002. *The Scribe Speaks? Colophons in Early English Manuscripts*. H. M. Chadwick Memorial Lectures 12 (Cambridge: Department of Anglo-Saxon, Norse, and Celtic, University of Cambridge).

Gatch, Milton McC. 1986. 'King Alfred's Version of Augustine's *Soliloquia*: Some Suggestions on its Rationale and Unity'. In *Studies in Earlier Old English Prose*, ed. Paul E. Szarmach (Albany: State University of New York), pp. 17–45. Reprinted in *Old English Prose: Basic Readings*, ed. Paul E. Szarmach with Deborah A. Oosterhouse (New York and London: Garland, 2000), pp. 199–236.

Genette, Gérard. 1997. *Paratexts: Thresholds of Interpretation*, trans. Jane E. Lewin (Cambridge: Cambridge University Press).

Gittos, Helen. 2014. 'The Audience for Old English Texts: Ælfric, Rhetoric and the Edification of the Simple'. *Anglo-Saxon England* 43 (2014): pp. 231–66.

Gneuss, Helmut. 1986. 'King Alfred and the History of Anglo-Saxon Libraries'. In *Modes of Interpretation in Old English Literature: Essays in Honour of*

Stanley B. Greenfield, ed. Phyllis Rugg Brown, Georgia Ronan Crampton, and Fred C. Robinson (Toronto: University of Toronto Press), pp. 29–49.

Gneuss, Helmut, and Michael Lapidge. 2014. *Anglo-Saxon Manuscripts: A Bibliographical Handlist of Manuscripts and Manuscript Fragments Written or Owned in England up to 1100* (Toronto, Buffalo, and London: University of Toronto Press).

Godden, Malcolm. 1978. 'Ælfric and the Vernacular Prose Tradition'. In *The Old English Homily and its Backgrounds*, ed. Paul E. Szarmach and Bernard F. Huppé (Albany: State University of New York Press), pp. 99–117.

Godden, Malcolm. 1997. 'Wærferth and King Alfred: The Fate of the Old English Dialogues.' In *Alfred the Wise: Studies in Honour of Janet Bately on the Occasion of her Sixty-Fifth Birthday*, ed. Jane Roberts and Janet L. Nelson with Malcolm Godden (Cambridge: D. S. Brewer), pp. 37–51.

Godden, M. R. 2001. 'The Sources of King Alfred's Old English Version of Augustine's Soliloquia (Cameron C.B.9.41)', *Fontes Anglo-Saxonici World Wide Web Register*, https://arts.st-andrews.ac.uk/fontes/search.

Godden, M. R. 2002a. 'The Anglo-Saxons and the Goths: Rewriting the Sack of Rome'. *Anglo-Saxon England* 31: pp. 47–68.

Godden, Malcolm. 2002b. 'King Alfred's Preface and the Teaching of Latin in Anglo-Saxon England'. *English Historical Review* 117: pp. 596–604.

Godden, Malcolm. 2003. 'Text and Eschatology in Book III of the Old English Soliloquies'. *Anglia* 121: pp. 79–188.

Godden, M. R. 2007. 'Did King Alfred Write Anything?'. *Medium Ævum* 76.1: pp. 1–23.

Godden, M. R. 2008. 'King and Counselor in the Alfredian Boethius'. In *Intertexts: Studies in Anglo-Saxon Culture Presented to Paul E. Szarmach*, ed. Virginia Blanton and Helene Scheck. Arizona Studies in the Middle Ages and the Renaissance 24, Medieval and Renaissance Texts and Studies 334, in collaboration with Brepols (Tempe, Arizona: Arizona Center for Medieval and Renaissance Studies), pp. 191–207.

Godden, Malcolm. 2009a. 'The Alfredian Project and its Aftermath: Rethinking the Literary History of the Ninth and Tenth Centuries'. *Proceedings of the British Academy* 162: pp. 93–122.

Godden, Malcolm R. 2009b. 'Ælfric and the Alfredian Precedents'. In *A Companion to Ælfric*, ed. Hugh Magennis and Mary Swan. Brill's Companions to the Christian Tradition 19 (Leiden and Boston: Brill), pp. 139–63.

Godden, Malcolm. 2011. 'Prologues and Epilogues in the Old English *Pastoral Care*, and their Carolingian Models'. *Journal of English and Germanic Philology* 110: pp. 441–73.

Godden, Malcolm. 2013. 'Alfredian Prose: Myth and Reality'. *Filologia Germanica* 5: pp. 131–58.

Godden, Malcolm. 2013. 'Editing Old English Prose and the Challenge of Revision or, Why It Is Not So Easy to Edit Old English Prose'. In *Probable Truth: Editing Medieval Texts from Britain in the Twenty-First Century*, ed. Vincent Gillespie and Anne Hudson (Turnhout: Brepols), pp. 91–110.

Graham, Timothy. 2004. 'The Opening of King Alfred's Preface to the Old English Pastoral Care: Oxford, Bodleian Library, MS Hatton 20'. *Old English Newsletter* 38.1: pp. 43–50.

Grant, Raymond J. S. 1989. *The B Text of the Old English Bede: A Linguistic Commentary*. Costerus n.s. (Amsterdam: Rodopi).

Harting, P. N. U. 1937. 'The Text of the Old English Translation of Gregory's "Dialogues"'. *Neophilologus* 22: pp. 281–302.

Haug, Walter. 1997. *Vernacular Literary Theory in the Middle Ages: The German Tradition, 800–1300, in its European Context*. Trans. Joanna M. Catling (Cambridge: Cambridge University Press).

Heuchan, Valerie. 2007. 'God's Co-workers and Powerful Tools: A Study of the Sources of Alfred's Building Metaphor in his Old English Translation of Augustine's Soliloquies'. *Notes and Queries* n.s. 54: pp. 1–11.

Higham, N. J. 2006. *(Re-)Reading Bede: The* Ecclesiastical History *in Context* (Abingdon and New York: Routledge).

Hinton, David A. 2008. *The Alfred Jewel and Other Late Anglo-Saxon Decorated Metalwork* (Oxford: Ashmolean Museum).

Huppé, Bernard F. 1978. 'Alfred and Ælfric: a Study of Two Prefaces'. In *The Old English Homily and its Backgrounds*, ed. Paul E. Szarmach and Bernard F. Huppé (Albany, New York: State University of New York), pp. 119–37.

Irvine, Martin. 1994. *The Making of Textual Culture: Grammatica and Literary Theory, 300–1100*. Cambridge Studies in Medieval Literature 19 (Cambridge: Cambridge University Press).

Irvine, Susan. 2003. 'Wrestling with Hercules: King Alfred and the Classical Past'. In *Court Culture in the Early Middle Ages: The Proceedings of the First Alcuin Conference*, ed. Catherine Cubitt (Turnhout: Brepols), pp. 171–88.

Irvine, Susan. 2005. 'Fragments of Boethius: the Reconstruction of the Cotton Manuscript of the Alfredian Text', *Anglo-Saxon England* 34: pp. 169–81.

Irvine, Susan. 2015a. 'The Alfredian Prefaces and Epilogues'. In *A Companion to Alfred the Great*, ed. Nicole Guenther Discenza and Paul E. Szarmach. Brill's Companions to the Christian Tradition 58 (Leiden and Boston: Brill), pp. 143–70.

Irvine, Susan. 2015b. 'The Anglo-Saxon Chronicle'. In *A Companion to Alfred the Great*, ed. Nicole Guenther Discenza and Paul E. Szarmach. Brill's Companions to the Christian Tradition 58 (Leiden and Boston: Brill), pp. 344–67.

Irvine, Susan. 2017. *Uncertain Beginnings: The Prefatory Tradition in Old English*. H. M. Chadwick Memorial Lectures 27 (Cambridge: Department of Anglo-Saxon, Norse, and Celtic, University of Cambridge).

Irvine, Susan. 2018. 'The Protean Form of the Old English *Boethius*'. In *The Legacy of Boethius in Medieval England*, ed. Joey McMullen and Erica Weaver (Arizona: Arizona Centre for Medieval and Renaissance Studies), pp. 1–17.

Irvine, Susan. Forthcoming. 'The Idea of Decorum in the Old English *Dialogues*'. In *The Age of Alfred: Rethinking English Literary Culture c. 850–950*, ed. Amy Faulkner and Francis Leneghan. Studies in Old English Literature (Turnhout: Brepols).

Isaacs, Neil D. 1965. 'Still Waters Run *Undiop*'. *Philological Quarterly* 44: pp. 545–9.

Janson, Tore. 1964. *Latin Prose Prefaces: Studies in Literary Conventions*. Studia Latin Stockholmiensia 13 (Stockholm: Almqvist & Wiksell).

Jayatilaka, Rohini. 2012. 'King Alfred and his Circle'. In *The Cambridge History of the Book in Britain*. Vol. 1: *C. 400–1100* (Cambridge: Cambridge University Press), pp. 670–8.

Johnson, David F. 2006. 'Who Read Gregory's *Dialogues* in Old English?' In *The Power of Words: Anglo-Saxon Studies Presented to Donald G. Scragg on his Seventieth Birthday*, ed. Hugh Magennis and Jonathan Wilcox (Morgantown: West Virginia University Press), pp. 171–204.

Johnson, David F. 2007. 'Why Ditch the *Dialogues*? Reclaiming an Invisible Text'. In *Source of Wisdom: Old English and Early Medieval Latin Studies in Honour of Thomas D. Hill* (Toronto, Buffalo, and London: University of Toronto Press), pp. 201–16.

Johnson, David F. 2015. 'Alfredian Apocrypha: *The Old English Dialogues* and *Bede*'. In *A Companion to Alfred the Great*, ed. Nicole Guenther Discenza and Paul E. Szarmach. Brill's Companions to the Christian Tradition 58 (Leiden and Boston: Brill), pp. 368–95.

Jurasinski, Stefan. 2010. 'Violence, Penance, and Secular Law in Alfred's Mosaic Prologue'. *The Haskins Society Journal* 22: pp. 25–42.

Jurasinski, Stefan. 2012. 'Slavery, Learning and the Law of Marriage in Alfred's Mosaic Prologue'. In *Secular Learning in Anglo-Saxon England: Exploring the Vernacular*, ed. László Sándor Chardonnens and Bryan Carella (Amsterdam and New York: Rodopi), pp. 45–64.

Jurasinski, Stefan. 2015. *The Old English Penitentials and Anglo-Saxon Law* (Cambridge: Cambridge University Press).

Kendall, Calvin B. 1978. 'Bede's *Historia ecclesiastica*: The Rhetoric of Faith'. In *Medieval Eloquence: Studies in the Theory and Practice of Medieval Rhetoric*, ed. James J. Murphy (Berkeley, Los Angeles, London: University of California Press), pp. 145–72.

Ker, N. R. 1957. *Catalogue of Manuscripts Containing Anglo-Saxon* (Oxford: Clarendon Press).

Keynes, Simon. 1998. 'King Alfred and the Mercians'. In *Kings, Currency and Alliances: History and Coinage of Southern England in the Ninth Century*, ed.

M. A. S. Blackburn and D. N. Dumville. Studies in Anglo-Saxon History 9 (Woodbridge: The Boydell Press), pp. 1–45.

Keynes, Simon. 2015. 'Alfred the Great and the Kingdom of the Anglo-Saxons'. In *A Companion to Alfred the Great*, ed. Nicole Guenther Discenza and Paul E. Szarmach. Brill's Companions to the Christian Tradition 58 (Leiden and Boston: Brill), pp. 13–46.

Kiernan, Kevin. 1996. *Beowulf and the Beowulf Manuscript*, rev. ed. (Ann Arbor: University of Michigan Press).

Kim, Suksan. 1973. 'A Collation of the Old English MS. Hatton 20 of King Alfred's *Pastoral Care*'. *Neuphilologische Mitteilungen* 74: pp. 425–42.

Lapidge, Michael. 1996. 'Latin Learning in Ninth-Century England'. In his *Anglo-Latin Literature 600–899* (London: The Hambledon Press), pp. 409–54.

Lapidge, Michael. 2003. 'Asser's Reading'. In *Alfred the Great: Papers from the Eleventh-Centenary Conferences*, ed. Timothy Reuter (Aldershot, Hants.: Ashgate), pp. 27–47.

Lapidge, Michael. 2006. *The Anglo-Saxon Library* (Oxford: Oxford University Press).

Liebermann, Felix. 1908–10. 'King Alfred and the Mosaic Law'. *Transactions of the Jewish Historical Society* 6: pp. 21–31.

Lockett, Leslie. 2022b. 'Towards an Understanding of the Lost Exemplar of Augustine's *Soliloquia* Consulted by the Translator of the Old English *Soliloquies*'. *The Journal of Medieval Latin* 32: pp. 81–153.

Love, R. C. 'Vita S. Gregorii (L.E.102)'. 1997. *Fontes Anglo-Saxonici: World Wide Web Register*, https://arts.st-andrews.ac.uk/fontes/, 22/09/1997, accessed December 2021.

Love, Rosalind C. 2012. 'The Latin Commentaries on Boethius's *De Consolatione Philosophiae* from the 9th to the 11th Centuries'. In *A Companion to Boethius in the Middle Ages*, ed. Noel Harold Kaylor, Jr. and Philip Edward Phillips (Leiden and Boston: Brill), pp. 75–133.

Magennis, Hugh. 1999. *Anglo-Saxon Appetites: Food and Drink and Their Consumption in Old English and Related Literature* (Dublin: Four Courts Press).

Magoun, Francis P., Jr. 1948. 'Some Notes on King Alfred's Circular Letter on Educational Policy Addressed to his Bishops'. *Medieval Studies* 10: pp. 93–107.

Magoun, Francis P., Jr. 1949. 'King Alfred's Letter on Educational Policy According to the Cambridge Manuscripts'. *Medieval Studies* 11: pp. 113–22.

Marsden, Richard. 1995. *The Text of the Old Testament in Anglo-Saxon England*. Cambridge Studies in Anglo-Saxon England 15 (Cambridge: Cambridge University Press).

Meaney, Audrey. 2006. 'Old English Legal and Penitential Penalties for Heathenism'. In *Anglo-Saxons: Studies Presented to Cyril Roy Hart*, ed. Simon Keynes and Alfred P. Smyth (Dublin: Four Courts Press), pp. 127–58.

Minnis, A. J. 1988. *Medieval Theory of Authorship: Scholastic Literary Attitudes in the Later Middle Ages*. 2nd ed. (Aldershot: Wildwood House).

Mitchell, Bruce. 1987. *Old English Syntax*. 2 vols (Oxford: Clarendon Press, 1985; rpt. with corrections).

Mize, Britt. 2008. 'Manipulations of the Mind-as-Container Motif in *Beowulf*, *Homiletic Fragment II*, and Alfred's *Metrical Epilogue to the Pastoral Care*'. *Journal of English and Germanic Philology* 107: pp. 25–56.

Mize, Britt. 2013. *Traditional Subjectivities: The Old English Poetics of Mentality* (Toronto: University of Toronto Press).

Molyneaux, George. 2009. 'The *Old English Bede*: English Ideology or Christian Instruction?'. *The English Historical Review* 124: pp. 1289–323.

Morrish, Jennifer. 1986. 'King Alfred's Letter as a Source of Learning in England in the Ninth Century'. In *Studies in Earlier Old English Prose: Sixteen Original Contributions* (Albany, New York: State University of New York Press), pp. 87–107.

Napier, A. S. 1887. 'Bruchstück einer altenglischen Boetius-Handschrift'. *Zeitschrift für deutsches Altertum und deutsche Literatur* 19: pp. 52–4.

O'Brien O'Keeffe, Katherine. 1990. *Visible Song: Transitional Literacy in Old English Verse*. Cambridge Studies in Anglo-Saxon England 4 (Cambridge: Cambridge University Press).

O'Brien O'Keeffe, Katherine. 2005. 'Listening to the Scenes of Reading: King Alfred's Talking Prefaces'. In *Orality and Literacy in the Middle Ages: Essays on a Conjunction and its Consequences in Honour of D. H. Green*, ed. Mark Chinca and Christopher Young (Turnhout: Brepols), pp. 17–36.

Oliver, Lisi. 2015. 'Who Wrote Alfred's Laws?'. In *'Textus Roffensis': Law, Language, and Libraries in Early Medieval England*, ed. Bruce O'Brien and Barbara Bombi (Turnhout: Brepols), pp. 231–54.

Orton, Peter. 2005. 'Deixis and the Untransferable Text: Anglo-Saxon Colophons, Verse-Prefaces and Inscriptions'. In *Imagining the Book*, ed. Stephen Kelly and John J. Thompson (Turnhout: Brepols), pp. 195–207.

Papahagi, Adrian. 2009. 'The Transmission of Boethius' *De Consolatione Philosophiae* in the Carolingian Age'. *Medium Ævum* 78.1: pp. 1–15.

Parkes, M. B. 1976. 'The Palaeography of the Parker Manuscript of the *Chronicle*, Laws and Sedulius, and Historiography at Winchester in the Late Ninth and Tenth Centuries'. *Anglo-Saxon England* 5: pp. 149–71.

Paz, James. 2017. *Nonhuman Voices in Anglo-Saxon Literature and Material Culture* (Manchester: Manchester University Press).

Pelteret, David A. E. 1995. *Slavery in Early Mediaeval England: From the Reign of Alfred until the Twelfth Century*. Studies in Anglo-Saxon History 7 (Woodbridge, Suffolk, and Rochester, New York: Boydell and Brewer).

Potter, Simeon. 1949. 'King Alfred's Last Preface'. In *Philologica: The Malone Anniversary Studies*, ed. Thomas A. Kirby and Henry Bosley Woolf (Baltimore: Johns Hopkins University Press), pp. 25–30.

Pratt, David. 2007. *The Political Thought of King Alfred the Great*. Cambridge Studies in Medieval Life and Thought, Fourth Series 67 (Cambridge: Cambridge University Press).

Pratt, David. 2007. 'Problems of Authorship and Audience in the Writings of King Alfred the Great'. In *Lay Intellectuals in the Carolingian World*, ed. Patrick Wormald and Janet L. Nelson (Cambridge: Cambridge University Press), pp. 162–91.

Pratt, David. 2012. 'The Voice of the King in "King Edgar's Establishment of Monasteries"'. *Anglo-Saxon England* 41: pp. 145–204.

Quain, Edwin A. 1945. The Medieval *Accessus ad auctores*'. *Traditio* 3: pp. 215–64.

Rauer, Christine. 2021. 'The Earliest English Prose'. In *Vernacular Languages in the Long Ninth Century*, ed. Alban Gautier and Helen Gittos. *Journal of Medieval History: Special Issue* 47: pp. 485–96.

Richards, Mary P. 1986. 'The Manuscript Contexts of the Old English Laws'. In *Studies in Earlier Old English Prose*, ed. Paul E. Szarmach (Albany: State University of New York Press), pp. 171–92.

Richards, Mary P. 2015. 'The Laws of Alfred and Ine'. In *A Companion to Alfred the Great*, ed. Nicole Guenther Discenza and Paul E. Szarmach. Brill's Companions to the Christian Tradition 58 (Leiden and Boston: Brill), pp. 282–309.

Robinson, Fred C. 1980. 'Old English Literature in its Most Immediate Context'. In *Old English Literature in Context: Ten Essays*, ed. John D. Niles (Cambridge: D. S. Brewer), pp. 11–29.

Robinson, Fred C. 1981. '"Bede's" Envoi to the Old English *History*: An Experiment in Editing'. *Studies in Philology* 78: pp. 4–19. Reprinted in his *The Editing of Old English* (Oxford: Blackwell, 1994), pp. 167–79.

Rowley, Sharon M. 2011. *The Old English Version of Bede's 'Historia Ecclesiastica'* (Woodbridge: Boydell and Brewer).

Rowley, Sharon M. 2015. 'The Long Ninth Century and the Prose of King Alfred's Reign' *Oxford Handbooks Online* (DOI: 10.1093/oxfordhb/9780199935338. 013.53, https://www.oxfordhandbooks.com/).

Sayers, William. 2008. 'King Alfred's Timbers'. *SELIM: International Journal of the Spanish Society for Medieval English Language and Literature* 15: pp. 117–24.

Schaefer, Ursula. 1992. *Vokalität: Altenglische Dichtung zwischen Mündlichkeit und Schriftlichkeit* ScriptOralia 39 (Tübingen: Gunter Narr).

Schreiber, Carolin. 2015. '*Searoðonca Hord*: Alfred's Translation of Gregory the Great's *Regula Pastoralis*'. In *A Companion to Alfred the Great*, ed. Nicole Guenther Discenza and Paul E. Szarmach. Brill's Companions to the Christian Tradition 58 (Leiden and Boston: Brill), pp. 171–99.

Shippey, T. A. 1979. 'Wealth and Wisdom in King Alfred's *Preface* to the Old English *Pastoral Care*'. *English Historical Review* 94: pp. 346–55.

Sims-Williams, Patrick. 1990. *Religion and Literature in Western England, 600–800*. Cambridge Studies in Anglo-Saxon England 3 (Cambridge: Cambridge University Press).

Sisam, Kenneth. 1953a. 'The Publication of Alfred's Pastoral Care'. In his *Studies in the History of Old English Literature* (Oxford: Clarendon Press), pp. 140–7.

Sisam, Kenneth. 1953b. 'An Old English Translation of a Letter from Wynfrith to Eadburga (A.D. 716–17) in Cotton MS. Otho C I'. In his *Studies in the History of Old English Literature* (Oxford: Clarendon Press), pp. 199–224.

Sisam, Kenneth. 1953c. 'Addendum: The Verses Prefixed to *Gregory's Dialogues*'. In his *Studies in the History of Old English Literature* (Oxford: Clarendon Press), pp. 225–31.

Smith, Scott Thompson. 2012. *Land and Book: Literature and Land Tenure in Anglo-Saxon England* (Toronto, Buffalo, London: University of Toronto Press).

Stanley, E. G. 1970. Review of Carnicelli's *King Alfred's Version*. *Notes and Queries* o.s. 215: pp. 109–12.

Stanley, E. G. 1988. 'King Alfred's Prefaces'. *The Review of English Studies* n.s. 39: pp. 349–64.

Stanton, Robert. 2002. *The Culture of Translation in Anglo-Saxon England* (Cambridge: D. S. Brewer).

Stephens, Mary Isabel. 1960. 'A Study of the Old English Preface' (PhD diss., University of Pennsylvania).

Szarmach, Paul E. 2005. 'Alfred's *Soliloquies* in London, BL, Cotton Tiberius A.iii (art. 9g fols. 50v–51v)'. In *Latin Learning and English Lore: Studies in Anglo-Saxon Literature for Michael Lapidge*, ed. Katherine O'Brien O'Keeffe and Andy Orchard. 2 vols (Toronto, Buffalo, London: University of Toronto Press), II. 154–79.

Szarmach, Paul E. 2012. 'Boethius's Influence in Anglo-Saxon England: The Vernacular and the *De consolatione Philosophiae*'. In *A Companion to Boethius in the Middle Ages*, ed. Noel Harold Kaylor, Jr. and Philip Edward Phillips (Leiden and Boston: Brill), pp. 221–54.

Szarmach, Paul E. 2015. 'Augustine's *Soliloquia* in Old English'. In *A Companion to Alfred the Great*, ed. Nicole Guenther Discenza and Paul E. Szarmach. Brill's Companions to the Christian Tradition 58 (Leiden and Boston: Brill), pp. 227–55.

Thijs, Christine. 2007a. 'Close and Clumsy or Fanatically Faithful: Medieval Translators on Literal Translation'. In *Transmission and Transformation in the Middle Ages: Texts and Contexts*, ed. Kathleen Cawsey and Jason Harris (Dublin: Four Courts Press), pp. 15–39.

Thijs, Christine B. 2007b. 'Early Old English Translation: Practice Before Theory?' *Neophilologus* 91: pp. 149–73.

Thomson, R. M., in collaboration with M. Winterbottom. 1999. *William of Malmesbury, Gesta Regum Anglorum, The History of the English Kings*. Vol. 2: *General Introduction and Commentary* (Oxford: Clarendon Press).

Thomson, R. M., with the assistance of M. Winterbottom. 2007. *William of Malmesbury, Gesta Pontificum Anglorum, The History of the English Bishops.* Vol. 2: *Commentary* (Oxford: Clarendon Press).

Thornbury, Emily V. 2014. *Becoming a Poet in Anglo-Saxon England* (Cambridge: Cambridge University Press).

Torkar, Roland. 1981. *Eine altenglische Übersetzung von Alcuins de Virtutibus et Vitiis, Kap. 20: Liebermanns Judex Untersuchungen und Textausgabe mit einem Anhang: die Gesetze II und V Aethelstan nach Otho B. xi und Add. 43703.* Texte und Untersuchungen zur englischen Philologie 7 (Munich: Wilhelm Fink).

Treharne, Elaine M. 2016. 'Invisible Things in London, British Library, Cotton Vitellius A. xv'. In *Textiles, Text, Intertext: Essays in Honour of Gale R. Owen-Crocker*, ed. Maren Clegg Hyer and Jill Frederick (Woodbridge: The Boydell Press), pp. 225–37.

Treschow, Michael. 2007. 'Wisdom's Land: King Alfred's Imagery in his Preface to his Translation of Augustine's *Soliloquies*'. In *Divine Creation in Ancient, Medieval, and Early Modern Thought: Essays Presented to the Rev'd Dr. Robert D. Crouse*, ed. Michael Treschow, Willemien Otten, and Walter Hannam. Brill's Studies in Intellectual History 151 (Leiden: Brill), pp. 257–84.

Troncarelli, Fabio. 1981. *Tradizioni perdute. La 'Consolatio Philosophiae' nell'Alto Medioevo* (Padua: Antenore).

Waite, Greg. 2000. *Old English Prose Translations of Alfred's Reign.* Annotated Bibliographies of Old and Middle English Literature 6 (Woodbridge, Suffolk, UK, and Rochester, NY: D. S. Brewer).

Waite, Greg. 2014. 'Translation Style, Lexical Systems, Dialect Vocabulary, and the Manuscript Transmission of the Old English Bede'. *Medium Ævum* 83: pp. 56–103.

Waite, Greg. 2015. 'The Preface to the Old English Bede: Authorship, Transmission, and Connection with the *West Saxon Genealogical Regnal List*'. *Anglo-Saxon England* 44: pp. 31–93.

Weaver, Erica. 2016. 'Hybrid Forms: Translating Boethius in Anglo-Saxon England'. *Anglo-Saxon England* 45: pp. 213–38.

Westgard, Joshua A. 2010. 'Bede and the Continent in the Carolingian Age and Beyond'. In *The Cambridge Companion to Bede*, ed. Scott DeGregorio (Cambridge: Cambridge University Press), pp. 201–15.

Wheeler, Stephen M. 2015. *Accessus ad auctores: Medieval Introductions to the Authors (Codex latinus monacensis 19475).* TEAMS Secular Commentary Series (Kalamazoo: Medieval Institute Publications).

Whitelock, Dorothy. 1960. *After Bede.* Jarrow Lecture (Jarrow: Jarrow Parish Council). Reprinted in *Bede and His World: The Jarrow Lectures 1958–93*, ed. Michael Lapidge. 2 vols (Aldershot: Variorum, 1994), I.35–50.

Whitelock, Dorothy. 1962. 'The Old English Bede'. *Proceedings of the British Academy* 48: pp. 57–90.

Whitelock, Dorothy. 1966. 'The Prose of Alfred's Reign'. In *Continuations and Beginnings: Studies in Old English Literature*, ed. E. G. Stanley (London: Nelson), pp. 67–103.

Whitelock, Dorothy. 1969. 'William of Malmesbury on the Works of King Alfred'. In *Medieval Literature and Civilization: Studies in Memory of G. N. Garmonsway*, ed. D. A. Pearsall and R. A. Waldron (London: The Athlone Press), pp. 78–93.

Whitelock, Dorothy. 1979b. 'Some Charters in the Name of King Alfred'. In *Saints, Scholars, and Heroes: Studies in Medieval Culture in Honour of Charles W. Jones*, ed. Margot H. King and Wesley M. Stevens. Vol. 1: *The Anglo-Saxon Heritage* (Collegeville, Minnesota: Hill Monastic Manuscript Library, St John's Abbey and University), pp. 77–98.

Whobrey, William T. 1991. 'King Alfred's Metrical Epilogue to the *Pastoral Care*'. *Journal of English and Germanic Philology* 90: pp. 175–86.

Wilcox, Miranda. 2006. 'Alfred's Epistemological Metaphors: *eagan modes* and *scip modes*'. *Anglo-Saxon England* 35: pp. 179–217.

Williams, Ann. 2014. 'Land Tenure'. In *The Wiley-Blackwell Encyclopedia of Anglo-Saxon England*, ed. Michael Lapidge, John Blair, Simon Keynes, and Donald Scragg, 2nd ed. (Chichester, West Sussex, and Malden, MA: John Wiley and Sons).

Wormald, Patrick. 1977. '*Lex Scripta* and *Verbum Regis*: Legislation and Germanic Kingship, from Euric to Cnut'. In *Early Medieval Kingship*, ed. P. H. Sawyer and I. N. Wood (School of History, University of Leeds), pp. 105–38.

Wormald, Patrick. 1991. 'In Search of King Offa's "Law-Code"'. In *People and Places in Northern Europe 500–1600: Essays in Honour of Peter Hayes Sawyer*, ed. Ian Wood and Niels Lund (Woodbridge: The Boydell Press), pp. 25–45.

Wormald, Patrick. 1999. *The Making of English Law: King Alfred to the Twelfth Century*. Vol. 1: *Legislation and its Limits* (Oxford and Malden, MA: Blackwell).

Yerkes, David. 1977. 'The Text of the Canterbury Fragment of Werferth's Translation of Gregory's *Dialogues* and its Relation to Other Manuscripts'. *Anglo-Saxon England* 6: pp. 121–35.

Yerkes, David. 1986. 'The Translation of Gregory's *Dialogues* and its Revision'. In *Studies in Earlier Old English Prose*, ed. Paul E. Szarmach (Albany: State University of New York Press), pp. 335–43.